The Paradoxical Republic

Austria is a labyrinth everybody knows their way about in.

—HELMUT QUALTINGER

THE PARADOXICAL REPUBLIC
Austria, 1945–2005

Oliver Rathkolb

Translated from the German by

Otmar Binder, Eleanor Breuning,
Ian Fraser and David Sinclair-Jones

Berghahn Books
New York • Oxford

Published by
Berghahn Books
www.berghahnbooks.com

German edition
© 2005 Paul Zsolnay Verlag Wien
Die paradoxe Republik: Österreich 1945 bis 2005
by Oliver Rathkolb

English-language edition
© 2010 Berghahn Books

Library of congress cataloging-in-publication data

Rathkolb, Oliver.
    [Paradoxe Republik. English]
    The paradoxical republic : Austria, 1945-2005 / Oliver Rathkolb ; translated from
the German by Otmar Binder, Eleanor Breuning, Ian Fraser and David Sinclair-Jones. —
English-language ed.
        p. cm.
    Includes bibliographical references and index.
    ISBN 978-1-84545-639-9 (hbk. : alk. paper)
    1. Austria—History—1955- 2. Political culture—Austria—History. 3. Austria—Politics
and government—1945- 4. National characteristics, Austrian. 5. Austria—Social conditions.
6. Austria—Economic conditions—1945- I. Title.
    DB99.2.R36713 2010
    943.605'3--dc22

                                                                    2009025364

British Library cataloguing in publication data

A catalogue record for this book is available from
the British Library.

Printed in the United States on acid-free paper

ISBN 978-1-84545-639-9

Contents

⌒

TABLES

⌒

FIGURES

~~

ILLUSTRATIONS

Abbreviations

AG   Aktiengesellschaft (Stock Corporation)
AKH   Allgemeines Krankenhaus Wien (Vienna General Hospital)
ARGE   Arbeitsgemeinschaft (consortium)
ASVG   Allgemeines Sozialversicherungsgesetz (Comprehensive Social
        Security Law)
AZ   Arbeiter-Zeitung
BAWAG   Bank für Arbeit und Wirtschaft AG
BSA   Bund Sozialistischer Akademiker (Association of Socialist University
        Graduates)
BZÖ   Bündnis Zukunft Österreich (Alliance for Austria's Future: national
        conservative political party founded by Jörg Haider in 2005)
CDU   Christlich Demokratische Union (the German Conservative Party)
CIC   United States Army Counter Intelligence Corps
CV   Cartellverband (Catholic student fraternity organization)
DAF   Deutsche Arbeitsfront (German Labour Front, the Nazi Trade Union
        Organisation)
DDSG   Donau Dampfschiffahrtsgesellschaft (Danube Shipping AG)
DÖW   Dokumentationsarchiv des Österreichischen Widerstands
        (Documentation Archive of Austrian Resistance)
EC   European Community
ECSC   European Coal and Steel Community
EEA   European Economic Area
EEC   European Economic Community
EFTA   European Free Trade Association
EMU   Economic and Monetary Union
ERP   European Recovery Program
FAM   Free Austrian Movement
FDP   Freie Demokratische Partei Deutschlands (the German Liberal Party)
FPÖ   Freiheitliche Partei Österreichs (Austrian Freedom Party)
KPÖ   Kommunistische Partei Österreichs (Austrian Communist Party)

NSDAP Nationalsozialistische Deutsche Arbeiterpartei (National Socialist German Workers' Party)
ÖAAB Österreichischer Arbeiter- und Angestelltenbund (Austrian Federation of Workers and Employees)
OECD Organisation for Economic Co-operation and Development
OEEC Organisation for European Economic Cooperation
ÖGB Österreichischer Gewerkschaftsbund (Austrian Trade Union Association)
ÖIAG Österreichische Industrieholding AG (Austrian Industry Holding Stock Corporation)
ÖMV Österreichische Mineralölverwaltung (Austrian Mineral Oil Authority)
ORF Österreichische Rundfunk Gesellschaft (Austrian Broadcasting Corporation)
OSCE Organization for Security and Co-operation in Europe
OSS Office of Strategic Services
ÖSV Österreichischer Skiverband (Austrian Ski Federation)
ÖVP Österreichische Volkspartei (Austrian People's Party)
RAVAG Radioverkehrs-AG (forerunner of ORF)
RSHA Reichssicherheitshauptamt (Reich Main Security Office)
SDAP Sozialdemokratische Arbeiterpartei (Social Democratic Workers' Party)
SEA Single European Act
SN Salzburger Nachrichten
SPD Sozialdemokratische Partei Deutschlands (the German Social Democratic Party)
SPÖ Sozialistische Partei Österreichs (Social Democratic Party of Austria)
UNRRA United Nations Relief and Rehabilitation Agency
USIA Upravlenie Sovetskim imuščestvom v Avstrii = Administration of Soviet Property in Austria
VdU Verband der Unabhängigen (Federation of Independents, national-liberal political party, 1949-1955)
VGA Verein für Geschichte der Arbeiterbewegung (Association for the History of the Workers' Movement)
VOEST Vereinigte Österreichische Eisen- und Stahlwerke (United Austrian Iron and Steelworks AG)
WAZ Westdeutscher Allgemeiner Zeitungsverlag
WEU Western European Union
ZIB Zeit im Bild (TV news programme)

Preface

The year 2005 was an exciting one for the Republic of Austria. There were no fewer than three jubilees to celebrate: 1945 (war's end, liberation and start of the Second Republic), 1955 (signature of the State Treaty and Neutrality Act) and 1995 (EU entry). Exhibitions in Schloss Belvedere, in the Schallaburg and in hundreds of local museums sought to draw in the masses. And again Vienna's Staatsoper, which commemorated its reopening on 5 November 1955 with a state ceremony and star conductors from all over the world, presented itself, as it had fifty years earlier, as *the* place in Austria for remembrance. The war's end in 1945 and the proclamation of Renner's provisional government on 27 April 1945 were highlighted in the media and by politicians, as were the liberation of the Mauthausen concentration camp in early May 1945 and the forty-eight subsidiary concentration camps throughout Austria. Towns, villages, factories, institutions, organizations and political parties all positioned themselves historically and endeavoured to reinterpret their past. Additionally, the year of remembrance offered the last chance for eyewitnesses to establish their accounts in the collective memory.

'History sells': but how much critical historical awareness did the various historical performances, whose motto might be 'Turn off the future, turn up the past' (Jesse Sykes), really bring about?

This book will seek to portray ten important developments and structural elements of the Second Republic, combining the findings and debates of recent decades with an academic analysis. It is intended to offer an intensive, sometimes subjective, but always clear insight into the collective memory of Austrians, men and women, and especially to stimulate reflection about identity and democratic consciousness. It is not the by now almost obligatory negative account of the State that is to be the focus, but a critical discussion of the foundation and reconstruction myths of the Second Republic, again meant to arouse contradiction and reflection. It will not deal in parlour patriotism, but rather offer an open-minded, open-ended assessment of the Second Republic's achievements, and its mistakes. The Austrian identity is part of this, as is the specific development of democracy and the Austrian economic miracle. The international context will always be at the centre of the interpretation. Austria, which as a nation felt itself for far too long to be a sort of island, is not one any longer; indeed, in many respects it is a kind of Atlantis, whose traces and artefacts will be highlighted in this volume.

A picture will also be sketched of the most important political actors, against the background of the political party landscape. This will no doubt upset quite a few wishful notions and historical traditions, but at the same time it will bring various new facets into view. The importance of women, not even covered in most histories, in the predominantly women's elections of 1945 that decided the political shape of the Second Republic will be appropriately reflected in all ten sections.

Democracy and politics without art, culture and the media are inconceivable; especially in a small country like Austria, these are seismographs for the extent of open democratic debate. Throughout the text the focus will repeatedly fall on the attitudes of Austrian men and women towards democratic politics. Since the *demos* determines the present, and the future, of our republican polity, the question of democratic consciousness and corresponding attitudes receives much attention. In 2004 a survey on Austria's authoritarian potential was specially commissioned for this book; its findings are juxtaposed here with actual historical developments since 1945.

The historical origins of Austrian neutrality and current attitudes to it form one of the ten viewpoints, as do European identity and Europe policy. One oft-neglected but important feature of the history of the Second Republic is social policy, the Austrian welfare-state model. It helped greatly towards building an identity quickly and creating acceptance for the mini-State. But in addition the picture also brings in the importance of political pasts for current politics (from the monarchy via the dictatorial regimes of Dollfuß and Schuschnigg to National Socialism, reconstruction and the Kreisky era). In conclusion, future trends will be summarized, and an assessment of various earlier futurologies given.

This book would not have come about without a very understanding publisher, Herbert Ohrlinger, and a constructively critical while also very sensitive editor, Brigitte Hilzensauer; to them go my special thanks. For desk editing I wish to thank Maria Wirth and Agnes Meisinger. Special thanks go to the translators of the German version, Otmar Binder in Vienna, Eleanor Breuning in London, Ian Fraser in Florence and David Sinclair-Jones in Sao Paulo.

Vienna, November 2008
Oliver Rathkolb

The translation and editing work has been financed by the Austrian Federal Ministry of Science and Research (MR Alois Söhn) and the Department of Cultural Affairs of the City of Vienna (Prof. Hubert Christian Ehalt).

Austrian Identity

*Between National Pride, Solipsism
and European Patriotism*

'… we are left with no option but to give up of our own accord the
very idea of an Anschluss.'[1]

—CHANCELLOR KARL RENNER

After the end of the First World War in 1918, the decisive political forces in
Austria unreservedly supported parliamentary democracy and the abolition of
the monarchy, but the mini-state met with great scepticism. The phrase 'the State
nobody wanted' precisely expresses this doubt about the economic and nation-
state viability of a state that with the break-up of Austria-Hungary had shrunk
from around fifty to seven million inhabitants. The desire for 'Anschluss' with the
now also democratically organized German Reich ran through all the political
parties, but it was not accepted by the victorious Allied powers (France, the U.K.
and the U.S.) in 1919 and met with only half-hearted support in Germany too.

The ensuing decades were marked by the increasing militarization of political
debate and radicalization of political conflicts (for example, the 1927 Ministry
of Justice fire) in the midst of prolonged social and economic crises. The authoritarian course taken by Christian Social Chancellor Engelbert Dollfuß, with the
elimination of Parliament after 4 March 1933, ended in a civil war beginning
on 12 February 1934 and led to the banning of the SDAP (Social Democratic
Workers' Party). The objective of repelling National Socialism, in power in Germany since 1933, through a dictatorial regime failed. The National Socialists'
terrorist attacks continued, and Dollfuß himself was murdered in July 1934 in
an unsuccessful putsch attempt. His successor, Kurt Schuschnigg, aimed first at
compromise with Hitler's Germany (with the July 1936 agreement) and continuation of the dictatorship. The cautious opening up to the banned 'left' and the
trade unions in late 1937 came too late, however, and brought the same fiasco as
did a plebiscite scheduled for 13 March 1938 '[f]or a free and German, indepen-

dent and social, Christian and united Austria', which Hitler forbade. The unopposed entry of German Wehrmacht troops on 12 March 1938 definitively ended the mini-state. Some 200,000 people on the Heldenplatz cheered Adolf Hitler as 'liberator'. Immediately, the first waves of arrests began: 50,000 Austrian men and women, political opponents as well as Jews, fell victim to these terror actions. This also set the framework for the plebiscite held on 10 April 1938 to decide the 'Anschluss'. Its almost hundred per cent result (99.6 per cent) was the outcome of opportunism, ideological conviction, massive pressure and perfect propaganda, along with occasional falsification of the counts.

Despite the accommodation to the Nazi regime that ran through all social classes, many forms of resistance crystallized, mostly in reaction to the dominance of Reich Germans and the negative consequences of the German Wehrmacht's expansion campaigns throughout Europe. After liberation by the Allies – mainly the Red Army in the East and U.S. units in the West – it was not, however, Austrians' own responsibility and collaboration in the Holocaust and the war that stood at the centre of debate in Austria, but their situation as victims, as prisoners of war, bombing casualties and targets of Nazi repression. Even the sufferings of the Jewish population – some 130,800 Jewish men and women had been driven into exile, with around 65,000 murdered or dead from other causes – were quickly repressed by references to Austrians' own sufferings and misfortunes.

The national historical memory took its origin from the shock the 'Ostmarkers' got in 1938 when they were integrated into the National Socialist German Reich not as an elite but a mere provincial society. Since the Nazi Party leadership had deliberately rejected the special role the Austrians had constructed for themselves as the 'better German Kulturnation', there rapidly came, especially with the growing military defeats after the battle of Stalingrad in 1942–43, an emotional severance. By 1945 hardly anyone was still publicly questioning the State's separation from Germany. But no strong separate identity as a small country had yet been formed.

This ambivalent position is manifest from the very first statement by Chancellor Karl Renner, a classically German-nationalist Dual-Monarchy Social Democrat. To the officials in the Chancellery on the Ballhausplatz on 30 April 1945, he declared:

> [T]he idea of Anschluss as put forward in 1918, 1920 and subsequent years meant something quite different from what Hitler created. According to their idea the Austrian people were to join the community of all German peoples as a federation member with its State intact, as a Federal State in accordance with the Weimar constitution … It was Adolf Hitler who first of all falsified the Anschluss and got it wrong, and in the end gambled it away for ever. The three world powers [the U.S., USSR and U.K.] agreed to restore an independent Austria, all other States in the world have with very minor exceptions joined them, and we are left with no option

but to give up of our own accord the very idea of an Anschluss. This may well be hard for quite a few of us, but on the other hand, after what has happened, after this dreadful catastrophe, what is now a *fait accompli* is for all of us at the same time a release and a *fait libérateur*.[2]

Now Austria actually was, as it would always have liked to be, a 'special case' at the centre of world politics, specifically because of its chance geographical position between the bloc systems in the Cold War. At the same time the notion grew that Austria would be noticed with corresponding attention by the new Western superpower, the United States. As one German politician wrathfully put it in 1952, 'instead of acknowledging their share of responsibility, they want to be coddled like a bullied child';[3] but this was nonetheless not a topic in geopolitics. Overestimation of the international significance of the Austrian question, combined with an unvoiced bad conscience, continues to this day, very much as a sort of national solipsism mediated through and strengthened by the Austrian press. Politics too conveys the false impression that, for instance, U.S. decision makers and media are constantly observing developments in Austria. This might occasionally have been true for the period up to 1955; but despite Waldheim and Haider, Austria is, in the United States, seen rather more as a land of music or as the setting for the Trapp family saga *The Sound of Music,* as long-range studies of the media document.

Austria's neutrality after 1955 lent its self-obsession a permanent and special status. Austria was regarded as a bridge between East and West, the appropriate venue in the 1970s for talks aimed at reducing tensions. It is only an apparent contradiction that a pan-Austrian national consciousness flourished particularly in the active foreign policy era of Bruno Kreisky, when internationalism was in vogue. Its worldwide recognition and reputation strengthened the identity of the mini-state, though provincialism and permanent self-overestimation had by no means had their teeth drawn. The end of the Cold War and integration into the EU then resulted in an abrupt end to Austria's special role, already markedly reduced in the 1980s. EU entry, but also the consequences of globalization, plunged the self-absorbed Austrians into deep crisis. Suddenly there was a need to accept new realities and decision-making processes, which led increasingly to frictions as Austria's special political and economic role from Cold War times was markedly reduced, or disappeared entirely. For instance, the anti-nuclear policy that Austria had inscribed on its banners after the referendum that decided against the opening of the Zwentendorf nuclear power station in 1978 failed vis-à-vis the Czech Republic, Slovakia and Slovenia, since Austria was unable to mobilize any lobby in the EU – e.g. against starting up Temelín.

This trend is strengthened by global developments, as documented in a June 2003 study by the Washington-based Research Center for the People and the Press after questioning 66,000 people in forty-nine countries.[4] This very repre-

ILLUSTRATION I.I
'Tourist Paradise Austria.' Advertisement of Austrian Tourism.

sentative cross-section of the world public – without mini-states like Austria – agrees, across all age groups, that globalization brings with it a loss of traditional cultural identities. Thus, in Germany, for instance, 69 per cent of those surveyed saw their traditional way of life as endangered, while 68 per cent of Italians – like 53 per cent of the French – favoured cultural protectionism to safeguard the 'national' culture. Such developments have still stronger effects in small states with a relatively young national identity. In this sense, then, Austria is in the global mainstream of identity development, but with even more intense reactions in crisis periods.

In a talk with the author of this volume, Viola Breit, driven from Vienna with her family in 1938, once used the word 'solipsism' to describe the national self-image of her former compatriots. This aptly catches the essence of the way most Austrians currently view themselves: from a standpoint of permanent self-absorption. In my opinion this Austrian solipsism is a constant, handed down from the last decades of the monarchy. Then, a German-speaking minority dominated the other national majorities (with the exception of the Hungarians after 1867). The territory of today's Austria, with the imperial capital and residence of Vienna, was elevated into the centre of all activities and developments in the monarchy, while real developments in the outside world were ignored by the dominant national group, as regards both the nationality question and economic and political developments in Europe. The declaration of war in 1914 despite inferior military and socioeconomic capacities was the first culminating point of this misestimation and baseless exaggeration of the country's actual capabilities.

Clear traces of solipsism are also to be found in surveys on national pride. Even before the referendum on Austria's EU entry, opinion surveys documented extremely marked national pride for Austrians, both men and women, surpassed in an international comparison only by the U.S. population.[5] It also became clear that this national pride was often based on such arguments as 'beautiful landscape' (increasingly associated with high environmental awareness) and the traditional popular and high culture. Three 'pillars' of Austrian identity mentioned in this context are landscape, culture (both high culture and popular culture) and – still – neutrality. It is noteworthy that the 'medical school' continues to hold a very high position. Sports successes, originally very important (in the 1950s), have been losing importance since 1980, while sports stars themselves continue to rate very highly on the scale of recognition.

Austria's political system and constitution, however, are not among the standard markers on Austria's mental identity map. This is in striking contrast to Germans, but also Americans, who have never lost confidence in their (as such in great need of renewal) eighteenth-century constitution. In Austria, by contrast, 'faith' in politics disappeared after the Kreisky era: in 1987 only 27 per cent of those surveyed still called Austrian politics an achievement to be proud of (as against 72 per cent in 1980).[6] In October 2000 the crisis continued: only 27 per cent of Austrians were content with the political situation. Again, trust in politicians by comparison with doctors (91 per cent approval), teachers and policemen (76 per cent each) was extremely low in 2004 (15 per cent).[7] This puts Austria on a level with Hungary (14 per cent), though well above Germany (6 per cent), Italy (9 per cent) and Poland (6 per cent). In this connection, though, there are regional differences, partly coinciding with the regional identity of Austrians, the older root of the national identity. Thus, while in 2000 27 per cent indicated political contentment overall, in Tyrol the figure was only 19 per cent, but in both Styria and Vorarlberg it was 36 per cent; Vienna stood at the average.[8]

At the same time – almost in a countermovement – Austria's record national pride rose, as mentioned, still further on a European comparison, by at latest 1990[9] (1. Poland, 2. Austria, 3. Britain, 4. Hungary, 5. Norway and Spain, 7. Sweden, 8. Italy, 9. Czechoslovakia, 10. Federal Republic of Germany); by 1995 it had risen even higher (1. Austria, 2. Norway, 3. Britain, 4. Spain, 5. Germany, 6. Italy, 7. Sweden, 8. Czech Republic, 9. Hungary, 10. Poland). One thing to give us pause here, though, is that on questions indicating negatively coloured patriotism (chauvinism in the classical sense) and national superiority, in 1998 Austria came first, ahead even of the United States, followed by Bulgaria, Hungary and Canada. (In the ranking for positively-associated patriotism Ireland came before the United States, Canada and Austria, as well as New Zealand.)

It emerges even from this simple listing how strongly outside events can influence national feelings when it comes to social and economic crises, as in Poland or Hungary since 1989. Anyone imagining that the economic and cultural globalization that, even before the fall of the Iron Curtain, had reached Eastern Europe and the Soviet Union (albeit in weakened form) would render national attitudes less important was wrong. Quite the contrary: the more strongly the actual or presumed effects of globalization and European integration affected people's lives, the more intensive became the reaching back to narrow, traditional national value systems. This can be very well shown in the history of the area in the Habsburg Empire that present-day Austria occupies: with the very first globalization at the end of the nineteenth century in the wake of the industrial revolution, radical nationalism escalated as a simple, but ultimately catastrophic, answer to far-reaching social and economic change.

In addition to a theoretical, 'internal' definition of nation and identity, it is absolutely necessary for Austria to take into account the various external frameworks in the area of integrated economies, international politics and cultural transfer. Thus, sociologist Max Haller[10] and linguist Ruth Wodak[11] have analysed theories of the nation and identity concepts from theoretical and critical viewpoints, while historical and political discourses have been considered by political scientists such as Anton Pelinka or historians such as Ernst Bruckmüller and Gerald Stourzh. The trend in the primarily historical and only most recently sociological debate[12] is going in the direction of defining the Austrian nation as a nation state, a 'political community of opinion'. According to Ruth Wodak, this distinguishes itself 'deliberately from traditional, conservative or indeed racist concepts such as "cultural nation", "linguistic nation" or "community of descent"'. Particularly against the background of the renationalization debates of the last ten years, however, the question arises whether theory here may perhaps have developed an ideal form that has not been confirmed by experience, notably in such debates as those on migrations or EU enlargement. Austrian society, and increasingly also the three big political parties – foremost among them, with their unmistakable radicalism, the FPÖ or BZÖ – have been manifesting plainly cultural national elements.

Max Haller brings the complex theoretical discourses down to a single denominator: 'the concept of the "nation state" stresses the political community of all citizens living on the territory of the State and their equal rights and duties; the concept of the "cultural" or ethnic nation the similarity or relatedness of the members of a nation as regards language and culture, morals and customs, up to blood relationship through common descent ... It seems reasonable in this connection to equate the concept of the nation state with an "open" society and that of the "ethnic" or "cultural" nation with a "closed" one.' The very definition shows, though, that in the subjective experience of nationality the two tendencies come into contradiction, with the various mixed positions being determined primarily by international developments, but also by internal Austrian changes. In this sense the Austrian identity is still in constant flux, while it is particularly the most recent national and international confrontations that will bring about a basic decision as to where the Austrian identity is headed, between globalization and enlargement of the European Union.

Below, I hope to bring out certain specific features of the nation of Austria, which at the war's end in 1945 had scarcely any strongly marked, tangible identity, but a mere forty-five years later – that is, within one or two generations – perceived itself fully as a cultural nation and a nation state. This rapid nation-building process, while indubitably among the riddles of the Second Republic, is seldom as intensively subjected to investigation as is the social and economic reconstruction after 1945, although in this area especially some self-examination might be very much in order. I intend to consider which elements have formed the Austrian identity since 1945. To this end, it is necessary to define certain central strands by which the identity of the population – which can very definitely be distinguished from the self-perception of the elites and the political decision makers – can be enquired into.

Non-impartial (Pro-Western) Neutrality, the State Treaty and Minor Statehood

A result that may at first sight seem surprising was given by a survey done by the Sociological Studies Association in October 1995 on the question 'Since when has there been a free Austria?' Of those surveyed, 87 per cent named the year 1955 and not that of liberation by the Allies, 1945; out of these 87 per cent, 52 per cent opted for 15 May 1955, the date the State Treaty was signed, and 35 per cent for 26 October 1955, when the Neutrality Act was passed in Parliament. Ten years of Allied administration, which through Marshall Plan aid and joint control of political structures played an extremely important role in constituting the Second Republic, continue to be perceived merely as 'occupation' or else repressed from the collective memory.

Since the 1960s, in education and at political events in particular, the State Treaty and the Neutrality Act have been presented and celebrated as central documents of the state's foundation. But as early as 1956 – on the eleventh anniversary of the declaration of independence on 27 April 1945 – the context of the state's foundation was emphasized: 'Austria is free'.[13] Leopold Figl's famous sentence was again to be a motif at many events in 2005; by contrast with 1955–56 and the 1960s, however, it was now not the Neutrality Act but liberation from the Allies' 'occupation regime' that was at the centre of public debate. While the original security-policy and international-law components of that neutrality have long been deemphasized, nonetheless the economic and social progress in reconstruction and the heyday of social and political contentedness in the 1970s are brought directly into connection with them. Bruno Kreisky's concept of an active and self-confident neutrality policy, and his efforts as chancellor to discuss foreign-policy questions and issues broadly and publicly, proved especially successful in deeply rooting this transformation of neutrality into a code for prosperity, security and international reputation in the collective awareness. Accordingly, it was with contentment – but not without an undertone of warning against exaggerated nationalism – that Kreisky said in his farewell speech to Parliament on 28 September 1983: 'All groups today stand up for our flag, and take their hats off when our national anthem is played. No one any longer questions Austria's viability. A new, very peaceful and calm patriotism has emerged.'

By the mid 1960s, political decision makers were already recognizing and promoting the importance of neutrality as a constitutive element in the making of the nation. In this sense, the Act on the Austrian National Day, passed on 25 October 1965 (which only three ÖVP and FPÖ members from Vorarlberg did not vote for), was an important, politically symbolic step on the long road to a final farewell to the latent dreams of Anschluss. It 'filled' the empty 'flag day' with neutrality. An active foreign policy was thus seen in the Austria of the 1960s also as a means of promoting identity. The ÖVP–SPÖ Grand Coalition and the ÖVP-only government under Josef Klaus after 1966 were jointly responsible for this course. Stronger internationalization was designed to counteract the still-present pan-German tendencies, and the national code for internationalization was 'neutrality'.

A glance at the opinion surveys of the time will show that the identity-building process was really only just starting: in 1964, 15 per cent strictly opposed the notion of a separate Austrian nation, 23 per cent felt the nation was gradually coming into being, and 47 per cent accepted the concept of an Austrian nation.[14] Whereas immediately after the jubilee year of 1955 and the attainment of state sovereignty 49 per cent were in favour of an Austrian nation but 46 per cent still felt like part of the 'German people', in a political context the debates became clearer: thus on 28 June 1967 FPÖ Federal Party Chairman Friedrich Peter expressed his rejection of a 'National Day', since there could only be a 'State Day'. His second successor, Jörg Haider, born in 1950 and therefore a representative of the second generation in the FPÖ, was still saying on 8 August 1988 in an ORF (Austrian Radio/TV) domestic report that 'the Austrian nation was an abortion, an ideological abortion. For belonging to a people is one thing, and belonging to a State quite another.' Later the FPÖ rallied, on Haider's instructions, behind a conservative, '*heimattreu*' [faithful to the homeland] Austrian patriotism, though with primarily German culturally defining features.

As we know, there was no referendum on either Austria's state sovereignty in 1945 or the Neutrality Act. In the first case the Allies decided; in the second it was Austrian political elites in the ÖVP – supported, if hesitantly, by the SPÖ. The FPÖ by contrast voted against perpetual neutrality, since this meant giving up the basic pan-German position and embarking on national (not just state) independence. There is therefore relatively little information on public consciousness of neutrality at this point in time; at any rate, there was a broad majority against any further involvement in wars of aggression, as in the First and Second World Wars. The central question was thus more whether neutrality would continue to guarantee the dominance of ideological, cultural and economic integration with the West, along with radical anti-communism.

Anti-communism: A Repressed Component of the Austrian Identity

Anti-Russian stereotypes were present in the Austrian area as of the late nineteenth century. After the Bolshevik revolution in Russia in 1917–18 and the proclamation of the German-Austrian Republic on 12 November 1918, they escalated into still more radical forms as anti-Bolshevism and anti-communism. National Socialism perfected the racist connotation of the Slavic '*Untermensch*'. The marauding, raping soldiers of the rearguard of the Red Army that freed Austria in 1945 finally provided a traumatic confirmation of many a prejudice.

After the Second World War, demarcation from the neighbouring states' communist system was an essential element in Austria's strengthening of its faith in small statehood. The claim of an alleged constant communist threat internally and externally was skilfully played off, particularly vis-à-vis the United States. It enabled a maximum of financial and political support to be secured without the U.S. seeking to change economic and political structures in line with its own model. Thus, Austria got one of the highest per capita quotas of Marshall Plan aid, even though Austria's economic structure was not truly reformed, nor state influence reduced. As regards the state's obligations, the threat card was long played adeptly in order to postpone payments (for example in respect of Jewish compensation demands or the claims of American, British and other oil companies). The anti-communism that relativized all legal and political constraints also meant that grossly suspect former NSDAP elites or technical people from the Nazi arms industry could be integrated 'in the national interest', while, for instance, artists who had worked in the New Theatre in the Scala or for the Soviet film industry or the 'Russian Hour' on the radio RAVAG, and thus become tarred with the communist brush, were blackballed. In many cases all they could do was emigrate to the GDR.

One important event for Austria's identity-building in this connection was the alleged communist coup attempt in September/October 1950. In 1997, the Salzburg historian Ernst Hanisch asked the hypothetical question whether '68-influenced historiography might have underestimated the 'danger of a communist seizure of power in Eastern Austria'. [15] This put him in the same camp as the ex-president of the Austrian trade-union federation and former SPÖ minister of the interior Franz Olah, who in 2005 was still vehemently defending the position that the mass strikes by the KPÖ (Austrian Communist Party) in September and October 1950 had been a coup attempt. All available sources and the well-nigh

ILLUSTRATION I.2
The Soviet Headquarters at Wiener Ringstraße (Palais Epstein)

unanimous conclusions of relevant scholarly analyses rule out such an aim for the plan as unrealistic; but the 1950 'coup attempt' remains a still-present myth despite the numerous studies, a myth that cannot be overlooked when thinking about the Austrian identity of the post-war generation.

This does not mean, though, that there had been no planning in that direction. Newly available Soviet documents confirm that sections of the KPÖ leadership did seriously discuss a solution on the pattern of the emerging partition of Germany as an option.[16] But on 13 February 1948 the two top KPÖ officials, Johann Koplenig and Friedl Fürnberg, who were in Moscow to report, received a political dressing-down from Andrey Zhdanov, the Politburo member responsible for questions concerning foreign Communist parties. From the Soviet viewpoint it was not a possible partition of Austria and continuation of the Soviet presence there that were in the interests of the KPÖ and the Austrian population, but the conclusion of the State Treaty and the withdrawal of all the Allies. While many eyewitnesses, such as Franz Olah, perceived the events of October 1950 as a coup attempt, two years earlier a division of the country had in fact been discussed. It was prevented by the USSR; but this recollection has not become part of the collective memory in Austria.

Since most historical, sociological and political-science studies tend to sideline geopolitical aspects, anti-communism as an essential component in the relative stability of Austrian post-war society in the extremely volatile reconstruction phase is largely ignored. Yet even after the collapse of the communist bloc this question still plays a part in public opinion, as could and still can be seen in, say, the prejudices against the Central and Eastern European EU applicants. The confrontation over the Temelín nuclear power station brought in yet older prejudices vis-à-vis the Czechs, reaching back to the nationality conflicts of around 1900. These images were preserved in the ice of the Cold War, to reemerge after 1989. Neither school nor university has been able to exert any modifying influence on these national stereotypes handed down for three or four generations – not that they wanted to.

All in all, then, in my view anti-communism has a much more important unifying function both at elite level and in social discourse since 1945 than, for instance, the myth of the 'Lagerstrafe', that is, the traumatic memories of Nazi concentration camps or jails shared by men who were later to become ÖVP and SPÖ functionaries.

Demarcation vis-à-vis Germany and Eastern Europe: The Wicked 'Prussian'

The exclusion of all debate, even in theoretical terms, about a 'pan-German' option, which might in fact have started up again among the social democrats, was followed through consistently after 1945 and firmly kept to. Allied pressure, along with the clear logic that the thesis of having been a victim of military aggression by Hitler's Germany in 1938 required the governing parties to drop the idea of Anschluss, prevailed – at first primarily as a useful state doctrine aimed at fending off reparation demands as well as at keeping Jewish restitution and especially compensation claims financially low and delaying over satisfying them. Anyone not willing to share this state doctrine was disciplined, as was, for instance, the editor in chief of the socialist *Linzer Tagblatt*, Dr. Alois Oberhummer, after an article of 7 February 1946 headed 'Good Austrians – Good Cultural Germans.' In this article he defended the Austrians' membership in the German cultural nation, on the grounds that the 'Austrian people' consisted of many nations. The SPÖ party leaderships in Vienna and Linz immediately distanced themselves from this article, and the U.S. administration briefly imposed a publication ban on the paper. Perhaps the most prominent Social Democratic official in exile, Friedrich Adler, was by contrast still railing from abroad in 1955 against Austria's independence as a state. In 1945 he had called in vain for a plebiscite on the repeal of the 1938 Anschluss. The Utopia of a pan-German revolution on the basis of 1848 had thus not yet been laid aside by many, but in practical politics it no longer played any part.

As opinion surveys showed, however, this ban on discussion was broken after 1949 by the Association of Independents (VdU), in whose hands the idea of unity degenerated into extreme German nationalism of a right-wing conservative stamp. Open and more intensive discussion of Austria as a German cultural nation might perhaps have averted the long shadows of this debate, which reached right into the 1970s and 1980s.

Paradigmatic examples of the heavy stress placed on detachment from everything German as a state doctrine of the Second Republic can be found in the cultural-policy debate after 1945. The very image of Austria in exile was defined primarily by backward-looking, classically-oriented cultural activities, becoming in many cases not too far removed from the grotesque image of Austria in the era of the 'corporate state'. The ideas of State Secretary for Mass Education, Schools and Education Ernst Fischer, a communist who had brought a sort of anti-Prussian ideology for Austria back from exile in Moscow, even enthused the former editor in chief of the Christian Social central organ *Reichspost,* Friedrich Funder: 'The Communists have found a very gifted representative in government in the person of Dr. Fischer … The strongly Austrian note he repeatedly strikes is, I feel, genuine.'[17] Under Fischer, a decree of 3 September 1945 even brought in a subject entitled 'language of instruction' (instead of 'German'), a measure mostly wrongly ascribed to his successor, the ÖVP Education Minister Felix Hurdes, since the decree was not actually implemented on certificates till after the elections in November 1945. The ÖVP in turn did not just rely on rather laughable national gestures, but instead aimed at a radical 'Austrification' in schooling, mostly referring back to the pre-1918 baroque and imperial heritage, with a strongly Catholic overlay. For school teaching, for instance, the 'Programmatic Guidelines' summarized the objective as 'total permeation ... with Austrian ideas'. At the same time there were calls for 'the most intensive work on building up the Austrian Nation', to form 'a strong, proud Austrian national and cultural awareness'.[18]

This radical cultural-policy demarcation vis-à-vis the 'Prussianness' of the eighteenth and nineteenth centuries was intensified by the Allied policy of deporting all 'Old-Reich Germans', i.e. people who before 13 March 1938 had been German nationals, back to Germany. Hundreds of thousands of 'Reich Germans', men, women and children, were – without any arguments about their share of political responsibility – transported from Austria to Germany in 1945–46, with families frequently being broken up. The leading German theatre and opera director Peter Stein recalls with amazement the radical Austrification he went through as a child in Salzburg, as does the German psychoanalyst Horst Eberhard Richter, sent back to the 'Reich' from Tyrol as a former Wehrmacht soldier.

Sudeten German refugees were let in by Austria only extremely reluctantly and in small numbers; Renner's Provisional State Government and the then Lower Austrian Provincial President Leopold Figl, for instance, called for immediate closure of the border with Czechoslovakia by the Red Army. Even people from Southern Bohemia and Moravia with old Austrian roots were not to be allowed to enter Austria. Of course, the food supply situation in 1945 was catastrophic, and additionally there were almost two million refugees already residing on Austrian territory. On the other hand, the debates in the Provisional State Government voiced wholesale condemnation of all Sudeten Germans as National Socialists, whereas there was a much more understanding attitude towards Austria's 'own' Nazis. Alarming reports of the refugees' plight changed nothing in the government's attitude: 'The transports are totally disorganized ... Some transports arrived with the dead falling out of the waggons.'[19] On 9 January 1946 Chancellor Leopold Figl once again declared in the Council of Ministers that no exceptions should be made to the deportations of Sudeten Germans and 'Volksdeutsche': 'This expulsion of aliens should start in Vienna, followed by Lower Austria, and then all the Reich Germans and Volksdeutsche from Hungary, Romania and the East should be brought to this camp. This will of course mean big problems, particularly as regards provisioning. The Russians have to date registered over 92,000 aliens who are to be expelled from the Russian zone. Several tens of thousands will have to be added to this number. If 160,000 to 180,000 people can be got out of Vienna, Lower Austria and Burgenland, that will considerably ease our food situation for the future.'[20]

Such actions were also felt as symbolically clearing individual Austrians from co-responsibility in the terror, aggression and annihilation policies of National Socialism. The point here is by no means about collective responsibility, but about actually dealing with the many perpetrators in one's own State community. U.S. opinion surveys of Austria soon after the war's end showed how deep-rooted the social processes already were that overnight pronounced almost all Austrians to be 'victims' and victors, without awaiting the outcome of the political and legal clarification of the share of Austrians in the Nazi terror and expansion regime, and in the Holocaust. The question 'Do you believe the whole Austrian people shares guilt for the war, because it let a government come to power that wanted to plunge the world into war?' was answered yes in December 1946 by only 4 per cent, and by 15 per cent with partial affirmation. The clear majority, 71 per cent, saw no shared guilt at all, while 10 per cent gave no opinion.[21] Today there are some – as will be shown in Chapter 9 on the basis of empirical studies – who hold a 'main perpetrator' doctrine. This is equally one-sided, but ultimately a delayed consequence of that broad apologetic process that in the 1960s led in jury trials to totally unjustified acquittals of war criminals like Franz Murer and others.

In the 1950s and into the 1960s, relations between West Germany and Austria were fairly tense, although Austria's return to economic independence had rapidly accelerated after 1955. In this period the Austrian victim doctrine had concrete repercussions on the nationalization of German property and on the complex negotiations about the restitution of German 'private property' in Austria. It was not only these negotiations that were dominated – from the viewpoint of the German Foreign Office – by 'anti-German elements'. All responsibility for the Second World War and the Holocaust (and consequently all compensation claims) was passed on to the Federal Republic of Germany. On the question of sequestered German property, the Republic of Austria similarly defined itself as a victim and endeavoured to nationalize as much formerly German property as possible by way of compensation. Chancellor Konrad Adenauer did not conceal his feelings over so emphatically anti-German a stance on the part of Austria in these negotiations over assets, and said at the time to then State Secretary Bruno Kreisky: 'So, Austrian property in Germany? You know, Mr Kreisky, if I knew where Hitler's bones were to be found I'd gladly return them to you as Austrian property.'[22]

It was only in relation to the national anthem that Austria did not manage to assert its old/new cultural superiority vis-à-vis Germany. Particularly the socialists in the government opposed the revival of the old Haydn tune, so as to avoid symbolic partial restoration of the monarchy. As the Tyrolese ÖVP Member of Parliament Franz Gschnitzer said resignedly in 1952 about the new anthem: 'All honour to Mozart – but noble inanities and a saccharine ode do not an anthem make.' By now, though, Germany had usurped the old anthem, and Austria had lost it 'out of fear and cowardice'.[23] So there was nothing for it but to go for the unloved new tune – after internal investigations by the Education Ministry had 'absolved' Mozart of the accusation of anti-Catholic freemasonry.

Demarcation vis-à-vis the Slavic Roots

It is a paradox that this small state, with a population accurately defined by former Austrian ÖVP Foreign Minister Lujo Tončić-Sorinj as a Slavic mixture with chance German dominance, has an extremely negative attitude towards its Slavic neighbours. The oft-stressed 'Mitteleuropa' nostalgia, with a hint of nostalgia for the monarchy too, remained confined to the elite and never corresponded to public opinion in Austria. It is hard not to feel that many Austrians are here denying their own or their family's roots. Thus, in November 1999 – just after the elections to the national assembly – only 31 per cent favoured Poland's inclusion in the EU, whereas Poles had a much more positive image of Austria, deriving from the high point of neutrality in the 1970s (though after February 2000 this fell from a previous 60 per cent expressing sympathy to 41 per cent).[24] The degree of assent to the Czech Republic's entry was somewhat higher, but at 36 per cent well below a majority, as was the 45 per cent for Slovenia. Only Hungary reached 56 per cent in its favour. References to a shared past within the monarchy were scarcely rated positively, while many a historical preference, and dislike, seems to have been preserved, such as the sympathy for Hungary and the rejection of the Czechs, but also the great coolness towards Poland. The weeks of blockades and demonstrations along the Czech border against the start-up of the Temelín nuclear power plant widened this rift with the Czech people still further, but without these prejudices relations would likely not have deteriorated as they did.

There is also a problem in the fact that in connection with pro-EU propaganda in 1994–95, a background scenario of threats from 'the 'East' was pushed, without any rational explanations: the talk was chiefly of criminality, 'insuperable poverty' and 'large-scale migrations'. Only in an EU framework – said the Europe White Paper from the chancellor's office – could these threats be countered. Academics too initially made no rational contribution here, calculating, on the basis of inadequate fundamental data with no backing in experience, totally absurd migration potentials that rendered debate yet more acrimonious. The subsequent attempts at rationalization using more precise information and methods produced hardly any real effect on current discourse.

Since the wave of refugees from Hungary in 1956, Austria has been fond of presenting itself, both at home and abroad, as a country of asylum. In 1987, for instance, then Interior Minister Karl Blecha talked of how 'we in Austria have taken in 1,966,000 people as a country of first asylum', and of how around a third of these had been fully integrated.[25] The same minister was even at the time obliged to admit, however, that 'Austria takes in refugees with such open arms because we know that 80 per cent of them do not want to stay here at all'.[26] Although until 1918 it had been the product of intensive internal migration within the Habsburg monarchy, Austria in the interwar years was already no longer regarding itself as a country of immigration, and the Second Republic defined itself, despite de facto immigration of over a million, exclusively as a neutral country of asylum. Refugees were not primarily to be integrated into Austria, but passed on as quickly as possible to countries of immigration like the U.S., Canada or Australia. This extremely important restriction was not, however, incorporated in the image-building, whether in 1956 (Hungary), 1968 (invasion of Czechoslovakia by Warsaw Pact troops) or 1981 (imposition of martial law in Poland).

The end of the Cold War brought with it the crumbling of that pillar of Austria's identity that consisted in its role as a 'country of asylum'. In early March 1990 a vehement debate on the refugee problem broke out, led up to by public pronouncements by Social Democratic officials and Social Democratic Interior Minister Franz Löschnak about exploding refugee numbers. Of course the asylum seekers, many of them in reality economic refugees, were a politically sensitive topic, but the populist media strategy only made matters worse and failed to solve the underlying problem. Particularly the mass media – foremost, but by no means alone, the *Kronenzeitung* – heightened fears and prejudices with wildly exaggerated figures and individual stories. It has to be noted that the *Kronenzeitung* is the by far largest member of the yellow press, with up to 2.3 million readers on Sundays, in a country with 8 million inhabitants.

Even in the new Europe, enlarged to twenty-five member states since 2004, the Austrian trend towards marking itself off from neighbouring countries and the former nationalities of the Habsburg monarchy has continued, indeed even intensified. Only some sort of depth psychology can by now see this trend as a result of nineteenth-century nationality conflicts or of traumatization from being reduced to an insignificant, crisis-ridden petty state after 1918. I regard as more relevant the fear of social and economic crisis as a consequence of EU enlargement. Prosperity and the welfare state have contributed decisively to rapid identity-building; but this important pillar of identity – small state means social and economic as well as political security – seems from the Austrians' viewpoint to be threatened by the new competitors in the East. The fact that the Austrian economy earned high profits in this area after 1990 is blocked out, finding a place only in the business pages and political Sunday speeches. With no public response, such statements as that by Economics Minister Martin Bartenstein, that some 40 per cent of Austrian growth is to be attributed to the fact of having opened up to the East, sink without a trace.[27]

The Austrians' Welfare State: A Limited Community of Solidarity

As to the public memory, what predominated in collective recollection at the end of 1999, looking back over the twentieth century in answer to a question about 'events that particularly affected your family', was the 'hardship in the postwar period' (35 per cent of those surveyed). Only after that came 'hardship before the Second World War' (30 per cent), the entry of the German troops in 1938 (20 per cent), job loss in the 1980s and 1990s (19 per cent), persecution by the Nazi regime (12 per cent), expulsion at the end of the war (12 per cent), the First World War (11 per cent), the end of the monarchy (6 per cent), the economic crisis of the 1920s (6 per cent) and the civil war in the 1930s (6 per cent).[28] Here we can already see clear generation-specific memory trends, which need not correspond at all to real long-term effects on the political culture of the Second Republic. It is accordingly best to look more closely at the role attaching to social and economic expansion in identity-building in Austria, which ranks among the ten richest industrialized countries but in which at the same time enormous numbers of people – around a million out of eight million inhabitants – are threatened by poverty. The daily *Kurier* reduced the relevant statistics to a single graphically terse negative denominator: 'In Austria more and more are earning less and less.' Particularly hard hit by this negative development are women, who – by contrast with other welfare-state systems – earn markedly less in Austria than do men.[29] Foreigners, men and women, earn relatively even less.

The year 1945 is equated in Austrians' collective memory with the reconstruction of the economy. Fairly exactly, the first income growth going beyond daily needs is set in the 1960s, while the Kreisky era is seen as the high point of social satisfaction too. Worries about retirement and pensions, and about jobs, continue to be the central themes for politics here. Defence of the relatively high standard of living, as it stood at the end of the Cold War, is not only reflected through fears (which are then also expressed in electoral support for nationalist positions) but is also increasingly being translated into a mood of radical and emotional demarcation. Over 60 per cent of Austrians, both men and women, were firmly convinced in 2002 that EU enlargement would bring them disadvantages. At the same time they felt exasperated and powerless, since the enlargement process was already irreversible. Taken all round, support for the EU in Austria in February/March 2004 had fallen markedly:[30] Austria's EU membership was rated a 'good thing' by 30 per cent and a 'bad thing' by 29 per cent; 36 per cent felt it was neither good nor bad. EU membership on the whole was seen as a benefit for Austria by 38 per cent, and as a disadvantage by 47 per cent. Since autumn 2002 there has been a continuous decline in the approval rate, with the February/ March 2004 values being the poorest since the Eurobarometer measurements began (1995–96).

The fact that in Austria, by contrast with Germany or Spain, open brutal attacks against 'foreigners' are not currently happening is no reason to rejoice. Many people have already forgotten that the murder of four young Roma (gypsies) in Burgenland and the other attempted killings by the loner Franz Fuchs were definitely influenced by the tenor of the debates on migration and immigration. One other phenomenon that allegedly disproves hostility towards foreigners is Austrians' generosity in donating, especially for charitable and humanitarian purposes, which is extremely high – even in a European comparison. This is not, however, really connected with a genuine feeling of solidarity, but is the descendant of traditional Catholic 'poor relief', perfectly addressed by such organizations as Caritas and the Red Cross, as well as the TV campaign 'Neighbour in Distress'. And it changes nothing in the high degree of demarcation vis-à-vis both immigrants and the non-German-speaking neighbouring peoples. The fact that many refugees from the wars in former Yugoslavia – 150,000 or more – were allowed into Austria is in my view the result of a basic political and media consensus against the Milošević regime in Serbia. Here the Cold War again played a part – Serbia being the last bastion of communism in Europe, and into the bargain an enemy from before 1914 and afterwards – as did Austria's traditional role as a country of refugee transit. If the political debate at the beginning of the refugee waves had at the same time focused on integration into Austria, the topic would have exploded. No one had originally expected, or addressed, the fact that the refugees would also in large part stay in Austria.

Austria as a Nation of Culture

The self-image of Austrians as a closed cultural nation was reflected in 1980 in a survey on 'Austria as the bearer of a great cultural heritage',[31] a claim to which 47 per cent assented. In 1987, 45 per cent indicated agreement with this idea, while 74 per cent of those surveyed additionally stressed Austria's cultural heritage in general. An analysis of opinion surveys from 1980 through 1987 shows a steady rise in the importance of – mostly traditional – art and culture for the national ego in Austria, with the popular arts (operetta, folk music) to the fore, followed by classical music and theatre; only the importance of Austrian medicine let it squeeze in at second place between these two. The reasons for this special emphasis on cultural values, involving intensive assent to an ethnic identity, lie in the shift in that identity which took place after 1989. Whereas the 1980s and 1990s had brought a further strengthening of nation-state discourses (Austrian patriotism), the ensuing migration and asylum debate ended in sharp demarcation. This trend additionally offered psychological reassurance after entry into the European Union in 1995. And the government's EU entry campaign carried a correspondingly patriotic appeal, with its central slogan 'Austria is Europe'.

It is significant here that the cultural achievements of the monarchy were redefined as Austrian, i.e. de facto 'Austrianized': the diverse roots of today's state society in a multi-ethnic state and in the migration and assimilation processes of the turn of the century mostly remain confined to academic discussions. This is also connected with the fact that the monarchy has no place in public awareness of the Austrian nation. The 'usable' identification elements from the Habsburg period are transferred entirely separately into the Second Republic, without taking any account of their historical interrelations with a broad area of peoples and cultures. This is the result of strictly republican school teaching that only ever situates historical images, from the Babenbergs to the Habsburgs, within the borders of the post-1945 small state. Vienna and today's Austria are to the fore as the site for these images.

At least since 1945, Austrians have no longer been taught to think and act in terms of large spaces. It is no coincidence that perhaps the internationally best-known politician of the Second Republic, Bruno Kreisky, always derived his approaches in his thinking from the Empire, to which he felt much attached because of his family origins. Putting it somewhat provocatively, the broad success of an Austrian identity brought a 'Swissification' in basic mentalities, which at the moment is leading to difficulties in adapting to globalization and acting in a European context. The centre of political action is no longer international connections – as in the Cold War or the times of détente and Ostpolitik – but specifically Austrian national interests. Popular culture and sport are increasingly dominating the political setup too. In 2000, for instance, one expert, the opinion researcher Rudolf Bretschneider, opined that only Austria as the land of traditional culture could be successfully 'sold' abroad.[32] It was only by this circuitous route that present-day aspects might, piecemeal, be conveyed. If, then, in the 1970s Austria was to be made ready to receive Europe, nowadays, evidently, it is Europe that is to be made ready to receive Austria. Tourism publicity has of course over the decades repeatedly changed the packaging, but the marketing content continues to follow guidelines from the 1950s, defined in one guide that appeared in 1955 by the following components: 'Haydn, Mozart, Beethoven, Schubert, Burgtheater, Staatsoper, Philharmoniker, Vienna Boys' Choir and the Salzburg Festival.' The foremost cultural policy-maker of the late 1950s and early 1960s, Heinrich Drimmel, summarized this backward-looking concept as follows: 'The country's material life requires representative culturalism. The image of the Festivals, the marble façades of the palaces of culture, act more persuasively to shape opinions politically in a mass democracy than the pressing need to … overcome … the shortfalls in support for scientific research and artistic activity.'[33] The economic upswing in the 1950s favoured this development, on tourism-oriented economic grounds too. At the same time, traditional high-culture activities raised the national self-confidence, as evinced by the reopening of the Staatsoper and the Burgtheater in 1955.

It was only at the end of the 1950s that resistance arose against these sociopolitical constraints, strengthened still further by opinions published in the print media and by reactionary trends in broadcasting. This resistance developed in group niches in the underground scene, but also in Catholic circles and in individual 'resistance centres' in several of the provinces, for instance in Graz. In the 1960s these manifold forms of artistic opposition and cultural protest were sup-

pressed, sometimes even with the use of police-state methods – to the applause of
the media and the public. But the underlying social unease at this development,
which was also part of the 'siege mentality' of Austria's political culture, emerged
increasingly clearly. In the 1970s this social pressure was to lead to a radical
shift in the artistic and cultural policy strategies of government bureaucracies and
political decision makers. This, however, in no way meant that the underlying
conservative, reactionary mood had disappeared overnight.

From the Victim Myth to the Sole Perpetrator Myth

Sociological analyses of the Austrian identity reflect the fact that official Austria, and soon the public too, defined itself primarily and almost exclusively as
a victim of the Nazi regime and of the Second World War. Historians such as
Robert Knight or Gerhard Botz and Albert Müller, as well as the group around
the linguist Ruth Wodak, instead stress the importance of the victim myth in
underpinning the identity of a great postwar majority in Austria. In construct-
ing a broad, undifferentiated 'victim' majority out of surviving soldiers from the
Second World War and the 'home front' generation (the great majority of whom
were women), numbers of conflicts from the interwar years were buried. Under
the slogan 'cover the graves, but do not forget', this postwar project was to become very relevant, especially in the Cold War. It was not until the 1970s and
finally the 1980s that this repression of memory collapsed, under the impetus
of reassessment of the Holocaust in the U.S. and thereafter in Europe too. Both
there and here, a more critical debate on National Socialism developed. And
there were correspondingly negative press reports on the reception of the war
criminal Walter Reder, an ex-SS Obersturmbannführer freed in Italy, by FPÖ
Defence Minister Friedhelm Frischenschlager.

When it then came out in the U.S. media as well as in Austria that the ÖVP
presidential candidate and former UN Secretary-General Kurt Waldheim had
covered up his wartime past as a well-informed staff officer in the Balkans, an
international and national debate ensued about Austria's victim role in the Second World War. After Waldheim's election – de facto confirmation of the victim
doctrine by a majority of voters – Austrian foreign policy encountered difficulties
both in the U.S. and in Western democratic states in general. Although protocol bestowed on him the title of the State's First Man, Waldheim received no
invitations to visit Western Europe or the United States and was diplomatically
isolated.

Today Austria is beginning to see itself confronted with an additional phenomenon: the constructs of the victim doctrine are eroding, but at the same time
a section of the political elite is striving, through unreserved acknowledgement of
the formerly marginalized Jewish victims, but also of the sufferings of Roma and

Sinti gypsies and others, to uphold the victim narrative, with these persecuted minorities as it were standing in for Austria. That this is at least indirectly serving as a compensatory element in the collective memory is plain to see. It was around this political trope that the discussion of the Resistance in an official symposium in Parliament in January 2005, at the start of the Year of Remembrance, revolved: instead of critical reflection on Austrian perpetrators, men and women, in the Holocaust and the Nazi terror machinery or the German Wehrmacht, it was again – as it had been back in 1960–65 – the Austrian Resistance that was stressed. This approach ultimately also meant ruling out any direct facing up to the history of the perpetrators.

A Country of Asylum and Immigration against Its Will

In the International Year against Racism, 1997, the EU Commission did an EU-wide survey in order to determine racist potential empirically. After Belgium (22 per cent) and France (16 per cent), Austria took third place on the EU's negative scale, with 'very racist attitudes' among 14 per cent of the population. For the 'quite racist' figure, Austria at 28 per cent stood in fourth place, after Belgium (33 per cent), France (32 per cent) and Denmark (31 per cent). There were lower rates of reported non-racists (26 per cent in Austria) only in Denmark (17 per cent), Belgium (19 per cent), Finland (22 per cent), the Netherlands (24 per cent) and France (25 per cent).

The survey showed that 44 per cent of Austrian men and women are still caught up in the thought patterns of racism, without any broad enlightenment and discussion campaign having been started. Austria can, as we have shown, be classed as a country of asylum and immigration against its will. Austria today, with around 8.1 million inhabitants, is home to some 740,000 men and women with a migration background; between 1985 and 1996 some 425,000 entered the country. Since 1997, rigid residence requirements have aligned further inflows primarily towards family reunification. Surveys show that fear and rejection are disproportionately strong particularly where markedly fewer foreigners live. Moreover, only 14 per cent of Austrians estimate the proportion of foreigners correctly, with most (24 per cent) underestimating it very considerably. This means, however, that it is not actual personal evaluation or direct contact that are important for the images of foreigners, but irrational and emotional conceptions.

The economic growth of the Second Republic would have failed had there not – applying the criteria of demography – been immigration since 1945. Thus, between 1989 and 1994 the number of foreigners rose to 700,000 (8.9 per cent), especially after the collapse of the Iron Curtain and in the wake of the Balkan wars. Previously, recruitment of foreign labour – mostly from Yugoslavia and Turkey – had by 1974 raised the proportion of foreigners to 4.1 per cent (as in

1951, when the alien contingent consisted primarily of not-yet-naturalized Sudeten Germans and other ethnic Germans). Numbers then stayed almost constant at 300,000 until 1981.

In the debate on immigration and EU enlargement, which for years now has often been vehement, it is repeatedly claimed that Austria cannot possibly be anti-foreigner, since after all it took in large waves of refugees in 1956 and 1968. But the fact is that of the some 200,000 Hungarians who entered, only just over 30,000 stayed in Austria. In 1968 too Austria functioned more as a transit country: 160,000 Czechs and Slovaks stayed only briefly in Austria, around 10,000 filed for asylum, and 600 had been naturalized by 1970. It was not just the KPÖ press that was then raving against the refugees; the willingness for integration on the part of Austrians was very low even in a Cold War context. Austria's gain in reputation in Western Europe and the U.S. was by contrast high, as a neutral country that had positioned itself ideologically clearly on the side of the West. Not that Austria's willingness to help should be denied: on the contrary, it redounds to its credit, and in 1956 was associated with great political courage too. But it ought not to be adduced in our present context as an indication that Austrians were highly willing to integrate foreigners.

As regards Austrian emigrants, the Republic retained a negative attitude in the immediate postwar period. Chancellor Karl Renner wrote that rapid restitution

ILLUSTRATION I.3

When good intentions meet reality: Poster of 'Aktion Mitmensch' designed to promote tolerance of ethnic minorities and sponsored by the Austrian Advertising Industry (1973). The words allude to the Slavic origin of many Austrians.

of stolen property was undesirable, lest the 'Jewish masses' flood back. His successor, Leopold Figl of the ÖVP, himself a concentration-camp survivor, began in 1947 to come out fairly openly against émigrés' demands, since they had sat out the Second World War in safety. Vice-Chancellor Adolf Schärf frequently railed against the presence of Jewish DPs in hotels in Bad Gastein. Here it should however also be noted that especially the U.S. occupiers, and the British, prevented the entry of Austrian émigrés into Austria until 1946. Only in exceptional cases were permits granted. They too regarded the exiles as material for social-policy debates, but stability in the Cold War was more important than implementing human rights and building a living democracy.

Folk Culture in the 'Land of Dancers and Waiters'

Not long after 1918, Arthur Schnitzler stated[34] that the Austrians, that is, the German-speaking 'remnant' of the Habsburg monarchy, would increasingly see themselves as the musical, light-hearted heirs of the shattered multiethnic Empire. Anton Wildgans, in his 1929 'Discourse on Austria', recast this as a new theory of cultural superiority because of 'race mixture': 'the Austrian is, by language and original descent, a German, and as such has repeatedly offered German culture and nationality the most valuable services in every area of human action and creation; but his Germanness, however convincedly and faithfully he holds to it, is less unambiguous and brittle in him, because of the mixture of many types of blood and historical experience, but on the other hand all the more conciliatory, cosmopolitan and European.' The Salzburg Festivals of the 1920s perfectly conveyed this idea, and the country profited, in the 1920s and then especially in the 1930s, through tourism resulting from this self-definition.

After 1945 tourism began once again to become an essential component of the economy. Marshall Plan money and the ensuing ERP loans were purposefully invested in the appropriate tourism infrastructure. Between 1948 and 1950 the number of overnight stays had already risen from 11 to 16 million. (For comparison, in 1993 128 million overnight stays were recorded, with Austria able to offer a total of 1.15 million beds.)[35] In the balance of payments the revenues derived from tourism have secured an important, if not the most important, role. It is noteworthy that the overall performance of the Austrian economy is in the public mind totally dominated by tourism, which is actually only one component of it. Thus, in 1987, 91 per cent of Austrians named tourism as the major achievement in Austria, followed by the lower crime rate and the high level of social security.[36]

This 'success rate' no doubt has its background also in the continuing strong ties to one's region and 'soil': although the agricultural sector has since 1945 rapidly lost in importance, 'agricultural' codes continue to play an important part. This can also be seen from comparisons between news magazines and film self-portraits and the films used in tourist advertising in the 1980s and 1990s. The reference back to nature is an essential thing for the Austrian identity; only the packaging is different. This extends into politics too, where for instance the Austrian Farmers' Union, despite its ever-shrinking membership numbers, plays a disproportionate role in ÖVP decision-making. In recent years this trend has increased still further, as a consequence of the ever-commoner second homes in country or village areas. In political marketing, pseudo-folk 'traditional' local dress has acquired an important media function that was not there in the 1970s and 1980s.

Since the 1990s '*Heimat*' marketing has been pursued, as was already the case in the 'corporate state'. Then, regional '*Heimatwerke*' were used to try to package a primarily peasant folk culture or, in many respects (e.g. the regional costumes), to create it in the first place. The political objective was cultural defence against and demarcation vis-à-vis not only National Socialism, but also socialism and Bolshevism. The Nazi regime too sought to operate with traditional, peasant-conservative value patterns using folk culture. After 1945 folk culture served as a barrier against the Allies' 'foreign' cultural influences, especially against jazz and other forms of American 'unculture' (as it was termed) in the U.S. zone in Salzburg and Upper Austria.

One can find endless confirmation of the effects in history-of-mentality terms of the inclusive and therefore also exclusive tendencies of organized '*Heimatkultur*' after 1945. The importance of this reproduction of an artificial folk culture, reduced in films to total kitsch, for identity-building should not be underestimated, especially in demarcation vis-à-vis Germany. What this means is that the '*Heimatkultur*' of the 1950s helped to develop an Austrian identity and support the move away from '*deutsch*' nationalism; at the same time, though, it helped to conserve nationally dominated prejudices (often in turn based on the constructs of radical '*deutsch*' nationalism from the late nineteenth century).

Between Regional Identity and Consumption-oriented Non-identity

While in 1987 the Viennese, Lower Austrians and Burgenlanders saw themselves as committed to a strong local patriotism, they also displayed the highest level in Austria of pan-Austrian national consciousness, markedly higher than the Tyrolese, Vorarlbergers or Carinthians. In the year 2000, however, Western Austria had gained in patriotism; currently Carinthians, Vorarlbergers and Styrians are the proudest of Austria, and the Viennese have slipped down to last place.[37]

This regional disproportionality can be found very clearly as early as the period after 1945, with, by contrast, the 1970s especially bringing stronger harmonization. Behind this lay a clear political objective of Bruno Kreisky, who in exile in Sweden had realized the importance of regional identity (for instance among soldiers who had deserted the German Wehrmacht for Sweden). And it was the provinces, not the all-powerful Vienna Party, that took Kreisky to the top of the SPÖ. As chancellor he accordingly sought to promote the development of infrastructure in the western provinces, which in turn led to electoral shifts in favour of the SPÖ. And in this way he ultimately also strengthened the sense of a pan-Austrian identity. Surveys document that the pan-Austrian identity was certainly strongest in 1980, only to be weakened again later by regional competition.[38]

Correspondingly, the attempts in 1995–96 to celebrate a thousand years of Austria were a failure. Are we today perhaps seeing the first developments in the direction of a postnational diversification of Austria along regional fault-lines? At the same time, the real political powers of the provinces have declined since EU accession, and calls are heard here and there for a cutback on expensive provincial parliaments and governments. It may at least for the short term be doubted that this loss of competences and power by the provinces will be replaced through EU regional policy.

Yet no trend in the direction of a European consciousness is currently evident in Austria. And Robert Musil's ideas about 'world citizenship' find a response only among a few elites (often Green-voting men and women). Whether the EU citizens on the territory of today's Austria may one day, as under the monarchy, identify with the bureaucratic centre – now Brussels – as a focus of loyalty remains to be seen. Around a third of seventeen- to nineteen-year-old Austrians, male and female, have at any rate no national loyalties at all, but instead follow the marketing codes of the consumer society. And this group shows a corresponding susceptibility to populist political marketing.

Summary

There is nothing flabbier than identity discourses. One has to be agree with Ernest Gellner: nations were invented in modern times and are the outcomes of social construction processes. National identities are in constant flux, and they change over time. Nonetheless, it is possible to venture a stocktaking for Austria, in which the strands of identity can be seen to operate with differing intensities.

The central anchor of today's Austrian identity was already there in the nineteenth century: the extremely high degree of political, socioeconomic and cultural concentration of all that happened in the monarchy on the small German-speaking core country, which, along with the Hungarians, ruled as a minority over several national majorities. Even after 1918 this Austro-solipsism continued, in total denial of the international realities and in the belief that all Germany was waiting for the 'Anschluss'. The Austrians of the interwar years felt they were in fact the better 'cultural Germans', and made every effort to isolate themselves in

Europe from the democracies and seek alliances with fascist Italy and authoritarian Hungary.

Outside the elites, the national identity of the small state of Austria, which after 1945 – by contrast with the interwar period – everybody wanted, was initially a construct. It was primarily defined in antithesis to Germany (culturally, to the German Reich and Prussia), on the basis of a propaganda declaration, the Moscow Declaration of 1 November 1943. This proclamation by the foreign ministers of the United States, USSR and UK described Austria as the first victim of Hitler's aggression, but at the same time called for resistance, because of shared responsibility for the Second World War. After 1945 the degree to which Austrians had contributed to their own liberation needed to be assessed. But no assessment came, since by 1946 the Cold War primarily required, from a Western viewpoint, stability, not democratic experiments. The Soviet Union too was in agreement with the status quo.

The economic and social crisis brought a 'regression' to the times before 1933, though with at least formal suspension of the differences between the Christian-Social camp (now the ÖVP) and its socialist counterpart (the SPÖ, with no united front with the KPÖ). To strengthen the small state's identity and stress achievement potential vis-à-vis other countries, high culture was strongly emphasized, and rebuilding the Burgtheater and Staatsoper figured as a national concern. At the 'Ostarrîchi' celebrations in 1946, Austria was also again officially rebaptized as a cultural great power, with allusions to examples from the authoritarian 'corporate state' and with a strongly Catholic-Habsburg keynote. In 1946, then, as before 1938, a signal was to be sent to the German cultural nation.

The most successful identity metaphor was, however, undoubtedly the country's neutrality, associated with an economic upswing presided over by the social partnership. This for the first time really instilled positive, tangible content into the sense of a 'special role' for Austria. In the cultural sphere, despite a theoretical fixation on the nation state and despite de facto immigration, it was subliminal codes hinting at great mistrust of strangers and foreigners that dominated. Till 1970 recourse was not made to the multiculturalism of the Habsburg monarchy; on the contrary, all scientific and cultural achievements of the 'melting pot' of Austria-Hungary were Austrianized. 'Modernity' remained entirely excluded and had to be reimported into Austria via foreign publications such as those of William Johnston and Carl E. Schorske. It was not until the tenure of Bruno Kreisky, with his strong affinity – despite his being a Social Democrat – for the broad territory of the Austro-Hungarian Empire, that these Catholic-conservative and imperial constructs broke down and there came a slow, gradual opening in the direction of the moderns from around 1900 and thereafter.

In 1986 the possibilities of integration into the Western European area (EC, later EU) began – partly as a consequence of the economic problems connected with adapting nationalized industry to the emerging globalization – to take on increasingly clear outlines. At the same time Mikhail Gorbachev's glasnost and perestroika loosened the fetters of the Cold War, and the Soviet Union acquiesced to EU accession by Austria. Yet, notwithstanding the overwhelming majority of yes votes in the EU referendum of 1994, the Austrian identity has narrowed inwards still further since 1989. The referendum result was ultimately a yes to maintenance of the standard of living, but it did not mean any European broadening of the Austrian identity. Austria's special role in the Cold War was long played out. At the same time a cleavage grew between political elites, who wanted to abolish neutrality so as to join NATO or the WEU, and the population. This vexed phase of Austrian politics was dominated by exclusion and hostility towards outsiders, without the political elites and the mass media uniting to consistently oppose the clear signs of open verbal racism. Such impressive actions as the torchlight parade on 23 January 1993 ultimately lacked sociopolitical staying power and enlightening impact in the clash with xenophobia.

Surveys carried out in 2008 confirm that the European identity in Austria is as weakly developed as ever.[39] Only 28 per cent saw the EU as a 'good thing'; in the EU of twenty-five only Britain took an even dimmer view (29 per cent). The gap between contentedness with democracy in Austria (64 per cent contented, 32 per cent not contented) and scepticism about the EU (40 per cent contented, 46 per cent not contented) has increased since 2003. At the same time, the exclusive national identity is booming: 50 per cent of Austrians see themselves as being only Austrians in the near future, and 36 per cent as Austrians and Europeans. In no other EU country at the time were there such strong trends in the direction of exclusively national identity.

Against this background, it becomes clear that Austria is currently in a difficult transformation phase. The national identity recently attained, with its connotations of extremely positive social and economic components, is in competition with three massive changes in the socioeconomic environment: globalization, European integration and European enlargement. That is why Austrians are currently reacting so strongly by withdrawing into national and often even regional identity clusters.

NOTES

1. Gertrude Enderle-Burcel, Rudolf Jeřábek and Leopold Kammerhofer (eds.). *Protokolle des Kabinettsrates der Provisorischen Regierung Karl Renner 1945. Vol. 1,* (Horn-Vienna: Verlag Österreich, 1995), 55.
2. Ibid.
3. Constantin Goschler, *Wiedergutmachung. Westdeutschland und die Verfolgten des Nationalsozialismus (1945–1954)* (Munich: Oldenbourg, 1992), 270.
4. http://people-press.org/reports/display.php3?ReportID=185 (accessed 1 June 2005).
5. Compare *profil* 28, 6 July 1998, referring to Tom W. Smith and Lars Jarko, *National Pride: A Cross-national Analysis* (NORC/University of Chicago, 1998).

6. Gerald Stourzh and Peter A. Ulram, *Österreichbewußtsein 1987* (Vienna: Dr. Fessel & Co, Institut für Meinungsforschung, 1987), 28.

7. See *Der Standard*, 11 August 2004, 6.

8. *News* 43, 26 October 2000, 57.

9. Smith and Jarko, *National Pride* (FN 5).

10. Max Haller (ed.), *Identität und Nationalstolz der Österreicher. Gesellschaftliche Ursachen und Funktionen. Herausbildung und Transformation seit 1945. Internationaler Vergleich* (Vienna: Böhlau, 1996).

11. Ruth Wodak, *Zur diskursiven Konstruktion nationaler Identität* (Frankfurt/Main: Suhrkamp, 1998).

12. Friedrich Heer, *Der Kampf um die österreichische Identität* (Vienna: Böhlau, 1981); Felix Kreissler, *Der Österreicher und seine Nation* (Vienna: Böhlau, 1984); Albert Reiterer, ed., *Nation und Nationalbewußtsein in Österreich* (Vienna: Verband d. Wiss. Ges. Österreichs, 1988); Anton Pelinka, *Zur österreichischen Identität. Zwischen deutscher Vereinigung und Mitteleuropa* (Vienna: Ueberreuter, 1990); Gerald Stourzh, *Vom Reich zur Republik: Studien zum Österreichbewußtsein im 20. Jahrhundert* (Vienna: Wiener Journal Zeitschriftenverlag, 1990); Ernst Bruckmüller, *Nation Österreich. Kulturelles Bewußtsein und gesellschaftlich-politische Prozesse* (Vienna: Böhlau, 1996).

13. http://derstandard.at/?url=/?id=1944961 (accessed 1 June 2005). These words were not spoken on the balcony of the Belvedere castle, but later on in the Marble Hall.

14. Compare Peter Thaler, *The Ambivalence of Identity: The Austrian Experience of Nation-Building in a Modern Society. Central European Studies* (West Lafayette, IN: Purdue Univ. Press, 2001), 167–172.

15. Ernst Hanisch, 'Überlegungen zum Funktionswandel des Antikommunismus. Eine österreichische Perspektive', in *Zeitgeschichte im Wandel. 3. Österreichischer Zeitgeschichtetag 1997,* ed. Gertraud Diendorfer, Gerhard Jagschitz and Oliver Rathkolb (Innsbruck-Vienna: Studien Verlag, 1998), 39.

16. See Wolfgang Müller, '"Genosse Filipov" und seine österreichischen "Freunde". Kommunikationslinien, Strategiedebatten und Entscheidungsmechanismen im Verhältnis zwischen KPÖ, Sowjetbesatzung und UdSSR 1946–1951', in *Osteuropa vom Weltkrieg zur Wende,* ed. Wolfgang Müller and Michael Portmann (Vienna: Verlag der Österreichischen Akademie der Wissenschaften, 2007), 153–159.

17. Friedrich Funder to Richard Schmitz, 14 September 1945, 2. Austrian State Archives, HHStA SB Nl.

18. Robert Kriechbaumer. Von der Illegalität zur Legalität. Die ÖVP im Jahr 1945. Politische und geistesgeschichtliche Aspekte des Entstehens der Zweiten Republik (Vienna: Multiplex Media Verlag, 1985), 290.

19. Enderle-Burcel et al. (eds.), Protokolle des Kabinettsrates, 209.

20. Enderle-Burcel, Gertrude and Rudolf Jerábek. Protokolle des Ministerrates der Zweiten Republik. Kabinett Leopold Figl I, Vol. I (Vienna: Verlag Österreich, 2004), p. 26.

21. Heinz P. Wassermann, *Naziland Österreich!? Studien zu Antisemitismus, Nation und Nationalsozialismus im öffentlichen Meinungsbild* (Innsbruck-Vienna: Studien Verlag, 2002).

22. Bruno Kreisky, *Zwischen den Zeiten. Erinnerungen aus fünf Jahrzehnten* (Berlin: Siedler, 1986), 449.

23. Oliver Rathkolb, 'Vom Freimaurerlied zur Bundeshymne', in *Begnadet für das Schöne. Der rot-weiß-rote Kulturkampf gegen die Moderne,* ed. Gert Kerschbaumer and Karl Müller (Vienna: Verlag für Gesellschaftskritik, 1992).

24. Österreichische Gesellschaft für Europapolitik. *Die EU-Erweiterung aus der Sicht der Österreicher und unserer Nachbarn* (Vienna: Self Publishing, 1999), 43, and Österreichische Gesellschaft für Europapolitik. *Osterweiterung am Prüfstand* (Vienna: Self Publishing, 2001), 10.

25. Cited in Gernot Heiss and Oliver Rathkolb, ed., *Asylland wider Willen. Flüchtlinge in Österreich im europäischen Kontext seit 1914* (Vienna: Jugend & Volk, 1995), 7.

26. *Der Standard,* 17 May 1990, 8.

27. http://www.zeit.de/2004/25/EU-_85sterreich (accessed 1 June 2005).

28. *Der Standard,* 31 December 1999, A6.

29. The wage difference stood around 33 per cent in 2002, women earning an average gross amount of €1,279 and men €1,904 per month – with additional regional variations. In Vienna the difference was lowest, around 24 per cent.

30. http://europa.eu.int/austria/factsheets/040712_eb61_text.pdf (accessed 1 June 2005).

31. Fessel GfK Institut für Marktforschung, *ORF Qualitätsmonitoring 1999. Das Kunst- und Kulturverständnis der Österreicher* (Vienna: GfK, 1999); Dr. Fessel & Co. Institut für Meinungsforschung, *Österreichbewußtsein 1987* (Vienna: Dr. Fessel & Co, 1987), 28–29.

32. Statement during the International Culture Conference 2000, notes of the author.

33. Cited by Martin Wasmair, *Österreich, schau auf deinen Schilling und behüte den lieben Gott! Kulturpolitische Rückschau auf ein Erfolgsrezept der ÖVP,* see http://www.igkultur/kulturrisse/1046078977/1046162765 (accessed 1 June 2005).

34. Arthur Schnitzler, *Tagebuch 1917–1919* (Vienna: Verlag der Österreichischen Akademie der Wissenschaften, 1985), 218.

35. Kurt Luger and Franz Rest, 'Mobile Privatisierung. Kultur und Tourismus in der Zweiten Republik', in *Österreich 1945–1955. Gesellschaft, Politik, Kultur,* ed. Reinhard Sieder, Hans Steinert and Emmerich Tálos (Vienna: Verlag für Gesellschaftskritik, 1995), 661.

36. Ibid., 666–667.

37. Dr. Fessel & Co., *Österreichbewußtsein 1987,* 29.

38. Thaler, *Identity,* 172.

39. Eurobarometer 69, 'Public opinion in the European Union. First results, June 2008', http://ec.europa.eu/public_opinion/archives/eb/eb69/eb_69_first_en.pdf (accessed 1 June 2005).

CHAPTER 2

Peculiarities of Austrian Democracy

The Austrian form of controlled democracy, typified by two big, dominant party blocs and the social partnership and termed *Proporz* (proportional), or concordant, democracy, was certainly a special case of the generally rather restricted development of democracy in Europe after 1945; by the 1960s many were already talking, in exaggerated language, of a demo-dictatorship. But this development had its reasons. In the collective self-image of Austrians, the Second Republic had been constructed as the deliberate opposite of the conflict- and violence-oriented First Republic, and the collaboration of the big political blocs retained its positive associations right into the 1950s.[1] It was not till the 1960s that there arose an increasingly widespread resistance to the Grand Coalition of the ÖVP and SPÖ, and in the 1980s to the social partnership too. Here, however, the question arises as to how far this gradual opening up of authoritarian decision-making structures was also associated with open and progressive democratic political attitudes on the part of the sovereign in any parliamentary democracy – the voters. This is a touchy question from which political science tends to shrink away.[2] To be sure, it does study socioeconomic value shifts and the developments in the camps that make up the right-left-centre spectrum of the party landscape, but the basically authoritarian views of voters are concealed in imprecise value typologies.

How can the syndrome of authoritarian attitudes in the sovereign voter be defined for the twentieth century? In the first years after 1945 a group of social scientists – Max Horkheimer, the Austrian exile Else Frenkel-Brunswick, Daniel Levinson and Nevitt Sanford – under the leadership of Theodor W. Adorno at the University of California in Berkeley developed an analysis and questionnaire model for this.[3] Adorno himself, however, did not really like the methodological background of the project, which was influenced by early studies of Erich Fromm and psychological models. Central to it is the authority scale (F-scale, F standing for fascism). The Berkeley group endeavoured on the basis of differentiated opinion surveys of a white, urban population in the United States to measure latent authoritarianism, in their view the basis for the mobilization of the masses by National Socialism but also by other fascist movements, and in its ultimate consequence the foundation for the Holocaust.

The Authoritarian Personality

Following these studies, what is meant by 'authoritarian personality' is a type that exhibits several patterns of attitudes and may be described as follows:

- Conventional in standards: obedience and absolute respect for authority are to the fore here, and severe punishment of breaches of norms is also part of this factor. Strictly formal thinking in terms of the rule of law also belongs here. Of further significance are a repressive sexual morality and a belief in the importance of material wealth. This conventionalism of standards continually flares up in condemnation of modern art. Exaggerated nationalism is likewise strongly marked.
- Desire for power and strength and rejection of and contempt for the weak: this includes the call for a 'strong man', the search for scapegoats and images of an enemy (Jews, strangers, foreigners, etc.), anti-Semitism and glorification of the Second World War. A typical feature is strong irrationalism, symbolized by belief in astrology or invisible powers. Social Darwinism ('survival of the fittest') flourishes in this environment, as does pronounced militarism, both of which also mark everyday life and social relations. In the scientific areas it is primarily applied research that counts as useful, while social and human sciences are seen as 'useless' – unless, as historical science often does, they serve to legitimize the prevailing system.

It should be made clear that latent authoritarianism in itself by no means automatically implies authoritarian forms of government, and that accordingly quite strong authoritarian trends may be present even in formally well-functioning democracies. The United States of the 1950s, on the structures of prejudices among whose population this opinion research is after all based, is a good example of a situation of this kind. It is reflected in, for instance, the sharp clashes over the abolition of racial segregation in the 1960s, which came close to leading to a new civil war in the South of the United States. At the same time, though, U.S. democracy and especially the committed civil rights movement were capable of gradually changing this authoritarian development and combating it politically.

But what attitude towards the basic democratic values on which the functioning of the parliamentary system of the Second Republic rests is present in the sets of values of Austrian men and women? It was only sixty years ago that the Allies – especially the Red Army, U.S. units and British soldiers, but also individual Austrian resistance groups – defeated the Nazi regime. The parliamentary system reestablished after the National Council elections of November 1945 had already been completely destroyed in 1933–34 by the Dollfuß regime. Nor, before 1918, can there be any talk of a functioning democratic (constitutional) monarchy: the fairly representative Reichsrat remained a rump, was prorogued in 1914 and was not convoked again until 1917, by the Emperor Karl.

Anyone looking at the educational traditions inherited from the monarchy will immediately be struck by the strongly authoritarian brand of obedience and compulsion in the social system as a whole. Nothing was changed here by the occasionally more open educational concepts of the interwar period that were mostly confined to Vienna, such as the Glöckel reform – other than breeding a counter-elite that initially remained marginal. The authoritarian Dollfuß-Schuschnigg regime smashed this alternative, and to present-day eyes progressive, opening in the educational sphere. National Socialism saw off what little was left and utilized the available authoritarian traditions to militarize society as a whole. Even in the face of the primacy of political and especially economic reconstruction after 1945, there came further 'obedient decades'. Not till the late 1950s did resistance stir – especially in youth culture – and then, in the 1960s, take on a political colouring, though it never came close to the explosive force of the youth and protest movements in France or West Germany.

Even with redemocratization after 1945, pro-dictatorship ideological patterns remained latently present. Thus, in June 1948 the U.S. occupation administration tested the 'popularity' of Communism and National Socialism in its zones in Vienna, Linz and Salzburg. Three years after the war's end, 26.4 per cent of respondents in Linz, over 43.2 per cent in Salzburg and up to 35.6 per cent in Vienna voted openly in favour of National Socialism. Both in Vienna and in Salzburg, just over 50 per cent opted for 'neither', and only in Linz was the dismissal of authoritarian ideologies stronger (62.8 per cent). In another survey 39.3 per cent favoured a democracy, 23.7 per cent a socialist republic (by which most of them meant a social-democratically governed, anti-communist republic, while the U.S. researchers were thinking of a communist regime), 3.3 per cent a dictatorship and a noteworthy 15.9 per cent the monarchy (with 17.8 per cent abstentions).[4] Here too, then, a latent authoritarian potential is manifest, with observers like the political scientist Hans J. Morgenthau in the 1950s additionally criticizing the authoritarian structures of the Austrian universities.[5] Nonetheless, even he remained hopeful: despite numerous pointers to 'clericalism and corporate-state traditions from those times', in his view the practice of the 'forced' Grand Coalition and control by the Allied administration would prevent the return to an authoritarian course.

The question therefore arises as to how Austrian society managed this transition from authoritarian-dictatorial regimes to democracy. In 1966 many Social Democrats, such as Bruno Kreisky, still feared that after the end of the Grand Coalition authoritarian traditions might prevail in the ÖVP and accordingly wanted at almost any political price to continue the cooperation. As far as parliamentarianism and the social partnership were concerned, these fears did not prove justified: the ÖVP-only Klaus government did not call into question the system of informal balancing of interests and settlement of conflicts through the social partnership any more than Kreisky's socialist-only governments did later.

This area remained sacrosanct, and the corresponding communication channels among a small group of decision makers remained intact and were even expanded. Basically, the impression conveyed is indeed that in everyday political life – apart from temporary ideological differences of opinion – the social partnership grew under non-coalition governments.

At the end of the 1960s in Austria there was an open debate on democratic reform, carried on particularly by the opposition SPÖ and conservative or independent media and experts.[6] Here too the focus was more upon improvements to the democratic system than the development of democratic attitudes among the voters, men and women. In principle the rights of parliament and of parliamentarians were to be strengthened, and also citizens' rights vis-à-vis the administration and the executive. The social partnership as such was not criticized, though regulation of this informal balancing of interests was brought up for discussion.

Authoritarian Potential in 1978

It was not until 1978 that the question was posed of voters' specific attitude patterns as distinct from electoral behaviour on any given occasion,[7] but the topic soon disappeared from sight, apart from two articles in the short-lived magazine *Extrablatt*. The general lack of interest in an evaluation of authoritarian potential in Austria was no doubt connected with the high levels of voter assent to the Kreisky government. The SPÖ did not want directly to antagonize the sovereign voter, and the ÖVP could not because of its weakness. Kreisky himself, however, recognized the basic problem, as can be seen, for instance, from his initiative in founding an association against anti-Semitism. The pre-1938 national trauma – the Dollfuß-Schuschnigg regime and the civil war – was on the other hand to remain firmly banished to the realm of history and, by the late 1970s, was only capable of getting historians excited. Still stronger was the unconscious anxiety about addressing the authoritarian potential stemming from the Nazi period (apart from anti-Semitism research and academic studies). No one yet ventured to bring the social-policy level into the debate; that was not to happen till the clash over Kurt Waldheim in the mid 1980s.

In recent years it has occasionally happened that the theme of authoritarianism in Austria has been reopened via youth research (mostly by foreign authors).[8] But even the most recent study of democracy offers hardly any differentiated evaluations of this basic attitude, since the 'right-left' dichotomy is to the fore. This, in line with empirical findings, has in my view nothing to do with authoritarian potential.

Snapshots of individual forms of expression of basic authoritarian positions such as anti-Semitism and/or xenophobia demonstrate that continuities from the first half of the twentieth century are still to be found in the second, and now even third, post-war generation. The sociologist Hilde Weiss has depicted in her empirical study on the shift in attitudes to minorities in Austria from 1984 to 1998 how 'anti-Semitism and xenophobia, however, certainly draw on a common underlying attitude – namely, an authoritarian thinking that tends also to be oriented antidemocratically and ideologically to the right, and is associated with nationalistic positions'.[9] These syndromes of prejudice cannot be radically changed by 'isolated' enlightenment and information alone; that can only be done by changing the syndromes of the basic authoritarian attitude. This is compounded of a multiplicity of limitations and marginalizations in the classical modern democratic system, associated with 'ethnocentrism ... nationalist self-overestimation ... aversion to a universalism that grants freedoms to minorities too'.

The syndrome, as found for Germany by the above-mentioned research group around Theodor W. Adorno in the first post-war years and confirmed for the elite in Austria in 1952 by political scientist Hans J. Morgenthau,[10] can be seen even today, in the third postwar generation. Its latent potential explodes politically in socioeconomic crisis situations or periods subjectively perceived as such. This view is supported by recent surveys of 15- to 24-year-olds in Germany, measuring latent xenophobia in relation to the proportion of foreigners in the population. In Austria there was by contrast a differentiated and in part surprising result, despite the high proportion of first-time voters choosing the FPÖ in the 1990s. The FPÖ had inscribed a number of these authoritarian codes on its banners (especially in the area of aliens and migration policy, the law-and-order mentality and an ethnocentric nationalism). When, however, authors Ferdinand Karlhofer and Gilg Seeber questioned a total of 2,500 young people between the ages of fourteen and nineteen in autumn 1999 for the 'Youth and Democracy in Tyrol' study, they found only a hard core of 12 per cent of authoritarian young people who could be classed as FPÖ sympathizers.[11] Fifty-three per cent of respondents were identified as confirmed democrats, 17 per cent as sceptics and 18 per cent as vacillating democrats. Here it again emerged that personal life circumstances – positive and optimistic job prospects – markedly increased the level of support for democracy (57 per cent as against 50 per cent) and that the proportion of 'consent to authoritarianism' fell notably in this category (from 16 per cent to 9 per cent). This, however, means that it is not young FPÖ or BZÖ voters that automatically constitute the core group where authoritarian potential is located, but that the latter is to be met with in intermediate strata.

Although the two big parties' camps are heavily eroded, extreme authoritarianism has in general decreased even by comparison with twenty years ago. Thus, in 1980 24 per cent still thoroughly favoured the idea of having a 'strong man' instead of a parliament, whereas in 1991 the figure was 22 per cent and in November/December 1997 only 18 per cent.[12] Most recently, in November/December 1997, only three indicators were used (positive attitude to obedience, acceptance of 'leader figures', authoritarian upbringing of children), leading to the classification of 8 per cent of the population as definitely authoritarian, while 51 per cent were definitely non-authoritarian. Yet, even taken in isolation, the inconsistency with the answers to the question about parliament versus strong man shows an inexplicable difference. My basic thesis – that personality-related authoritarianism need not be connected with political ideas and electoral behaviour – was confirmed.[13] However, to conclude from this that the potential is disappearing because the proportions of the radically inclined are getting smaller is in my view not permissible: from 1978 up to the current study cited in Chapter 10 there have been no further comprehensive, differentiated surveys of the various factors of the authoritarian syndrome, which, moreover, quickly intensifies when there is a mood of economic pessimism.

Since the 1980s, in the wake of the globalization debate and EU accession, a new phenomenon has made its appearance: authoritarian codes are operating more effectively, even if no real change in the overall social situation perceptible to all is occurring. Additionally, such codes must be modern and attractively packaged, if they are to be got across politically. Traditional authoritarian slogans and marketing strategies from the times before 1945 can now continue to work only on extreme-right marginal groups, so the symbolic language has changed – notwithstanding occasional 'slips into historical reference'.

Since the mid 1980s, which for me already show a reawakening of European nationalisms, even the mere fear of negative change has sufficed to strengthen authoritarian trends once again. One important element in this connection is Austrians' strong need for security, which is accorded an extremely high value, both socially and as regards anything defined as 'criminal'. This can be clearly seen in the increasing hostility to immigration and the strong mistrust of EU enlargement eastwards, which go hand in hand with fears about jobs and about a rise in criminality.

In the comprehensive authoritarianism survey of 1978 too, it was not radicalized former Nazi officials that were to the fore, but average voters, both men and women. This allowed the conditions for take-up of anti-democratic, authoritarian codes and propaganda to be analysed. Authoritarian inclinations were to be found among SPÖ voters primarily on themes indicating a bias towards convention and irrationalism, as well as latent aggressive potential vis-à-vis marginal groups and minorities, with SPÖ core voters here even coming out ahead of FPÖ supporters. The latter were in turn well ahead of SPÖ and ÖVP voters on glorification of the Nazi past and on anti-Semitism.

In 1978 Austrian society was 'controlled' and socially stable as far as acceptance of formal rule-of-law provisions was concerned. The surveys showed, however, that a number of specific reforms of the Kreisky era in the justice sector met with no broad assent. Even the death penalty, already abolished before 1970, would have been approved again had there been a referendum. The liberalization of the criminal law similarly did not remotely correspond to any broad social predilection.

The image of 'the Austrian' in 1978 shows an unexpectedly strong continuity of authoritarian codes, with the following peaks: 80 per cent 'yes' versus 4 per cent 'no' felt that 'criminals are too mildly punished today'; 74 per cent versus 4 per cent favoured 'obedience and respect' as important virtues for children; 68 per cent versus 16 per cent wanted a ban on entry by 'deprived foreign young people'; 67 per cent versus 16 per cent were for more severe punishment of trans-vestites and of sexual abuse of young people; 60 per cent versus 19 per cent felt that only 'the reintroduction of the death penalty could put a stop to terrorism'; 51 per cent versus 16 per cent still saw the 'natural role as housewife and mother' as 'the true fulfilment for women'; and 47 per cent versus 19 per cent agreed that 'people can be divided into two classes: the strong and the weak'. Further, 46 per cent versus 21 per cent agreed that 'if we could get rid of vagrants and crooks, most of our society's problems [would be] solved'.

This stocktaking – a year later, in 1979, Bruno Kreisky was to celebrate his biggest electoral success – runs counter to the SPÖ government's programme in both theory and practice. The disparity points to an extremely high authoritarian potential, but one suppressed by the welfare state's security package plus an active job-security policy. It was particularly the potentially authoritarian SPÖ voters who remained loyal to Kreisky, since his welfare state model seemed more impor-tant than the liberal reform of the justice sector carried out by Justice Minister Christian Broda or the democratization of other areas of life, up to and including artistic freedom.

Kreisky himself, who was accepted as a leader personality and even revered by many, was perhaps more aware than anyone else of these authoritarian continu-ities. He was accordingly very cautious about going to the limits in social-policy discourse. How vehement the reactions of the authoritarian potential could be was shown in 1972, when in the mixed-language area of Carinthia a large num-ber of the bilingual road signs put up in implementation of Article 7 of the State Treaty were torn down and violent riots ensued. Kreisky, in his attempts to give political support to the provincial president in Klagenfurt, Hans Sima, met with sometimes openly hostile rejection, even from SPÖ members. Subsequently he reduced his original commitment on this issue and let Sima drop too.

Authoritarian Potential and Freedom of the Arts

The area of the modern-art debate in particular brings out the latent authoritarian potential in all its aggressiveness. Whenever social and political taboos are bro-ken, there are vehement discussions accompanied by radical slogans (de facto au-thoritarianism expressed in words). They disappear fairly quickly, only to appear again all the more violently at the next opportunity. An analysis of the 'art scandals' in the 1970s makes this clear, especially in the area of the yellow press. The debate about modernity also offers rich illustrative material on how authoritarian attitude patterns stemming from the monarchy, the First Republic and National Socialism turn up again in the Second Republic. In 1983 Bruno Kreisky spoke, in one of his last speeches as chancellor, about a historical report on freedom of the arts, which had only become one of the fundamental rights on 12 May 1982, by a unanimous resolution of the National Council on a constitutional Act ('Article 17a of the Federal Constitution: artistic creation, the supplying of art and the teaching thereof shall be free.') Between the law and the constitutional reality there were, however, still differences: for instance, after a complaint by a right-wing extremist on 18 November 1983 the film *Das Gespenst* [The Ghost] by Herbert Achternbusch was impounded pursuant to § 36 of the Media Act ('Attempted denigration of religious doctrines'). Despite appeals, the ban on showing this film still applies today, under a Supreme Court decision.

A few years later the first performance of Thomas Bernhard's *Heldenplatz,* on 4 November 1988 in the Burgtheater, led to furious domestic-policy disputes and an anti-Bernhard media campaign headed by the *Kronenzeitung.* FPÖ Party Chairman Jörg Haider called for a performance ban and the expulsion of the German Burgtheater director, Claus Peymann, while ÖVP Federal President Kurt Waldheim spoke of 'gross insults to the Austrian people', ÖVP Foreign Minister Alois Mock advocated a performance ban, and liberal ÖVP Vice-Chancellor Erhard Busek favoured a public boycott. The list could be continued. It shows, even in this fragmentary form, how authoritarian slogans enter daily politics when works of art do not fit conventional standards. Today, Bernhard's *Heldenplatz* is already considered a classic.

From 'Democratic Miracle' in the Cold War to 'Outdated Model': The Rise and Uncertain End of Austrian Concordance Democracy

Several international observers of Austria's political structures – especially in the United States – interpreted the first centre-right coalition of the Second Republic, which took office in 2000, as a reaction against the static *Proporz* (proportional holding of offices) system in which the SPÖ had allegedly been dominant since 1945, and thus as a change to be regarded as positive for democratic politics. This meant forgetting the dominance of the ÖVP right up until the 1970s: indeed, from 1945 to 1970, i.e. for twenty-four years, this had been the party that supplied the chancellor, governing for four years on its own and for twenty in a Grand Coalition with the SPÖ. It had also dominated the provinces except for Vienna and Burgenland, plus Carinthia until the 1980s. But all that lingered in political observers' memory in the year 2000 was the SPÖ, which had for a good six months of 1945 as well as from 1970 to 1999, i.e. for twenty-nine years, supplied the state (later the federal) chancellor, governing for thirteen of those years alone and for a further thirteen in a second Grand Coalition with the ÖVP. The fact that after 1986 the ÖVP took a very decisive share in determining the direction of coalition policy evidently remained repressed.

A closer look at how the country was assessed internationally brings out, though, that the 'special case of Austria', which took until the 1990s to have two strong political parties, was rated negatively. This criticism of lack of political change was not altered at all by the two big parties' efficiency in cooperation through the social partnership. They had – said the critics – acted untransparently, and were not legitimized by direct elections either. Yet into the 1980s the 'Austrian social partnership' system was regarded as a miracle of political stability and economic growth in a state that had hardly been credited with such chances for its future in 1945.

This change in evaluation (paralleled by what had become an unfavourable assessment of Austrian neutrality as 'free riding' at the expense of the Western defence community) was a product of the transformation phase after the ending of the Cold War in 1989. Yet by the 1950s it was already clear to political analysts that the Austrian post-war structures by no means amounted to a classical liberal-democratic system. As Hans J. Morgenthau, already cited, commented dryly on his fact finding mission to Austria in October 1951: precisely because of these specific authoritarian structures (and the Grand Coalition), 'the radicalism of communism and neo-Nazism was kept within bounds', without the voters having moved away from these parties.[14]

In 1952 an internal report on the 'un-American structures' of decision making processes in Austria's economy caused a great stir.[15] This – inadvertently published – report by a subordinate member of the Economics Division of the U.S. embassy, entitled 'The Restraint of Competition in the Austrian Economy', was intended to point out structural shortcomings whose removal was deemed essential in order to be able to secure further funds from the Marshall Plan. In practical political terms, though, the report was nothing but an internal game plan, with no real objectives or consequences for Austria. Even in the context of Marshall Plan aid, it was primarily economic stabilization rather than restructuring of the economy that was aimed at. Stability had to be a basic goal if Austria's integration into the West was to be secured; and the concentration of economic power, with nationalized big banks, nationalized industries, trusts and the 'Kammerstaat' (neo-corporatist system), though criticized, was quite deliberately accepted.

It would, however, be a mistake to think that in 1945 the trench warfare of the First Republic was simply forgotten. Austrian politicians' readiness for conflict in 1945 was greater than the successful formation of an all-party government might at first sight suggest. Thus, Renner attempted in the first talks before 27 April 1945 to exclude the ÖVP or at least limit its influence by pointing to its authoritarian roots, a line the Soviet political officers did not accept. Stability had priority, from the viewpoint of both the Soviet Union and the United States; political competition was allowed only within the tripartite ÖVP-SPÖ-KPÖ pattern.

Among Austrian decision makers what dominated was not, as is often assumed, their common experience in the concentration camps; the decisive factors were the current situation, the manifold constraints imposed by the Allied administration and the grievous socioeconomic problems, all of which had to be dealt with alongside the process of rebuilding the state. The oft-invoked 'Geist der Lagerstraße' served primarily as an explanation and justification vis-à-vis their own voters as to why the conflicts of the First Republic, ending in the dissolution of Parliament, the bloody civil war of February 1934 and the political persecution of Social Democrats and Communists, suddenly no longer mattered. There was of course a strong personal tie among former concentration camp inmates, but it remained largely confined to the ÖVP, since important SP liaison people from the camps (like the Schutzbund [Republican Defence League] leader Alexander Eifler) had perished. In particular the Austrian National Committee in the concentration camp of Mauthausen, consisting of the pro-ÖVP former political prisoners Hans Becker, Hans Hammerstein-Equord and Bruno Schmitz, the Social Democrat Alfred Migsch, the Communists Ludwig Soswinski and Heinrich Dürmayer, plus Hans Maršálek for the Vienna Czechs, was to play no real political role for the ÖVP or SPÖ.[16]

One further priority in connection with securing stability in 1945 was 'experience', which however also meant political reliability, or adaptability. This particularly characterized Chancellor Renner, whose pan-German nationalist tendencies around 1938, which had also led to public and journalistic hobnobbing with the Nazi regime, were almost never mentioned in 1945.

The Austrian concordance or *Proporz* democracy was thus, as our evidence shows, an outcome of both internal Austrian and geostrategic constraints, in a country where the most recent elections had been held in 1932. Despite this lack of tradition, and in a political vacuum, a handful of men – women remained totally marginalized – with support from the Soviet military authorities in eastern Austria alone, brought about the restoration of structures dating from the pre-1933 period.

The *Proporz* idea as such was traditionally connected with the exercise of control in Austria. Thus, Renner had even before 1914 advocated the introduction of *Proporz* in a proportional representation system, which by contrast with majority voting tends not to produce clear majorities and to encourage fragmentation of parties: 'a system which, while letting the majority rule, still procures appropriate representation for the minority'. In the 1920s attempts had been made to create a transparent '*Proporz* cabinet', but it was not until 1945 that this system was achieved, with even the KPÖ forming part of this complex mechanism for dividing up power and control in Renner's Provisional State Government. This meant in practice that every state secretary had at least two undersecretaries allotted to him as control and communication adjuncts. *Proporz* extended to the civil-servant level too, and it should be noted here that this afforded Social Democrats their only opportunity to gain a foothold in a civil service dominated exclusively by Christian Socials or conservative German nationalists.

Proporz acted as a sort of shock-absorber system for the still-existing social pillars in Austria, the conflict potential of which was canalized in this way. Both 'camps', pro-ÖVP and pro-SPÖ, could thus count on making a career in their respective political spheres of influence, and on being accepted and promoted even in ministries and departments not 'controlled' by political friends. Continual negotiation, and reciprocal checks, gradually softened up the closed political system dating from pre-1938 in the administration and judiciary. In this way, the system of *Proporz,* though much abused today, had an important stabilization function. The first resistance to it began in the late 1950s and in the 1960s, when the system had been increasingly reduced to the mere allocation of posts and housing and scarcely held any implications of objective political competence or ability to reform any longer. The opposition to *Proporz* was particularly strong in the media sector, where since the mid 1950s it had come to be very rigidly applied. For instance, the news programmes of the broadcasting corporation RAVAG were each controlled by two party journalists, with matters once even coming to fisticuffs when an overly one-sided news bulletin was broadcast. With the beginning of television in 1955 the *Proporz* spectrum broadened in the direction of a 'black frequency' (continuation of the ÖVP's primacy in radio) and 'red screen' (television with SPÖ-nominated directors). The broadcasting popular initiative of 1964, essentially launched by the *Kurier,* its chief editor Hugo Portisch and other print media not directly belonging to a political party, was a first attempt to mobilize the public against this total carve-up of power in state radio and television.

ÖVP Chancellor Josef Klaus gives an unvarnished sketch of these abuses in the first Grand Coalition:[17] 'The *Proporz* system continued the practice of the total arrogation to themselves of power in the State by the coalition parties: appointments to posts, subventions, even government and official delegations travelling abroad had to maintain the 1:1 ratio.' Even the Austria TV weekly newsreel had, as a state propaganda medium, to have two directors (each with a service car), and the lengths of time for which each ÖVP or SPÖ representative appeared in a newsreel spot were exactly measured, to guarantee parity.

The positive aspect of *Proporz,* on the other hand, was that no single socio-political model could – like the Catholic-conservative one in the First Republic after 1920 or the Social Democratic one in Vienna until 1934 – be pursued exclusively. While nationalized industry was ideologically controversial, in practical politics it was accepted by the ÖVP too. And the leading positions in nationalized industry and the nationalized big banks with their own industrial complex were allocated, sometimes in great detail, so that after a clear advantage had initially been enjoyed by the ÖVP, by the mid 1950s the SPÖ had attained a sort of parity (see Table 1).

The problem with *Proporz* in the 1950s and 1960s was that the original reciprocal checking function had given way to a total division of power. This circumstance also explains the 1966 election result, which gave the ÖVP a bigger share of the vote especially in the sector of first-time voters and women: it had been more convincing in indicating that it wanted to break out of this system. After 1970 Bruno Kreisky made known his willingness to reduce the dominance of the parties in important power positions by bringing in independent ministers and personalities (e.g. Rudolf Kirchschläger or later Erich Bielka as foreign minister). The appointment of the former ÖVP Finance Minister and Parliamentary Party Chairman Stephan Koren as president of the Austrian National Bank was another indication of this intention. In the foreign-policy bureaucracy Kreisky – by contrast with the ÖVP foreign ministers of the Grand Coalition – also promoted non-party candidates. For instance, Klaus's former secretary Thomas Klestil worked as a diplomat on implementing the plans for an international conference centre.

The second SPÖ-ÖVP Grand Coalition (1986–2000) perpetuated the old *Proporz* system once again, especially in the matter of appointing top civil servants. Now the criticisms of this way of dividing up of power were all the more

TABLE I

Comparison of the party affiliations of board members of the nationalized industry 1964 and 1980/1981 (per percentage)

	1964				1980/1981			
	SP	O	VP		SP	O	VP	FP
VV^c	50		50	VV^F	63	25	12	
GV	48	3	49	GV	46	5	49	
AV^D	52		48	AV	33	11	56	
GA^E	<50		>50	GA^E	53	2	42	3

Abbreviations

VV EXECUTIVE CHAIRMAN	SP SOCIALIST PARTY OF AUSTRIA
GV EXECUTIVE COMMITTEE MEMBERS	VP AUSTRIAN PEOPLE'S PARTY
AV CHAIRMAN OF THE SUPERVISORY BOARD	FP FREEDOM PARTY OF AUSTRIA
GA NON-EXECUTIVE BOARD DIRECTORS	O NEUTRAL

a) BOARD OF DIRECTORS (ELIN-UNION 1979) ÖIAG (AUSTRIAN INDUSTRIES COMPANY) AND DEPENDENT COMPANIES

b) EXECUTIVE COMMITTEE MEMBERS OF ÖIAG AND SUBSIDIARY COMPANIES

c) ZIMMERMANN DECLARES ONLY IN 14 OF 22 COMPANIES AN EXECUTIVE CHAIRMAN

d) SCHIFFSWERFT LINZ AG AND SCHIFFSWERFT KORNEUBURG AG HAD A JOINT MANAGEMENT BUT SEPARATE BOARDS OF DIRECTORS

e) INCOMPLETE DOCUMENTS

f) THERE WAS NO EXECUTIVE CHAIRMAN NAMED IN WTK (WOLFSEGG-TRAUNTHALER-KOHLENWERKS AG)

Source: Peter Gerlich, Wolfang Müller (ed.): Zwischen Koalition und Konkurrenz. Braumueller: Vienna 1983

effective. While in 1986 Chancellor Vranitzky came up with a coalition agreement revolving around technical matters and endeavoured to push the personnel questions always associated with *Proporz* into the background, in practice obstacles to this approach quickly arose and then escalated, particularly towards the end of the coalition under Chancellor Viktor Klima. And though the ÖVP often skilfully got its candidates through, in the public mind the SPÖ was criticized as solely responsible for *Proporz* – for instance, in decisions by high officials.

The ÖVP-FPÖ coalition effective as of 2000 announced a 'new-style *Proporz*', meaning that losses of powers were to be expected especially for civil servants counted as belonging to the SPÖ. On boards and supervisory boards of the ÖIAG (the holding company for state-owned industries), comprehensive personnel changes were carried out. By contrast with the 1970s, when, though SPÖ governments dominated the central management of nationalized industry, ÖVP sympathizers were fairly strongly represented on the boards and supervisory boards of industry, now one strong political party, the SPÖ, was plainly being squeezed out. In this sense American conditions have arrived but again divided according to coalition interests between two parties. Independent managers with no ÖVP or FPÖ sympathies are similarly kept almost entirely excluded from this schema. In this connection the formal party membership plays less of a role than actual ideological affiliation.

Presidential or Parliamentary Democracy?
Federal Presidents since 1945

After the FPÖ-ÖVP coalition took office in February 2000, the conflict between president and Parliament or government, which up till then had in practice been latent, came to a head. President Thomas Klestil had not only, in the run-up to the formation of the FPÖ-ÖVP government, supported continuation of the SPÖ-ÖVP Grand Coalition from the start, but had also sought other options for forming a government without the FPÖ. This gave rise, among both the domestic and the international public, to an exaggerated image of the Austrian federal presidency quite out of line with the real powers of the office. It was noteworthy at any rate that this capacity of the president for single-handed decisions, problematic in terms of democratic politics, was welcomed internationally in the FPÖ-ÖVP case, whereas in Austria polls showed the president's popularity figures falling. Evidently Austrians had failed to realize that since 1929 the president had no longer been a mere 'state notary'. But when in the upshot he did act, in the above-mentioned case absolutely in conformity with the constitution, many were painfully affected, to say the least.

Theoretically the Austrian president, by virtue of the 1929 constitutional reform with its semi-authoritarian features, and of his legitimation by direct popular vote (the 'Austro-Hindenburg model'), holds powers, in crisis or pivotal situations such as forming a government, that might resemble those in a parliamentary presidential republic. But the 1920 constitutional system does not correspond to the U.S. or French model. Austria's real constitution (the social-partnership regulatory mechanisms) has so far limited such conflicts to a few individual cases, which are, however, worth reviewing in a historical analysis, since they show the 'explosiveness' of this 1929 constitutional reform.

Thomas Klestil himself had already explored the issue after his first election as ÖVP candidate in 1992 – in 1998 he was reelected as a non-party candidate. He wanted then to obtain a legal opinion to clarify whether these powers of decision making and leadership dating from 1929 might not also apply to the new EU mechanisms after Austria's EU entry. On the basis of the legal advice he was given, there were for a while conflicts with then SPÖ Chancellor Franz Vranitzky, who would not let Klestil contest his claim to represent Austria on the European Council. Ultimately the chancellor won; the real constitution and EU usages were on his side.

The presidency of Thomas Klestil's predecessor, Kurt Waldheim, had been overshadowed by another sort of conflict between federal president and federal chancellor. Since Waldheim, because of the debate about his wartime past, was not invited on state visits to Western Europe and was on the 'watch list' in the U.S., i.e. could not travel there privately, it was then-Chancellor Vranitzky who had to represent Austria externally. This period clearly strengthened the position of the chancellor and reduced the president's influence even with his supporters as his time in office went on.

Chancellor Bruno Kreisky in turn, in a friendly but nonetheless tough dispute about the legal powers of the president, secured an opinion from the Constitutional Service that confirmed the primacy of the chancellor. President Rudolf Kirchschläger, the non-party foreign minister who had been put forward by Kreisky as SPÖ candidate, tried increasingly in his second term in office (after 1980) to exert specific influence over civil-service appointments. Especially after the end of the Kreisky single-party government in 1983, in the SPÖ-FPÖ Small Coalition phase in 1983–86 and in the discussion over Kurt Waldheim's role in the German Wehrmacht, Kirchschläger strove to assert himself as a moral authority. Despite these moral stances (which, however, always avoided any specific taking of sides and therefore quickly disappeared from the political debate again), while in office Kirchschläger remained an aloof political prophet, going unheard when, shortly before his death, he warned against FPÖ participation in government under Jörg Haider's auspices.

The office was exercised equally correctly, and with scrupulous precision though reticently, by the former Socialist mayor of Vienna, Franz Jonas (1965–74), although he was disliked particularly by the bourgeois elements for his proletarian origins and for having left the Catholic Church, and was also subjected to humiliation during the election campaign (as various jokes document). During the formation of the first SPÖ minority government in 1970 he stayed in the background, and in 1966 he accepted the ÖVP single-party government.

It is noteworthy that all the presidents – most recently Thomas Klestil and especially Heinz Fischer – subscribed to the social-partnership basic consensus between the two big parties, the ÖVP and SPÖ. This is clear from the career of Adolf Schärf, who in 1957, rather against his will, was 'elevated' to the presidential candidacy. A group around Felix Slavik, Franz Olah and Bruno Kreisky had persuaded Schärf, after twelve years as vice-chancellor and SPÖ chairman, to swap this power position for the gamble of a federal presidency election campaign and the office of president. Schärf knew about the rules of the game and the loss of power that this office entailed. In both 1959 and 1960 he worked massively and successfully for a continuation of the Grand Coalition.

One of the most active and perhaps 'difficult' presidents of the Second Republic was Theodor Körner. A former general and chief of the general staff of the Isonzo army in the First World War, he had since 1924 been a member of the Social Democratic Party. As mayor of Vienna from 1945 to 1951 he helped to shape reconstruction. But whereas he was an advocate of the policy of pardoning ex-NSDAP members, at the same time he supported the modern, open-minded cultural policy of the KPÖ city assessor for culture, Viktor Matejka. During the Cold War his almost naive admiration for the Soviet dictator Stalin seemed particularly explosive: it was only with difficulty that he could be restrained in 1953 from attending a memorial celebration arranged by the Austrian-Soviet Society in honour of the dead Soviet head of state and government. Whereas in 1945 he was defending ex-Nazis, he later by his unyielding stance blocked a coalition pact with the umbrella party of the 'oldtimers' (NSDAP members or sympathizers) and the electoral association of independents (forerunner of the FPÖ) already fully negotiated by Raab. This was indubitably one of the most significant turning-points in the Second Republic, resulting in the continuation of the Grand Coalition and the curbing of the right-wing nationalist camp until 1986.

While Körner was the first Austrian president actually legitimated by popular vote since 1929, Karl Renner had in 1945, because of the organizational overload due to the National Council elections on 25 November, still been elected president unanimously by the Federal Assembly. Renner attempted, by setting up a de facto Second Council of Ministers under his leadership, to establish an informal presidential regime, but was brought back into line by vice-chancellor Schärf as early as 1946. However central his role as state chancellor may have been in 1945, Renner was still marginalized in his domestic role as federal president. By contrast, his talks with journalists and the articles he published abroad – for instance in *Foreign Affairs* – certainly did command an audience.

Federalism, Centralism or Division: Options in 1945

In 1945, the establishment of a Provisional State Government with powers in the Soviet zone only meant the possibility that Austria might be divided. There were signals, particularly from Western Austria and the Tyrol, centring on the wartime Tyrolese resistance groups and the provincial president, Karl Gruber, that there were indeed thoughts of separation should it not be possible to arrive at participation in government in Vienna. The founding of a 'Democratic Joint Party' by Gruber was an attempt to establish a strong 'Western' movement. It sought to recruit both former Home Defence and former NSDAP members, in marked contrast to the strong anti-Nazi tendencies of the new 'Vienna ÖVP' around Lois Weinberger. At the same time, Gruber presented his joint movement as liberal, aiming at a clear separation of church and state and also coming out against Christian-Social traditions. Denazification in Tyrol was handled very personally, with individual assessments and examples being made, not through a structured policy. After July/August 1945 Gruber, who had no roots in the Christian Social Party and came from a Social Democratic family, was integrated by means of his contacts into the ÖVP, where he increasingly began to influence ÖVP stances – especially at the interprovincial conferences. One important aspect here was the strengthening of the provinces as against the central federal administration.

What lay behind this question of the provinces versus Vienna in the structural-policy area was the question of whether in Austria after 1945 there ought to be strong centralism or not. In this connection, State Chancellor Renner in particular tried in his early memorandums to argue that the opposition between 'Red' Vienna and the 'Black' provinces had in the interwar years led to increasing political gridlock. The interprovincial conferences in September/October 1945 definitively set the course towards a centralist federal state, though not one as tightly organized as Renner had originally imagined. The traditional opposition between the provinces and the centre in Vienna was, in the first years after the Second World War, no longer to be so clearly apparent, since in the coalition government both the ÖVP (the dominant force after the 1945 November elections) and the SPÖ, dominant in Vienna and later also in Carinthia and then in the late 1960s in Burgenland too, were represented. The interests of the provinces were increasingly being channelled directly along the Grand Coalition route, thereby rendered harmless politically and often barely surfacing.

The real political influence of the provinces on the parties runs, particularly in the ÖVP but in the SPÖ too, much more along this route than through constitutional rights. For instance, Bruno Kreisky was elected SPÖ party chairman in 1967 chiefly because of a strong lobby from the provinces. And their influence remained correspondingly dominant into the 1970s. At the same time, however, the provinces' voter potential constituted a major element in the changes that in 1966 gave the ÖVP and in 1970 the SPÖ, in each case the most promising reform party, an absolute or relative majority. Especially in municipalities with under 5,000 inhabitants, the desire for change was great, leading to corresponding switches of allegiance by voters. And Bruno Kreisky, who as mentioned owed his rise in the SPÖ to the provinces, very deliberately located infrastructure measures there. The 'deep Black' Tyrol was especially favoured, since here the need to catch up was great. Putting it somewhat provocatively, it was not the ÖVP, traditionally strongly rooted in the provinces, but the SPÖ under Kreisky that in the 1970s contributed to infrastructure shifts that also in part led to unexpected flows of voters towards the SPÖ. In the ÖVP, by contrast, in recent decades the influence of the provinces – except for Vienna – has grown markedly, to compensate for the fact that no top provincial officials are any longer also ÖVP chairmen; neither Karl Schleinzer, Josef Taus, Alois Mock, Erhard Busek nor Wolfgang Schüssel can be termed classic 'province politicians' in the mould of Leopold Figl or Josef Klaus. And the influence within the party of the provincial bigwigs, i.e. the ÖVP provincial presidents, has become correspondingly stronger.

But the provinces also resorted to the use of stronger legal instruments to assert their new importance, with an initial high point consisting in a citizens' initiative and referendum on federalism, starting from Vorarlberg. More rights for provinces in the new provincial constitutions of the late 1980s document this further development, which went through a transition after EU accession and the voluntary delegation of many powers to the European Union. Subsequently, there have been repeated debates about the provinces' loss of political significance since EU entry. On the one hand, the traditional, historically defined provincial assemblies and provincial governments are no longer in line with the new context. On the other it is pointed out that the EU itself wishes to strengthen the regional level further and expand it. In 1997, then Styrian ÖVP Provincial Councillor Gerhard Hirschmann made a proposal for reform: pointing to Bavaria, which with ten million inhabitants gets by with a quarter of the Austrian political apparatus, he called for a reduction in the number of provincial assemblies and provincial parliamentarians by setting up EU-compatible regions. The reaction to this was vehement and without exception negative: Austria must not be divided into three regions.

The provincial identities, which especially in Western Austria and Carinthia have become yet stronger in recent years, will no doubt prevent the realization of any such adaptations to the actual European constitution for some time to come. The various cross-border regional initiatives such as ARGE Donauländer (Working Community of the Danube States), ARGE Alpen-Adria, ARGE-Alp or the Lake Constance Conference are totally embryonic, and in part remain mere paper tigers. Vis-à-vis Austria's Central and Eastern European neighbours, initiatives are developing only slowly and are nowhere near comparable with the big Franco-German regional economic areas. In connection with enlargement in 2004, however, the EU laid down such strong guidelines that even the mental reservations in Austria are decreasing and corresponding cooperation is being sought.

Constitution: New or Old? Turning Points in 1945

In party discourse in 1945 the strong legal continuities with the period before 1933 were by no means a foregone conclusion. Among others, émigrés in the Soviet Union had done some thinking about the specific constitutional framework for Austria's resuscitation. The juridical approach taken in 1945 by, for instance, one of the leading KPÖ functionaries in exile, Ernst Fischer – perhaps while still in Moscow – avoided any direct constitutional discourse and called for the 'formation of a provisional national assembly', to be made up of candidates of the 'freedom front (Communists, Social Democrats, Catholics, bourgeois democrats and non-party people)', who would then be elected 'in various appropriate ways'.[18] From among them a provisional government should be recruited and then confirmed by this provisional national assembly. The 'chairman' might be a non-party person ('university professor' or the like), flanked by a 'three-man presidium: a Communist, a Social Democrat, a Catholic (or perhaps a bourgeois democrat).' Émigrés too should be included, as well as pre-war Austrian politicians such as Seitz, Kunschak or Körner – here, by contrast with a speech delivered in Moscow in 1944, he no longer mentioned Renner.[19] Fischer had then had in mind Hans Kelsen (in the United States) and Josef Dobretsberger (in Turkey) as possible politically integrative figures to be brought back quickly from exile. Wilhelm Miklas, as the last Austrian Federal President before the Nazis assumed control, was to appoint this provisional government and then retire. A sort of rump parliament dating from 1933 as a constituent body was ruled out by Fischer, inter alia because no Communist Party members had then been in Parliament. The provisional National Assembly should have an advisory role.[20]

Fischer's ideas, interestingly, corresponded in part with those of Karl Renner, even though under quite different political auspices. In his letter of 17 April 1945 to the Christian Social politician Karl Kollmann, Renner emphasized that, as the last president of a free Parliament and first state chancellor of the Austrian Republic in 1918, he was holding himself in readiness to 'organize the Second Republic'.[21] Renner explicitly based himself on the 1920 constitution but disputed 'the legality and the political advisability of all the amendments to it, especially those since 1934'.[22] In a memorandum headed 'Probleme I: Politik' ('Problems I: Politics'), probably written before 19 April 1945, Renner remained vague on the constitutional question. Like Fischer, he rejected the 'idea that what is involved is merely a restoration, i.e. a return to the situation before 1933 and 1938'; 'it is about the future, the building of a new order, the achieving of socialism [sic]'.[23] With regard to electoral laws he advocated those of 1918, not 1920, tightened by provisions intended to prevent splinter parties. He opposed further autonomy for the provinces, as already mentioned, since they had 'abused it after 1920 to continually blackmail Vienna, continually undermine the State government' etc.[24] Renner also managed to put through his formulation for the independence declaration of 27 April 1945, with its rather general wording in relation to constitutional matters: 'Art I. The democratic Republic of Austria is hereby restored and shall be established in the spirit of the 1920 constitution.'[25] That meant that all the constitutional options were still kept open.

Renner came into conflict with his party colleague Adolf Schärf over his proposed constitutional innovations. The latter developed the idea of restoring the pre-1933 constitutional position, while at the same time keeping, by means of a 'provisional constitution'[26] for a period of six months until the elections, to a centralist, tight handling of the Provisional State Government, which should act as both supreme executive and legislative body. The state chancellor and the three state secretaries without portfolio would form the Political Cabinet Council, which would handle the duties of the federal president.[27]

The KPÖ instead sought to prevent the passing of the Constitutional Transition Act 1945 and opposed autonomy for the provinces. Nonetheless, in the decisive vote Renner put pressure on the KPÖ to follow the unanimity principle in the Cabinet Council or leave the Cabinet. The KPÖ representatives therefore voted for the act with reservations, since they refused to comply with the call to resign.[28] In the course of the debate the KPÖ still tried to argue against the 1929 amendment but was outvoted here too, since the amendment had been adopted correctly in formal terms, even though it did not politically suit Schärf, for one.[29]

This constitutional non-debate in 1945 turned into a permanent situation, with the 1929 constitutional amendment that had derived from the authoritarian storms of the interwar years remaining in force, albeit with most of its political 'fangs' drawn. By now, many amendments of detail have made it incomprehensible to any but experts. Corresponding amendments in EU law and the future EU constitution have made the situation even less clear, so that the question arises as to how far the constitution is accepted by the people at all. It is already plain that Austrians do not regard their constitution as an important element of their identity by any means, yet this dangerous fact has not elicited any appropriate democratic political responses. Meanwhile, despite direct elections, the European Parliament is even more remote. Neither the debate on a European constitution nor the work of the Austria Convention has found any broad public resonance. And the chances of any fundamental revision of the Austrian constitution are correspondingly small. Whether the European constitution might at least spark off some new advance in European consciousness in Austria remains to be seen, and is still totally uncertain.

The Beginning and (Apparent) End of the Social Partnership

Very much to the discomfiture of some important economists and political scientists, in Austria more strongly than in other Western European countries an interest-balancing system formed of institutionalized lobbies of blue- and white-collar workers (the trade unions and Chamber of Labour) and private employers (Association of Industry and Chamber of Commerce) has proved effective. While cracks in this system have become clearly apparent, especially in the Second Grand Coalition phase of 1986–99, the position of the U.S. economist Mancur Olson[30] has remained valid: wherever, as in Austria, the two major economic-policy lobbies act together, their respective group interests will balance out in favour of a policy that stimulates the economy.

We shall attempt now to throw some light on the obscurities of the social partnership that helped to bring about the social and economic development of the Second Republic (against a background of favourable international conditions).

One decision important for the success of the social partnership came as early as late April 1945, namely the drawing by representatives of the SPÖ, ÖVP and KPÖ of an institutional lesson from the picture of fragmented and ideologically compartmentalized craft unions under the First Republic, by setting up a centralist, tightly organized trade-union movement. Before 1945 in the ÖVP there had been debates in the underground on whether to reestablish the Christian trade unions, but younger ÖVP trade unionists around Lois Weinberger and Erwin Altenburger managed to prevail. On the SPÖ side, the man who was to become the ÖGB (Austrian Trade Union Federation) president, Johann Böhm, led the way; in late 1937 he had belonged to a group attempting, together with activists from the Schuschnigg regime, to set up a defensive movement against the Nazi regime. In many formal respects there were continuities with the post-1934 authoritarian unions as well as with the German Labour Front (DAF), but always within a clearly democratic framework, albeit with a basically centralist orientation.

By 1946, however, ideological controversies and efforts at demarcation vis-à-vis a Communist unitary trade union were already becoming apparent, although the KPÖ was in places, particularly in Soviet-administered enterprises, strongly represented at the works-council level. It similarly became clear that the ÖGB and the Socialist faction that dominated it after making electoral gains would more likely choose the option of cooperation over that of challenge through strikes (despite the great social problems, in 1946 only 35 per cent of strikes were recognized by the ÖGB).

Alongside centralization, stronger integration into the SPÖ than had been the case before 1933 was a further important element. Böhm, like SPÖ Vice-Chancellor Adolf Schärf, took the view that leading SPÖ trade unionists (and representatives of the Chamber of Labour) should also belong to the SPÖ party executive and the Socialist parliamentary faction, and be correspondingly represented in government. This kind of accumulation of personal power could, in times of economic and social crisis, facilitate the making of rapid decisions with few actors involved. The ÖVP too integrated the decision makers in its trade union organization (and its Chamber of Commerce representatives), and after 1947 Julius Raab and the Chamber of Commerce increasingly came to prevail over the 'old' economic-policy decision makers from the First Republic and 'corporate state', represented by Renner's adviser Viktor Kienböck.

The institutionalization of this extraparliamentary decision making process in the form of an 'economic directorate' (which consisted of the presidents of the ÖGB, the Association of Industry, the Chamber of Labour and the Chamber of Commerce), while in line with the political reality, was nonetheless abolished by the Constitutional Court in 1951 on the grounds that it represented a formal circumvention of the parliamentary system. The fact remained, though, that decisions on major economic and social topics were taken by the actors in this group and merely ratified or refined in detail by government and Parliament.

While the ÖVP was not greatly interested in a legal codification of the social-partnership institutions and decision making processes, the ÖGB under Böhm attempted to entrench them. This then succeeded – despite much resistance from, among others, the SPÖ leadership around Schärf and SPÖ party whip Bruno Pittermann – with the founding in 1957 of the Parity Commission for Wage and Price Questions. It had been preceded in 1956 by a strike wave, the biggest in the history of the Second Republic until the year 2000. The establishment of the Advisory Council for Economic and Social Questions in 1963 was similarly a sort of political 'canalization' of the pressure from strikes. Whenever social-partnership processes were institutionalized, this was in reaction to strike movements; in the case of the 1963 regulation, it took the somewhat authoritarian form of an agreement between ÖGB President Franz Olah and Chancellor Julius Raab.

It is noteworthy that the successors to Franz Olah and Julius Raab in the ÖGB and Chamber of Commerce respectively were elected at around the same time: Anton Benya became ÖGB president in 1963, and Rudolf Sallinger president of the Chamber of Commerce in 1964. These two were to be the major actors in decision making for the next twenty-three years, a fact reflected in a regular early-morning appointment. In the periods of both the ÖVP single-party government – which was when the forty-hour-week was adopted – and the SPÖ single-party government in 1970–83, the importance of this cooperation continued. The real political primacy of the social partnership in economic and welfare – but not social – policy questions was perhaps best represented by the fact that Anton Benya remained president of the National Council from 1971 to 1986. Here the social partners had a solid, clearly defined lobby of MPs in both big parties. Ministerial posts in SPÖ governments were allotted on an appropriate scale to trade union officials, and when the ÖVP was in power to members of the Chamber of Commerce. This power conglomerate was indirectly given democratic legitimation by elections, but these were elections to the respective interest groups, not to the National Council.

The narrow defeat in the vote on the Zwentendorf nuclear power station, massively promoted by the ÖGB, and the disputes about the Hainburg Danube power station in 1984 were the first visible crises to shake this system. Although in 1986, after the brief interlude of the SPÖ-FPÖ coalition, the social partnership was once again extended, political initiative now increasingly shifted to the government level of the new Grand Coalition. There were points of friction over the reorganization of nationalized industry, reaching their culmination in 1996 with the resignation of Finance Minister Ferdinand Lacina, which was motivated in part also by demonstrations by top ÖGB officials against some measures by him. On the question of the EU's eastward enlargement, resistance built up in the ÖGB too after 1997–98, with calls for long transition periods to protect the home labour market. And when it came to pension reform in 1997 the social partnership failed glaringly, since the opposing interests no longer seemed capable of being reconciled.

In seeking to compare the Austrian social-partnership path with other models of the modern welfare state aimed at balancing interests, what strikes one in relation to Scandinavia, say, and especially Sweden, is that there the influence of the government and parliament has been stronger than the dominance of the social partners in Austria, especially in the 1960s. By contrast with other continental European welfare states, however, Austria has been able to turn its relatively high taxes into actual high employment; Germany, Finland, Belgium and even Sweden do less well on this count. Moreover, Austria has more jobs in private service firms than the high social security contributions might lead one, in a European comparison, to expect. Below the line, as matters have turned out since 1945, Austria actually did invest tax receipts in achieving a better employment level.[31] This success came, however, at the expense of income distribution, with Austrians, and women especially, earning less than the European average – here Austria in 1995 stood below the average for the fifteen EU member states in full-time jobs, just ahead of Ireland, Greece, Portugal and the Netherlands. The excellent employment rate in international comparison was partly achieved by somewhat lower wage rates since 1945, with women, as mentioned, being particularly disadvantaged in Austria – as they still are.

The ÖVP-FPÖ coalition since 2000 has rendered the ÖVP–Chamber of Commerce axis more fragile, an effect already visible earlier in the relationship between the SPÖ and the trade union movement. The FPÖ, or BZÖ, in turn began both in the Association of Industry and in individual sectors to attack the 'business monopoly' of the ÖVP and correspondingly to develop lobbying activities here. How far the traditional social partners may manage on individual questions to join together in a temporary alliance against the government of the day remains to be seen, but it is conceivable that they will do so in the debates on a new intergenerational contract (long-term reform of social security and pensions). The social partnership will no longer attain any permanent formulation of policy comparable to that which prevailed in its heyday from the 1960s through the 1980s. Yet total collapse seems unlikely as long as in both the ÖVP and the SPÖ the fundamental pillars of this alliance for reconstruction remain politically effective, even if the range of action of top party officials, as opposed to those of trade unions or other interest groups, has grown markedly broader.

Notes

1. Anton Pelinka and Sieglinde Rosenberger, *Österreichische Politik. Grundlagen – Strukturen – Trends* (Vienna: WUV Univ. Verlag, 2000), 60.
2. David F. J. Campbell, ed., *Die Qualität der österreichischen Demokratie. Versuche einer Annäherung* (Vienna: Manz Verlag, 1996)
3. Theodor W. Adorno, 'Scientific Experiences of a European Scholar in America', in *The Intellectual Migration: Europe and America, 1930–1960,* ed. Donald Fleming and Bernard Bailyn (Cambridge: Harvard University Press, 1969), 338–370.
4. Oliver Rathkolb, 'NS-Problem und politische Restauration. Vorgeschichte und Etablierung des VdU', in *Verdrängte Schuld. Verfehlte Sühne. Entnazifizierung in Österreich 1945–1955,* ed. Sebastian Meissl, Klaus-Dieter Mulley and Oliver Rathkolb (Vienna: Verlag für Geschichte und Politik, 1986), 76.
5. Oliver Rathkolb, 'Hans J. Morgenthau und das Österreich-Problem in der letzten Phase der Truman-Administration 1951/1952', in *Geschichte zwischen Freiheit und Ordnung. Gerald Stourzh zum 60. Geburtstag,* ed. Emil Brix, Thomas Fröschl and Josef Leidenfrost (Graz-Vienna-Cologne: Böhlau 1991), 277–298.
6. Karl Heinz Ritschel, ed., *Demokratiereform. Die Existenzfrage Österreichs* (Vienna: Zsolnay Verlag, 1969).
7. I appreciate that both Professor Josef Weidenholzer, who coordinated this study together with the historian Karl R. Stadler in 1978, and the director of the public opinion institute IFES, Imma Palme, granted access to the raw data and the complete poll.
8. Thomas Claus, Ferdinand Karlhofer, Gilg Seeber and Cocky Booy, 'Jugendliche im Spannungsfeld von Demokratie und Extremismus. Tirol, Sachsen-Anhalt und Holland im Vergleich', in *Demokratie, Modus und Telos. Festschrift für Anton Pelinka,* ed. Andrei S. Markovits and Sieglinde Rosenberger (Vienna: Böhlau, 2001); http://homepage.uibk.ac.at/homepage/c402/c40205/JuP.pdf. (accessed 1 June 2005).
9. Hilde Weiss, '*Alte und neue Minderheiten. Zum Einstellungswandel in Österreich (1984–1998)', SWS Rundschau 40 (2000): 25–42.*
10. Rathkolb, 'Hans J. Morgenthau', 277–298.
11. Claus et al., 'Jugendliche im Spannungsfeld', 78.
12. Günther Ogris, 'Einstellungen der österreichischen Bevölkerung zur Demokratie. Demokratietheorie und Demokratieverständnis in Österreich', in *Demokratietheorie und Demokratieverständnis in Österreich,* ed. Manuela Delpos (Vienna: Passagen-Verlag, 2001), 198.

13. Ibid., 174.
14. Rathkolb, 'Hans J. Morgenthau', 277–298.
15. National Archives, College Park, Maryland, Record Group (NA, RG), Johnstone to Ambassador, 5 May 1952. 84, Vienna Legation Files, Box 3178, Folder 350.
16. Oliver Rathkolb, ed., *Gesellschaft und Politik am Beginn der Zweiten Republik. Vertrauliche Berichte der U.S.-Militäradministration aus Österreich 1945 in englischer Originalfassung* (Vienna: Böhlau, 1985).
17. Josef Klaus, *Macht und Ohnmacht in Österreich. Konfrontationen und Versuche* (Vienna-Munich-Zürich: Molden Verlag, 1971).
18. Austrian Institute for Contemporary History, Vienna, Ernst Fischer Papers, NL-38, Do 126, Manuscript, 'Die Vorarbeiten zur Herausbildung einer provisorischen Nationalversammlung', 1.
19. Wilfried Aichinger, *Sowjetische Österreichpolitik 1943–1945* (Vienna: Österreichische Gesellschaft für Zeitgeschichte, 1977), 133.
20. Austrian Institute for Contemporary History, Vienna, Ernst Fischer Papers, NL-38, Do 126, manuscript, Die Vorarbeiten zur Herausbildung einer provisorischen Nationalversammlung.
21. Adolf Schärf, *Österreichs Erneuerung 1945–1955. Das erste Jahrzehnt der Zweiten Republik* (Vienna: Verlag der Wiener Volksbuchhandlung, 1955), 31.
22. Ibid., 32.
23. Austrian Institute for Contemporary History, Vienna, Karl Renner Papers, NL 1–3, DO 721, Folder 9: Manuskript Probleme I: Politik.
24. Ibid., 4.
25. Eva-Marie Csáky, ed., *Der Weg zu Freiheit und Neutralität. Dokumentation zur österreichischen Außenpolitik 1945–1955* (Vienna: Österreichische Gesellschaft für Außenpolitik und Internationale Beziehungen, 1980), 37.
26. Enderle-Burcel et al. (eds.), *Protokolle des Kabinettsrates der Provisorischen Regierung Karl Renner 1945, Vol. 1,* 80–90.
27. Schärf, *Österreichs Erneuerung*, 49–53.
28. Ernst Fischer, *Das Ende einer Illusion. Erinnerungen 1945–1955* (Vienna: Molden, 1973), 81.
29. Enderle-Burcel et al. (eds.), *Protokolle des Kabinettsrates der Provisorischen Regierung Karl Renner 1945, Vol. 1,* 64–66 and 75.
30. Compare Peter Neidhart, 'Historische Analyse ausgewählter österreichischer Interessensvertretungen anhand der Erklärungsansätze von Douglass North und Mancur Olson' (Phil. diss., Vienna University of Economics and Business, 2003).
31. Scharpf, Fritz W and Vivien A. Schmidt (eds.). Welfare and Work in the Open Economy, vol. 1, (Oxford: Oxford University Press, 2000), 266.

CHAPTER 3

'Austria Can Beat Everything, If It Only Wants To'

Myth and Reality of Austrian Economic Policy since 1945

Post-war Options

On or near 21 April 1945 – with war and persecution not yet over – the Social Democratic politician Karl Renner was writing his first post-war memorandum in Schloß Eichbüchl near Vienna. Entitled 'Probleme II: Volkswirtschaft' (Problems II: The Economy), it listed four areas: restitution; currency, prices, and wages; money; and war victims, war damage, and reparations.[1] The future state chancellor, not yet so designated by Stalin, came to the conclusion that given the 'enormous burdens' to be expected in these four areas, 'which one has to despair of being able to bear … the most radical socialization measures' would have to be enforced. In particular Renner, the former first state chancellor of the Republic of Austria in 1918–20, was opposed to any general 'restoration of the past,' since otherwise, in his view, 'the coming generation will innocently hunger and bleed for all eternity for the sins of the past.' Here, though, he had in mind not just reparations such as those after the First World War, but also any far-reaching integration of the surviving Jews into the post-war economy, for which restitution would have been a first prerequisite.

Specifically, Renner wanted to use state aid to support especially the agricultural sector and in principle also the commercial and retail sector (though without restoring the businesses the Nazi regime had expropriated, primarily the property of Jewish owners). By contrast, 'big industrial, agricultural and commercial enterprises' were, against compensation, to be made state property, as were all financial and credit institutions. Private rental housing was also to be taken over by the municipalities against compensation. Renner's domestic economic policy was thus clearly going in the direction of far-reaching nationalization. The factories and assets seized in 1934 and 1938 had to be restored to the 'workers', in order to 'return to the bearers of the proletarian reconstruction movement a guaranteed basis of existence'. The 'restitution of stolen Jewish assets should ... not be to the individual victims, but to a joint restitution fund' 'so as to avert a massive, sudden influx of expellees'.

Renner's economic policy option for the domestic economy could of course equally well have looked different. The brainpower and experience of exiles, male and female, could have been deliberately planned into the reconstruction process, as is currently the case in many transformation economies of the former USSR and the once-communist eastern bloc. But in 1945 Renner, like most decision makers of the time, still cherished prejudices about the control of the economy by Jews. For party-political reasons too, Renner opposed any return of exiles of Jewish origin; the reason for this was a latent anti-Semitic feeling that in the First Republic had been liable to stigmatize the Social Democrats in the propaganda of the Christian Socialists and German Nationalists as the 'Jewish party' (while the workers' party in turn did not shrink from anti-Semitic excesses in its anti-capitalist argumentation).

This economic concept reflected mainstream opinion, oriented as it was towards narrow national autarky and no longer – as under the monarchy – thinking in terms of large areas and networks. To put it plainly: Renner, as a pragmatic right-wing Social Democrat, could make nothing of the internationalism of someone like Otto Bauer, a tradition not to be taken up again until the advent

ILLUSTRATION 3.1
An adult's food ration for one week in late 1945/early 1946.

of Bruno Kreisky. Only in the area of Central European customs-union projects were there a few ideas in 1945–47, for instance from ÖVP Foreign Minister Karl Gruber or from Julius Deutsch, a prominent Social Democrat back from the United States. These projects for forming at least a customs and commercial union with neighbouring Eastern European states all failed because of the Cold War, which was already increasingly perceptible in 1946–47, in the shape of the ideological confrontation between Soviet communism and the Western system under U.S. leadership. In 1945, however, these options would still have been entirely reasonable; they were seriously discussed both in exile circles and in the Allies' postwar planning.

Though Renner was subsequently unable, in concrete negotiations on his comprehensive socialization plans, to get his way entirely with the ÖVP – especially in the areas of big landholding and rental housing – the nationalization of 'key industries' was all the same agreed by late 1945. The ÖVP's main reason for consenting to a measure that contradicted that party's basic ideological concept was the fact that a return to the old monetarist economic concepts of the Christian Socials had already been ruled out by 1945, in view of the problems and opportunities that many experts saw in a government-guided transformation of the Nazi armaments industry. For the Western Allies – especially the United States – their assent was already a first signal of the beginning of the Cold War, and of Austria's integration into the West and its stabilization. But achieving these goals ultimately meant government planning and management of the former 'German assets' and the building up of a relatively autarkic and protected Austrian domestic economy on a new 'heavy-industry basis'.[2]

In most states of Europe after 1945, a strongly government-controlled and partly even directly managed economy initially came to prevail, in consequence of continuities from the war economy and times of scarcity: a completely different starting position compared with the period after 1918. It would seem that the 'golden age' of high growth rates prior to 1973 – as the British social historian Eric Hobsbawm calls it – ran in parallel with this abandonment of the basic concept of the period after the First World War. Then, the European states had on the one hand ended the age of the first globalization – with open currency transactions and free trade – in favour of inward-looking nation states. But in the autarkic home economy they had nonetheless cut back on government influence and allowed free play to private capitalism. In Austria, especially after 1920 and the end of the first Grand Coalition between Social Democrats and Christian Socialists, this meant that a hard-currency policy was aimed at. Private property and the private economy, however – except for a few sectors – acted without regulation or control. Not until the 1930s were there the first signs of government interventionism, for instance in connection with the rehabilitation of the Creditanstalt-Bankverein after its collapse in 1931, or the first job-creation programmes, which even contained elements of deficit spending in a Keynesian sense.

It should be noted that after 1945 this decision to exert increased government influence did not necessarily end up in nationalization and centralization. In Austria too, economists – particularly on the American side – discussed breaking up the remaining, largely formerly German remnants of the industrial conglomerates and running them in the form of medium-sized firms. The objective was to be a sort of Austrian Switzerland, with a strong finished-goods industry. This concept was, for example, discussed in connection with the Linz works of the former Reichswerke Hermann Göring AG, but it met with resistance from both U.S. economic officials, who wanted to keep a large enterprise as U.S. property, and local political elites. Here one can see that the pressure from the grassroots to create as many jobs as possible quickly, with government support, was very strong and cut across all the parties. At both the level of the Renner provisional state government and the provincial level, nationalization of the key industries, but also of the oil and electricity business, increasingly gained majority support. The big banks too were to be covered; the insurance companies by contrast were left out. This also meant a strategic turn in the direction of transformation of the primary industry built up or expanded particularly under National Socialism; it was to profit enormously from the boom in the steel industry in the late 1940s and 1950s. But this dream scenario was not yet foreseeable in 1945; the decision thus certainly also involved risks.

An important element in this reversal of trend by comparison with pre-1938 was also the uncertainty about the future of the 'German assets', which, according to the Potsdam resolutions of August 1945, could be claimed by the Allies as de facto reparations. The Soviet Union especially interpreted this concept very broadly, subsuming under it even the sequestered assets that in 1945 were under German management (including Jewish-owned enterprises stolen between 1938 and 1945). In the area of the Soviet Zone in Vienna, Lower Austria and Burgenland and the Mühlviertel alone, the 'German property' covered 450 firms with (in 1955) 50,000 blue- and white-collar workers, around 10 per cent of Austrian industrial capacity.[3] After 1946 the Western Allies ceded fiduciary administration of these firms to the Austrian Republic, including the gigantic Alpine-Montan Konzern (steel, coal and ore) in Upper Austria, Styria and Carinthia. The Soviet Union by contrast seized the German assets in its zone in February 1946 and placed them under Soviet administration through the USIA organization ('Upravlenie Sovetskim imuščestvom v Avstrii' = Administration of Soviet Property in Austria).

The Western Allies took this political step for two main reasons. First, all measures were to be taken to separate Austria definitively from Germany and ensure the viability of this small state. Second, the logic of the Cold War required that Austria should be integrated into the Western, U.S. sphere of influence and stabilized, while sole responsibility for blocking the Allies' withdrawal was placed on the Soviet Union.

The Unexpectedly Rapid Upswing

But how was it possible for real GDP to double between 1946 and 1950 and to have risen to a third above the prewar level as early as 1951? Despite a slight falling off in 1951–52 – partly because of the Korean War – growth rates between 1953 and 1957 attained an average of 7.7 per cent, and from 1968 to 1975 5.6 per cent annually. In public awareness this undisputed achievement of reconstruction is mostly attributed to internal factors, especially the industrious Austrian workers. These male-dominated memories marginalize the major role of women in reconstruction, or reduce it to 'rubble women' clearing up the debris. In fact, neither the Nazi war economy nor the reconstruction economy could have functioned without women.

The Austria-related reconstruction myth is especially readily employed in public debates on enlargement of the European Union, being as it were held up as a mirror to Eastern European new EU member states or future candidates for accession, with the basic theme running: 'Work harder, then you'll do better, and if you're as good as we are you'll be able to join.' The structural factors by contrast speak a more differentiated language, with the 'individual worker', male or female, being only one stone – even if an important one – in the mosaic of a truly explanatory model. Internal Austrian as well as international factors were relevant for Austria's reconstruction and its status as one of the most successful small industrial countries in the world, namely:

- the inheritance of the National Socialist arms industry ('German assets');
- human capital derived from training and management before 1945 and the nationalized industries;
- European growth and the end of the 'viability debate';
- Allied aid and the Marshall Plan, the European Recovery Program (ERP), i.e. food aid before and after the ERP aid, and after 1947 financial investments and productivity enhancement;
- a stringent currency stability policy in 1945–51;
- a radical wage and price policy at the expense of wage earners;
- the social partnership;
- the first period of Austro-Keynesianism with the Raab-Kamitz approach;
- the second period of Austro-Keynesianism in the Kreisky era, together with a strong infrastructural push;
- adaptation through restructuring and EU accession in 1986–95;
- globalization and privatization, with unknown outcome.

The Example of Kaprun: An Explanatory Model for the Above Structural Factors

All the schoolbooks since the 1950s, newsreels from 1950 to 1955 and many other publications have featured one outstanding example of Austria's reconstruction achievements: the Kaprun high alpine power station in the Tauern massif. Over a dozen Kaprun films ensured that this reconstruction myth became rooted in the collective memory of the 1950s and 1960s. The 1970s then found their own symbols of achievement, such as the Arlberg tunnel and UNO City. Since then, the Kaprun myth has lost some of its lustre – perhaps partly because it now runs counter to ecological thinking, which at any rate since the Zwentendorf nuclear power debate has rendered the marketing of such huge power stations a more or less lost cause.

The Kaprun power station, while conceived even before 1938 in several plans, which were partly the product of megalomania, began actual building only under the National Socialist regime. Hermann Göring himself cut the first sod on 16 May 1938, after announcing in Vienna, the construction of 'an enormous power station in the High Tauern'. Since this had been a PR stunt underpinned by no specific planning or financing, implementation of the project had to be prepared in great haste. In disregard of all legal requirements (building permit, water-rights permit etc.), preliminary work was begun on the spot; building of the station itself began in May 1939 and was completed in 1944.

By 1945 around a third of the allocated budget had been invested in the Kaprun project, inter alia for ropeways, shafts, roadways etc.; some 50 per cent of the Limberg dam had been completed. The construction firms in the ARGE Tauernkraftwerke had increasingly been employing foreign forced labour, including well over 2,000 Polish, Belgian, French and Russian prisoners of war and 8,500 foreign civilian workers (1,800 Poles, 1,000 Russians, 1,400 French and 1,500 Italians), as well as thirty Jewish forced labourers. Only some 1,100 citizens of the German Reich are to be found in the statistics. The figures on deaths on this extreme building site vary; at least fifty-six deaths of foreign forced labourers are documented through 1945 (of a total of up to eighty-three victims), while between 1946 and 1951 a total of seventy-eight workers lost their lives in accidents or avalanches.

Kaprun and the further expansion of hydroelectric power constituted a major component of economic reconstruction and the viability of the Second Republic. A high percentage of the investments from the Marshall Plan accordingly went to the completion of Kaprun.[4] In media presentations U.S. economic aid and Austria's own efforts were particularly stressed, while the performance of the foreign forced labourers and prisoners of war was mostly glossed over, although this factor was not suppressed in the firm's internal publications. Not till the late

Das große Aufbauwerk beginnt

ILLUSTRATION 3.2
Map of Austria's industrial potential, Berliner Illustrirte Zeitung, *1938.*

1990s was the theme of 'forced labour and the heritage of the National Socialist period in the economy' fully confronted.

The power-station building in the Alps and the involvement of Marshall Plan aid also stand for the beginning of state investment and infrastructure measures that can later, especially in the era of Finance Minister Reinhard Kamitz, be seen specifically as a preliminary stage of Austro-Keynesianism. Of course Kamitz primarily represents a liberal-conservative and strictly 'anti-social liberal' approach, though with marked government input into financial and economic policy.

The Heritage of the National Socialist Arms Industry and Nationalized Industry

In his 1967 study *Society and Democracy in Germany,* the late Ralf Dahrendorf conclusively argued that the National Socialist regime had left revolutionary traces in the German economy that had long-term effects on the postwar society of the Federal Republic of Germany.[5] This was evident, amongst other things, in the failure of the attempts of the second postwar chancellor, Ludwig Erhard, to modify corporatist – semi-state – structures inherited from the Nazi period in such way as to enable liberal reforms in the direction of an open market economy not under state influence. What actually became established instead was a system strongly marked by central government, Länder and municipal influences, with powerful federal and semi-public institutions. Altogether, they added up to a very effective regime of public influence and control over the economy in the Federal Republic.

Although the car industry, of particular importance for the creation of the West German economic miracle, remained privately owned (e.g. Volkswagen), it was politically shielded against foreign takeovers, and at the same time foreign car industries (e.g. that of the U.S.) were discriminated against in the Federal Republic. Well into the 1980s Volkswagen kept a number of monopoly-type advantages over non-German competitors (for instance, in relation to trade in spare parts), and even the Social Democrat-dominated trade union IG Metall negotiated moderate wage settlements.

In Austria the directly state-owned portion of the economy was certainly higher than in the Federal Republic, since enterprises controlled by (private and public) German owners had come under government administration in 1945. After 1955 these largely became public property. The strong planned-economy approach of the post-war economy displays clear traces of the Nazi period, exemplified, inter alia, in the continued employment of the same specialists.

Apart from the anti-Semitic prejudices already discussed, the trend in the direction of a nationalized economy also hindered the making of total restitution to Jewish owners. While some small and medium-sized enterprises were restored, the surviving Jewish owners, mostly living abroad, still had huge legal problems to cope with. The 'Aryanizations' were not silently 'glossed over', but the legal disputes were dominated by the efforts of the justice and financial authorities to offer settlement by way of compensation rather than restitution. With regard to the eighty or so small banks and exchange offices that had existed before 1938, moreover, the aim was a radical 'clean sweep' – a frightening term, but one that grasps the brutal core of this policy. Hardly any banking concessions were issued to the pre-1938 Jewish owners (e.g. the Bank Gebrüder Gutmann). In most cases these banks had already been liquidated before 1945. Most claims for restitution and trading permits thus failed for lack of capital and because of competition from the domestically controlled banks after 1945, although these were really just as bankrupt. This scenario was not, however, confined to Austria. In France a similar line can be traced; there, only the big credit institutions with Jewish owners were readmitted, and liquidated banks were hardly ever reinstated.

To cut a long story short: Austrian economic policy in the first years after 1945 largely indirectly continued the 'Aryanization' policy of the Nazi regime in its structural effects. Though one of the great Austrian economists, Joseph A. Schumpeter, had made the importance of entrepreneurship a central point of his analyses, the founding fathers of this republic de facto excluded entrepreneurs of Jewish origin from the reconstruction process. The Second Republic wished to do without this human capital. This can be seen in Renner's plans, which, while providing for compensation for the stolen property, did so with a time lag and through shares in a fund, not through restitution in kind. For this reason it took a while before the restitution legislation was passed (under pressure from the Western Allies); the step of actually making restitution, a step towards a new style of coexistence, was one many did not want to take.

A second step that might have facilitated the reintegration of the expelled economic elites was likewise not taken: Austrian citizenship was automatically restored only to those who had held it before 12 March 1938 and who had resided permanently on Austrian territory since 27 April 1945. All others – thus also the exiles – had to reapply for citizenship in order to take up normal residence in Austria. This form of discrimination was not lifted until 1995, under the Vranitzky government. Since then Austrian citizenship can easily be regained by exiles and their descendants; they are not required to give up their former citizenship. In 1945, though, the deprivation of citizenship – loss of Reich nationality based on pre-1938 Austrian nationality – was confirmed, at least for the time being.

That this also meant the loss of an active and successful group of private business people with international connections was apparently not clear to the decision makers in 1945, but it becomes very evident in today's economic structure. Below we shall deal with this most-suppressed facet of the history of Austrian enterprises.

The Unused Options

For foreign marketing purposes, the Austrian economy readily has recourse to the Habsburg monarchy and its baroque setting, for some twenty years now enriched with remnants of the Vienna moderns of around 1900, from Klimt via Schiele to Otto Wagner and Josef Hoffmann. Left to one side is the fact that the centre of the monarchy, the imperial and dynastic capital city of Vienna, has a second kind of modernity to show: the 'Gründerzeit' (period of boom in new businesses) around the turn of the century brought out an interesting aspect of Austrian entrepreneurial culture that has a special appeal in today's 'third Gründerzeit'.

The French economist Jean-François Vidal rightly notes similarities between the internationalization of financial and currency flows from 1880 to 1913 and today's globalization since the 1970s and especially the 1980s.[6] Using the examples of figures for international goods and capital movements (foreign investments) and of deregulation measures, he finds structural parallels. Vienna was also booming around the turn of the century as a banking and stock-exchange centre, and companies founded in Prague were moving their head offices to Vienna. Herbert Matis locates a 'second Gründerzeit' between 1896 and 1913, when average annual growth in gross domestic product amounted, for a period of thirty years up to 1913, to 1.89 per cent per annum.[7] The First World War, with its nationally compartmentalized war economies, ended these first approaches to a global, open economy – then still with its centre in London – and the break-up of Austria-Hungary after 1918 reduced the opportunities available to the Vienna business groups. Nonetheless, channels of communication and finance remained intact; a number of firms were able at least to keep their subsidiaries in Eastern Europe and headquarters in Vienna above water. National Socialism and the Cold War destroyed these socioeconomic and cultural structural survivals from the times of the Dual Monarchy.

In the economy (as was also the case with the moderns in art) migration effects were to be observed around 1900 that enabled the financial and trading hub that was Vienna to emerge as an urban centre. And here too the proportion of assimilated Jews – many of them no longer members of their religious community – was very high. A close look at the break-up of big groups in 1938 reveals – and not just in the case of the family of Louis and Alfons Rothschild – a highly modern network, seen from today's perspective, of Central European business groups (despite the economic crisis, inflation and nationalistic economic policy after 1918). These structures, though broken up during the National Socialist period, were not definitively destroyed until the nationalizations in the communist states. In Austria too, despite restitution legislation, they were revived in only a few cases, such as Karl Kahane's mining group or the Bunzl-Biach group, which however no longer belongs to the founding family.

Internationally, Austria's reputation suffers from its not being reckoned as an entrepreneurial country. Thus, one of the U.S. authors of the *Area Handbook* published in 1994 by the Library of Congress maintained that Austria had never had an entrepreneurial capitalist tradition, and that most Austrian firms produced only for the home market or at best for the neighbouring region (particularly the EU, and especially Germany and Italy). The fact that Austrian business played only a modest role from 1945 until very recently is also connected with the fact that after 1938 all the Jewish-owned big business groups were broken up and de facto expropriated, with only part of the proceeds of liquidation reaching the original owners. And restitution policy after 1945 was not aimed at bringing the business families – to the extent they had survived – back to their homeland.

European Growth and the End of the Viability Debate

An element that is hardly ever taken into account in the development of Austria's post-1945 separate identity – as contrasted with Germany's – is the fact that there were now no longer any debates about the viability of this small state such as those that had often served in the interwar years to justify integration with Germany. As we know, the Allies prevented this, as they did the project for a customs union; Germany's economic influence nonetheless grew steadily.

After 1945 the Anschluss was not only exorcized by Austrians because of their negative experiences under the Third Reich (as the future socialist Vice-Chancellor

Adolf Schärf put it as early as 1944), but the German part of the economy, which had long outgrown the rest, was simply expropriated. Many Austrians saw this as a sort of reparation made to Austria by the legal successor to the German Reich, without considering the extent of their own collaboration. In the economic sphere the total takeover of the German assets in the Western occupation zones laid the basis for a new start, at least in budgetary terms – the slate having been cleaned, as it were, by bankruptcy proceedings. This revolutionary act – not legal succession, but seizure – was certainly one of the essential preconditions for Austria's economic reconstruction. Not till some years after the State Treaty of 1955 had been signed was an assets agreement reached with the Federal Republic of Germany, following tough negotiations (the Kreuznach Agreement of 1961); by contrast, private German property – referred to as 'minor German assets' – was hardly restored at all. The pre-1938 holdings of German firms were also treated as lapsed.

A psychologically significant factor in the transformation of German enterprises, many of which had suffered war damage or had, in eastern Austria, been partly dismantled by the Soviets, consisted literally in declarations of bankruptcy. All enterprises, in both the industry and service sectors and in banking, began their activity with an initial balance sheet expressed in schillings (based on the relevant Reichsmark balance for 1944). In the real economy many of the receivables carried forward had long ceased to be recoverable but continued to appear on the balance sheet, or else the Republic of Austria took on outstanding claims against the German Reich and against German firms. Often the impression is that a kind of notional bankruptcy was deemed to have taken place, so that a sort of accounting new start could be attempted. This was an important process for consolidating a market economy, even though it was not based on any underlying assets.

Allied Emergency Aid, the Marshall Plan and the Cold War

Reconstruction would have been impossible without the Allied and international food supplies made available between 1945 and 1947. The rate at which reconstruction happened would have been unthinkable had it not been for the ERP Marshall Plan funds. These facts have totally disappeared from public and even political awareness. Until spring 1946 the Allies fed the inhabitants of their respective zones, though in many industrial areas of Lower Austria, for instance, the population subsisted on a mere 900 calories per day. Altogether, domestic food supplies officially covered only 40 per cent of the meagre rations, while the black market and foraging trips to farms close to urban centres boomed.[8] And the assistance campaign through UNRRA (United Nations Relief and Rehabilitation Agency) was to last only until mid 1947.

It is certainly true that the loading of 'occupation costs' onto the Austrian budget during the process of post-war consolidation was a burden; on the other hand, Allied aid measures for 1945–46 amounted to an estimated 200.3 million dollars, 91.6 million of it from UNRRA, which in 1947 was still sending aid goods valued at 44 million dollars to Austria (Tables 2 and 3).

At latest from 1947, it was clear to decision makers in the United States that only the rapid economic integration of the former enemy powers of Germany (western zones) and Austria, as well as economic support from the Western Allies, could prevent Soviet dominance from spreading in Europe and confine the Soviet sphere of influence to Eastern Europe. Originally, in the case of Germany a 'severe' and controlled postwar system had been announced, centred upon the four D-Programmes (demilitarization, denazification, decartelization and democratization), but in Austria after autumn 1945 at the latest, the U.S. authorities were much more conciliatory in their approach.

The Marshall Plan (European Recovery Program, ERP), a comprehensive reconstruction programme with a cost of some 14 billion U.S. dollars, was intended to stabilize particularly France and Britain, but also Italy, the Netherlands and West Germany, economically and socially. Two-thirds of the resources in the loan and credit programme went to these countries (a quarter to Britain, a fifth to France and a tenth each to Italy and West Germany). Fourfold occupied Aus-

TABLE 2

External aid until the signing of the Austrian State Treaty in 1955
(quoted in million dollars)

AMOUNT	1945	1946	1947	1948	1949	1950	1951	1952	1953	1954	1955[4]
ERP (EUROPEAN RECOVERY PROGRAM) – DIRECT AID	686.6	-	-	94.3	194.2	119.5	127.6	91.4	38.5	19.8	1.5
ERP (EUROPEAN RECOVERY PROGRAM) – INDIRECT AID	269.6	-	-	3.3	95.6	83.1	76.0	11.6	-	-	-
UNRRA (UNITED NATIONS RELIEF AND REHABILITATION ADMINISTRATION)	135.6	91.6	44.0	-	-	-	-	-	-	-	-
USA – WAR DEPARTMENT	38.0[1]		38.0	-	-	-	-	-	-	-	-
CONGRESS- AND INTERIM AID	156.1[1]	-	54.6	101.5	-	-	-	-	-	-	-
AID FROM CANADA	3.4	-		3.4	-	-	-	-	-	-	-
BOOTIES AND OVERAGE GOODS	86.9[1]	-	30.7	56.2	-	-	-	-	-	-	-
GIFT PARCELS	69.5[1]	-	29.9	19.6	9.3	4.1	2.4	2.4	1.8	-	-
OTHER AID SHIPMENTS	55.6	24.8[2]	28.2	1.5	1.0	0.1	-	-	-	-	-
OVERALL	1,585.1	200.3[3]	225.4	279.8	300.1	206.8	206.0	105.4	40.3	19.8	1.5

1 WITHOUT POTENTIAL SHIPMENTS 1945 AND 1946 2 AID FROM ALLIED SOURCES 3 ESTIMATES 4 JANUARY UNTIL APRIL

TABLE 3

Utilization of the foreign economic aid until the year 1955 (quoted in million schilling)

	ERP-funds	Other auxiliary accounts	Overall	Percent
Currency hedging	125	725[1]	850	6.5
Federal investments	1.529	538	2.067	15.9
Industrial investments	6.137	600	6.737	51.8
Agriculture and forestry	1.360	-	1.360	10.4
Subsidized housing	504	50	554	4.3
Tourism	305	-	305	2.3
Technical aid and stimulation of efficiency	296	-	296	2.3
Promotion of exports	163	-	163	1.3
Others	684	-	684	5.2
Releases overall	11.103	1.913	13.016	100.0

1 Including 650 Million Schilling of congress- and interim aid

Source: Franz Horner: Probleme der österreichischen Währungspolitik. Ph.D. Thesis, University of Freiburg 1964, p. 123.

tria received the second-highest ERP aid per head of population after Norway, which was to cause some geopolitical friction. This financial aid was used to buy raw materials, foodstuffs and new technologies, but it also went towards balancing Austria's state budgets. The United States in turn created new markets for itself and assisted in reconverting its domestic war economy to a peacetime one. However, the Marshall Plan did not bring about fundamental change in well-established economic state structures, as the examples of France and Austria show; that is, the U.S. economic model was not exported.

Despite its enormous financial volume, the Marshall Plan, which began to run only in late 1948 after the establishment of the OEEC (Organization for European Economic Cooperation), charged with the distribution of funds and also responsible for economic and monetary policy cooperation, would not by itself have been able to set the European economic upturn in motion. Still, it undoubtedly promoted its rapid development, and above all provided social cushioning for economic reconstruction while at the same time weakening the left-wing extremist and Communist parties in Europe.

Given the social-policy goals of the ERP, the Soviet Union quickly changed its initial wait-and-see position and forced other Eastern European states within its sphere of influence, like Czechoslovakia, to remain aloof from the programme. Stalin for his part sought new ways to bind the Eastern European satellite states more strongly to the communist bloc: after the setting up of the Communist Information Bureau (Cominform) in January 1949, the Council for Mutual Economic Assistance (COMECON) was founded, which promoted in particular the orientation of the national economies to the Soviet model – without regard for national traditions and differences.

The Marshall Plan had by contrast been conceived as a geopolitical programme carried out by economic means, and it moreover compensated for losses that the Austrian economy was suffering as a result of its separation from its traditional economic hinterland, already perceptible after 1945. In the country itself the option for integrating Austria politically and economically into the Western bloc had already become tangible by September/October 1945. While Austria's foreign trade with the eastern bloc was still 22 per cent in 1946, it had fallen to 10 per cent by 1955, while the proportion of trade with Western Europe – after 1950 particularly with the Federal Republic of Germany – rose to 58 per cent; by contrast, trade with Czechoslovakia fell from 19.1 per cent in 1946 to 1.5 per cent of the export sector in 1955.

The Marshall Plan not only served as an instrument of stabilization and compensation in this reorientation of Austria's foreign trade but also enhanced the traditional infrastructure differences between the eastern and western parts of the country, since officially no ERP funds at all could be allocated to eastern Austria. Nonetheless the federal government managed, with the toleration of local U.S. authorities, in part to circumvent the instructions from the U.S. Congress not to allot any ERP funds to communist states. Thus, between 1950 and 1955 Vienna and Lower Austria received 5.8 per cent and 5.3 per cent respectively of the ERP money, and Burgenland 2.2 per cent; the western provinces were plainly favoured here (Tyrol 29.6 per cent, Salzburg 19.5 per cent and Upper Austria 9.2 per cent), something that was in part connected with the government's investment focuses – for instance on the construction of power stations and on tourism. The east-west difference continued even after 1955, so that the 'Golden West' had a higher standard of living to offer, despite regional and occupational variations.

Economic Exploitation and Social Restoration

The Soviet Union's intention to carry out massive economic exploitation in Austria – on paper aimed primarily at the 'German assets' and German arms industries – can readily be documented, starting with the famous Moscow Declaration of 1 November 1943, where the Soviet diplomats changed their line on Austria's political responsibility for the Second World War. Whereas until late 1943 this matter had automatically been seen in terms of exclusive (Reich) German responsibility, stronger emphasis was henceforth to be laid on specifically Austrian political co-responsibility. Behind this lay very practical intentions, as even the political debate in the exile Free Austrian Movement (FAM) in London, dominated by exiled Communists, shows. The FAM unreservedly addressed the consequences deriving from co-responsibility: payment of reparations to the Soviet

Union and a tough denazification policy after liberation.[9] Evidently the Soviet
planners had realized that reparations from Austria would be justified and could
be pushed through the international conferences only in the case of shared guilt.
Initially the Soviet Union itself, as opposed to the KPÖ, had no great interest in
the 'Nazi question' beyond the prosecution of war criminals. The stability of a
bourgeois society willing to adapt was much more important to it than revolutionary social processes.

For economic reasons, Soviet diplomats were still trying in late March 1945 to
take control of another zone in Austria, namely Styria and Carinthia, with the Alpine Montan conglomerate affiliated to the Reichswerke Hermann Göring. They
based this change of mind first of all on political considerations: strengthening
Soviet influence on Yugoslavia and weakening British influence, as well as envisaging 'real chances for a small zone for Yugoslavia in Southern Austria', or for that
country to take part in the occupation with symbolic units. But economic arguments were also relevant: a map of Austria captured by Soviet intelligence suggested there were more aircraft factories and steel and nonferrous metal plants, as
well as power stations, in Styria and Carinthia than in Lower Austria.[10]

One important theme in Soviet-Austrian relations during and after liberation
from National Socialism was thus the nature and extent of the Soviet 'right of
plunder'. On 12 May 1945 Marshal Tolbukhin had talks with Karl Renner about
various large plants from which the Red Army wanted to remove technical installations and raw materials. From the Soviet viewpoint, this meant specifically
that the 'seized Reich German plant' was to be carried off as compensation for
the destruction and dismantling of Soviet industry up to the Volga.[11] Tolbukhin
also claimed that Austrian manpower would anyway be insufficient to keep these
works operational now that the foreign workers who had been exploited in many
of them – deported 'Fremdarbeiter', i.e. forced labour – had gone. 'Light industry
that the people needs, the food industry, urban utilities, in a word, the whole industrial apparatus that serves the people's needs and which did not belong to the
Germans', was to remain.[12] Altogether in 1945 requisitions estimated at 1,135
billion schillings were carried out; of that, around 700 million schillings' worth
concerned enterprises with German involvement. In Lower Austria and Vienna
alone, the total loss of machines amounted to 650 million schillings (mostly in
the steel and metal working industries).[13]

In daily political contacts between Austrian politicians and Soviet officers, the
dispute over the Soviet sequestration policy (the 'plunder question') intensified.
Both Karl Renner and Theodor Körner, the mayor of Vienna, tried to defend
the economic interests of the extremely shaky Austrian economy in the eastern
Austrian territory. Despite assurances that only plants newly installed after 1938
would be dismantled, the Soviets in practice carried off the factory installations
lock, stock and barrel.[14] It may be stated by way of summary that the Soviets'
economic exploitation policy in Austria was supposed to compensate exclusively

for the heavy wartime losses suffered by their own economic infrastructure, losses to which many thousands of Austrians in the German forces had contributed. The sometimes suggested hypothesis of a 'Trojan horse' policy[15] does not, however, stand up, and was already refuted by Martin F. Herz, who had personally experienced the immediate post-war era as a secret-service officer and later as a U.S. diplomat.[16] Herz conducted a number of background interviews in 1945, which are supported by a wealth of reports from the Office of Strategic Services (OSS).[17] Nevertheless, during the Cold War the hypothesis came to prevail that the exploitation policy was a smokescreen for political objectives. At the Moscow Foreign Ministers' Conference in April 1947 the suspicions that the Soviet Union wanted to politically destabilize Austria through its reparation demands was decisive for the outcome of the negotiations. The U.S. High Commissioner Mark W. Clark accordingly blocked a possible version of the State Treaty involving substantial financial compensation to the Soviet Union.[18] This would have weakened Austria economically and increased the likelihood of a Communist seizure of power from within.

Before the Cold War set in in Austria too in February 1946, the Soviet leadership signalled a willingness to co-operate in some areas of the exploitation of the 'German assets'. For instance, 'Aryanized' enterprises, i.e. those stolen from Jewish owners, were in part being run once again by their pre-1938 owners, at least provisionally.[19] In the sphere of the oil industry, there were intensive negotiations from August 1945 on a joint venture. The Republic of Austria, still consisting only of Lower Austria, Vienna and Burgenland plus the Mühlviertel in Upper Austria – as we know, Renner's Provisional State Government as yet had no powers in the Western Allies' zones – was to contribute 13 million U.S. dollars, whilst the Soviets' share (12 million dollars) was to take the form of the oilfields they claimed in eastern Austria. The project, also linked to a Soviet-Austrian commercial treaty, ultimately foundered upon a 'coalition' that cut right across the Austrian party elites of both SPÖ and ÖVP and the interest groups. Federal Chancellor Karl Renner (SPÖ) voted for the Soviet-Austrian Project, Adolf Schärf (SPÖ) against; Julius Raab (ÖVP) supported Renner, whilst Eduard Heinl (ÖVP) instead presented the U.S. and British reservations and political pressures that in September 1945 caused the negotiations to collapse.[20]

Whether this sort of joint-venture solution would have paid off economically is hard to say in retrospect. That the Soviet Union intended a creeping Communist seizure of power as in Eastern European states like Hungary, Romania etc. can now be disproved on the basis of the Soviet documents. At any rate, Austria had until 1958 to pay, out of its national wealth, de facto oil reparations to the Soviet Union, which until the State Treaty of 1955 were not even checked or quantified, since the Soviet oil and mineral administration managed the exploitation of the wells on its own. In 1955, because of overproduction, annual output was estimated at 3.7 million tonnes. Between 1955 and 1958 6 million tonnes of crude with a value of 2.7 billion schillings had to be delivered to the Soviet Union.[21] Since in 1945 the Soviet Union had offered a fifty-fifty split of net profits, it would seem that despite the high initial investment a considerable gain for the Austrian economy would have been possible.

One interesting but almost totally forgotten chapter of Austria's postwar economic history is the integration of the formerly Soviet-administered industries (USIA enterprises) in Lower Austria, Burgenland and Vienna. These 400 or so industrial and agricultural enterprises – among them the Erste Donau-Dampfschiffahrtsgesellschaft (DDSG) and the oil administration – were, as already mentioned, placed under Soviet administration after the failed negotiations. The transfer of profits to the Soviet Union from this part of the German assets resulting from dismantlings and seizures, plus the settlement consignments and payments under the State Treaty of 1955 after the return to Austrian control of the USIA enterprises, amounted to between 1,547 and 2,647 million U.S. dollars according to the latest estimates, corresponding to around twice the total Marshall Plan contributions of altogether 909 million dollars.[22] Losses from the booming shadow economy are of course not included here. They affected the Western zones in equal measure.

The takeover of these USIA enterprises, among them the Soviet oil administration (today's OMV) and the Vienna Film Studios at Rosenhügel, as well as the DDSG and industrial enterprises in the glass, leather, iron and steel, metal working and machine- and vehicle-building sectors, might partly be compared with the integration of the former GDR into the Federal Republic of Germany. Especially in Vienna and Lower Austria these enterprises represented 30 per cent of the local industrial capital, in some sectors a large part of the Austrian total (for instance, 40 per cent of the iron and steel industry and 32 per cent of the metal working industry). Politically, these industries were KPÖ strongholds. The SPÖ in particular accordingly endeavoured to bring about integration with the greatest possible circumspection, to avoid political conflicts in Lower Austria, Burgenland and parts of Vienna. Investment requirements in these industries after 1955 were also high, since the Soviet owners had barely invested in them.

Oil was another area where Austria's national economy was unsuccessful in its efforts to bring all national resources in the raw materials sector together under state control for reconstruction. Anglo-American and Dutch oil companies had acquired drilling rights before 1938 but scarcely used them; as early as 1946 they began again to lay claim to the oil deposits massively exploited by the Nazi regime. The United States in particular supported these demands, and in 1955 in the decisive negotiations on the State Treaty the U.S. pushed through an additional document of its own, the Vienna Memorandum. Despite the fact that they were based on highly controversial legal premises, the Austrian government accepted these claims in a sort of political blanket assurance. While Bruno Kreisky in particular, as state secretary and later as foreign minister, tried to reopen the legal question, he failed because of U.S. pressure. In 1958 the release of credits from the Marshall Plan repayment funds was even stopped in order to force the Austrian side to yield. The claims were in fact accepted in the 1960s, which laid the basis for extremely heavy Austrian dependence on international oil companies – especially through the filling station network, but at times in price setting too. By contrast with the de facto reparations to the USSR and its settlement demands, however, this loss of assets on the overall balance sheet of the Republic is hardly discussed.

Monetary and Stability Policy, 1945–51

In the National Socialist period – especially after the German attack on Poland and the start of the war – a strictly state-controlled economy was imposed. Prices, wages, foreign trade and all international finance and currency transactions were monitored by the authorities and required their approval. Immediately after Austria's liberation in 1945 all the bank tills were closed; not until the Tills Law of 3 July 1945 could payment transactions resume, at least in eastern Austria, the area run by the Renner government. Balances from before 3 July were 60 per cent frozen as old balances; account holders could access the remaining 40 per cent, but only up to a maximum of 150 Reichsmarks per month. The Soviet Allied Administration had made only limited funds (200 million Reichsmarks) available to the Austrian National Bank for distribution to the bank and savings-bank sector.

It was only by means of a radical break, the Schilling Law of 30 November 1945, that the huge amounts of Reichsmark banknotes and 'Allied military schillings' in private hands could be verified and exchanged for new schilling notes. Altogether there were between 8 and 15 billion Reichsmarks in circulation in the small territory of the Austrian state, far too high a money supply for the new national economy. Only a maximum of 150 Reichsmarks per person was permitted to be changed into the new schilling notes. The rest was paid into accounts or savings books and was freely accessible; balances from before the set date of 22 December 1945 were 60 per cent frozen, with only limited access to the remainder. This highly technical procedure makes it clear that the pre-1938 monetarists had come to prevail. Real property was much less involved in this legally based state bankruptcy, which is how the whole budget position in the early years should be viewed. Viktor Kienböck, who had already headed the National Bank from 1932 to 1938, was the dominant figure here, Renner having brought him on board. The drafts of the laws cited are in Kienböck's handwriting.

Special problems were, as already mentioned, caused by the occupation costs. Thus, 1.5 billion schillings had to be paid to the Allies in 1945. In 1946 35 per cent of total expenditure was appropriated as a fixed sum. The only way to raise it was by drawing on the Treasury. The 1947 Currency Protection Law enabled the hitherto only formally frozen balances to be definitively withdrawn and the 40 per cent remainders converted into government bonds. That it was ultimately possible to reduce the gigantic money supply sufficiently to bring goods volumes and prices into harmony was only partly connected with this law. The measure once again affected only money owners and not owners of real property.

Radical Wage and Price Policies and the Social Partnership

Despite the monetarist mechanisms now in place, it was not possible to get inflation under control. For this reason, in 1947 the three business chambers and the trade union federation became actively involved in Austrian economic policy, resorting for the first time in Austrian economic history to a voluntary but binding wage-price agreement. Farm prices and wage rates were fixed, and the resulting supplements were calculated according to the motto 'who earns more gets more'. In 1946–47 the cost of living rose by 130 per cent, but net collectively bargained wages by only 83 per cent. This shows very clearly that the ÖVP had once again got its way and that it was motivating performance, and not by any means social progressiveness, that ranked foremost.

A comparison with 1985 should illustrate purchasing power in 1950: how much bread or meat could an industrial worker buy for an average month's pay, and how much by comparison did a suit cost? Monthly pay in 1950 was 1,149 schillings (thirteen times per year), which could buy 400 kg of bread or 70 kg of meat, compared to 840 kg of bread or 140 kg of meat in 1985. In 1950 it bought one suit; in 1985, five suits.

This policy, which by no means banished inflation, led to vehement discussions that in 1950 escalated into the great September/October strikes. Even today the facts that these strikes were heavily pushed by the Communist Party of Austria and that the USIA enterprises played a major part in them cause them still to be interpreted as a 'putsch attempt', since even the Federal Chancellery was besieged. All the detailed archival studies show, however, as already mentioned, that by this time there was no longer any plan for a Communist seizure of power and that the Soviet occupiers were not promising any support for such a notion.

The putsch metaphor (while it cannot be denied that many people may well have felt the sometimes violent clashes actually to be a putsch attempt) proved a perfect instrument for finally freeing the Social Democrats from the suspicion that they were planning to form a united front with the KPÖ. Since the trade unions, and especially the builders' and woodworkers' union under the future Interior Minister Franz Olah, played an active part in ending the strike, the Social Democrats could definitively lay claim to being an anti-communist grouping – despite various attempts in later election campaigns (e.g. in 1966) to raise the spectre of a 'people's front'.

Today the wage and price agreements are portrayed as successful measures accepted by all, but closer consideration shows a rather different scenario, since the burdens for wage earners were bigger than for other income groups. The first agreements were only an emergency measure, which slowed inflation somewhat and gradually brought it under government control. The fifth wage and price agreement, concluded in 1951 – the mere fact it was the fifth in quick succession in itself shows the endemic instability of the situation – was already a failure, with prices exploding upon the conclusion of the agreement. The economist Wilhelm Weber dryly noted the 'failure of a planned economy in freedom'.[23] In part, expected price increases were even calculated into the wage increases.

Despite ERP aid, the capital market was so limited that not nearly enough was invested in broad reconstruction. Private businesspeople invested in their own firms, while the government credit-guidance commission instead saw big projects that did not always match real needs as the main focus of its investment activity. Prestige projects like the rebuilding of the Staatsoper and the Burgtheater, or economically questionable ones like completing the high-alpine Kaprun power station, tied up large resources. The symbolic significance of these projects for the will for reconstruction and the self-image of Austrians should not, however, be underestimated.

The tradition of wage and price agreements, but especially also the process of extra-parliamentary decision making between the big interest groups of labour and employers, gave rise to an institutional structure: the Parity Commission for Price and Wage Questions of 1957, the corresponding Wages Subcommittee of 1962 and finally the Advisory Council for Economic and Social Questions. While this specific feature of influence exerted by the associations on a government-guided or controlled market economy was in line with the European trend after 1945, in Austria it took a special form, particularly because central figures in the social partnership often played multiple parts in government, parliament and interest groups. The number of real holders of power was thus very small. Economic policy objectives were dominated by short-term strategies; only rarely were there long-term planning decisions.

The lack of long-term structural planning – one of the weaknesses of the first postwar decade – was partly a result of both the everyday and the survival problems of the 1945–53 stabilization phase. The presence of the Allies, and of strong competition between group interests that ended ultimately in compromises, played a role here. One typical lack that persists today because of this long-term planning deficit is the extremely low budget share allotted to research. Even in the 1960s there was still not even a medium-term planning scenario for university education. Not till 1968 were research statistics brought in, by the ÖVP single-party government under Klaus. In 1966–67 the relevant figure for research and development was only 0.6 per cent. Research expenditure had risen by 1981 to 1.17 per cent, but by 1994 it had dropped to 1.15 per cent.

One particular weakness in Austria in an Organisation for Economic Co-operation and Development (OECD) comparison is, moreover, not just the low public expenditure – around half the research and development expenditure is borne by the public, and by central government – but the below-average share by comparison with other European countries of research funds from private business, which is only partly explicable by the modest size of many of the firms. To some extent, this may be connected with the cautious ('economizing') entrepreneurial tradition in post-1945 Austria. The Austro-centrism of the reconstruction period impinged very negatively on business and managerial culture, although there undoubtedly were successful examples of return on investment: for instance, the well-known Linz-Donawitz process, a basic oxygen steelmaking process developed by Vereinigte Österreichische Eisen- und Stahlwerke (VOEST) in the 1950s. Not until recent years has the interest in expansion of Austrian small and medium-sized firms grown stronger; the foreign-capital share in Austrian firms has also been growing since 1989 at least. However, an OECD study showed that research expenditure by Austrian industry in 1997, measured as a percentage of domestic product, was still well below the EU average. Only after EU entry did successive Austrian governments try to raise the amounts allocated to research and development. One political problem here is that these issues do not rank high among voters.

Forerunners of Austro-Keynesianism and the Raab-Kamitz Approach

Anyone clicking on the ÖVP website in 2000 was immediately confronted in the historical section with the Raab-Kamitz approach as an essential feature of post-1945 reconstruction. Now, however, the very name Kamitz is not to be found even in the virtual archives on the ÖVP homepage. Obviously, he does not fit in with the new neoliberal tradition-building.

In fact reconstruction was made up of several components, one of which was the Raab-Kamitz approach. Together, the strong man of the ÖVP, Julius Raab, who became federal chancellor in 1953, and the head of the economic-policy section of the Federal Chamber of Commerce, Reinhard Kamitz, who was finance minister in 1952–60, largely set the course of economic policy for the first postwar years. It was clear to both that monetary-policy measures or wage and price agreements alone could not manage to stem the ever-rising inflation and that unemployment was not falling either. The key economic data for the years 1951 to 1960 document the problems and the economic trends very clearly.

In this connection we must address a ticklish topic that both structurally and in content requires reference back to the period of National Socialist rule. In 1933 Reinhard Kamitz earned a degree in economics in Vienna and began his career as an academic employee of the Austrian Institut für Konjunkturforschung (Institute for Business Cycle Research), then headed by Oskar Morgenstern.[24] In 1938 Morgenstern was removed for racist reasons; he was later to have an internationally respected career in the United States as a professor of economics at Princeton. Like most expellee intellectuals he was not involved in the first years of reconstruction; not until the 1960s did the then Foreign Minister Bruno Kreisky, himself a former exile, and Finance Minister Kamitz bring Morgenstern into the founding brain trust of what is today the Institute for Higher Studies. Morgenstern, one of the most important 'games theorists' in economics and mathematics, remains influential even today. His study *Theory of Games and Economic Behavior,* published in 1944, is still regarded as one of the classics of economics.

Kamitz is by contrast barely known now even in Austria, and his Austro-centric studies are long forgotten; only the Raab-Kamitz approach still means something, at least to political insiders. Nonetheless, his essential significance merits attention, though without whitewashing his political biography. In 1938 Kamitz tried to preserve the independence of the Austrian vis-à-vis the Berlin Institut für Konjunkturforschung, but failed. In 1938–39 he nevertheless rose rapidly: he obtained his *Habilitation* in December of the Anschluss year and in November 1944 became an associate professor at the Hochschule für Welthandel (now Vienna University of Economics and Business Administration). From 1939 he worked in the Gauwirtschaftskammer (Regional Economic Chamber) in Vienna, becoming its head in March 1944. Under his leadership it produced an extensive project to expand the 'Ostmark economy' into Southeastern Europe. In his journalistic writings at the time he concentrated on the need for government guidance of the economy to enhance 'Wehrkraft' (defensive capacity). He joined the NSDAP, thus taking up the tradition of his German-nationalist father, who in 1934 – presumably because of his political affiliations – had been pensioned off early as president of the Administrative Court.

Kamitz, who evidently used the NSDAP as a career springboard but seemingly fought no ideological battles in the Nazi period, belonged from the very outset among the strategic economic-policy thinkers of the Second Republic. Initially, however, because of his NSDAP membership, he was employed only as an ordinary technical consultant in the Vienna Chamber of Commerce. In 1947 he moved to the Bundeskammer der gewerblichen Wirtschaft (Federal Economic Chamber), where his close political cooperation with Julius Raab began. In 1948 he was definitively amnestied, and once he was finance minister he was given his NSDAP party documents, his so-called Gauakt, as a gift from the socialist interior minister, Oskar Helmer. The U.S. denazification authorities had, however, already noted its main contents, which we have used in this book.

The type of the young, ambitious and energetic economic-policy manager with an academic background, able to adapt politically to any system, was much in demand in the postwar period. Another trait of Kamitz's was that he was able to implement his concepts as policy manager, not just analyse them theoretically. In his approach to economic policy he was no monetarist. He brought a number of the deficit-spending elements of the first phase of the National Socialist regime in 1938–39 into the debate; evidently he had learned from the mistakes of the pure monetarism of the interwar years. Kamitz carried elements of the state investment policy of the Nazi period over into his post-war concepts to combat the mass unemployment of that period. Recasting Schärf's phrase about the political sphere, one might even say that National Socialism had driven monetarism and Manchester liberalism out of the Austrian elite.

Around the turn of 1950–51 prices rose by 40 per cent within a few months, while the purchasing power of the schilling fell by a comparable amount. In 1952 Austria had the second-highest inflation rate of all OEEC states. The Raab-Kamitz approach was the only way to turn this phase of reconstruction, harmful to wage earners and therefore ultimately to the whole economy, into part of a 'normal', socially acceptable economy. In 1953 a balanced budget was produced by dint of making cuts in government investments. In the short term, the price for this step was high: in January 1953 the unemployment rate rose to 285,000 (an annual average of 8.7 per cent). The slumps in growth had primarily to do with the flagging of the initial boom at the start of the Korean War.

But the Kamitz approach to achieving a market economy, a controlled opening up of economic structures under government guidance, was able to make headway within the Grand Coalition only once the SPÖ had been given a concession: a ten-year government investment programme for the expansion of hydroelectric power, the telephone network, roads and the railways. This too was an outcome of *Proporz* in its content, but because of the structurally vital investments involved it had positive effects on economic reconstruction. Kamitz had no particular interest in either wealth redistribution or the privatization of state enterprises. Three tax cuts were intended to encourage the individual to more effort, and a de facto devaluation of the schilling in 1953 boosted foreign trade, since it made exports cheaper. In 1958, however, he went a step further, even imposing a budget policy along the lines of Keynesian anti-cyclical policy and increasing government indebtedness (9 per cent of nominal GNP in 1957, 14.7 per cent in 1959). It is interesting that at the time it was particularly the SPÖ that heavily criticized this budget policy and pushed for balanced budgets.

It was typical of the Austro-centric economic-policy debate that European economic integration was considered only marginally. For instance, Austria was present only as an observer in the European Coal and Steel Community (ECSC). In part, this lack of interest in the development of the ECSC, the core of today's European Union, was connected with the USSR's Austrian policy. In the case of Austria the Soviet Union had, by contrast with its veto for Finland, Czechoslovakia and other Eastern European countries, accepted the policy of a 'soft' approach to participation in the Marshall Plan as a chance for economic stabilization (after all, indirectly the USIA enterprises profited from this too). By contrast, the ECSC, and after 1957 the European Economic Community (EEC), always remained an economic area largely dominated by the Federal Republic of Germany. From the USSR's viewpoint, accordingly, accession or even just association (as aimed at, for instance, in 1960–63) would be a breach of the State Treaty because of the ban on an Anschluss. A brief push by Foreign Minister Figl in 1956 to seek membership in the ECSC, the negotiations with the EEC in the late 1950s and those in the 1960s in their entirety were accompanied by continual Soviet threats. The post-war trauma – the Anschluss as the beginning of renewed German expansionism – remained relevant, and was still coming up even in the talks held with Gorbachev and Foreign Minister Shevardnadze in the late 1980s and in the 1990s.

To return to the first developments in integration in 1958 and 1959, when there was an intensive debate in Western Europe on a closed EEC market, Austrian decision-makers began increasingly to pay attention to this new situation. At the same time, it should not be overlooked that Austria, like, say, Britain, had underestimated the rapid development of the EEC in the direction of a functioning and closed economic community. In 1960, as a sort of 'stopgap', EFTA, the European Free Trade Association, which alongside Britain also included Austria, Switzerland, Sweden and others, was founded. The project for a pan-European free trade area covering EEC members and their Western European neighbours plus Britain had proved impossible to realize. All the same, EFTA enabled alleviation of some of the negative effects on the Austrian economy deriving from non-membership in the EEC. But it was not till the outline agreement of 1972 between the EEC and EFTA that some real bridge building came about, leading to a gradual reduction of economic barriers. The 'provisional' EFTA was, however, to remain effective and important for Austria right up to the 1990s and EU entry.

Keynesianism in the Kreisky Era

Two features predominate in the Austrian public memory of the Kreisky era, that is to say, the period of the socialist single-party government from 1970 to 1983: one, international recognition and reputation as a neutral small state with a chancellor extremely active in foreign policy, and two, debt policy. This section will look at the question of the economic objectives and consequences of Social Democratic economic policy in the 1970s. It would seem important in this connection to make the international setting clear.

It must be pointed out that Austro-Keynesianism as an economic-policy strategy was not an issue in the run-up to the 1970 elections. While Kreisky was able to assemble a group of experts around Ernst Eugen Veselsky, who developed concrete concepts in regard to social and economic policy questions, they all remained within the framework of the basic social-partnership consensus. This was the first occasion on which Hannes Androsch stood out politically, when in the final phase of political debate on the experts' programme he very rapidly developed a financing concept and also successfully defended it within the party. It proposed neither supposedly socialist objectives, such as radical income redistribution, nor the repeatedly discussed adoption of the French model of a planned economy ('*planification*'). Especially in the first years after 1970, by contrast, elements of the social wage (free school transport, free schoolbooks, free pre- and postnatal medical checks, marriage grants) were introduced to alleviate low incomes. At the same time, though, all incomes were raised, because these measures were not means-tested – another clear indicator of the basic social-partnership consensus, which in the Kreisky era worked particularly effectively, even though the SPÖ had no absolute majority in Parliament. The drawback of this system – for instance, by comparison with other states with a highly developed welfare system – is that income differences in Austria are relatively large (and particularly affect women, who continue not to receive equal pay for equal work). The Swedish high-tax model was deliberately not aimed at here; Kreisky feared for his working majority. Those conservative and independent voters who had primarily chosen him rather than the SPÖ would in that event probably no longer have voted for him.

Since 1962, the last grand coalition had already been confronted with a recession in Austria, leading to rising budget deficits, disadvantages for Austrian exports from non-participation in the first closed European market of the EEC, a crisis in nationalized industry and indications of problems in the full-employment strategy. The new finance minister in the single-party ÖVP government, Stephan Koren, sought in 1967 to counter this recession, which was also in part due to international developments in the area of European integration. Despite his academic and ideological preference for economic liberalism, he deployed a package of active measures in an endeavour to reverse the trend. Koren, who had held chairs in Innsbruck and at the Hochschule für Welthandel in Vienna and been state secretary in the ÖVP single-party government, consolidated the Austrian budget by cutting expenditure and raising taxes. The surpluses obtained were used to stimulate the economy. But the benefits went ultimately to the socialist single-party government under Bruno Kreisky.

The first phase of deficit spending in the second Kreisky government after 1973 was an economic-policy reaction to the first oil price shock in 1973 and had nothing to do with socialist planning. The recession from 1973 to 1975 ended the golden age of the long boom in Europe and the U.S. (thus, whereas in the 1960s Austria had hit annual growth rates of almost 5 per cent, in 1973 it achieved only 2.6 per cent). The term 'Austro-Keynesianism' was first used to describe this policy ex post facto in the late 1970s by the state secretary in the last Kreisky government, the economist Hans Seidel. In practical political terms it was an active strategy developed in 1973–74, in a 'combination of demand management, incomes policy and hard-currency policy', to counter the supply-side shock of the oil price rises.[25] As regards economic policy, this approach was a final – and in the short term, thoroughly successful – attempt to make the most of the possibilities of a small 'insular economy with foreign-trade relations'[26] and swim against the world economic tide: as it were, to dive under the negative effects of the first oil price shock.

Hannes Androsch, the finance minister who put his stamp on this phase, rightly called this specific economic policy 'a policy mix that could also have been termed "Austro-monetarism"'. As a consequence of the hard-currency policy, the schilling was tied to the deutschmark. Nonetheless, the term Austro-monetarism is an exaggerated formulation, even if the hard-currency policy remained an essential factor for stabilization. It is interesting that Androsch today makes his differences of opinion with Bruno Kreisky on this point responsible for his break with the chancellor, who tended more towards an independent strategy of not necessarily following every revaluation of the deutschmark, thus improving export possibilities. It is true that Kreisky – motivated partly by his personal friend Hans Igler, president of the Federation of Austrian Industry – pressed for a somewhat softer currency, to promote export business.

The 'policy mix' achieved clear successes in the area of unemployment rates. Whereas in 1973 Austria and OECD Europe had had similar rates (1.2 per cent as against 3.5 per cent), by 1979 the gap had already grown larger (2.0 per cent as against 6.2 per cent), and by 1983 it showed a marked structural contrast (4.4 per cent as against 10.4 per cent).[27] It became increasingly clear that Kreisky himself, as well as a number of his ministers and the social partners, were emphasizing this employment priority in part in order to stabilize the whole democratic edifice. The occasional complaints from private business and industry did nothing to change this. The negative experience of the mass unemployment of the interwar years had created a basic consensus after 1945, as Kreisky himself continually emphasized. Here it can be seen that he had been much struck by the positive experience of Sweden.

In the long-term perspective, it should not be forgotten that Austria, by contrast with many other European states, even today does not have high core unemployment; elsewhere, because of rationalization effects, it can hardly be reduced any further, even in growth phases. The original postwar automatic assumption that growth equals higher employment has, since the 1980s, failed to work without additional measures.

A second expected effect of deficit spending, which was however already planned before 1970 and embodied some of Koren's ideas, concerned the 'modernization' of the Austrian economy. This strategy was symbolized by the SPÖ's election slogan in 1970: 'Make Austria ready for Europe'. The 1970s were the period in the Austrian economy when most of the infrastructural measures (transportation, schools, hospitals, housing schemes) on which the economy still rests today were taken. Austria's traditional technology deficit and extremely low research and development promotion rates were, on the other hand, only slightly improved.

The structural problems, then, were stabilized in the 1970s but not eliminated. While Kreisky and his team – starting from the pre-1970 plans of the SPÖ's 1,400 experts – tried to make nationalized industry more competitive by pooling capacities in the areas of the steel industry and mining (a trend towards concentration seen at that time in many European countries), the concept failed. In the wake of the international economic crisis and the second oil price shock after 1978–79, a repeat of the 1973–74 'dive' was no longer possible. Both Kreisky and his new Finance Minister Herbert Salcher sought, in a surprise coup in 1982, to be completely open with voters before the elections: a tax package was to bring about budgetary rehabilitation. This package, whose core was a tax on capital gains, perfectly usual in Europe – a so-called withholding tax – was worked out at the chancellor's holiday home on the Spanish island Majorca. Immediately, the media slogan 'Majorca package' was born. The withholding tax became a focus for attacks on Kreisky in the tabloids, only to be introduced ten years later.

In this constant to and fro over taxing interest on savings, the confidentiality of the bank book, which was to continue to be protected even from the taxman, played its part. The European Union was eventually to put an end to this special chapter of Austrian attitudes to saving by sheer brute force, and banking secrecy, which certainly can be abused for money laundering and tax evasion, is gradually being lifted.

A Savings Mentality versus Investment-mindedness

Political discourse and public opinion ignore the fact that while budget deficits rose in the 1970s, the investments thereby made possible benefited the economy as a whole. This situation is connected with two factors: party-political polemics by the ÖVP and the specific Austrian savings mentality. The latter was a central element in the National Socialist war economy and in the scarcity economy of reconstruction after 1945. Before 1945 attempts were made by the most varied propaganda means to extract the last pfennig from the pockets of those on the 'home front' through collections ('Winter Aid'), economies and ersatz products – right up to the sawdust schnitzel – without endangering the regime's stability. In 1945 the Provisional State Government began in its turn to use every means to raise savings rates, and it similarly promoted national reconstruction saving at many levels. In schools saving was 'learned' through many campaigns (the Spare-froh [Happysave] cartoon figure, magazines etc.), but neither in the Nazi period nor during reconstruction was there any statement as to what these funds, collected in a broad national effort, were to be used for: in the one case to prolong a war of aggression, in the other for a reconstruction that in its first stage was carried by the lower and middle incomes, rather than, say, by real-estate capital.

Perceptions in the 1970s were dominated by the idea that this deficit spending was 'buying' jobs. The fact that long-term investments were also being made was ignored. This partly also explains why research and development expenditures remained far too low for an industrialized country in the medium and long term. The political elites were afraid of focusing on them because they feared voters might interpret them as injuring the savings myth. Yet there are plenty of examples of how public investments and industrial-park projects can succeed in the stable Austrian production climate. Thus, Bruno Kreisky as chancellor sought to remedy one of Austria's major disadvantages after 1945 – that despite successful examples like Steyr it had no car industry of its own – through his pet project, the Austro-Porsche. Feasibility studies very soon showed that it was too late for this step but that there were clear opportunities in the area of the automotive supplies industry. Both General Motors and BMW in Steyr developed corresponding projects with public support. In 1999 BMW-Steyr drew up a balance sheet for the project – by then twenty years old – which showed that since 1979 a total of 23 billion schillings had been invested in this particular plant; by the turn of the century, the 2,400 employees of BMW-Steyr, Germany's biggest Austrian trading partner, were bringing an annual 8 billion schillings (net) into the trade balance.[28] The post-war emigrant Frank Stronach also took advantage of the specific incentives in the 1980s and 1990s available for his Magna group in Styria, and then also took over large parts of Steyr.

A careful analysis of the budget deficits shows, moreover, that 48 per cent of the Austrian government's financial debt was taken on between 1970 and 1983, but 46 per cent of it accumulated in 1984–88, the latter partly to rehabilitate nationalized enterprises and banks. The myth of 'debt making' with no investments will not die until clear investment and research support is clearly identified, positively commented on and promoted.

Adaptation of Reconstruction Structures and EU Entry

Austria's major problem in the years after 1978 was certainly that it did not, in either the state or the private sector, manage to respond proactively enough to the first clear indications of globalization and the end of the national and European 'insular economy' with restructurings and adaptations. Here it should be borne in mind that the European Community was entering a period of considerable turbulence. This forced it to respond with a new integration push in order not to fall behind the United States and Japan in global competition, especially because the United States was apparently increasingly shifting its interests to the Pacific area with its extremely high growth rates. The late 1970s and early 1980s were the heyday of what was known as Euro-sclerosis and Euro-pessimism.

A few of the factors that go towards explaining this turbulence and the response to it may be given as follows: the reaction to *perestroika* and *glasnost* in the USSR, but also to the increasing economic predominance of the Federal Republic of Germany; the Green and disarmament movements; increasing mobility and headlong development in international currency and share trading as well as in commodity trade and tourism. Essential parts were certainly also played by EU Commission President Jacques Delors, with his French *dirigiste* traditions, along with the British pragmatism of Lord (Arthur) Cockfield. Regarding the practical political implementation of the resultant objectives, one should mention, despite their differing political instruments, the conservative Chancellor Helmut Kohl in Germany, the socialist President of France François Mitterrand, and the neoliberal conservative Prime Minister of Great Britain Margaret Thatcher. In the background, various top managers of multinational European companies did their bit. These business groups were expecting a liberalization push, coupled with the economic and political homogenization of Europe, to provide the necessary impetus for the emerging global economic competition with big Japanese and U.S. concerns.

In Austria the SPÖ-FPÖ Small Coalition of 1983–86 under the new federal chancellor, Fred Sinowatz, had no time to prepare the reorganization of traditional economic structures. The broad protest movement against the Danube power station at Hainburg showed very clearly what new political forces had to be taken into account. The priority for economic growth demanded particularly by the unions no longer fitted in with the social values that were being expressed in the active protest and resistance campaigns. While the dispute over the Zwentendorf nuclear power station was still able to be 'channelled' by the dominant political elites through a referendum, the political breakthrough of the Green movement was no longer stoppable: government, SPÖ and unions had all proved too inflexible and slow. Confrontation had entered political awareness.

In nationalized industry it was also evident that the portents of globalization and the end of the 'insular economy' (both for Europe and for Austria specifically) had come: in 1973 – fully in line with the trend to concentrations in the steel sector in Europe and the U.S. – a huge concern had been formed through the merger of VOEST in Linz and Alpine Montan AG. Its CEO, Heribert Apfalter, attempted after 1978 to compensate for the first setbacks by broadening the scope of VOEST's business, inter alia to armaments sales, which were highly lucrative. Speculation in oil futures by the VOEST subsidiary Intertrading and chemicals subsidiary Merx were part of this strategy of covering losses through risky transactions. It was typical of this misbegotten Austro-expansion approach that the risks were totally underestimated and that top managers of Intertrading barely spoke and/or understood English.

As early as the Kreisky era, from 1981 onwards, the nationalized group, which had made an essential contribution to the reconstruction of the Second Republic (through both jobs and the value-added revenue of private and public supplier firms), was receiving subsidies from the budget, amounting to 26.1 billion schillings between 1981 and 1985. In autumn 1985 it became clear that – despite prevarication in management statements – VOEST-Alpine AG, a wholly owned subsidiary of ÖIAG (Österreichische Industrieholding AG) and, with 50,000 white- and blue-collar employees, the biggest Austrian company (100,000 people were employed in the whole ÖIAG framework), was going to show a loss for the year of 12 billion schillings. The Austrian Republic, and thus ultimately the taxpayer, was responsible for that through state guarantees to the tune of a total of 71 billion schillings (not counting the interest burden!). There have not yet been precise studies on how decisions were taken, on the involvement of politicians at national, provincial and municipal levels alike, or on what responsibility attaches to political actors, trade union representatives and works councils. Public opinion has made top politicians in general, and Kreisky specifically, responsible for the crisis of nationalized industry because of his set objective of full employment. A detailed picture can come only from precise source-based historical analysis. But the findings of the Noricum trial of VOEST and Noricum managers, accused of breaching the Neutrality Act, at any rate show how wide managers' room for manoeuvre was. At the same time, though, they were faced with the basic problem of not being able to reduce workforces to any great extent, and because of the size of the firm they were overtaxed by complex decision-making processes.

The dismissal of the whole board by the relevant minister, Transport Minister Ferdinand Lacina, brought the conflict between shareholder representatives and the board of directors into the open. This led to the development at the company level of a new form of cooperation, marked by strong separation between owners' and management's responsibilities. At the same time the VOEST group was split into smaller units and the ÖIAG group reduced in size through sales and management buyouts, and subsequently by the first steps towards stock-exchange listing and privatization. While this halved the employment directly attributable to the ÖIAG – in 1998 it had only 50,000 employees – the jettisoned companies also still offered employment. VOEST Alpine Stahl AG, which had its Initial Public Offering in 1993 (but is still controlled by ÖIAG through shareholdings) developed so successfully that in 1997 it might even have taken over the German firm of Preussag Stahlbereich, had not the future German chancellor and then minister-president of Lower Saxony, Gerhard Schröder, intervened to stop it.

The urgency of the need to reorganize the by now obsolete nationalized industries was partly connected with the fact that various economic structures dating from the monarchy were still in place, proving an obstacle in global competition as well as showing up weaknesses in top management. In 1945 the most important banks in Austria, the Creditanstalt-Bankverein and the Länderbank, had been definitively brought into state ownership. The broad spectrum of industrial holdings had in part already existed under the monarchy, and had despite the collapse of 1931 been retained in the interwar years too. Politically, influence in these nationalized banks was clearly divided: the Creditanstalt-Bankverein was run by a managing director close to the ÖVP, and the Länderbank by directors affiliated with the SPÖ. In the late 1970s this 'arrangement', as it was known, began to falter. Once Hannes Androsch, who had left the third Kreisky government as the result of a dispute, was appointed the Creditanstalt's managing director, there was even an open break with *Proporz*. (Following a conviction for tax evasion in 1988 he had to give up the position and was replaced by a conservative banker, Guido Schmidt-Chiari.) Androsch's former cabinet chief, Franz Vranitzky, was entrusted with reorganizing the Länderbank, which had experienced heavy turbulence in the early 1980s as a result of bad loans. Both the Creditanstalt and the Länderbank had increasingly been drawn into the general crisis because of their industrial holdings. Here too major problems with management emerged.

One fact often overlooked is that in this phase of recession a multiplicity of private bankruptcies and failures showed the limitations of modern management in crisis situations, while the political full-employment strategy made itself felt only through the acquisition of credit for private firms. This filtered perception is of course connected with the high proportion of the working population that was employed in nationalized industries right into the 1980s. Thus, in 1980 630,000 people, 22 per cent of all those at work in Austria, were employed in 6,846 industrial firms, accounting for 30 per cent of the gross national product; over 110,000 belonged directly to companies in the ÖIAG Group. The area of industry controlled through the big nationalized banks, the Creditanstalt-Bankverein and Länderbank, employed a further 60,000.[29] The 6,846 medium-sized and smaller industrial firms, along with 3,000 commercial enterprises also contributing to industrial production (with 145,000 employees), were decisively involved in the economic upswing, but like nationalized industry they were susceptible in times of crisis to adjustments and bankruptcies.

Almost forgotten today are the bankruptcies of the early 1980s, such as those of Österreichische Klimatechnik (2.8 billion schillings in liabilities) or of Eumig (2 billion schillings in losses), to mention only the biggest among the insolvencies. In 1980 there were a total of 1,169 insolvencies in Austria, in 1995 there were 2,043 and in 2003, 2,957. In 1992 insolvency liabilities were twice the size they had been only two years earlier, at around 23.6 billion schillings. In 1993 this figure rose to 32 billion schillings.[30] Creditor claims in the year 2000 – 9.2 billion schillings (€660 million) – were one-quarter borne by firms, the remainder being covered by banks, the revenue, health-insurance schemes and employees. These negative repercussions on banks and credit institutions of losses sustained by private, but also nationalized, firms were another factor leading to the crises of the Creditanstalt-Bankverein with its industrial holdings and of the

Länderbank. Altogether in 1985, for instance, the Austrian Republic gave the Creditanstalt guarantees to the value of 10.126 billion schillings in respect of losses by firms in which it had holdings.[31] The failures of both private and state firms showed that a reconstruction management that had grown up in a growth-oriented, protected, insular economy had in many cases failed to come to terms with the growing international crisis, or with sharper competition than it had been accustomed to. Only a younger, more internationally skilled generation of managers was able to get a grip on these structural changes in the late 1990s and to operate more efficiently in international markets – not that this ruled out further mega-bankruptcies. The limitations of socialist managers became clear in the Konsum bankruptcy of 1995, with altogether 26 billion in liabilities. A comparison of private, public and semi-public businessmen and managers who had experienced bankruptcy shows hardly any differences of an ideological nature.

Foreign opinion, however, continued to take a positive view of the Austrian reconstruction miracle even in 1981, which was a real crisis year. A meeting organized by the conservative American Enterprise Institute in Washington, D.C., even described Austria in 1981 as a European reincarnation of the Japanese economy in many areas.[32] Industrial growth since 1945 had been greater in Austria than in any other OECD state except Japan. Despite many differences compared with that country (a considerably larger state sector, higher rate of government investment) there were certainly parallels in the 1980s in terms of political stability and the balancing of political interests. In the meantime, though, the picture has radically changed to Japan's disadvantage, as regards both economic crisis and business collapses, and gigantic corruption scandals. Here Austria has remained an isle of the blessed.

In public discourse in Austria, however, the underlying structural problems were initially not discussed. Attention was confined to homemade scandals. The Androsch case was a classic example of the responsiveness even of individual figures to the headlong developments in the mass-consumption decade of the 1970s. Hannes Androsch, one of the greatest political talents of the Second Republic, had been called into government in 1970 by Kreisky and made the youngest finance minister in the Republic's history. Only a few years after he took office he had a new villa built in Neustift, a posh residential district; its alleged financing by an 'adoptive uncle' and tax evasion in the 1980s, since confirmed by Austria's highest court, were to be his downfall. Androsch and his lawyer Herbert Schachter dismiss the trial as political justice;[33] even today it remains unclear whether the adoptive uncle, Gustav Steiner, was really rich or not. The facts are that Steiner's family had lost its fortune after the First World War and that he had been driven into exile in Britain. Androsch was a typical child of the times, wanting to profit quickly from wealth and the contacts of the reconstruction generation; thus, in his case too financing came via his family's capital and connections. As a businessman he was later to adapt perfectly to the restructuring phase, develop his networking further and build up an economically highly successful business: his AT&S Group ranked 215th among Austria's 1,000 biggest firms, and Österreichische Salinen AG was 761st.

Another affair concerned the new General Hospital in Vienna. Despite the fact that the necessary expertise in supervision and monitoring was lacking at that time in Austria – and not only there, for similar problems were to be found in Germany too – the attempt was being made to carry through mammoth projects in line with the trends. Even an economic sector that was obviously on the way down, namely agriculture, was caught up in this wave of scandals in the post-Kreisky era: wine growers had for years 'sweetened' the wine in hazardous ways to meet customer taste, namely by adding the poisonous substance diethylene glycol. Even in the U.S., Austrian wines thereupon disappeared from the shelves (only to return after 2000 with great success as the products of new young wine growers).

The Grand Coalition's Last 'Great Leap': EU Entry in 1995

In the late 1970s the then European Community's economic figures (for instance, for growth and employment) had fallen compared with Japan's. In the early 1980s the other global competitor, the United States, overtook the EC area. In world trade too, the share of the Twelve fell despite enlargement to the Southeast and South in the 1980s to include the young democracies of Greece (1981), Spain and Portugal (1986).

Against the background of the threat of the EC's global marginalization, political response came from the European Parliament with its adoption in 1984 of the 'Draft Treaty Establishing the European Union'. In December 1985 the European Council in Luxembourg decided on reform of the EC bodies, enhancement of its powers and the legal embodiment of European political cooperation in the Single European Act (SEA). The economic-policy objective of the SEA was to create a 'genuine' common market by 1992. Comprehensive deregulation, the taking down of various administrative barriers and the forcing of real competition were to secure falling prices, higher demand and productivity and more expenditure on research. Unemployment, which was higher than in the U.S. and Japan, was thereby to fall automatically.

Austria too found itself increasingly embraced by these global developments in the economic sphere. While in 1974 it had still been possible to counter the negative effects of the first oil crisis on jobs and the economy, the second oil crisis had created major problems in the nationalized industries. As part of the economic restructuring measures of the mid 1980s, it was also necessary to respond to the biggest trading partner, the European Community. In the political sphere, the ÖVP had already in late 1985 signalled a willingness to join the EU. This was also part of a strategy developed by Andreas Khol to prevent the surrender to the SPÖ of either foreign policy making, so long and successfully dominated by Kreisky, or the success story of the active neutrality policy. Meanwhile, in the 1960s the ÖVP had already pursued a course of placing the interests of economic profit before those of the neutrality policy (for instance, until the late 1960s negotiations on association with the EEC, even though ultimately unsuccessful, had been conducted solo, without the other neutrals Switzerland and Sweden).

After 1986 a new-type Grand Coalition headed by Franz Vranitzky (SPÖ) – with the Foreign Ministry led by the ÖVP party chief and Vice-Chancellor Alois Mock – began a reorientation of Austria's Europe policy. Though especially in the SPÖ – and particularly among Social Democratic trade unionists – there were reservations about an excessive degree of integration, in 1989 agreement was reached: Austria would apply for accession.

Between Globalization and Privatization

It will yet be some time before the public consciousness realizes that Austria's insular economy was already definitively tied in to the internationalization process by the late 1970s. The headlong development of communications and computer technologies in the 1990s lent global dimensions to flows of both capital and information. At latest with EU entry in 1995 – but in many areas ever since the pegging of the schilling to the deutschmark – a number of economic-policy guidance mechanisms were transferred to the European Union or to individual EU institutions, particularly in the spheres of budget and monetary policies.

International financial markets continue at present to be very strongly dependent on American financial giants and the U.S. stock exchange, whether reacting randomly or in accordance with specific market interests. What is missing – as was the case before the first globalization thrust in 1880–1913 – is a regulatory framework for the financial and currency markets.[34] In crisis phases, even at the height of global deregulation of commodity and labour markets, we see only ad hoc, never structural, political intervention. Particularly the seven biggest industrial countries (the G7) are on such occasions again given the role of 'currency fire brigade', as on 22 September 2000.[35] A surprise support purchase of billions of euros by the U.S. Federal Reserve and Japanese and European central banks was aimed at stopping the fall of the euro, which had dropped by 30 per cent against the dollar since its introduction in January 1999, and starting a rising countertrend. In 1998 the central banks intervened in favour of the Japanese yen, whose crisis had hit the whole Asiatic area and China hard economically. Earlier, in 1985, the U.S. dollar had been supported, but it did not really recover until the mid 1990s. Since April 2002 the dollar has been falling against the euro, especially because of the continuing – and growing – American budget and balance of payments deficits.

This excursus into the by no means always rationally acting currency markets is intended to make clear that the long-customary monetary and currency policy is a thing of the past. Austrian interests can henceforth be represented only in an EU framework. It is only in alliances with other small and midsized states that the continuing national interests of the large states – above all France and Germany – can be brought together in a European compromise of interests. While at the old central-state level possibilities for exerting influence and control are somewhat reduced, the EU is strengthening the trend to regionalization, not necessarily in the sense of the region being the equivalent of the old nation state, but rather of the delegation of public tasks to subordinate bodies. This trend is perceptible in Austria in two ways. Firstly, since EU entry there have been repeated vehement debates on whether the federal loss of powers following EU entry ought not to mean bringing the provincial parliaments together into administrative bodies for new 'mega-regions', so as to save costs here too. Secondly, the discussions on financial adjustments between the centre and the provinces, and the often fierce clashes on the amount of payments to be made by the provinces to beef up the federal budget, very clearly reflect the political scenario of the future in the economic-policy sphere as well.

Despite the basically anti-enlargement domestic policy debates of the 1990s and since 2000, the Austrian economy was already benefiting even before the actual enlargement to the EU Twenty-five. Thus, the Institute for Economic Research has calculated that around 60,000 jobs have been created as a result of the new export markets. Whereas in 2003, for instance, there was a negative balance of trade with the Czech Republic and Slovakia (minus €218 million and minus €235 million respectively), the surpluses with Slovenia (€690 million), Hungary (€579 million) and Poland (€355 million) were huge. It was these that made it possible to build up a wide-ranging banking infrastructure in Eastern Europe (Bank Austria Creditanstalt in alliance with HVB, Erste Bank, Raiffeisen). In insurance, the Wiener Städtische is the leading Austrian insurance group in this geographical area, with a total premium volume of some four billion euros in 2003. Around 30 per cent of Austrian investments abroad in 2003 went to Slovenia, where Austrian firms also form the biggest block of foreign investors. Some 23 per cent went to Croatia, where again Austria stands in first position overall, and 20 per cent each to Romania and Bosnia-Herzegovina, with the same ranking. In Slovakia (14.1 per cent of Austria's foreign investments), Hungary (11.1 per cent) and the Czech Republic (10 per cent), Austrian firms occupy third place in the international investors' lists. All around, by 1999 Austria was already the fifth-biggest foreign investor in Eastern and Central Europe – after Germany, the United States, the Netherlands and France.

Nonetheless, in the area of modern technologies (from electronics to biotechnology) there is certainly a need to catch up. Will Austria – as partly happened in the nineteenth century with the industrial revolution – now also miss the digital revolution, despite this recent eastward expansion? Anyone acquainted with the dismally low rates of use of e-commerce by Austrian firms will understand that there is a need for action here. However, there are thoroughly satisfactory growth rates for Internet users and use of PCs as purchasing instruments, though here too the U.S. is in advance of Europe. Altogether, the United States is five years ahead of Europe in the digital revolution.

Summary

Nationalization after 1946 was largely influenced by the Cold War, with regard to both ownership structures and reconstruction as such. In all zones the 'German assets' were originally under Allied administration, but in the western zones they were handed over to the federal government. Although nationalization contradicted the idea of a capitalist economic system, it was accepted even by the United States as a political measure against the Soviet Union, which in its zone ran the enterprises classified as 'German assets' itself.

In public awareness in Austria it is especially the Kaprun myth that has taken root: the belief that Austrians were able to cope by themselves, even under extreme conditions. Indirectly, this exaggerated small-state economic thinking was strengthened by the Austro-Keynesianism of the 1970s. Increasing state expenditure was regarded as a national economic-policy weapon of defence against world economic crises, against unemployment, and in the late 1970s even against neoliberalism à la Thatcher and Reaganomics. After the first oil-price shock of 1974, the Kreisky government sought successfully to fend off the negative repercussions of this global crisis, and particularly to prevent a rise in unemployment. But the attempt to fend off the effects of the second oil-price crisis in 1978 instead only prolonged the nationalized industries' structural problems; these became capable of resolution only in the second half of the 1980s and early 1990s (also in the sphere of the then still nationalized banks). Nonetheless, core unemployment was kept relatively low in a European comparison, and infrastructure measures that were taken are still effective today.

In the memories of Austrian men and women it is only the welfare-state aspects and the 'budget deficits' from this phase that still feature; the fact that from an international viewpoint an industrial-policy miracle took place between the 1960s and 1970s has been forgotten. The internationally renowned political economist Peter J. Katzenstein, however, stated in 1981 that, looking at the economic figures for the 1970s and the growth rates in the 1960s, one might argue that Austria was a 'European incarnation of Japan'.

The environment changed radically with EU entry and the Maastricht Treaty. The state's financial and economic freedom to manoeuvre was considerably reduced, compared with what it had been in the 1970s and 1980s. Political debate continues, however, to be dominated by the autarky myth, which even goes as far as discussion of leaving the EU without its proponents encountering massive public rejection. In public awareness the fact of the aid that was afforded to reconstruction after 1945 has gone missing, as has the fact that the phase of prosperity and infrastructure investment could not have been financed without the long growth phase up to 1973 or the existence of a nationalized industry sector. Still vivid, though, are the budget deficits, which have been rising again especially since the 1980s and after the first successful savings made in 1998 in the Grand Coalition's pre-election budget, because of an ineffectual tax reform (with the active and driving collaboration of the ÖVP) and voter-oriented extra expenditure.

In the midst of globalization and advancing European integration, Austria is thus confronted with the phenomenon of a public consciousness that continues to believe in national autarky, and is indeed continually being politically reinforced in this belief, especially by the FPÖ and now the BZÖ (Alliance for Austria's Future), which the FPÖ has spawned. In the specific case of Austria, what we see is a prosperous society that has lost its historical memory of the reasons for that prosperity. It is not able properly to grasp the transformation problems of EU enlargement or the chances for Austria to shake off its marginal position for the first time since 1918 and become effective as a central country in a larger association. This is in part connected with the fact that along with its small-state national identity, it has developed a small-state economic consciousness too.

NOTES

1. Austrian Institute for Contemporary History, Vienna, NL-2, Renner.
2. Compare Eduard März and Maria Szecsi, 'Stagnation und Expansion. Eine vergleichende Analyse der wirtschaftlichen Entwicklung in der Ersten und Zweiten Republik', *Wirtschaft und Gesellschaft* 2 (1982): 321–344.
3. Eric Solsten and David E. McClave, eds., *Austria: A Country Study,* 2nd ed. (Washington, D.C.: Headquarters, Department of the Army, 1994), 122.
4. The Austrian electricity industry received 2,961 million Austrian schilling in ERP loans, covering 70 per cent of total investment. The Tauern power plant obtained nearly 50 per cent of this amount, 1,428 million Austrian schilling: cited after Georg Rigele, 'Der Marshall-Plan und Österreichs Alpenwasser-Kräfte: Kaprun,' in *80 Dollar. 50 Jahre ERP-Fonds und Marshall-Plan in Österreich 1948–1998,* ed. Günter Bischof and Dieter Stiefel (Vienna: Ueberreuter, 1999), 196–197.
5. Simon Reich, *The Fruits of Fascism: Postwar Prosperity in Historical Perspective* (Ithaca, NY: Cornell Univ. Press, 1990), 305–308.
6. Jean-François Vidal, 'Internationalisierung, Regulation und politische Ökonomie. Ein Vergleich der Perioden 1880–1913 und 1970–1995', *Kurswechsel* 1 (1998): 23–33.
7. Herbert Matis, 'Handel, Gewerbefleiß und Industrie', in *Die wirtschaftliche Entwicklung Österreichs,* ed. Hannes Androsch and Helmut H. Haschek (Vienna: Brandstätter, 1987), 144.

8. Hans Seidel, 'Österreichs Wirtschaftspolitik und der Marshall-Plan', in Bischof and Stiefel, *80 Dollar*, 67.

9. Helene Maimann, *Politik im Wartesaal. Österreichische Exilpolitik in Großbritannien 1938–1945* (Vienna: Böhlau, 1975), 198–201 and 225–229.

10. Stiftung Bruno Kreisky Archiv, Vienna, Sondersammlung Russische Akten, Smirnow, Nowikow, Roschtschin und Basarow an Wyschinskij, 29 March 1945.

11. Enderle-Burcel et al., *Protokolle des Kabinettsrats*, 135–136.

12. Ibid., 13.

13. Otto Klambauer and Ernst Bezemek, *Die USIA-Betriebe in Niederösterreich. Geschichte, Organisation, Dokumentation* (Vienna: Selbstverl. d. NÖ Inst. für Landeskunde, 1983), 6–7.

14. Oliver Rathkolb, ed., *Gesellschaft und Politik am Beginn der Zweiten Republik. Vertrauliche Berichte der U.S.-Militäradministration aus Österreich 1945 in englischer Originalfassung* (Vienna: Böhlau, 1985), 272.

15. William Lloyd Stearman, *The Soviet Union and the Occupation of Austria: An Analysis of Soviet Policy in Austria, 1945–1955* (Bonn-Vienna: Siegler, 1962), 112–128; William B. Bader, *Austria between East and West* (Stanford, CA: Stanford Univ. Press, 1966), 77–109.

16. Martin F. Herz, 'The View from Vienna', in *Witnesses to the Origins of the Cold War*, ed. Thomas Taylor Hammond (Seattle: Univ. of Washington Press, 1982), 161–185.

17. Rathkolb, *Gesellschaft und Politik*, 268–359.

18. Gerald Stourzh, *Um Einheit und Freiheit. Staatsvertrag. Neutralität und das Ende der Ost-West-Besetzung Österreichs 1945–1955* (Vienna-Cologne-Graz: Styria Verlag, 1998).

19. Compare the fate of the factory of Jungbunzlauer in Laa an der Thaya.

20. Karl R. Stadler, *Adolf Schärf. Mensch, Politiker, Staatsmann* (Vienna: Europa Verlag, 1982), 226–231.

21. Karl Ausch, *Licht und Irrlicht des österreichischen Wirtschaftswunders* (Vienna: Verlag der Wiener Volksbuchhandlung, 1965), 100; Stearman, *The Soviet Union and the Occupation of Austria*, 156.

22. Dieter Stiefel, 'Coca-Cola kam nicht über die Enns: Die ökonomische Benachteiligung der sowjetischen Besatzungszone', in Bischof and Stiefel, *80 Dollar*, 126.

23. Cited by Franz Honner, *Probleme der österreichischen Währungspolitik* (Freiburg/Schweiz-Zell am See, unpublished dissertation, University of Fribourg 1965), 48.

24. Hildegard Hemetsberger-Koller, 'Reinhard Kamitz', in *Die Politiker. Karrieren und Wirken bedeutender Repräsentanten der Zweiten Republik*, ed. Herbert Dachs, Peter Gerlich and Wolfgang C. Müller (Vienna: Manz Verlag, 1995), 257–265.

25. Hans Seidel, 'The Challenge of Small Size. Austria's Economy – Today and Tomorrow', in *Austria. Past and Present*, Hannes Androsch and Helmut H. Haschek (eds.) (Vienna: Brandstätter, 1986), 158–185.

26. Ibid., 161.

27. Felix Butschek, *Die österreichische Wirtschaft im 20. Jahrhundert* (Vienna: Österreichisches Institut für Wirtschaftsforschung, 1985), 159 and 210.

28. *Der Standard*, 13 September 1999, 19.

29. Oskar Grünwald, 'Austrian Industrial Structure and Industrial Policy', in *The Political Economy of Austria: A Conference Held at the American Enterprise Institute in Washing-*

ton, DC, on October 1–2, 1981, ed. Sven W. Arndt (Washington, D.C.: American Enterprise Institute, 1982), 130–135.

30. Ernst Chalupsky, 'Strategisches Controlling. Unternehmenssanierung' (Linz: Institut für Treuhand- und Rechnungswesen, unpublished paper, 1994).
31. Franz Kubik, 'Creditanstalt-Bankverein. Von der führenden Bank des Landes zur internationalen monetären Visitenkarte Österreichs', in *Bank Austria Creditanstalt. 150 Jahre österreichische Bankengeschichte im Zentrum Europas,* ed. Oliver Rathkolb, Theodor Venus and Ulrike Zimmerl (Vienna: Zsolnay Verlag, 2005).
32. Statement of Peter J. Katzenstein in Arndt, *The Political Economy of Austria,* 151.
33. Cf. the statements in Robert Kriechbaumer. *Die Ära Kreisky* (Vienna-Cologne-Weimar: Böhlau), 204, 485–542, and Lieselotte Palme. *Androsch. Ein Leben zwischen Geld und Macht* (Vienna: Molden, 1999), 278–295.
34. Vidal, 'Internationalisierung', 23–33.
35. *New York Times,* 23 September 2000, 1–2.

CHAPTER 4

Ten Chancellors,
and Not One a Woman

It is not the object of this chapter to present a comprehensive biographical and political analysis of the federal chancellors of the Second Republic.[1] Taking the top decision makers as examples, their characteristics will be compared, and their individual qualities highlighted as demonstrated in major political decision making since 1945. The chancellors will thus be taken as a barometer of majority political opinions, but also as a measure of attempts to implement long-term policy objectives running counter to the political trend. One important characteristic in this connection is the capacity to recognize potential creative opportunities early and make full use of them, as well as, in some cases, to go beyond the limits of these options.

Karl Renner, the Man with Two Faces

It is still today a riddle how a 75-year-old pensioner, who had already been a Reichsrat member under the monarchy and served as State Chancellor in the first republican period from 1918 to 1920, was able in 1945 to reemerge from the political wilderness that was the small, sleepy town of Gloggnitz am Semmering. World opinion too was surprised on 27 April 1945 by the establishment of a provisional government under Renner's leadership. With only Stalin's fiat in his pocket, Renner and his team developed centralized state structures overnight. These were successfully imposed on the partly separatist political movements in the provinces, and vis-à-vis the extremely mistrustful diplomats and politicians in the U.S., U.K. and France, without the backing of any real power machinery such as a police force or army, in a rump state beset by extreme social and economic problems. In fact, for many months this fragile governing coalition ruled only Vienna, Lower Austria and Burgenland.

Seen in retrospect, the experiment worked so well solely because Renner played only very briefly with the idea of a socialist 'revolution', which would have marginalized the former Christian Socials in the new ÖVP. Renner recognized that the Soviet Union was not prepared to depart from the three-party SPÖ-ÖVP-KPÖ schema, which it had already endorsed, and on the question of a revolutionary new constitution too tended rather to hark back to the pre-1933 position. Originally Renner was thinking of a strong central state that would be able to politically disempower the Christian Social, conservative-dominated federal provinces. After only a few weeks he found he had exhausted the limits of his political scope for action, in which he had skilfully used the veterans of the senior conservative bureaucracy – very much to the displeasure of young Christian Socials, who regarded Renner's openly displayed aversion to the 'corporate state' and its functionaries as a provocation, particularly when seen in the light of his own 1938 vote for the Anschluss.

Renner also established permanent working contacts with old bureaucrats the National Socialist regime had discarded, such as Heinrich Wildner, who as general secretary controlled the Foreign Affairs Division in the State Chancellery. This ability to win officials over to his side brought him freedom to manoeuvre and act, especially in this phase of reconstruction.

In the economic-policy sphere he even reached back to a pre-1933 enemy of the Social Democrats, former Finance Minister and National Bank President Viktor Kienböck. By June 1945 he was already working with him on financial documents to be submitted to the Council of State. At this point serious differences of opinion between the two men were emerging on the question of nationalizing the big firms and banks. Kienböck did not reciprocate the esteem he was held in by Renner and described him as a man 'inexperienced and unteachable in economic matters', from whose draft laws on financial matters he had been at pains to remove the 'worst, "stupidest" bits'.[2]

At the same time it was clear that Renner must rapidly make contact with the Western Allies, if only to restore the unity of the small state. Nonetheless he corresponded with Stalin in extremely confidential, even devoted tones, so as to build up Soviet support, and succeeded in getting on good terms with the Soviet officer corps. Simultaneously he endeavoured, through a purposive media offensive in the West pointing out the catastrophic economic conditions, looting and rapes taking place in the Soviet zone, to get the other Allies to Vienna quickly and extend the government's powers to western Austria. His mediator in this extremely sensitive question, which could of course have ended with Renner's replacement by the Soviets, was the Austrian socialist Ernst Lemberger. A fighter in the French Resistance under the *nom de guerre* of Jean Lambert, he now relayed authentic information on the rapes and the economic exploitation of eastern Austria by Soviet troops to Paris and London, as well as to Sweden. From there these reports quickly made it into the world press, as well as into numerous political reports. News of Austrian sufferings under the Soviets even reached the

ILLUSTRATION 4.1

*The 'founding fathers' of the Second Republic in front of the Liberation Memorial
at Wiener Schwarzenbergplatz: Leopold Figl, Karl Renner, Ernst Fischer;
in the background, the Mayor of Vienna Theodor Körner between
Colonel General Gusev and Major General Krainyukov.*

desk of U.S. President Harry S. Truman. Renner had skilfully run an international media campaign from the shadows, without exposing himself or openly provoking the Soviets.

This daring seesaw policy, which caused anxious excitement among experienced diplomats at the Ballhausplatz and even meant a temporary 'cooling of affections' on the part of the Soviet political officers, was successful. The first portents of the Cold War and the pressure to set up an Allied Commission in Vienna forced the Western Allies to deal with the Renner government, which they had originally called a Soviet puppet government. At the same time the chancellor also created a pan-Austrian basis at the two provincial conferences regarding laws and regulations both planned and already enacted, and an expansion of the government to include western Austrian politicians.

If Karl Renner had turned up at the war's end in western Austria before a U.S. commander, he would very quickly have been sent packing. The Americans' plans, as set forth in their *Handbook Austria,* provided initially for only small local administrations on the basis of appointments made by the local commanding officers. Pan-Austrian parties, politicians and elections were to be allowed only after a comprehensive review of leading figures and under a strict licensing procedure. The Soviet Union had a quite different concept: not a slow, controlled resumption of democracy, but immediate restoration of structures on the basis of a fixed three-party schema. That this specific form of people's-front strategy also kept alive the distant goal of a 'socialist', i.e. communist, transformation was a thought present at least in Soviet and communist minds; other political actors, too, were well aware of this long-term planning.

The fact that Renner had belonged before 1934 to the pragmatic right wing of the Social Democrats and as former state chancellor had a name that meant something to at least a large proportion of the Austrians weighed heavier in public opinion than recollection of his conduct in 1938 or of his 'German' nationalism. Since most Austrian men and women of voting age had also voted for the Anschluss in 1938 in a plebiscite staged under manifest political and media pressure, but thought rather differently in 1945, Renner was well suited to personify typically Austrian thinking and conduct, and he was therefore also an integrative figure.

Within the SPÖ the local leading party founder members, mainly from Vienna and Lower Austria (including the Revolutionary Socialists) began after only a few weeks to consider the question of the return of exiles, many of them expelled from Austria in 1934, the rest after 1938. Given the Western Allies' policy of allowing entry to their zones only extremely restrictively and upon application, this in practice meant that the return especially of politically committed exiles required an official invitation. Schärf and Renner kept very quiet on this question, partly for fear of competition, partly because of ideological reservations, since both had earlier belonged more or less to the political centre. While, for instance, such experts as the star journalist Oscar Pollak were fetched back from London – Schärf wrote to him as early as 29 August 1945 that he was pencilled in as editor in chief of the *Arbeiter-Zeitung* – such invitations and clear promises of integration were few and far between.[3] In Pollak's case possible ideological reservations within the party were set aside, since the *Arbeiter-Zeitung* definitely needed an experienced editor in chief if it was to succeed in the 'political media war'. Pollak was able not only to secure a further permit for his wife Marianne, but also to invite ten other Social Democrats to return to Austria from exile in Britain, all of them urgently needed experts and technical people such as the economist Karl Ausch, the future Nationalrat member Karl Czernetz and the lawyer Wilhelm Rosenzweig, as well as the future secretary of the SPÖ for Vienna, Hella Hanzlik.[4]

In other cases, for instance in connection with the return of former Municipal Treasurer Hugo Breitner, who had been a much more prominent politician of the interwar period than Schärf, the leading Social Democrats long kept a low profile. Breitner himself tended to believe that it was the former Christian Socials who prevented his return, as he had been the target of anti-Semitic Christian Social agitation in the interwar years.[5] In practice this did not really bother the ÖVP in 1945. It was the SPÖ top functionaries who were actually back-pedalling, and when Breitner finally received an official invitation and thus also the chance of a U.S. permit, it was too late: he had died in exile.

This is only one of many cases already described in detail by Otto Leichter, Adolf Sturmthal and others.[6] Bruno Kreisky suffered similar treatment, which, however, he revealed only indirectly in his memoirs. He returned to Vienna with some difficulty via Vorarlberg and the French zone in early 1946, but was then, following intensive talks with the party leadership, sent back to Sweden. Kreisky represented this mission to himself as an important job, coordinating reconstruction assistance in Sweden as Number Two in the Austrian Embassy. In fact it was an evident downgrading. Nevertheless, Kreisky was extremely active in Sweden and also politically very successful in acting on behalf of Social Democracy as the representative of an exile association. The reasons for his de facto relegation lay not, as in Breitner's case, in his prominent position between the wars, but probably rather in his reputation as a pragmatic leftist of Jewish origins whose anti-communism was unacceptable in an alliance partner in 1946, particularly to the left-wingers grouped around Erwin Scharf.

Many other formerly prominent socialists were not invited back, and in 1946 deep-seated anti-Semitic tendencies continued to be discernible in this policy (one that also drew on experience of Christian Social anti-Semitic propaganda of the interwar period, when Christian Socials, National Socialists and the Greater Germany group had agitated against the Social Democrats as the 'Jew Party'). As Friedl Schorsch, a bank official at the Wiener Bankverein, former trade unionist and active Schutzbund leader in the civil war in February 1934, found after his self-organized return from the U.S. on 3 July 1946: 'According to Hillegeist and many others in his area, Schärf and Helmer are beacons of anti-Semitism in the party, and in internal circles allegedly go on using all the old Nazi expressions.'[7] As a political associate of Federal President Theodor Körner, Kreisky too witnessed anti-Semitic jokes being made by Interior Minister Oskar Helmer as late as the 1950s and asked Schärf to get Helmer to stop.[8]

By contrast with Otto Leichter or Adolf Sturmthal, Kreisky took these snubs as a challenge. He hardly mentioned them in his letters at the time, and not at all in his memoirs. But he put everything into using his career in the Foreign Ministry and his very intensive reconstruction contacts not only to secure his physical and professional return to Austria, but also to achieve political reintegration into the SPÖ. Denazification was one of the essential problems confronting the political elite in the postwar period. But in the SPÖ's internal party debates Schärf and Renner did not get their way on this point, central in particular to the electoral struggle. Both in the party executive and in government the two of them voted for the mildest possible approach to former NSDAP members, but the youthful left around Central Secretary Erwin Scharf imposed a hard line. In the election campaign the SPÖ tackled this topic fairly aggressively, going as far as proposing exchanging ex-Nazis for prisoners of war held in Siberia. On the question of the rapid reintegration of Social Democratic political exiles, however, the young leftists kept quiet; they too were protecting the positions they had attained.

Leopold Figl, Chancellor of the Emotions

Renner's successor, Leopold Figl, the first federal chancellor endorsed by Parliament, was certainly, among the top representatives of the Second Republic, the one who was most strongly marked by torture in the concentration camps. As director of the Lower Austrian Bauernbund (Farmers' Federation; after 1937 his title was Reichsbauernbunddirektor) he, like many other Christian Social farming officials, sought to pursue a radically anti-Nazi course. He was arrested as early as 12 March 1938 and hauled off to Dachau concentration camp, where he was repeatedly tortured. He was not released till 8 May 1943. Thanks to the intervention of Julius Raab, Figl got a job in a construction firm and was even given a service car. In this position he began in 1944 to make tentative contacts with a view to a relaunch of the Bauernbund, but also possibly forming a new, non-socialist party. These efforts ended in renewed arrest after the assassination attempt on Hitler. Figl only barely escaped execution in 1945 in the Vienna District Court.

Figl's role was of immediate importance in the Provisional State Government, because as a Farmers' Federation official he was ideally placed to help solve the food-supply problem. In his capacity as provisional provincial president of Lower Austria the topic of food again played a central part. In 1945 it was not theoreticians of political democracy but people able pragmatically to organize survival that were needed. Supplying Vienna was considered the most important political objective in the first months, since food stocks had been plundered by the Viennese themselves and by deportee forced labourers before the Red Army arrived. The farmers of Lower Austria and Burgenland for their part became aware of their new market power, and it took a number of efforts to secure even remotely adequate rationing, with rations well below the minimum and a flourishing black market.

By contrast with former Education Minister Hans Pernter, originally assigned as advisor to Leopold Kunschak as ÖVP federal party executive chairman, Figl was the typical successful man of action. Moreover, since he held various positions he not only possessed a strong power base in the Lower Austrian Bauernbund, but was also considered less of a former '*Ständestaat*' (corporate state) figure than Pernter. Figl, forty-three years old in 1945, was a young politician compared with Kunschak (seventy-four), Pernter (fifty-eight) and especially that veteran of veterans, State Chancellor Renner. He also very deliberately stressed his concentration camp experiences and was to some extent the creator of the myth of the camp road, which, as already mentioned, was a leitmotif employed mainly by the ÖVP post-war elite. But Figl also used his camp imprisonment to dodge the debate about the '*Ständestaat*' and to lay down a narrow Austro-centric line on the question of the reintegration of exiles. In this connection Figl was much more suited than Renner to the task of building up the victim doctrine and getting it across internationally. In Renner's case, acceptance of National Socialism in 1938 in a public vote had been all too plainly visible, and was increasingly sharply criticized the longer the Allied administration lasted.

Particularly in the first years Figl was also an excellent communicator, not (like Renner) only in relation to the Soviet Union, but also to the United States. Important political Secret Service officers such as Edwin Kretzmann and Henry Pleasants were Figl's neighbours in Peter-Jordan-Straße, and frequent private meetings in the evening promoted the exchange of political information and the coordination of policies over a glass of whisky. Hundreds of pages of memos of talks are preserved in the U.S. archives and document this informal contact, which contributed greatly to the building up of trust. Figl's successor, Julius Raab, was neither to seek nor to master this form of communication.

But by 1951 Figl was already steadily losing political ground. Julius Raab was evidently pulling the strings in the background, and once Reinhard Kamitz was called in to be finance minister in 1952 Raab was de facto represented in the government as the 'power behind the throne', pushing for a market-economic and much more confrontational course. Figl was definitely made to take a back seat by Raab himself, perhaps his closest political friend, when the 1953 negotiations to form a government failed. By contrast with Figl, Julius Raab had by 1949 lost any fear of being in contact with former NSDAP functionaries and was holding secret talks on setting up a 'national' wing within the ÖVP, which ultimately came to naught. While Figl too in 1953 sought a coalition with the Association of Independents (VdU), he failed in this and was therefore replaced as candidate for chancellor by Raab while the coalition talks were still going on. In 1953 Raab seemed to be more successful; he developed a coalition pact with the VdU, which was, however, not accepted by the SPÖ. Federal President Körner clearly indicated that he would not admit such a latently Nazi party as the VdU into government. Körner was even regarded as 'intractable' in the SPÖ, for several people, among them Oskar Helmer, would certainly have been willing to explore the option of using the presence of a third party in government as a means of occasionally exerting pressure on the ÖVP.

ILLUSTRATION 4.2
Leopold Figl, a specifically 'Austrian' politician, with his family.

Leopold Figl was to continue to play a part until 1959 as foreign minister, but his creative days were over. Moreover, he had health problems that led, for instance, to a temporary collapse during the Moscow negotiations of 1955. Nonetheless he did manage to negotiate the co-responsibility clause out of the Preamble to the Austrian State Treaty on 14 May 1955, the day before it was signed. This was supposed to mean the definitive adoption of the unqualified victim doctrine for Austria, which was of course subjectively true for many Austrian men and women – including Figl himself – but applied also to those who had participated in the Nazi regime, the wars of aggression and the Holocaust and enriched themselves with the property of Jews and other victims of the regime. From Figl's viewpoint it meant an end to the long years of occupation since 1938. On 15 May 1955 he put this into unqualified terms in an undifferentiated way that would no longer be acceptable today, since public awareness of the Second World War, the Holocaust and National Socialism has after all changed: 'A thorny path of unfreedom lasting seventeen years has come to an end.'

In Austria's public consciousness Figl had won strong sympathies, symbolized in the balcony scene at the Belvedere with his words 'Austria is free' and in the State Treaty. This emotional relationship, which Figl was also able to achieve with international interlocutors, ought by no means to be underestimated. On the other hand, sources on the history of the State Treaty show that after 1953 his role was marginal and more representative than decisive. The driving force and trailblazer on the Austrian side here was Julius Raab. But it was only the affable Figl who stuck in the collective memory of Austrians: it is he, not Raab, who has become the Austrian people's chancellor, the chancellor of the State Treaty. Seemingly, many images of the cheerful, bibulous Figl reflected a sort of ideal or archetypal Austrian, who is typically also deeply rooted in the country.

From the Raab-Kamitz Approach to the Gorbach Interlude

It is one of the paradoxes of Austrian postwar history that a former Lower Austrian Heimwehr leader, Julius Raab, was to become the central figure in the decisive State Treaty negotiations. In the 1930s Raab not only belonged to a right-wing conservative paramilitary group, but also gave radical speeches displaying both anti-democratic and anti-Semitic radicalism. Thus he described the Heimwehr on 8 January 1929 as follows: 'We call ourselves Heimwehr ... Protection of house and home, of peaceful constructive work, of the German stock against the destructive legions of Semitic agitators – that is our objective ... Our forefathers created and defended our Christian, Germanic culture. The red plague has entered Austria and poisoned the soul of a large part of our people ... Finally, comrades, I call upon you: what is at stake is Austria, the German Ostmark of the great German fatherland. It is worth the price! Strike at the enemy! Upwards and onwards!'[9]

In retrospect Raab in 1962 saw the Heimwehr as 'wild brigand hordes';[10] personally he had already broken with the anti-democratic (fascist) Heimwehr organization in the 1930s, particularly over the debate on National Socialism. Similarly, the ideas of the 'Fatherland Front', into which the Lower Austrian 'storm troops' merged, were ultimately too authoritarian for him, and he protested against methods of surveillance. His appointment as trade minister in Kurt Schuschnigg's 1938 government was the signal for the adoption of an autonomous 'Austrian course', with a relative willingness to enter into a compromise of interests with the labour movement, though still on the basis of corporate-state structures and ideas. After his 'compromise' with Hitler's Germany in the July 1936 Agreement, Schuschnigg wanted to use Raab and the monarchist-minded law professor Ludwig Adamovich as a counterweight to the strongly pro-German or even openly pro-Nazi lobby in his government (Guido Schmidt, Edmund Glaise-Horstenau and Arthur Seyß-Inquart).

After the Anschluss Julius Raab considered emigrating, with his friend Clemens Holzmeister, to Turkey as a master-builder, but instead he stayed in the German Reich. Although the Nazi regime classed him as politically unreliable, it never arrested him – by contrast with other officials such as Leopold Figl or Felix Hurdes. During the Nazi period Raab kept a low profile and confined himself to the building trade, but he still maintained political friendships with people like Leopold Figl and also kept in contact with his pre-1938 political network.

In 1945 Raab, taking off from his role in 1938, was already an important ÖVP decision maker, rated as second only to Figl in relevance by political observers.[11] Very early on, Raab pushed through his concept of a strong third federation alongside the – in his eyes – 'leftist' Österreichischer Arbeiter- und Angestelltenbund (ÖAAB; Workers' and Employees' Federation) under Lois Weinberger and the Bauernbund under Figl. Originally a 'small-business federation' was planned, but Raab advocated a strong Austrian Business Federation, to embrace the self-employed who had been disunited before 1938, or before 1933, but also senior employees from industry, trade, crafts, banking and credit and the liberal professions.[12] In Parliament Raab, as chairman of the Business Federation after the November 1945 elections, controlled at least twenty-seven MPs, a considerable power base, which he extended still further as ÖVP whip. Included in the first Figl government as trade minister, he was not given a post in the subsequent government because of a British and Soviet veto on account of his membership in the Heimwehr and the last Schuschnigg cabinet. Nevertheless he remained a pillar of the grand coalition. The Soviet Union's exclusion specifically of Raab from government, despite the fact that in September 1945 he had still been pressing for an economic agreement with the Soviet Union and the setting up of Austro-Russian companies to exploit the oilfields, was connected with the Soviets' sudden bout of anti-fascism, which was also to affect former 'Austro-fascists'.

It is noteworthy that current historiography on the ÖVP is silent on most of Raab's closer political comrades, who determined the extent of his political power. Except for his economic-policy right-hand man from the Chamber of Commerce, Reinhard Kamitz, none of them now figures in the contemporary analytical literature. In this connection it has also been forgotten that Kamitz 'clearly came from the National Socialists' (Julius Raab, recording, 1962[13]). Kamitz, who was amnestied in 1948, can stand as an example, among many, of Raab's policy of bringing former NSDAP members as well as Pan-Germans into the Chamber of Commerce to enhance the ÖVP's economic competence.[14] While especially the ÖAAB under Weinberger protested – but stopped short of making a political issue of it – against this underhand integration of ex-NSDAP members, it was unsuccessful in 1952 in resisting the appointment of Kamitz as finance minister.

Kamitz had already been readmitted into the Vienna Chamber of Commerce in 1945, and moved in 1947 to the newly created Federal Chamber of Business; in 1950 he was appointed its deputy general secretary.[15] For Raab, Kamitz was essential to working out the wage and price agreements. Later, after 1953, the Raab-Kamitz approach also stood for balanced-budget policies, tax reductions, increased competition within a narrow regulatory framework, a controlled capital market and more flexibility in foreign trade.

By contrast with Figl, Raab had no fears of political contagion in the area of specialists, as in the case of Viktor Kienböck, finance minister during the 'Geneva restructuring' and Central Bank president until 1938. Kienböck was closely associated with what Raab dismissively called 'accumulation policy', referring to the hard-currency and gold-reserves policy the former had pursued despite exploding unemployment figures before 1938. He became a propaganda target for the SPÖ and KPÖ after 1945. Another of Raab's closest advisers was the Creditanstalt's Managing Director Josef Joham, a Cartellverband (Catholic student fraternity organization) confrère of Raab's who had come unscathed through not only the Nazi period but also corruption accusations after 1949 and the Second Republic's first parliamentary investigation. Kienböck, who had initially been promoted by Federal Chancellor Seipel, continued to be regarded as the *éminence grise* of finance and currency policy.

Raab began early to gather economic experts and key economic-policy figures round himself in the Federal Chamber of Business and the Business Federation. The Creditanstalt, with its huge complex of industrial holdings, was, along with the Länderbank, which was closer to the Social Democrats, to play a central role in nationalized banking and industrial policy in relation to reconstruction, but also in controlling the economy. In economic policy Julius Raab was no liberal, but rather an exponent of early social-partnership cooperation. He soon displayed an interest in closer collaboration with the Soviet Union. Particularly in regard to the oilfields in its zone that the Soviet Union claimed as German assets, he ended up taking a very pragmatic line, quite far removed from the majority approach of most politicians – namely, integration with the West. Raab supported Renner's negotiating line and in September 1945 suggested signing the agreement, basically already drafted, on joint Soviet-Austrian administration of the former German or German-administered assets. The prospecting rights of British and American oil companies dating from before 1938 were to be adjudicated by the Allies among themselves. Similar bilateral administrations could also be formed for the oil in the U.S. zone in Upper Austria and the British zone in Styria.[16] U.S. intervention, but also British blockades, the first signals of the Cold War, brought this agreement to nothing, although the old prospecting rights were not exactly uncontroversial legally. The matter of the British-American prospecting rights remained unclarified till June 1960, when the Allies' interests finally prevailed over Austria's (between 1955 and 1980 the parent companies of Mobil Oil and Shell Austria received net dividends amounting to over 1.2 billion schillings). The free crude oil delivered to the Soviets amounted by 1958 to a total value of some 2.7 billion schillings.[17] Joint administration of the German assets with the Soviet Union in eastern Austria would have brought advantages to the Austrian state budget, particularly in the tough reconstruction phase, given the extreme shortage of capital.

In 1948 Raab struck U.S. observers as a 'Manchester liberal', a politician of the old school who, despite his scepticism about democratic institutions and usages, had quickly grasped the realities of the day. He was seen as a hard but honest negotiator, able to keep to an agreement.[18] Basically Raab favoured the grand coalition with the socialists but sought to weaken their influence, without fearing any contagion from former NSDAP functionaries. On 28 May 1949 he headed an ÖVP delegation with Nationalrat members Alfred Maleta and Karl Brunner that negotiated with ex-Nazi officials on setting up a 'national wing'. The list of positions held by this group of 'formers' shows how politically dubious these people were: Manfred Jasser, Nazi propagandist and after 1945 publisher of the *Alpenländischer Heimatruf,* which was repeatedly banned for disseminating neo-Nazi propaganda; Wilhelm Höttl, historian, in 1938 a *Judenreferent* (desk officer for Jews) of the Nazi security service, later becoming deputy Gruppenleiter in its Foreign Department; Taras Borodajkewycz, historian, ex-Cartellverband member and Nazi informer, as a Catholic nationalist after 1955 professor at the then Hochschule für Welthandel (since 1975 the Vienna University of Economics and Business Administration), where in 1965 he sparked debates and demonstrations because of his anti-Semitic and neo-Nazi utterances; Erich Führer, as a lawyer prominent in Gestapo 'Aryanizations', after 1945 counsel for ex-Nazis; Walter Pollak, former Hitlerjugend leader; Theo Wührer, Adjutant to Ernst Kaltenbrunner, head of the SS Reich Security Main Office (RSHA), who was executed at Nuremberg.

The group's demands were, however, ultimately too high: for instance, shelving all measures against former National Socialists, and replacing Justice Minister

Josef Gerö. The ÖVP therefore swung round suddenly to an anti-fascist election campaign, pushed especially by the *Salzburger Nachrichten* and Raab's closest friend in the media, Gustav Adolf Canaval.[19] Simon Wiesenthal too was then working for Canaval, supplying material on old-Nazi networks. The voters reacted to this ÖVP tactic as they had to the SPÖ's anti-Nazi line in 1945: while the ÖVP remained the strongest force, it lost votes to both the VdU and the SPÖ.

Raab ended up by hewing to the line – the mirror image of the SPÖ's – of weakening the coalition partners by cooperating with the VdU, the electoral association of independents, a hotchpotch of former NSDAP members plus a few scattered liberals. When in 1953 Figl failed to make progress in the coalition negotiations, Raab took over leadership of the talks and already had a protocol of agreement settled with his main negotiating partner Hartleb, although in the notes kept for private use he wrote quite bluntly of 'nothing but Nazi demands'. Expansion of the coalition ultimately failed to come about, as already mentioned, because of the SPÖ and especially Federal President Theodor Körner, though in the unpublished notes he made for his memoirs Raab primarily suspected Bruno Kreisky, Körner's political secretary, of having been the 'middleman' who brokered this refusal.[20]

Raab had further sought to secure international endorsement for his controversial new policy towards the VdU. In 1951 he had called on the ÖVP internally to 'seek a way of linking up with the decision makers in the Republican Party, so as thereby to bring about a change in the Americans' policy'.[21] One of the ÖVP's early emissaries in this endeavour was the pro-ÖVP media man Fritz Molden, a former resistance fighter. On the sidelines of a visit to the United States by Foreign Minister Gruber during the transition period between the Truman and Eisenhower administrations, Molden tried to influence John Foster Dulles, to whom he had private access because of his marriage with Dulles's niece Joan, in favour of an ÖVP-VdU coalition after the 1953 Nationalrat elections. This was how the results were reported to Vice Chancellor Adolf Schärf by Ernst Lemberger, a Socialist member of parliament in contact with Molden:

> As far as I gather from Fritz Molden ... Dulles has also been spoken to about the possibility of an ÖVP-VdU coalition. The plan is to split the VdU after the elections, hive off the radicals (Stüber etc.) and form a coalition with the moderate group around Kraus; that would probably produce a bare majority. The people around Kraus were described to Dulles as thoroughly acceptable, as 'gentlemen'. Dulles's reaction seems to have been rather peeved; he fears that if SPÖ and KPÖ in opposition [sic], their common opposition role might lead to new ties that would create a dangerous situation.[22]

When in 1953 this triple coalition (ÖVP, SPÖ, VdU) was seriously up for discussion,[23] the U.S. indicated, in a demarche made directly with the Austrian chancellor, that the idea met with little favour. Moreover, both the Soviet Union and France would vote against recognizing such a government.[24]

Raab openly admitted in his memoir fragments that his aim of a coalition with the VdU was unachievable: 'The Americans were entirely on the side of the Socialist Party. They supplied it with material on the Joham case that was then being dealt with by an investigating committee of Parliament. The Socialists had far better relationships altogether with the Americans than the ÖVP, something due mainly to Jews and emigration.'[25] This assumption of Raab's, which also had an anti-Semitic and anti-emigrant subtext, by no means corresponded with reality, which is clearly shown by the State Department's internal documents.

As the new federal chancellor in 1953, Raab on the one hand was able to bring his economic-policy competence to bear; on the other he tried from the very beginning, through direct talks with Soviet officers, diplomats and politicians, to secure an end to Allied administration and the conclusion of a State Treaty. By April 1952 he had already called, in the ÖVP Federal Party Executive, for a cessation of the propaganda against the 'people's democracies'.[26] In the more favourable climate created by Stalin's death he managed to obtain a number of concessions from the Soviet Union. Indirectly he developed vague ideas about Austria being 'alliance-free', which Eisenhower in early 1954 combined with the

ILLUSTRATION 4.3
Julius Raab, the 'State Treaty Chancellor'.

option for armed neutrality on the Swiss pattern. Raab, who had served as an officer in the First World War on first the Eastern and then the Italian front, had a rather more pragmatic understanding of the East-West conflict and of neutrality. Here he argued in line with the former general staff officer and k.u.k. (imperial and royal) Colonel Theodor Körner, who in 1952 had said much the same thing about the 'Swiss example' and in November 1951 had come out against a 'unilateral attachment' of Austria.[27]

In 1953 it was clear that Raab (partly in the light of intensive consideration of the Finnish experience at a meeting with Urho Kekkonen, the Finnish centrist and then prime minister, on 14 August 1953) was, first, prepared to make high redemption payments (like the Finns), in effect reparations, to the USSR, and second, definitely wanted to keep Austria free of foreign troops. In 1953 the options still ranged from nonalignment to freedom from alliances to neutrality. Raab seemed more prepared to choose the Soviet option from these international-law variants, whereas the SPÖ around Schärf and Kreisky still, until 1955, wanted to avoid offending the Western powers. By contrast with the SPÖ, Raab had no worries about being associated with neutrality, despite the communist neutrality propaganda in 1951–53.

It was Raab's merit to have stuck consistently, despite the internal Soviet power struggles over the succession to Stalin, to his line at talks and negotiations. By contrast with all the diplomats and politicians of the Western Allies, and most of the Austrian ones too, he recognized that the February 1955 invitation from Soviet Foreign Minister Molotov to participate in direct talks between Austria and the Soviet Union would present a chance for a speedy solution to the prolonged negotiations. He was supported and motivated in this really only by the Austrian ambassador in Moscow, Norbert Bischoff, and not by the civil servants of the Federal Chancellery or Foreign Office. Bischoff, with his upper middle-class background, was regarded as a loner, sending Vienna glowing reports of the development of the Soviet Union. Despite these rose-coloured spectacles, or maybe because of them, he had the best of contacts. The negotiations held in Moscow in April 1955 led to a dexterous compromise, since on the one hand Raab, with the help of State Secretary Kreisky, was able to persuade Schärf to accept the neutrality model, and on the other Schärf saw to it that more precise and legally unobjectionable language was employed.

Raab's actions in the neutrality matter showed his authoritarian leadership style, manifest also in internal party debate. All the same, the SPÖ accepted Raab more readily than other ÖVP leaders, since he was well disposed to social-policy advances. It was only when the leading role of the ÖVP seemed threatened – as in 1952–53 – that Raab was willing to resort to party tactical manoeuvres involving the VdU.

After the conclusion of the State Treaty, Raab's neutrality policy came under a crossfire of criticism. Thus, on the occasion of Raab's speech on the adoption of the Neutrality Act in 1955, the writer and journalist Friedrich Torberg told the undercover CIA agent Klaus Dohrn:

> Obviously, all those who were only waiting to be able to dress their neutralism or fellow-travellerism in the garb of *raison d'état* will continue to hold to the text of the first Raab speech on 16 October, of which I said in my comment, with wide-eyed naivety, that it couldn't possibly have been meant seriously. It was so meant, of course, and its parliamentary amendment changed nothing in the fact that it sums up the basis of Raab's policy. Still, even in Raab's own party an unconcealed counter-tendency has already taken root, and he was even publicly disavowed by one of his own cabinet members … But this will not change anything in the 'grand line' for the present.[28]

Though Austria's uncompromising attitude during the Hungarian crisis of 1956 briefly silenced all the accusations levelled at the 'neutralism' of Raab's Eastern policy, the SPÖ Vice-Chancellor Schärf nonetheless stuck to his guns:

> Towards the end of 1955 it became clear to me that Raab, and with him part of the Volkspartei, wanted to go beyond the permanent neutrality proclaimed in the Constitutional Law and pursue a policy of neutralism that was in reality an Eastern policy. He surprised the Socialists one day with a request for a state guarantee for a loan to be made to the Lower Austrian provincial Volkspartei by the Russians amounting to 800 million schillings … In talks about it Raab repeatedly complained that he could find no understanding among the Socialists for his Eastern policy. He said history was giving Austria a unique opportunity to secure the role of mediator between East and West, which would make Vienna the crossroads of two worlds.[29]

In domestic policy Julius Raab's consistent line on the question of the State Treaty paid off for him only in the short term, in the early elections of 1956, which however changed nothing in the coalition of ÖVP and SPÖ. Raab put too much into courting the 'old middle class', concentrating increasingly on the groups that in the ÖVP too were strongly rooted in the federal structure: tradesmen, farmers and civil servants. But the Business Federation, Farmers' Federation and Civil Service Association were no longer keeping pace with the development of a modern industrial society, which by the late 1950s and especially in the 1960s was already leading to a social restructuring and slowly blurring traditional voting patterns further. In 1959 the SPÖ succeeded in presenting itself as the more modern and progressive party; for the second time since 1945 the SPÖ overtook the ÖVP in votes, though not in seats, since the electoral system favoured the biggest party.

Raab wanted to send out a radical signal and limit the Business Federation's power by replacing Finance Minister Kamitz. He therefore offered this ministry to the SPÖ, which chose Bruno Kreisky, then state secretary for foreign affairs in the Chancellery. Despite his strength within the party, Raab did not manage to get his way in the ÖVP party executive, so he indicated to the SPÖ and Kreisky that they could 'have' the foreign minister's post. Kreisky, however, wanted to accept this position only if in addition to the ministerial post he could also have a ministry of his own, separated from the Chancellery, and wide economic-policy powers in the question of integration in to the EEC. Until then the Foreign Office – as it was imprecisely termed – had been only a section of the Federal Chancellery, headed by a minister. Remarkably, Raab and Kreisky – two politicians with extremely different life stories and political styles – always harmonized very well on foreign-policy questions.

After 1959 a discussion of reform began in the ÖVP, pushed by provincial officials. The driving force here was the 'Neue Österreichische Gesellschaft' around former Foreign Minister Karl Gruber, who, having been dismissed in 1953 by Raab for his overly strong U.S. sympathies, was subsequently sent to the U.S. as ambassador. Other members were the Styrian provincial party chairman Alfons Gorbach, the president of the province of Salzburg, Josef Klaus, and the Business Federation parliamentarian Hermann Withalm. In 1961 Raab paved the way in the ÖVP for the rise of Gorbach, who in Withalm also got a committed general secretary.

Because of his anti-Nazi policy before 1938, Gorbach had suffered particularly under the Nazi regime, spending five years and eight months in Dachau concentration camp – together with, among others, the socialist trade unionist and future ÖGB President and Interior Minister Franz Olah. On the one hand he had become a committed grand coalitionist after 1945, but on the other he was soon advocating the integration of former NSDAP members without too much examination of their ideological past. Given his authentic victim story, it is not surprising that in 1952 he rapidly developed into a key proponent of the pan-Austrian victimhood doctrine.

In domestic policy Raab, who had remained president of the Chamber of Commerce, sought, after leaving the Chancellorship and handing over office to Gorbach, to compensate for the decline in his authority in his own party by strengthening the social partnership. Shortly before Christmas 1961 he reached an agreement with that other lone wolf, the SPÖ politician and Trade Union Federation President Franz Olah, about which he informed the party bodies only ex post facto. Yet it decisively set the course both for institutionalization and current economic policy.

Gorbach tried reshuffling the government so as to introduce new emphases into the ÖVP, which led to a turn away from Raab's forced centralism towards stronger tying-in of the provinces to the ÖVP ministerial team. Here we see the central phenomenon of the 1960s, namely that the political changes – especially in 1966 and 1970 – were basically due to the various ÖVP and SPÖ provincial organizations. The social and social-policy need to catch up was greater in the provinces than in the urban centres. Thus, for instance, the 1968 student movement in Austria amounted to little more than a tepid May breeze, apart from an activist leadership; the real desires for change were implemented politically in much more moderate forms at provincial level. And it was from the country, from towns with fewer than 5,000 inhabitants, that the necessary votes came to bring in the ÖVP single-party government in 1966, to elect Bruno Kreisky as party chairman and to give the SPÖ its election success in 1970.

Having the Styrian Alfons Gorbach as chancellor, the Salzburger (of Carinthian origins) Josef Klaus as finance minister and the Carinthian Karl Schleinzer as defence minister marked the integration of the provinces. On one point, however, Gorbach did not bow to the new trend in the ÖVP led by the party strategist Hermann Withalm and the Styrian ÖVP: namely, the notion of pushing the SPÖ out of government for the first time since 1945 by forming a coalition with the FPÖ. Although secret talks took place in 1962, Gorbach held to the 'old' coalition, and despite the two seats he gained in 1962 he formed another government with the SPÖ after three months of coalition negotiations, in which the main bone of contention was Kreisky's continuation as foreign minister. Gorbach pushed through his line by bartering this concession for counter-concessions by the SPÖ.

Ultimately, though, it was already clear at this point that Gorbach's replacement was now only a question of time, since Klaus was demonstratively refusing to accept government office and Withalm had not been present when the coalition agreement was signed. In 1963 a national party congress, held early, elected Klaus as the new ÖVP party chairman. By this time the end of the old consensus politics of the grand coalition was looming. In the Habsburg crisis – the question of granting Otto von Habsburg permission to enter the country without his renouncing his claim to the throne – the SPÖ itself had made use of the new coalition-free space, which had not existed in the Raab era, by voting jointly with the FPÖ in Parliament against the ÖVP. Altogether, the importance of Parliament in real political decision making processes increased somewhat after Raab's retirement. This too signalled an end to postwar developments, in favour of a more dynamic political discourse.

Josef Klaus, a Catholic Conservative Modernizer or a Social(-ist) Chancellor?

The provocative title above echoes an assessment by California's 'people's governor', Arnold Schwarzenegger, who said in a campaign speech on 1 September 2004: 'As a child I saw how Austria became a socialist country after the withdrawal of the Soviets.' When Schwarzenegger left Austria in 1968, Klaus's ÖVP single-party government already had half of its legislative term behind it. Nonetheless, young Arnold felt cramped and made for the free West.

There is a grain of truth hidden in this assessment made from afar after a lapse of thirty-six years, except that it should have proceeded from different premises: Austria in 1968, even under Klaus's ÖVP single-party government, was a state that did not really want to abolish social networks or the social partnership. In this sense Schwarzenegger ought to have talked about a 'social country'; but then the point would have been lost, and criticism of the unsocial U.S. system as a whole would have emerged. All the same, this exaggerated statement does reflect the narrowness of political and social life in postwar Austria. The young Schwarzenegger had been particularly impressed by the 1964 popular initiative on broadcasting, and his plebiscitary style as governor refers back to this experience in his old homeland.

Josef Klaus was the first ÖVP chancellor to belong to a younger generation of decision makers who were not strongly committed to the grand coalition by personal experience of the camps. At the same time he was, by contrast with Raab, who was a conservative Catholic, deeply rooted in the postwar Catholicism of Salzburg's Archbishop Andreas Rohracher. In 1947 he had joined the movement launched by the Catholic Church to reintegrate former NSDAP members. Before 1933 Klaus had been brought up in a 'Greater German' atmosphere, and as chair of the Catholic-German University Committee he did not even hesitate to engage in anti-Semitic agitation; how far these factors were influential here is unclear. At any rate, after 1933 he opposed the NSDAP and worked as secretary of the 'corporate state's' single trade union. From 1939 to 1945 Klaus served as a conscript in the German Wehrmacht, which made him the first and only chancellor of the Second Republic to have belonged to the 'veteran' generation. His successor Bruno Kreisky was to be the first and only exile in that office, whilst Figl and Gorbach had been camp inmates: these three could thus, with differing methods and goals, represent the comprehensive, unqualified victim doctrine of Austrian postwar society internationally and nationally.

Klaus, totally unknown politically outside the Catholic groups in Salzburg he had already been connected with during the war, managed to impose himself as a new political prototype. With assurance he pushed through a planned reconstruction programme in Salzburg; the conservative Christian cultural image associated with it manifested itself, for instance, in his commitment to the Salzburg Festival. But here he consistently opposed too leftist a modernism, for example coming out against the collaboration of the communist Bertolt Brecht with the Salzburg Festival.

As finance minister Klaus retained his image as a conservative planner and indeed enhanced it still further. In 1966 he skilfully brought his concept of 'restrained' reform into the election campaign; by contrast the SPÖ, because of its internal party tensions over Franz Olah, who had been expelled from the party after embezzling trade-union funds, and also because it had been recommended to the voters by the Communists, cut a very poor figure. Very quickly, though, it emerged that the image of modernity suggested by, for instance, the meetings of experts centred on Klaus ('Aktion 20'), were tempered in the actual work of government by extremely reactionary features. The endeavour was seemingly to oppose social trends by putting the brakes on. The Cartellverband (CV) dominated not only the government but also the top civil service, and 23 per cent of ÖVP parliamentarians belonged to it. At the same time, the CV was far from displaying the new realism many voters, men and women – especially women, and first-time voters – had been expecting. Thus, the non-party Justice Minister Hans Klecatsky offered a judicial reform programme that meant a return to extremely conservative legal concepts, with Catholic admixtures. A budget rehabilitation programme through tax increases planned by Finance Minister Koren, appropriate in itself, was very negatively received by the public; the boom that started in 1969 was to become noticeable only in the 1970s.

Bruno Kreisky, the Dialectical Chancellor

As with no chancellor of the Second Republic before him, all the internal political structural conditions spoke against Kreisky, but all the social and international trends weighed in his favour. Bruno Kreisky had left the Jewish faith in 1931, but his Jewish origins were perfectly well known in the Socialist Youth and the underground movement alike, in exile and after 1945. Because of the latent anti-Semitism already rampant during his student years, which escalated after 1938 and after 1945 was still operative in the background, Kreisky himself believed he could never reach the topmost positions in politics. As a code for this self-assessment he frequently used the phrase 'best Number Two', meaning he was able to become neither SPÖ chair nor chancellor. All the same, even from his middle-school days he had only one great goal: to go into politics. (His fellow-pupils at the Radetzky Gymnasium in Vienna rated him as a future Vienna city councillor, since that was the only place where there were still Social Democratic politicians of Jewish origins to be found in governing positions in the 1930s.)

As a Jew and an upper middle-class intellectual (through the relatives of his mother, née Felix, from Trebitsch in southern Moravia), Kreisky was in a minority position twice over and was accepted by the Socialist Youth only after long hesitation and several rejections. Kreisky did not hide his bourgeois background, but he did not want to be active politically in the usual circles frequented by young intellectuals – among them many students, male and female, of Jewish origin – the Socialist Middle-Schoolers' or Students' Associations. He wanted to be near the grass roots, workers' children and working youth, and was undeterred by unspoken (or, in private, thoroughly open) anti-Semitism. Even when he was voted out after a putsch in his local group in Vienna-Wieden and sent into the by no means risk-free wilderness of Tullnerfeld in Lower Austria, where the Christian Socials predominated, he saw this as a challenge, not a defeat. There he was also to learn one of the secrets of winning over voters: in Austria, trend-breaking Nationalrat elections are ultimately decided in the regional sphere and not in the big urban centres.

Kreisky was from his earliest youth what one might today call a knowledge manager. He read an incredible amount, especially when he was imprisoned for illegal political activities under the Schuschnigg regime, in 1935–36. At the same time he was an astute analyst of his environment, even using his time in jail to get closer to his fellow prisoners, in order to understand such people. Even before 1938 he also stood out for being fond of pursuing ideas that ran counter to the trends and for wanting to implement them. On one point Kreisky was ahead of many of his contemporaries – even among Social Democrats. He was never a radical 'German' nationalist, but saw himself as a product of the melting pot of the Austro-Hungarian monarchy. This was a major precondition for his thinking in broad international contexts, which furthermore, even in the 1930s, reached well beyond the Central European cultural area, through his interest in the anti-colonial movement and the Socialist International. In exile this sense of Austria was strengthened, partly against the background of the democratic and unpretentious patriotism that he experienced in his Swedish exile after 1938.

The fact that Kreisky, after his return in 1951, rose so rapidly to the political heights was pure chance. It had chiefly to do with Federal President Körner, whose political secretary he became; in this position he was able to attend the daily policy meeting of the top Social Democrats. In 1953 Schärf chose him to be state secretary, partly in order to send a positive signal to Körner, with whom there were latent conflicts. As state secretary, Kreisky was subsequently to play an important analytical and mediating role in the State Treaty negotiations; he very quickly developed into the SPÖ's foreign-policy brains. Yet he was to continue his career within the party in the Lower Austrian 'wilderness' – the party of 'Red Vienna' had rejected Kreisky even after 1945, despite interventions by Olah. In 1956 Kreisky entered Parliament as a Nationalrat member for St. Pölten.

As foreign minister, Kreisky surprised the political world and especially the voters by setting what had hitherto been an ÖVP theme, the South Tyrol question, at the centre of his activities. At the UN he energetically spoke on behalf of minority rights in South Tyrol, and he came near to a negotiated solution based on autonomy with Saragat. In the ministry too he did not pursue the usual party politics but relied on independent diplomats, including ÖVP members. Nonetheless, even at those times when his popularity reached increasingly beyond SPÖ core voters he was continually pilloried in the right-wing tabloids as 'emigrant' and 'Jew'.

But in truth Bruno Kreisky was able to maintain a public presence because of his special access to journalists of various political orientations. As early as the

ILLUSTRATION 4.4
*Minister of Foreign Affairs Bruno Kreisky visiting
American President John F. Kennedy, 1963.*

1950s he had been regularly contacting a core group of Austrian journalists and in effect integrating them gradually into his political operations. Kreisky was in this sense very Americanized, and he also profited from the Kennedy era. In the face of strong resistance from professional diplomats he hired PR experts who got him access to U.S. decision makers, such as a private interview with John F. Kennedy. Like Kennedy in the U.S., Kreisky was a product of the – delayed – post-war rebellions that had led in the United States to the Civil Rights Movement and in Europe to the variously nationally articulated student and youth confrontations. At the same time Kreisky was a shrewd political pragmatist, cautiously sounding out society's willingness to accept reforms. Whereas Julius Raab had dismissed television as 'that box' and left the directorship of ORF, the state television company, to the SPÖ under the *Proporz* arrangements, Kreisky very early recognized the importance of this medium, which in the late 1960s was gaining a growing audience in Austria. In the TV debates with Chancellor Klaus that have since gone down in television history, Kreisky dominated owing to his naturalness and ready repartee, as well as his efforts to put complicated things simply and meaningfully.

Like no other SPÖ party chairman since 1945, Bruno Kreisky was able within a few years to not only unite the party and draw fully once again on traditional SPÖ voter segments, but also to address young and intellectually flexible voters, male and female. In a speech immediately following his election as party chair (by 63 per cent of votes of the party executive and a respectable 70 per cent of those of party congress delegates), Kreisky indicated a number of basic political orientations that the Klaus government had also inscribed on its banners: for instance, the 'scientific analysis of social conditions', with particular importance being attached to computer technology. At the same time, however, he also indicated a readiness for ideological struggle: he intended to devote special attention to the problem of automation and the associated loss of jobs. Viewed retrospectively, the messages Kreisky was sending out then continued to apply in subsequent years too: modernity, but with the human being as the central focus; the use of scientific methods to develop political strategies; plus a minimum of fidelity to ideological principles, referring back to the interwar years and the great Austro-Marxists (a line that Adolf Schärf in particular, as well as Bruno Pittermann, had eliminated almost completely from their political vocabulary). At the same time he always positioned himself as a bourgeois humanist and avoided any semblance of class-struggle slogans, though without giving up the call for social change. In this way he strove to bring together highly ambivalent opposing positions.

Kreisky was quick to try to pacify the former leadership apparatus round Pittermann and Waldbrunner, and also the ÖGB President Anton Benya, who had attacked Kreisky particularly offensively at the party congress. Pittermann got a relatively free hand as parliamentary group chairman and in parliamentary opposition work, and remained president of the Socialist International. Thus Kreisky managed gradually to ease the extremely tense relations of 1966–67. With Karl Waldbrunner too Kreisky regained a good working relationship. On personnel questions Kreisky proved very conciliatory. For instance, the editor in chief of the *Arbeiter-Zeitung*, Franz Kreuzer, was sacrificed to the heavily critical trade-union and Vienna City Hall factions and replaced by the journalist Paul Blau, who was deeply rooted in the trade-union movement.[30] However, this internal pacification policy had a relatively high price and restricted Kreisky's scope for the composition of the first SPÖ minority government in 1970.

By contrast, on strategic questions the new party chairman strove to develop a line of his own. In his brief time as Lower Austrian provincial party chairman, Kreisky had already begun developing great plans for transforming the economic structure, with particular reference to the example of Hesse in the Federal Republic of Germany. Kreisky mandated Ernst Eugen Veselsky, head of the Advisory Board for Economic and Social Questions nominated by the Chamber of Labour, to set up committees of experts to draw up economic-policy programme guidelines. New, young experts, divided into eight working groups, were to develop proposals for a future SPÖ structural and growth policy, with a number of existing economic-policy taboos being broken and long-serving experts tending to be squeezed out.[31] With the resultant programme, perfectly pitched from the publicity viewpoint, Kreisky showed that the SPÖ possessed economic competence and was willing to involve non-party experts actively in its consideration of principles. Still today this idea continues to be copied – sometimes in slightly altered form – but the reform élan of the 1970s has never been equalled.

In its economic programme entitled 'Reforming the Austrian Economy: Performance, Growth, Security', which was adopted at the 1968 party congress, the SPÖ presented an agenda aimed at gradually eliminating the structural weaknesses of the Austrian economy and bringing the standard of living up to Sweden's. Keynesian approaches are not, however, yet to be found in this programme. The SPÖ's '1,400 experts' – in fact the core group was considerably smaller – included a group headed by Hertha Firnberg that developed a comprehensive 'human programme', containing strategies for 'health policy and environmental hygiene', tackling such environmental questions as water purity, noise reduction and food policy. Here too the SPÖ was focusing on future perspectives.

As well as a school and further-education programme, a wide-ranging university programme was developed, combining ideas and concepts contributed by professors then regarded as progressive, such as Rudolf Strasser in Linz or Hans Floretta and Fritz Fellner in Salzburg, with the strategies of active '68ers' (Peter Kowalski, Norbert Roszenich, Silvio Lehmann, Marina Fischer and Eva Kreisky).[32] The justice programme was drafted by a working group headed by Christian Broda. This concept of using experts was part of one of Kreisky's basic strategies: 'Our party is an open party. It is open to all who want to work with us.'[33] The concept also included a continuation of the accommodation with the Catholic Church, something the agnostic Kreisky consistently pursued. Such thorny issues as the decriminalization of abortion before a certain time limit were not discussed intensively before 1970 and would become important in domestic politics only in subsequent years.[34]

But it is by no means the case that these pragmatic concepts suddenly turned the SPÖ into a 'liberal people's party'. By 1969 it was clear that the SPÖ under Kreisky had maximized its voting potential among working-class men and women and was making optimum use of it after the expulsion of Franz Olah. In a poll taken at this time 59 per cent of worker respondents stated they were close to the SPÖ.[35] In addition, a trend became noticeable in 1970 among the higher educational strata (university graduates, those with secondary education), who were increasingly voting for the SPÖ (1969: 18 per cent; 1972: 29 per cent; 1977: 30 per cent). In 1970 women too began to turn steadily to the SPÖ in parliamentary elections (1969: 39 per cent; 1972: 45 per cent). Among young voters of both sexes the SPÖ had already reached an absolute majority by 1970.

The SPÖ's reform ideas, augmented shortly before the 1970 Nationalrat elections by an additional slogan relating to the length of universal national service – 'Six months is enough' – reverberated particularly in small municipalities hitherto dominated by the ÖVP, and more especially among the upper middle classes, women, white-collar workers and young voters. A total of 158,000 votes swung directly from the ÖVP to the SPÖ.[36] The core areas of SPÖ growth were, moreover, particularly affected by primary structural change. Peter Ulram has summarized the Nationalrat election results for 1970–79 as follows: 'The SPÖ thus managed to convert the social-liberal coalition of interests and values into a voter coalition that lasted more than a decade, and so to rise to become the hegemonic force in the Austrian party system.'[37]

One important factor in reaching the new voter strata was, as already mentioned, television. Between 1965 and 1970 private ownership of TV sets rose from 30 to 67 per cent, thus also enabling much more private formation of opinion away from the previous community television in the pub or at the neighbours', which was mostly tied to one or the other political camp. At the same time the broadcasting reform, decided with ÖVP and FPÖ votes on the basis of the popular initiative on broadcasting, brought about a professionalization of television under the conservative journalist Gerd Bacher, which also confronted politicians with new demands and new possibilities in the direction of greater Americanization. Bruno Kreisky mastered this medium much more effectively than had the chancellors before him, and anyway he had for decades had more frank and open contact with journalists than was usual in the 1950s and 1960s in Austria. He kept on supplying material, and also headlines, that could easily be turned into a 'story'. Moreover, his experience abroad as state secretary and foreign minister had endowed him with an easy style of political communication.

In ideological debates Kreisky tried to send signals of his own. Starting from the 1958 party programme, on which he had worked as part of the drafting committee though not decisively shaping it, he pursued his line of utilizing Austro-Marxist methods and theses as analytical tools, whilst in practical politics – in both economic and social-policy areas – seeking 'historic compromises'. After 1967 he pressed on with the exploratory talks already begun by Franz Olah and Felix Slavik in the late 1950s between open-minded representatives of the Catholic Church (especially Cardinal Franz König) and the SPÖ. The importance, for him, of taking the heat out of this conflict in which the Social Democrats seemed to be eternally involved can be seen from his assessment of the repercussions that would stem from the law on abortions that Justice Minister Christian Broda had pushed through against the express wishes of the Catholic Church and the ÖVP, and indeed of the SPÖ too. Kreisky was certain this would lead to a loss of votes at the next elections, but history has proved him wrong here; he underestimated the social dynamism at work in this area.

The core of his efforts, even in opposition, was the formulation of a new economic programme aimed at presenting, for the first time, the SPÖ's new pragmatic course and finally dispelling old images of social democratic politics dating from the interwar years that had remained operative even after 1945. In 1970 Kreisky heralded an 'economic programme of the Austrian Social Democrats, who after all have the name of being an especially radical, Austro-Marxist party ... that lays down the equality of all productive property.'[38]

It would, though, be wrong to believe that the 'Social Democrat' Kreisky – he rated this term more positively than the official appellation 'socialist' – had therefore abandoned social reforms and political visions. The first years of the SPÖ minority or single-party governments are marked by the implementation of thoroughly controversial political concepts. Kreisky and his ministers managed to get the measure of the whole of society's potential for reform and fill it with daily perceptible practical content (such as free school transport, free schoolbooks and so forth) to benefit socially disadvantaged groups. In many cases this did not have a redistributive effect, since all groups – irrespective of income – could claim these social benefits. It was only those receiving supplementary benefits or pensions who in the mid 1970s got specifically targeted increases.

The theoretical ideas of the SPÖ chairman and federal chancellor concentrated increasingly on putting 'social democracy' into practice; Kreisky called himself a 'centrist' and 'enlightener' in the positive sense. Nonetheless, the SPÖ stuck to its basic aspiration for a 'classless society', so as to have at least a theoretical corrective to the new socially divisive developments in the welfare state.

Kreisky's long-term political goal was by no means to make the SPÖ into a 'leftist people's party', although in 1972 at the Villach party congress he stated that '[t]here are many who want to go a great deal of the way with us, without at first wishing to subscribe to our whole set of aims and ideas.'[39] Especially in the course of the internal party debate on the new party programme, which took place in 1978, the SPÖ tried to fix permanently some new/old social-policy visions, not only to pacify those on the left within the party, but also in order quite deliberately to counteract abuse of power and of public funds by those in government. Austria's internal political scene in the late 1970s and early 1980s was increasingly dominated by affairs (like the AKH scandal) in which socialist politicians were involved. The clash between Kreisky and his vice-chancellor, finance minister and for years heir presumptive, Hannes Androsch, sparked off by the business expansion of the latter's trustee-administered tax consultancy 'Consultatio' and his ultimately court-proven tax evasion, was paradigmatic for Kreisky's failure in his efforts to establish a permanent reform process in all social sectors – and especially in the SPÖ. Kreisky's scale of values on this point, stamped with the puritanical social democracy of the interwar years, is hard to grasp today. He had – like his son Peter – refused to take up the legacy, running into millions, of the Felix family, which had been almost exterminated in the Holocaust, just as he never wanted to own the villa in the Armbrustergasse because this was 'unbecoming' for a Social Democrat.

Subsequently the Kreisky-Androsch clash escalated and partly crippled government work until 1980. Only after repeated attempts was Kreisky able to pre-

ILLUSTRATION 4.5
Kreisky, the foreign policy expert: Vienna talks on 9 July 1978. From left to right:
Willy Brandt, President of the Socialist International, *Anwar el-Sadat,*
President of Egypt, Bruno Kreisky, and Shimon Peres, Head of the Israeli Labour Party.

vail and induce Androsch to give up the vice-chancellorship and the Finance
Ministry and move to the Creditanstalt Bankverein. The number of mutual accusations put about and amplified by rumour mongers is legion and would call for a
separate study.[40] Both main participants briefly even announced their withdrawal

from their political positions: Hannes Androsch to an ORF television team, Kreisky in a handwritten note to Karl Blecha. Neither resignation announcement became public, however: Androsch's press secretary had the tapes withdrawn and recalled the authorization for the interview, whereas Kreisky crumpled up the letter and left it in his safe.

The decisive break came immediately after the death of President Franz Jonas in late April 1974, in a talk with Hannes Androsch and Leopold Gratz. Both offered – whether for reasons of seniority or with ulterior motives – to propose Kreisky as a candidate for the presidential elections. Kreisky perceived this as an affront, since he himself in January 1957 as spokesman for the 'young Turks' in the SPÖ had 'promoted' Adolf Schärf from the centre of power as vice-chancellor and party chairman to the symbolic power centre of the federal presidency. Neither Gratz nor Androsch was aware of it, but from then on Kreisky began to look suspiciously at every move by his favoured successor.

Fred Sinowatz, the Underestimated Chancellor

Kreisky's clashes with Hannes Androsch ultimately also represented a generational conflict about political morality and material wealth. A whole series of other possible successors to 'Sun King' Kreisky, who remained increasingly isolated in the party executive, fell victim to this clash. These conflicts seemed in the 1970s to have disappeared with the election successes, but they were in fact only temporarily papered over. In his thoughts about a change of generations, Kreisky now concentrated on two candidates: Interior Minister Karl Blecha and Education Minister Fred Sinowatz.

Whereas Karl Blecha, a former SPÖ general secretary, was regarded in public opinion as a left-wing party strategist, Sinowatz was very popular. As education minister he had adopted long-needed reforms and started a major building programme in the middle-school sector. He also had a well-established positive image in the public consciousness thanks to a skilful PR policy. As a former high party official and a Provincial Assembly Speaker in Burgenland, he was able to command a majority of all tendencies within the SPÖ.

Kreisky was convinced that Sinowatz could become a 'socialist Raab', but forgot here that the Austrians had never taken Raab to their hearts. Indeed, in today's collective memory Raab hardly plays a part, although it was he – and not Figl – who exploited the 'window of opportunity' to rapidly conclude the State Treaty and make the neutrality declaration. Sinowatz began by refusing the task allotted to him, but ended by accepting the burden. Accordingly, from the very first moment the public message was that Sinowatz had only accepted the tough duty of the chancellorship out of party discipline. Given such negative attitudes, his popularity figures began to fall within a year. Moreover, he was faced with having to lead a SPÖ-FPÖ coalition with no strong basis of confidence. Many SPÖ ministers still saw the FPÖ, which was on the way to transforming itself into a liberal party, as the old 'Nazi party' of the 1950s. And it was just this point that was ultimately to bring to naught Kreisky's experiment of using the SPÖ-FPÖ coalition to split the ÖVP and promote the emergence of a liberal fourth party resembling the FDP in Germany.

In 1985, during the Reder-Frischenschlager affair, Kreisky realized that the question of the Nazi past would play a central role in this government setup and sought to prevent this by means of diversionary tactics, as he had done in the 1970s. The war criminal Walter Reder had, on release from imprisonment in Italy, been welcomed personally with a handshake by the FPÖ Defence Minister Friedhelm Frischenschlager. For decades politicians of all colours as well as church dignitaries had been intervening in favour of Reder, who had been painted as a martyr by both right-wing extremists and the political right as such. A justly condemned war criminal and convinced German-nationalist, Reder was reinterpreted in public discourse as the last ordinary prisoner of war. Although he had been deprived of Austrian citizenship before 1938 as a member of the Austrian Legion and saw himself not as Austrian but as 'Greater German', he had Austrian nationality conferred upon him while in jail, on application by the Upper Austrian provincial government – in disregard of the legal provisions and after revocation of a negative ruling by the Interior Ministry. From then on his legal and postage costs were paid for him. Perhaps his lawyer's most important function was, in an unparalleled PR and letter campaign, to turn a German SS war criminal into an innocent Austrian prisoner of war.

Sinowatz had his hands full trying to keep the coalition together during the Reder-Frischenschlager debate, since some of his ministers, such as Finance Minister Franz Vranitzky and Minister for Nationalized Enterprises Ferdinand Lacina, indignantly condemned Frischenschlager's conduct. Frischenschlager himself saw the ceremony at the Graz airport more as a symbolic end to the war, yet even his right-wing party government colleagues attacked him for it. Fred Sinowatz in turn was well aware that Austrian society was facing a new, more intensive confrontation with the role of Austrians in the Nazi period, in the Second World War and in the Holocaust, but in contrast to Kreisky he underestimated the percentage of those willing to abandon the victim doctrine. The matter escalated in the debate over the presidential candidacy of Kurt Waldheim.

The question of who really brought the 'blot' that Waldheim had glossed over in his CV into political debate is still disputed today. Mostly it is only the domestic-politics version that is discussed, namely that the SPÖ and within it especially Chancellor Fred Sinowatz's *chef de cabinet*, Hans Pusch, had played this card so as to win the presidential elections. At any rate, it 'exploded' in the media with the publication of Waldheim's service documents and discussion of his possible SA membership simultaneously in the *New York Times* and in *profil*. The original file was preserved in the Austrian State Archives. The 'Waldheim affair' is analysed in more detail in chapter 9. For Sinowatz it marked the end of his political career, so he utilized the lost presidential election to push through his favoured candidate, Franz Vranitzky, as chancellor.

It would, though, be over-hasty to reduce Sinowatz's chancellorship to the Reder-Frischenschlager and Waldheim debates. To a certain extent, however, these public disputes about historical evaluations were reflections of major social and economic changes. The second oil price crisis had shown clearly that there were downsides to the nascent globalization; Europe saw itself on the whole on the economic losing side compared with the growth rates in Japan and in Asia in general. Austria's nationalized industry could not adapt fast enough to the new environment. Attempts, such as those by the VOEST trading firm Intertrading to improve the balance sheets of the Linz steel giant by making speculative gains in oil futures or trading in steel and machinery, failed, as did the arms deals embarked upon by the state-run firm Noricum, which were barred under the Neutrality Law. These sorts of scandal, which – as is often forgotten – were due to management initiatives, had the effect of preventing any structured reform policy from being implemented. But it was only dealing with the scandals – politically, in the media, or judicially – that would offer the room for manoeuvre needed to successfully carry out a transformation policy. The Sinowatz government was not to remain in power long enough to achieve this.

Sinowatz had no doubt recognized the problems of the times, but he was unable to translate this understanding into political terms, let alone get it across in the media. In his policy statement of 31 May 1983 he had already formulated a motto that, correct though it was, displayed his indecisiveness: 'I know … that everything is very complicated, as is this world in which we live and act … Let us, then, have the courage to acknowledge this complexity more than we have hitherto.' Meanwhile, many misinterpreted his ostentatious but honest modesty and his statement that private interests had to give way to party interests. This statement no longer suited a time that was focusing increasingly on strong individual leadership figures.

By contrast with his predecessor Kreisky, Sinowatz favoured a collective political decision making process within an inner circle, which included Leopold Gratz, Science Minister Heinz Fischer, and Interior Minister Karl Blecha. In a second circle, the SPÖ whip and trade unionist Sepp Wille and SPÖ General Secretaries Fritz Marsch and Peter Schieder played a part.

There were positive effects from a government reshuffle that brought in Franz Vranitzky, fresh from his success in restoring the Länderbank to financial soundness, as finance minister. Vienna's Mayor Gratz came back to central government as foreign minister. Both appointments were also interpreted as a move away from the Kreisky team of 1983, since Finance Minister Salcher, at the height of his dispute with Hannes Androsch, had to go, as did Foreign Minister Erwin

Lanc. Kreisky commented extremely negatively on the changes. As for public opinion, surveys between October 1984 and October 1985 certainly show support for the Small Coalition and what was now the Sinowatz team, but the crisis of the state industries late in 1985 dashed the upbeat mood.

On one matter of importance for Austria's future political structure, namely repeal of the Nuclear Prohibition Act, Sinowatz showed considerably less skill. With his reconstruction-generation mentality, he and a clear majority of the government wanted to start operating the Zwentendorf nuclear power station, in which 14 billion schillings (over a billion euros) had already been invested. It was not the FPÖ alone that withheld support; the SPÖ motion in favour got only a one-vote majority in Parliament when a two-thirds majority would have been required. Talks with the social partners failed, and the ÖVP would not agree. This commitment to an environmentally obtuse energy policy also gave the signal for the slow rise of the Green Party and the increasing turn of young voters away from the SPÖ. The sharp controversy over the planned Danube power station at Stopfenreuther Au near Hainburg had already triggered youth and elite resistance – and aroused the *Kronenzeitung* – against Sinowatz and his energy policy. Sinowatz decided at the last minute on a Christmas break for reflection, in order to avert violent on-the-spot confrontations, and in 1985 extended this break indefinitely.

The Zwentendorf and Hainburg cases had very clearly shown that Sinowatz was imbued with the reconstruction and growth mentality of the postwar era. While he noted the new social movements, he was no longer able to embody them in political objectives. Moreover, the pressure from the trade unions and

ILLUSTRATION 4.6
After the presidential election of Kurt Waldheim, Fred Sinowatz (right) steps down as chancellor and is followed by Franz Vranitzky.

the social partners to give priority to what they claimed to be absolute economic necessity was too great.

Sinowatz displayed great adroitness in his choice of a successor and in the timing of his departure from politics. The day after Kurt Waldheim was elected president, he resigned as chancellor, though not as SPÖ party chairman, and nominated Finance Minister Vranitzky as his successor. Besides his highly positive basic media presence – even if he always kept his distance from journalists – Vranitzky was able to deploy his economic competence successfully. Almost more important, however, was his unambiguous aloofness from the German-nationalist backslidings of various FPÖ networks centred on Carinthian provincial assemblyman Jörg Haider. Once the latter had pushed his way up to the party leadership at the party congress in Innsbruck in 1986, Vranitzky terminated the SPÖ-FPÖ coalition.

Franz Vranitzky, the Crisis Manager

Franz Vranitzky's father, Franz, was an ironworker by trade who, after unemployment between the wars and war service in the German Wehrmacht, was close to the KPÖ until 1956. His mother Rosa had, with much effort, anxiety and affection, brought Franz Vranitzky and Inge, his sister, through the war years. Despite great financial difficulties he was able to go to high school and then study at the Hochschule für Welthandel; in the summer holidays he worked as a builder. Not until he became an employee of the Austrian National Bank – a job his mother got him through personal contacts – did Vranitzky join the SPÖ. His spell at the Nationalbank seems to have left him with a preference for grand-coalition scenarios.

This biographical excursus is important for a better understanding of the varied perceptions of Vranitzky by the public. Never a classic party functionary and/or professional politician, he had far more proletarian roots than did many SPÖ officials. Having managed, for the young Finance Minister Hannes Androsch, to bring calm and efficiency into the cabinet, in early 1980 he took up the post of deputy CEO of the then still nationalized Creditanstalt-Bankverein, where he was replaced – without prior notice – by Hannes Androsch when the latter left the federal government. Vranitzky went on to become CEO of the Länderbank, which was nationalized like the Creditanstalt but was only half its size. Because of imminent losses on loans to major private clients such as Eumig, Funder and Österreichische Klimatechnik, the bank was facing a crisis that threatened its survival. Vranitzky put these difficulties right and had set the bank on the road to recovery when Fred Sinowatz brought him into the SPÖ-FPÖ coalition as finance minister in September 1984.

Despite the numerous crises Vranitzky proved a calm finance minister, acting skilfully in terms both of financial technique and economic policy. Like Sinowatz, he displayed great mastery, when Sinowatz offered him the chancellorship, in choosing Ferdinand Lacina as his successor as finance minister. As minister for nationalized enterprises, Lacina had proved himself in the crises of VOEST Alpine and Chemie Linz. Vranitzky and Lacina were linked by a shared basic anti-Nazi attitude that went far beyond Sunday speeches: Lacina had been prominent in the revelation of the anti-Semitic machinations of the Welthandel professor Taras Borodajkewycz and had also taken clear positions in the debate concerning the Reder-Frischenschlager affair. Against the background of the steadily smouldering Waldheim debate, this was important emotional cement.

Vranitzky therefore had no problem terminating the unloved SPÖ-FPÖ Small Coalition after the 'seizure of power' within the FPÖ by Jörg Haider with its clearly right-wing nationalist overtones. Despite poor poll figures Vranitzky risked calling early elections in 1986 and still managed – with the loss of ten seats and a 43.12 per cent share of valid votes cast – to fend off the ÖVP. Their party chairman Alois Mock was plainly very disappointed at the ÖVP's 41.29 per cent, but ultimately acquiesced to a grand coalition, though personally he was rather less than keen on it. The by now openly radicalized FPÖ this time obtained 9.73 per cent, doubling its share of the vote with a skilfully populist election campaign making particular use of criticism of the grand coalition. Mock's attempts to form a coalition with the FPÖ failed, allegedly because of the lack of a majority in the party executive, since many ÖVP leaders and especially business figures were clear that a number of choices had to be made for the Second Republic: from a repositioning vis-à-vis European integration to a transformation of nationalized industry and a new attitude on the part of Austrian men and women to their role in National Socialism.

Internationally, Vranitzky succeeded with his de facto representation abroad of the president, who had become a symbol in the West of an Austria repressing its Nazi past. Waldheim's election campaign statement – 'I only did my duty' – and the defensive tirades of his supporters, many of whom did not even shrink from anti-Semitic attacks, had consolidated this image. Nor could critical speeches now improve the situation; Waldheim had already lost both international reputation and credibility.

In domestic policy Vranitzky endeavoured cautiously – or for many observers, too hesitantly and slowly – to induce Austrians to face up fully to National Socialism. There had been concrete proposals since 1986 – one from the renowned journalist Hugo Portisch – to point the way by means of a public statement, but Vranitzky kept on waiting. In retrospect this hesitation seems tactically wise, since a step of this kind needed to meet with broad public response and acceptance. And Vranitzky long sought an appropriate occasion to proclaim this about-face. In July 1991 he used a parliamentary debate on the war in Yugoslavia to bring up the past war in a self-critical manner. For the first time under the Second Republic, a federal chancellor cautiously yet unmistakably disowned the

Austrian victim doctrine in its unqualified version, without forgetting those who had been in the Resistance or fallen victim to Nazi terror.

At the same time he strove to achieve a détente in relations with Israel, already strained since the mid 1970s because of Kreisky's Middle Eastern policies and totally disrupted since Waldheim. Vranitzky used the opportunity afforded by a speech at the Hebrew University in Jerusalem to repeat his statement and amplify it point by point. At home, though, the components of the Vranitzky coalition – both SPÖ and ÖVP – suffered a painful defeat in the 1994 general elections.

Viktor Klima, the Austro-Blair with an Expiration Date

After Franz Vranitzky had elegantly reversed the attempts by his popular Transport Minister Rudolf Streicher to send him into a presidential election campaign and 'persuaded' Streicher to stand instead, he called the head of personnel at Österreichische Mineralöl Verwaltung (ÖMV), Viktor Klima, into the government as transport minister. After Ferdinand Lacina's resignation, however, Klima, who came from a Social Democratic background but apart from his role at ÖMV had no experience of party or ideological work, moved to the Finance Ministry. As finance minister he was soon able to improve his public image, as various surveys show. By contrast with Vranitzky, who was always concerned to keep his distance, both within his own party and vis-à-vis his coalition partner, and seemed primarily interested in policy-oriented interaction, Klima developed a very personal and friendly style. Commenting on Vranitzky's voluntary retirement in 1996, several party grandees, such as Mayor of Vienna Michael Häupl, felt that Chancellor Klima's entry into office had brought 'more warmth' into the party. Moreover, Klima had stood up well in a television confrontation with the populist Jörg Haider, who had previously begun to seem invincible.

The grand coalition and the new ÖVP Vice-Chancellor Wolfgang Schüssel were badly damaged by the sale of the 'black' Creditanstalt-Bankverein to the 'red' Bank Austria.[41] By contrast with all other privatization plans, Schüssel and with him the ÖVP thought only conservative bank groups and financiers close to the ÖVP should be allowed to bid for the Creditanstalt. However, their offers remained well below the value of the flagship of Austria's nationalized banks. Chancellor Klima implemented the sale in early 1997, and by doing so rang in the end of the grand coalition. Increasingly, in the first privatizations and in the reorganization of the state holding company ÖIAG, the SPÖ had questioned the ÖVP's economic competence; they were also more prepared to break with old proprietary and *Proporz* thinking – a tendency that was, if anything, to harm them in connection with the sale of Bank Austria to the German Hypo-Vereinsbank, and that led to enormous losses in the assets and liabilities position of the City of Vienna and of Wiener Städtische Versicherung (Vienna Insurance

Group). In 2005 the UniCredit Bank of Milan acquired the whole group as the wheel of globalization took another turn.

Klima sought through his jovial coalition style to bridge the differences with the ÖVP, without recognizing that they were increasingly looking forward to the end of the grand coalition. As chancellor he accomplished considerably less than he had as transport and finance minister, and his efforts to counter Haider's seemingly irresistible appeal by dint of hugs and back-slapping also ended in failure. The basic problem of the Klima era was that the proclaimed 'politics of warmth' ultimately ended up as a politics of shying away from confrontation. While Klima's PR kitchen cabinet, centred on Andreas Rudas as SPÖ general secretary and Josef Kalina as press spokesman, managed to get positive reportage on Klima in the *Kronenzeitung* and other newspapers, specific political content and/or objectives were left by the wayside. The dread of unpopular though necessary measures was ever more perceptibly enhanced by apprehension as to the *Kronenzeitung*'s reactions. The topic of EU enlargement was long kept in abeyance politically, as were the asylum and immigration issues. Skilfully, Haider began to poach on these unguarded political territories and in 1999 scored his biggest electoral victory. Klima by contrast pursued an extremely cautious election campaign and allowed all the rough edges to be smoothed away by his advisers, until the only issue left in the SPÖ election campaign (apart from the warm atmosphere) was the setting up of a commission on reforming the army.

Wolfgang Schüssel, the Surprising Chancellor

After the election of October 1999, which had disastrous results for the ÖVP – for the first time in its history it fell to third place, at 26.91 per cent, behind the FPÖ – Klima tried to steer negotiations once again in the direction of a grand coalition. But Schüssel had always seen Klima as the weaker partner; in this stalemate situation the ÖVP leader now developed a strategically perfect plan: forming a coalition government with Haider's FPÖ.

Schüssel – then economics minister – had already become acquainted with the weaknesses of the chain-smoker Viktor Klima. In the decisive EU accession negotiations on the transit question the latter had become as incapable of negotiating as had Foreign Minister Alois Mock.[42] Finance Minister Lacina and Economics Minister Schüssel had then saved the situation, but the public had been presented with the wrong heroes: Mock and Klima. It is said that in 1997, after the lost battle over the Creditanstalt-Bankverein, Schüssel had already proposed to President Thomas Klestil a sudden shift in coalition to the FPÖ, but in vain.[43] The idea was not new, and Alois Mock too would indeed readily have acted on it, but at the time Erhard Busek, the ÖVP chairman, categorically rejected any alternative involving the Haider FPÖ.

ILLUSTRATION 4.7
After the 'Sanctions' of the EU-14, T-shirts promoted a misjudged small country.

Despite the forceful disapproval of President Klestil, accompanied by demonstrations at home and the so-called Sanctions by the fourteen EU partners, Schüssel pushed his coalition through. In retrospect, it was only these reactions that stabilized the totally unequal partnership anyway. Indeed, the FPÖ was so short of personnel that it had to change its ministers almost monthly. It is uncertain how far this had been factored in by Schüssel, who, as a deft strategist, ended up by painting the manifest winners of the elections – the Social Democrats – as the losers. The fact is that he had learned how to operate the domestic political mechanisms from the Waldheim debate.

It will be some time yet before internal sources can clarify how the 'sanctions' by the EU Fourteen came about. They were not in fact based on EU law, but on a political punitive exercise. At the Stockholm Holocaust Educational Conference in January 2000 it was already clear that Schüssel was going to risk the coalition with Haider's FPÖ. A depressed and tearful Klima spread this message among the delegates, including the then Israeli Prime Minister Ehud Barak, German Chancellor Gerhard Schröder, and a number of other European heads of state. Ultimately the issue of right-wing populism was a European one, as much present in post-unification Germany as with Le Pen in France or the Front National in Belgium, to mention only a few states. Schröder himself stated in interviews that he had been motivated to act in Stockholm by the massive presentation of the Holocaust and the associated German guilt. In my view it was the Chirac-Schröder axis that 'invented' the sanctions, and Austria was not their primary target; instead, a pan-European message was to be sent.

But the campaign rather missed its mark. Although the sanctions were only symbolic ones affecting diplomatic and political representatives, the tabloid press and the ÖVP-FPÖ coalition enthusiastically blew the patriotic horn. Haider outdid himself in catering to the Austrian inferiority complex. As leader of the opposition, the inexperienced new SPÖ Chairman Alfred Gusenbauer basked in international acclaim and sought the ear of such EU bigwigs as Blair to protest against the new coalition, whilst at home the SPÖ initially left the 'Save Austria!' field totally to the ÖVP and was again stigmatized as a 'traitor to the fatherland'. Barely six months later an EU report pardoned the new government and – despite

ILLUSTRATION 4.8
The controversial 'Porsche Coalition': Jörg Haider and Wolfgang Schüssel demonstrating harmony after the formation of the government in 2000.

many critical observations – sanctioned the coalition ex post facto. In fact this report was really more of an artifice so as to be able formally to lift the sanctions.

Schüssel's strengths lay in his ability not to allow an inferior coalition partner to deflect him from steering his course relatively calmly and stoically. His 2002 election victory, surprising to many, was in fact basically connected with the presence of this inferior coalition partner, which was continually losing voter consensus everywhere, except in Carinthia. By keeping out of most conflicts and deftly intervening only occasionally, and mostly rhetorically, Schüssel succeeded in figuring as the still point in the government. In daily work too he managed to evade constraints.

Additionally, Schüssel and the ÖVP were able to erase from public discourse the memory of their participation in the grand coalitions since 1986. The paradigm example of this is the extremely costly and totally ineffective tax reform of 1999, which cost taxpayers a total of 32 billion schillings. The main lobbyist for it at the time was the ÖVP under Schüssel. Klima's lack of leadership qualities and the populist hankering after votes prevented any other solution and increased the budget deficit. After 2000, zero deficit was suddenly announced as the new doctrine, and the SPÖ was regarded as the party of budget sinners.

While Haider was aware that the FPÖ was ultimately only the puppet of the ÖVP, all he could achieve by a further move to the right would be new elections. The voters had long got used to this coalition of expediency, and Schüssel had even managed to draw the ex-FPÖ finance minister to his side as front man and finally obtain absolution for his pre-2000 sins. Karl-Heinz Grasser so skilfully sold the strict zero-deficit policy (seen by many economists as counterproductive) that even Gusenbauer, the leader of the opposition, suddenly wanted the principle of zero deficit incorporated in the constitution. That this fiscal policy meant a heavy tax burden and relatively high unemployment by Austrian standards was conveniently blamed on the past. But by 2004 Grasser had already moved away from this goal.

Schüssel's staying power, expressed inter alia in an ingenious strategy of delegation and a great deal of leisure time, had by then become recognized even internationally. His political objectives had already been set in the 1970s: less state intervention and more private initiative. For the sake of these objectives he increasingly sidelined the old social-partnership structures he had grown up in, mostly without getting himself actively involved in public debate on the matter. At the same time he warded off comprehensive structural changes that might have affected the ÖVP's core constituencies, as was evident in the case of pension reform and the exclusion from it of civil servants, but also in the farming sector. This is why the points of greatest friction with the FPÖ (now partly metamorphosed into the 'Alliance for Austria's Future' [BZÖ]) lie specifically within the sphere of welfare politics, where that party may lose its last remaining major voter potential.

Why No Female Chancellor?

Austria's domestic politics continues in terms of both presidents and chancellors to be typically male. Only once, in the coalition talks that took place during the crisis of 1999–2000, did Wolfgang Schüssel suggest the compromise of appointing Maria Schaumayer, the former president of the Oesterreichische Nationalbank, as SPÖ chancellor; however, Frau Schaumayer declined to accept the appointment on the grounds of age. In the SPÖ's discussion on who should become party chair, the former State Secretary, SPÖ General Secretary and Vienna City Councillor for Finance Brigitte Ederer had stated clearly around the same time that the SPÖ was not yet ready for a woman as its head. Since then the ÖVP has made an attempt, by putting up a woman as candidate for the post of federal president, to close this gap in Austria's post-war political development, but Foreign Minister Benita Maria Ferrero-Waldner had too polarizing an effect on women to be able to produce a 'female swing' and with it a majority. By contrast, at the provincial level women have succeeded in becoming provincial presidents for both the ÖVP and the SPÖ. It has more than once been evident that future political developments become apparent first at regional level. Business is occasionally ahead here: in 2005 Brigitte Ederer was appointed CEO of Siemens Austria.

The Chancellors' Leadership Qualities Compared

There is nothing harder than to sketch the still living chancellors of recent decades, and in particular it seems impossible for a source-based critical historian to analyse current office-holders in a historical context. What does seem thoroughly methodically legitimate is a comparison of the chancellors' political leadership qualities. Especially international political science, but also management consultancy and applied psychology, have fixed on empirically verifiable criteria here, so as to make it possible to develop a leadership profile. From the already vast literature and methodology, the following list of criteria has been distilled as useful, in the author's eyes, for a comparative analysis of the chancellors of the Second Republic. Seven key elements will be identified and assessed.

Authenticity

This area is especially often overlooked in today's political mise en scène. It is not enough to put on a perfect show; the voters, male and female, have – at least in the medium term – a sixth sense for performances that do not match the core of someone's real personality. This very much applies to Schüssel, who, while not cutting much of a figure in various popularity surveys, is rated authentic. With Klima the assessments were the other way round – high popularity figures, but not considered authentic. This was also one of the reasons for the election victory of the SPÖ presidential candidate Heinz Fischer, despite a number of points apparently militating against him (long party career, elderliness): his opponent, Foreign Minister Ferrero-Waldner, had been overly coached by her spin doctors so as to make her match the notional model, thereby losing authenticity.

Both Franz Vranitzky and Bruno Kreisky attained a high degree of authenticity. Both conveyed this in their unostentatiously elegant dress, with Vranitzky keeping an even greater distance between himself and his surroundings than Kreisky, but being seen in direct meetings with voters, both male and female and including workers, as authentic. With Kreisky there was the further point that he was able to infuse this authenticity with a high level of emotion. Vranitzky wanted to concentrate on material issues and problems and anyway had rather more crises to cope with than Kreisky in his first years as chancellor.

Fred Sinowatz appeared much too modest, conveying an authenticity that no longer suited an upwardly mobile, prosperous society. While the fact that he never moved away from his birthplace symbolized deep emotional attachment, it did not fit the zeitgeist of the 1980s. Josef Klaus had too much authenticity, making it hard for him to get himself across, particularly in the TV era that was by then dawning. Both Gorbach and Raab were authentic chancellors, but without much emotionalism, on which Leopold Figl seemed to have a monopoly. Karl Renner was automatically regarded as an authentic legend and monument in 1945, having been state chancellor after the First World War. For many he was also a sort of political fossil, yet both in 1918–20 and still more in 1945, he was extremely successful.

Integrity

This point is particularly important in the case of chancellors. In this connection Schüssel occasionally showed a nervousness that found expression in outpourings of insults, for instance his disparagement of the young 'Internet protesters' against the ÖVP-FPÖ coalition. Despite rumours to the contrary, he was not, as economics minister, connected with the payment of bribes, although there were contacts with a German arms wholesaler who had made donations to the CDU. However, many voters interpreted his formation of a coalition with the FPÖ under the right-wing populist leadership of Jörg Haider as a loss of integrity.

Both Klima and Vranitzky were regarded as having integrity, even if some criticized Vranitzky's acceptance of a Länderbank pension. Sinowatz had great problems defending his personal integrity, both in the Noricum trial for breach of neutrality through arms sales, in which he was charged and acquitted, and in the Waldheim affair.

Integrity was a central element of Kreisky's political strategy as a multiple outsider in the SPÖ and in society (Jew, exile, intellectual, diplomat); this factor also contributed to his attacks upon his heir presumptive, Hannes Androsch. Androsch's tax case, which was legally decided against him, constituted a breach of his moral criteria for Kreisky.

Klaus was a politician of absolute integrity, but for many voters he was too squeaky clean. No one applauded his swift resignation, and many interpreted it instead as evidence of political weakness. Gorbach, Raab and Figl too were able to score under this heading and remained politically unassailable. Renner's 1938 vote for the Anschluss counted as a black mark against him, but ultimately this did not matter, since he had acted the way a clear majority of Austrians had.

Fidelity to Principles

Specifically in the political sphere, this criterion is not essential to leadership. Where there are political upheavals, society readily tolerates breaches of principle – as with Karl Renner in 1938 – since they are also often supported or accepted by large parts of the population. Thus, even the political past of Figl and Raab in the authoritarian Fatherland Front (Figl) or the Lower Austrian authoritarian Heimwehr movement (Raab) did not count after 1945. Nor was the youthful anti-Semitism of Josef Klaus in the interwar years, which he sought to make up for after 1945 with emphatic philo-Semitism, an issue, nor the fact that Wolfgang Schüssel had long supported the grand coalition and helped to decide several major policy decisions taken by it.

What is more relevant when it comes to political fidelity to principles is stringent implementation of a clear political course, though such a course would, obviously, not succeed unless it met with general acceptance.

Making Active Contributions

In this area the need is above all to demonstrate political creativity. Increasingly, especially since Kreisky, policy advisors attempt, in line with developments in the economy, to attribute only key decisions to the chancellor; everyday business, with all its ups and downs, successes and failures, remains the responsibility of ministers. Up to Kreisky, who displayed particular activism – even intervening directly in the area of the nationalized industries – all the chancellors took similar initiatives. Josef Klaus contributed relatively little in any field of politics, as was also the case with Gorbach. Raab joined in actively at various levels, whereas Figl on the other hand tended rather to hang back here. Vranitzky too was regarded, especially in the second half of his period in office, as a ditherer. Klima sought primarily to convey the image of the active chancellor, but in practice he and his circle were extremely cautious, so as to ensure that no mistakes were made. Schüssel tended to delegate, and often said nothing even in heated political debates.

Cooperativeness: Team Spirit

Chancellor Schüssel was a master of delegation and therefore also enjoyed – by contrast with all his predecessors in office – a considerable amount of private leisure time. His leadership style was correspondingly team-oriented; but the co-alition partners developed strong tendencies to embark on a political life of their own, ending in 2003 in the coalition's collapse. Klima by contrast was unable to transpose his friendly 'coalition, new-style' to the level of practical work. Vran-itzky acted in typical business fashion, as if he were the team leader on a directo-rial board with clearly defined areas of competence, whereas Kreisky had more of an autocratic leadership style, recognizing all the same the specific responsibili-ties of such top ministers as Firnberg or Broda. And there were several decisions – for instance on the abortion question – that he accepted even though they ran counter to his convictions.

Pioneering Achievement

The pioneers of the Second Republic who have left deep traces in history are undoubtedly Renner, in connection with the refounding of the state in 1945; Raab, in connection with the State Treaty and neutrality in 1955; Kreisky as in-ternational communicator and domestic guarantor of social harmony and quiet Austrian patriotism; and also Vranitzky and Schüssel. Vranitzky, by going 'softly softly', achieved EU entry for a country that has really always concerned itself primarily with itself, and into the bargain he cautiously guided discussion on the National Socialist past and on the Holocaust onto new pathways. Schüssel has already gone down in history as a taboo breaker. Whether it was a specific strategy on Schüssel's part to 'tame' Haider and reduce the FPÖ's electoral suc-cess is something we shall not go into here. The primary objective was to squeeze the SPÖ out of government, no more and no less. Kreisky's project of making the FPÖ over time into a classical liberal party like the FDP had already failed, apart from the interlude when the Liberal Forum led by Heide Schmidt was rep-resented in the Nationalrat in 1993–99.

Ability to Communicate

In the sphere of communication, Bruno Kreisky was certainly the absolute super-star. As a journalist *manqué*, brilliant *raconteur* and solo entertainer he managed over a long period, through the media but also through a variety of personal contacts, to build up communication with various sectors of society. Additional-ly, Kreisky, a master of the telephone, himself spread his messages directly, and often even picked up the phone himself when it rang in his house. This access also let him control his political circle, which he began increasingly to distrust. He frequently used concrete examples drawn from everyday life, so as to irritate his ministers. Moreover, both in public appearances and on television he developed a sort of stage presence and thus attracted attention to himself.

It is no accident that Kreisky and Figl are by far the most popular chancellors in the collective memory of Austrians. Figl too, in his good years up to 1950, was an excellent communicator with the media of the times. Raab was more of a silent type who preferred to make decisions in autocratic fashion. Gorbach has left virtually no traces in this area. Klaus, however, though regarded as a good communicator at the small-scale provincial-president level, left behind a poor impression as chancellor of the first ÖVP single-party government both on television and in the print media. This allowed Kreisky to shine all the more, although he tended to monopolize direct conversations so that dialogue hardly ever happened. Still, with his gift of explaining complex situations simply, using well-chosen historical and topical images, the impression he left was mostly a fascinating one. Today that sort of strongly monologue-oriented style of communication would no longer be effective.

Sinowatz brought a good communicative style into his party and into government, but he failed to establish a close rapport with the public. Vranitzky, who came across very well in the media in his first years, had increasing problems moving onto the level of direct political debate; thus he avoided live confrontation with Jörg Haider, which was interpreted as weakness. Schüssel is viewed ambivalently in this area: he is seen as a brilliant speaker, but also as rather overbearing and by no means always skilful at dealing with journalists.

The Ideal Image and Its Reflection among the Voters, Male and Female

Modern leadership research[44] is increasingly recognizing that the model is in practice highly dependent on the audience. The decision as to what qualities ultimately constitute leadership criteria concerns society, not just those who exercise power or would like to put on a display of leadership. This level of interaction is often ignored by political analysts and political advisors so that their analyses apply only ex post facto. For instance, Sinowatz, at the start of his period in office, certainly fulfilled a number of leadership criteria, but at the same time, because of his modest, unpretentious self-presentation, he failed to meet voter expectations of the kind of leadership personality they had been accustomed to seeing in power since Bruno Kreisky – whether with approval or otherwise is irrelevant. Vranitzky did, especially in his first years, meet these expectations, before domestic political attacks increasingly put him on the defensive and he was pigeonholed as indecisive.

Bruno Kreisky by contrast persuaded public opinion to accept his policy decisions through a permanent 'pedagogical discourse', as Thomas Nowotny put it.[45] He appealed to the population's capacity for judgment and sense of responsibility; people were addressed as citizens with a creative role, not as mere voters. It was typical of him that the chancellor's cabinet was primarily concerned to follow up enquiries, requests and complaints from citizens and offer solutions that were as practical as possible. Only a tiny part of these activities came before Kreisky directly, but in a snowball effect the belief spread that one could at any time contact Kreisky by letter or telephone and get an answer that suggested or announced concrete measures. Only Jörg Haider in Carinthia continued to pursue a similar, and regionally highly successful, policy; however, by the time Haider died in a DUI car crash in October 2008, it had increasingly deteriorated into expensive event management, financed by the taxpayer.

The ascetic figure of Josef Klaus, because it was associated with a profound devoutness, evoked no particular response among young voters of either sex or from women, in the wake of the 1968 movement that spread to Austria too. Today, though, Wolfgang Schüssel's devoutness as an active Catholic who is even in the habit of going on retreats in a monastery comes over entirely positively, even if many critical voices are raised against this ostentatiously displayed Catholicism. Christian and generally right-of-centre gestures and statements have been on the agenda again since 2000, even though agnosticism is by no means a barrier to attaining a leadership role, as the election of the agnostic Heinz Fischer as federal president demonstrates.

Leopold Figl's style probably best matched the cheerful and fun-loving self-image of many Austrian men and women. From this viewpoint there is no room for either the real central actor in the decisive State Treaty negotiations, Julius Raab, or for others who did not fit the pattern.

But popularity alone does not make a leader, as was clearly evident in the 2002 elections. Surveys carried out in 2001 show that neither Schüssel as head of government nor the SPÖ leader Alfred Gusenbauer was seen as inspiring affection. At the time, both were equally short on personal popularity, while Schüssel had additional problems with his political line. Nonetheless, Schüssel plainly swung the elections in his favour, since he showed resoluteness and offered relative stability amidst the uncertainties of coalition-building.

NOTES

1. For such an analysis see Peter Pelinka, *Österreichs Kanzler. Von Leopold Figl bis Wolfgang Schüssel* (Vienna: Ueberreuter, 2001).
2. Archiv der Republik, Bestand Nachlaß Sammlungen, Diary of Heinrich Wildner, Transcript 1945, 86–87.

3. DÖW (Dokumentationsarchiv des österreichischen Widerstands) 17.153/II, Schärf to Pollak, 29 August 1945.
4. Helene Maimann (ed.), 'Die Rückkehr beschäftigt uns ständig. Vom Flüchten und vom Wiederkommen,' in *Die ersten 100 Jahre. Österreichische Sozialdemokratie 1888–1988,* (Vienna: Brandstätter, 1988), 241. For an overview see Heinz Kienzl and Susanne Kirchner, ed., *Ein neuer Frühling wird blühen. Erinnerungen und Spurensuche* (Vienna: Deuticke, 2002).
5. Wolfgang Fritz, *Der Kopf des Asiaten Breitner. Politik und Ökonomie im Roten Wien. Hugo Breitner – Leben und Werk* (Vienna: Löcker Verlag, 2000).
6. Adolf Sturmthal, *Zwei Leben. Erinnerungen eines sozialistischen Internationalisten zwischen Österreich und den USA,* ed. Georg Hauptfeld and Oliver Rathkolb in cooperation with Christina Wesemann (Vienna-Cologne-Weimar: Böhlau, 1989), 211–213.
7. The trade union leader Friedrich Hillegeist was imprisoned several times between 1938 and 1944 for political reasons and spent eight months in the Buchenwald concentration camp. In 1955 he was president of the International Federation of Private Employees, in 1959 vice-president of the Austrian Trade Unions; from 1945 to 1962 a member of the National Council in the Austrian Parliament and president of the Austrian Social Securities. Between 1961 and 1962 he served as vice-president of the Austrian National Council.
8. Oliver Rathkolb, Johannes Kunz and Margit Schmidt, eds., *Bruno Kreisky. Zwischen den Zeiten. Der Memoiren erster Teil* (Vienna: Kremayr & Scheriau, 2000), 427. Kreisky did not mention the name of Helmer, but the author was present when Kreisky told this story. This original version is documented on the tapes of the Kreisky Interviews stored in the Austrian Mediathek in Vienna.
9. Peter Bubenik, '1938 – Gefahr und Lehre', in *Julius Raab, Aussaat und Ernte,* Catalogue of the exhibition at the Benedictine monastery of Seitenstetten May 15 – October 26, 1992, 270–271.
10. Archives of Österreichische Gesellschaft für Zeitgeschichte, Material Julius Raab, 5th working session for a Julius Raab book, 13 March 1962, 4.
11. Martin Florian Herz and Reinhold Wagnleitner, eds., *Understanding Austria. The Political Reports and Analyses of Martin F. Herz* (Salzburg: Neugebauer, 1984), 87.
12. Ernst Bruckmüller, 'Die ständische Tradition – ÖVP und Neokorporatismus', in *Volkspartei – Anspruch und Realität. Zur Geschichte der ÖVP seit 1945,* ed. Robert Kriechbaumer and Franz Schausberger (Vienna-Cologne-Weimar: Böhlau, 1995), 295.
13. Archives Österreichische Gesellschaft für Zeitgeschichte, Material Julius Raab, 4th working session, 1 March 1962, 4.
14. Ibid., 5.
15. Hemetsberger-Koller, 'Reinhard Kamitz', 259.
16. Verein für Geschichte der Arbeiterbewegung (VGA), Nachlaß Adolf Schärf, Box 56, Verhandlungsprotokoll Nr. 29 über die Sitzung des Kabinettsrates, 5 September 1945, 5.
17. Oliver Rathkolb, *Washington ruft Wien. US-Großmachtpolitik und Österreich 1953–1963. Mit Exkursen zu CIA-Waffenlagern, NATO-Connection und Neutralitätsdebatte* (Vienna-Cologne-Weimar: Böhlau, 1997), 258.
18. Herz and Wagnleitner, *Understanding Austria,* 583.

19. Oliver Rathkolb, 'NS-Problem und Gründung des VdU', in Meissl, Mulley and Rathkolb, *Verdrängte Schuld,* 82–83.

20. Archives of Österreichische Gesellschaft für Zeitgeschichte, Material Julius Raab, 3rd Working Session for a Julius Raab book, 16 February 1962, 1.

21. Hurdes to Gruber, 2 May 1951. Niederösterreichisches Landesarchiv, Papers of Leopold Figl, 0130.

22. VGA, Schärf Papers, Box 49, Lemberger to Schärf, 4 December 1951.

23. Transcripts of Raab's calendar, 27 February 1954 (the originals are stored in the Stiftsarchiv Seitenstetten).

24. VGA, Amtsvermerk, 17 March 1953, Papers of Schärf, Box 49, Correspondence Lemberger.

25. Archives of Österreichische Gesellschaft für Zeitgeschichte, Material Julius Raab, Minutes of Interviews Raab-Jedlicka, 13 March 1962, 3.

26. Stefan Karner, Barbara Stelzl-Marx and Alexander Tschubarjan, eds., *Die Rote Armee in Österreich. Sowjetische Besatzung 1945–1955. Dokumente* (Graz-Vienna-Munich: Verein zur Förderung von Forschung von Folgen nach Konflikten und Kriegen, 2005), 763.

27. Gerald Stourzh, *Um Einheit und Freiheit. Staatsvertrag, Neutralität und das Ende der Ost-West-Besetzung Österreichs 1945–1955* (Vienna-Cologne-Weimar: Böhlau, 1998), 434 and 275.

28. Friedrich Torberg to Klaus Dohrn, 7 November 1955. The author thanks Mr. Frank Tichy, Abtenau, for a copy of this letter. With regard to Torberg's role in the cultural Cold War see Frank Tichy, *Friedrich Torberg: Ein Leben in Widersprüchen* (Salzburg: Otto Müller Verlag, 1995).

29. VGA, Papers of Schärf, Pa 28, Schärf, Geschichte, 1–2.

30. Bruno Kreisky, *Zwischen den Zeiten. Erinnerungen aus fünf Jahrzehnten* (Berlin: Siedler, 1986), 391.

31. Julian Uher, 'Das Wirtschaftsprogramm 1968', in *Austro-Keynesianismus in Theorie und Praxis,* ed. Fritz Weber and Theodor Venus (Vienna: Jugend & Volk, 1993), 58–60.

32. Heinz Fischer, *Die Kreisky-Jahre 1967–1983* (Vienna: Löcker Verlag, 1994), 51.

33. Cited after F. Buchegger and W. Stamminger, *Anspruch und Wirklichkeit,* 33.

34. Maria Mesner, *Frauensache? Die Auseinandersetzung um den Schwangerschaftsabbruch in Österreich* (Vienna: Jugend & Volk, 1994).

35. Cited after Christian Haerpfner, 'Die Sozialstruktur der SPÖ. Gesellschaftliche Einflußfaktoren der sozialdemokratischen Parteibindung in Österreich 1969–1988', *Österreichische Zeitschrift für Politikwissenschaft* 4 (1989): 375.

36. Peter A. Ulram, *Hegemonie und Erosion. Politische Kultur und politischer Wandel in Österreich* (Vienna-Cologne-Weimar: Böhlau, 1990), 238.

37. Ibid., 240.

38. Robert Kriechbaumer, *Parteiprogramme im Widerstreit der Interessen. Die Programmdiskussionen und die Programme von ÖVP und SPÖ 1945–1986,* Österreichisches Jahrbuch für Politik special edition 3 (1990): 441.

39. Sozialistische Partei Österreichs, ed., *Dr. Bruno Kreisky – Vom Heute ins Morgen. Rede vor dem Villacher Parteitag 1972* (Vienna: Sozialistische Partei Österreichs, Zentralsekretariat, 1972), 8.

40. Barbara Liegl and Anton Pelinka, *Chronos und Ödipus. Der Kreisky-Androsch Konflikt* (Vienna: Braumüller, 2004).

41. Bank Austria resulted from a merger of the Länderbank and Zentralsparkasse Vienna, both controlled by Social Democrats.

42. Joachim Riedl, *Der Wende-Kanzler. Die unerschütterliche Beharrlichkeit des Wolfgang Schüssel, Ein biographischer Essay* (Vienna: Czernin Verlag, 2001), 68.

43. Ibid., 101.

44. For the leadership debate in Austria see Anton Pelinka, 'Leadership. Zur Funktionalität eines Konzepts', *Österreichische Zeitschrift für Politikwissenschaft* 4 (1997): 369–376. For a leadership approach influenced by psychoanalysis see Irene Etzersdorfer, 'Persönlichkeit und Politik. Zur Interaktion politischer und seelischer Faktoren in der interdisziplinären 'Political-Leadership'-Forschung', *Österreichische Zeitschrift für Politikwissenschaft* 4 (1997): 377–392.

45. Thomas Nowotny, 'Aber was macht der Dumme schon mit dem Glück? Politische Leadership durch Bruno Kreisky', *Österreichische Zeitschrift für Politikwissenschaft* 4 (1997): 393–406.

CHAPTER 5

Austria's Media as a Political Test Lab

The Newspaper Tycoons of the Second Republic

On or about 7 April 1945 the Nazi regime shut down *Der Völkische Beobachter* and the *Neues Wiener Tagblatt,* the two newspapers catering for the Vienna area. Propaganda programmes on the radio were becoming severely curtailed by power failures. The first exploratory talks on establishing a new generation of newspapers were taking place against a background where Soviet, U.S. and British soldiers and isolated groups of Austrian Resistance fighters were mopping up pockets of German Wehrmacht and SS units. Soviet planning for the occupation had made advance provision for the speedy reestablishment of the mass media. On his return from Moscow, where he had spent the war years in exile, Ernst Fischer, the leading Communist functionary and former editor of the Socialist *Arbeiter-Zeitung,* was installed by Soviet political officers as the most important proponent of the foundation of new papers.

As early as 21 April 1945 the Red Army started publishing its own German-language newspaper, the *Österreichische Zeitung,* which was produced by an Austrian staff under the direct control of Soviet press officers and kept going until 1955. At the same time the Soviet political officer in charge, a Colonel Piterskiy, gave independent Austrian journalists permission to start a three-party newspaper. When this first appeared (23 April 1945), under the name of *Neues Österreich,* it anticipated not only Austria's declaration of independence (27 April 1945) but also the composition of its new government. The *Neues Österreich* was considered 'the mouthpiece of democratic reconciliation'. Separate party newspapers for the SPÖ, ÖVP and KPÖ were not part of the Soviet officers' original blueprint. The editorial offices in Seidengasse in Vienna's 7th district, today the Austrian headquarters of the almighty WAZ print media conglomerate, also housed the Soviet censorship authority in the person of a female captain by the name of Wichmann. The journalists listened enthusiastically to international radio programmes; in close collaboration with their news-starved readership they produced a highly sought-after paper for Vienna, which soon extended its reach to the rest of the Soviet zone of occupation. It took months for distribution to work without major hitches.

Even in those early days the stage was already being prepared for the first full-blown Austrian newspaper war. All three parties had nominated their representatives for the editorial board of *Neues Österreich:* Paul Deutsch, Karl Renner's brother-in-law and the former editor in chief of the *Wiener Allgemeine Zeitung* for the SPÖ; Paul Husinsky for the ÖVP; and the aforementioned Ernst Fischer, who remained in charge as editor in chief until 1947, for the KPÖ. The meetings of the editorial board were presided over by Rudolf Kalmar, a Catholic journalist and editor in chief of *Der Wiener Tag,* who had survived Dachau concentration camp. However, the concept of proportional representation was not a success in the world of print media, and each party clamoured for a dedicated 'instrument of propaganda', a paper of its own.

'A newspaper that gives three parties the chance to lie must come near to telling the truth.' This summary of the balancing act performed daily at the *Neues Österreich,* provided by one of its readers, glosses over the hardships of journalistic work. At least the first 50,000 copies sold in no time at all, which signalled the birth of a potentially respectable paper. Even though it was subject to censorship by Soviet officers, the fine-tuning that took place within the editorial board made it impossible to assign the paper to any one party. Karl Renner, the chancellor of the interim government, was quick to spot the 'danger'; early in July 1945 he expressed a keen interest in having the *Neues Österreich* transformed as quickly as possible into a 'literary product along the lines of the late *Wiener Zeitung*'. He preferred party newspapers because they were capable of putting across clear and unequivocal messages and of performing 'educational work'. The kind of 'professional pen-pushers and self-serving journalists' at work in the *Neues Österreich* were out of place 'in a time when no one has the leisure to enjoy or produce the fruits of intellectualism'. The *Neues Österreich* was only partly successful in warding off the 'benefits' with which it was always going to be force-fed, and the *Wiener Zeitung* was reborn as a paper in its own right.

On 1 August 1945 the advertising market, which was all-important for the foundation of any new paper, was painstakingly carved up between the *Neues Österreich* and the three party papers that first went to press on 5 August, aligned with the SPÖ, ÖVP and KPÖ respectively: the *Arbeiter-Zeitung, Das Kleine Volksblatt* and the *Österreichische Volksstimme.* For instance, a daily theatre programme was printed free of charge, whereas the publication of a full week's programme had to be paid for. Initially a shortage of pulp limited all papers to a circulation of 100,000. This meant there was no way for the *Neues Österreich* to remain anywhere near its previous maximum circulation of 360,000 and effectively put paid to the idea of an all-party paper.

As of August 1945 it became clear that the party papers had succeeded in securing the lion's share of that scarce commodity, pulp, for themselves. The graph below (Figure 1) shows the dominant position enjoyed in the aftermath of the war by the papers that openly declared their allegiance to one of the parties. Until 1956 and the end of the Allies' presence in Austria, the market share of party dailies was in excess of 50 per cent; in 1995, by which time their share had shrunk to below 3 per cent, their profile was minimal.

In view of these circumstances it is obvious how difficult it was for independent publishers such as Ernst Molden to obtain a licence for the publication of a paper. As of 27 July 1945 a three-party agreement put the party elites of the SPÖ, ÖVP and KPÖ in full control of the start-up procedure for print media. Pulp quota allocation, which received a legal basis in the shape of the Pulp Consumption Regulation Law (Papierverbrauchslenkungsgesetz) in August 1945, proved an effective tool for this purpose. Molden brought a well-known name and excellent political contacts to the fray. The son of the former assistant editor in chief of the *Neue Freie Presse*, Berthold Molden, he had been stigmatized under the Nazi regime as a 'half-Jew' but was spared direct persecution because of his marriage to Paula von Preradovic. He was therefore allowed to publish in the *Südost-Echo* during the Nazi era.

Molden's independent weekly, *Die Presse*, started publication in 1946 with a circulation of 55,000. It harked back to the tradition of the *Neue Freie Presse*, which was apparent also from the fact that 14,000 copies were distributed in neighbouring Eastern and Southeastern Europe, until the onset of the Cold War in 1947 closed that particular avenue. It took *Die Presse* until 19 October 1948 to switch to daily publication. The paper depended for financial support on business circles close to the ÖVP, in particular on the Mautner-Markhof (food and brewery) and on the Lauda (magnesite and other types of mining) conglomerates. The board of owners also included representatives of Maurigg (iron and steel) and Kapsreiter, the latter also holding a brief for Julius Raab, the powerful president of the ÖVP Business Federation. On some issues *Die Presse* was closer to corporate industry than to ÖVP headquarters in Vienna's Palais Todesco.

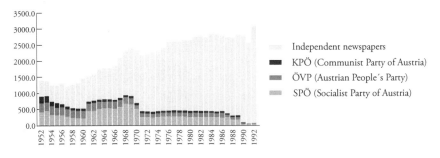

FIGURE I

Circulation of party daily newspapers compared with independent papers (times 1,000); figures rounded

ILLUSTRATION 5.1
*Increasing interest in news in the postwar period led to this line
in front of a newspaper kiosk.*

In the U.S. zone of occupation (Upper Austria and Salzburg) the run-up to
the foundation of a newspaper followed a different pattern. U.S. planning provided
for a strict system of newspaper licensing. In the first phase, German-language
papers were only permitted under direct U.S. supervision. The first paper in German appeared on 30 May 1945 under the name of *Österreichischer Kurier,* in
journalistic terms a mixed bag of copy supplied by the Information Service of the
U.S. Army, which was subject to censorship. As in Vienna, people on the far side
of the zone boundary along the River Enns were even more starved for news than
they were for food. In Zell am See, for instance, a queue that had formed outside
a food store quickly dissolved and re-formed in front of a newspaper kiosk the
moment it opened. In quick succession the same pattern could be seen in the
foundation (on 11 June) of the *Oberösterreichische Nachrichten* and the *Tiroler
Tageszeitung.* The *Österreichischer Kurier,* which had been conceived as a weekly,
was discontinued as of 7 June in favour of the *Salzburger Nachrichten.* U.S. press
officers remarked approvingly on how ready the Austrian staff members were to
toe the line and to follow U.S. guidelines to the letter.

It is interesting to note that the ideas discussed in concrete terms in the U.S.
press corps from August 1945 onwards included granting licences for party papers as well as for provincial ones and copying and enlarging the model of the

Neues Österreich, with its editorial board including all political parties plus the so-called *Unabhängigen,* members of the so-called Independent Party. Towards the end of September 1945 the *Oberösterreichische Nachrichten* was therefore handed over to an editorial committee in which all three parties were represented, together with the *Unabhängigen* in the person of Hans Behrmann and seventeen members in advisory roles. In Salzburg this model failed to work owing to the non-cooperation of the SPÖ and KPÖ. In the end the publishing licence was granted to one individual, a man whom the U.S. press officers had originally refused to clear for journalistic work despite the seven years he had to his credit in the Dachau and Flossenbürg concentration camps. As the former editor in chief of *Sturm über Österreich,* the propaganda publication of the Schuschnigg regime's Ostmärkische Sturmscharen, Gustav A. Canaval was considered to be lacking in basic democratic credentials. Yet he was finally granted the licence to take over the *Salzburger Nachrichten* together with Max Dasch, who was also rooted in the pre-1938 Christian Socialist movement and who had spent the years of the Nazi era at the head of a publishing company in Cracow, which came under occupation by the Wehrmacht after the German invasion of Poland. The *Salzburger Nachrichten* already boasted a circulation of 130,000.

The role that the owners of printing companies played behind the scenes was as important in the years after the war as it is today. In the case of the *Salzburger Nachrichten* the entity involved was the Katholischer Pressverein (with the archbishop of Salzburg, Andreas Rohracher, in the background), whose printing shops had been requisitioned in the Nazi era. It was this Catholic connection, and the fact that Canaval was personally on friendly terms with Julius Raab, that kept the *Salzburger Nachrichten* ideologically committed to the ÖVP party line. However, the paper very soon veered away from the course recommended by its founders, the U.S. authorities, with respect both to the political past of some of its editors and its attitude to National Socialism.

Gerd Bacher, the former CEO of ORF, called Canaval's *Salzburger Nachrichten* 'Austria's School of Journalism'. An astonishing number of journalists who went on to shape Austria's media landscape spent formative years in the editorial office of the *SN* after the war. A case in point is Viktor Reimann, a Catholic nationalist and one of the *Kronenzeitung*'s longest-serving columnists. As early as 1936 he had joined the outlawed NSDAP, and in spite of the four years he spent in prison in the Nazi era his basic instincts remained ultimately irrepressible, as is evidenced by his *Kronenzeitung* series 'The Jews' and by his contributions to controversies regarding the Second World War and National Socialism. He quickly made a name for himself in Western Austria as a vociferous critic of denazification legislation; moreover, he was one of the founders of the VdU (Verein der Unabhängigen), the political home for former members of the NSDAP. Bruno Kornel Skrehunetz, an ethnic German and former militant propagandist of Nazism, even rose to the position of an assistant editor in chief of the paper. During the

Second World War he had advocated the 'complete extermination of Jewry' and a 'defensive struggle' against the 'Bolshevism of the steppe' and 'barbaric American mindlessness'. Two former members of the press corps of the fascist Ustasha regime in Croatia – René Marcic, jurist and press and cultural attaché at Croatia's General Consulate in Vienna, who had fled that city, and Alfons Tomicic-Dalma, the last press attaché at the embassy of Croatia in Hitler's Berlin – both launched themselves on their respective careers from the editorial offices of the *SN*. Marcic was a legal philosopher and university professor in Salzburg, a fervent exponent of the idea of 'natural law' as defined by Catholic thinking in opposition to the 'legal positivism' advocated by Hans Kelsen and his Vienna school. Alfons Dalma, star journalist for the ORF as well as for *Die Presse* and *Die Welt,* was considered an expert on Italy particularly on account of his old connections to the Vatican.

And the list goes on: Hans (Johann) Thür, a former Hitlerjugend squad leader and editor at the *Völkischer Beobachter,* rose to become assistant editor in chief at the *SN* and editor in chief at the *Tiroler Tageszeitung.* The *SN* staff member Rudolf Bayr, who had been an editor on the staff of the *Völkischer Beobachter,* became head of the Culture and Science desk of Austria's state radio in 1971 and CEO of ORF Salzburg (1975–1984). Twelve staff members of *SN* had question marks placed against their names by the U.S. secret service on account of their Nazi political past. It was therefore no accident that the *SN* was vehemently opposed to the policies of denazification or that Dalma polemicized against 'Nigger soldiers'. In the Cold War, on the other hand, the *SN* took up an unambiguous position, as Canaval made quite clear in 1955: 'There are no communists or sympathizers in our ranks.' The line of the paper was no longer defined by a comprehensive discussion of National Socialism but by a political model with strong anti-communist as well as anti-socialist overtones.

While Canaval was always eager to pick a quarrel with the local ÖVP, he remained loyal to Raab and his policies at the federal level. He himself never realized plans to found a fourth Austrian political party, but one of the former leading members of his staff, Viktor Reimann, did just that with the help of another Salzburg newspaper editor, Herbert Kraus, who began to publish the monthly *Berichte und Informationen* in 1946. It was no accident that Canaval also took up the cudgels for one of the few Western European countries that remained a functioning dictatorship until well into the 1960s: he became acting head of the Austro-Spanish Society, which had been founded in 1956 by the former editor in chief of the Christian-Social *Reichspost,* Friedrich Funder.

Canaval and his circle are good examples of a particular problem that beset Austria's postwar development: if one leaves aside the short-lived, party-politically motivated polemics of the SPÖ, no attempt was made to confront and account for Austria's fate under the authoritarian Dollfuß-Schuschnigg regime. Groups like Canaval's became more and more vociferous in their opposition to communism, while the right-wing totalitarian tradition received no attention. This attitude prevented National Socialism, the Second World War and the Holocaust from being analysed and debated in critical terms, particularly as discussion of these matters was considered a danger to the new Austrian postwar order. This does not mean that the members of these journalistic old-boy networks were anti-democratic in their outlook, but it does show that authoritarian models were not considered to be unacceptable in a democratic context. For a long time international authoritarian developments met with positive coverage, as can be seen in reports and commentaries on South Africa, Portugal, Spain and Greece.

Ilse Leitenberger, who had been blooded on the staff of the NSDAP international periodical *Donauzeitung,* joined the *Salzburger Nachrichten* in 1946 and was polemicizing vehemently against denazification in Austria as late as 1985. Gerd Bacher, who by his own admission took great pains to establish himself as Austrian rather than German when he was on the staff of the *Salzburger Volkszeitung* after 1945, was an outspoken and unrelenting anti-communist. He was far less bothered by post-1945 European dictatorships: ORF staffers who filed critical reports on the dictatorship in Greece at the end of the 1960s were fired on his orders. So were the young freelance ORF journalists in the 1990s who reported on the involvement of one of Bacher's personal friends, Fritz Molden, in U.S. secret-service projects. The glories of anti-communism were not to be sullied. When topics such as war guilt or Austrian nationhood surfaced in the Waldheim controversy of the 1980s, Bacher was unable to muster any sympathy for the line taken by Catholic anti-fascists.

It did not take U.S. press officers long to realize that the ideology of the *SN*'s editorial team had within it a strain of traditional anti-Americanism. Charges of political impropriety had been brought by Austrian staff at the Public Affairs Office, a U.S. agency, against a VdU MP. When Canaval tried to get the head of the Public Affairs Office to refrain from pressing these charges, a U.S. official by the name of Hopman stopped the regular payments to Canaval that had been initiated by his predecessor. The MP concerned had defended Adolf Hitler in a speech and remained an unreformed National Socialist as late as 1953. Soon afterwards, Hopman was attacked by Gustav Zeilinger, another MP, for curtailing the time allowed to the VdU on the radio for election broadcasts; in this attack, Hopman was referred to as 'a certain Abraham Nathan Hopman', who was probably on the payroll of the 'Russians' anyway – had the U.S. not shipped arms to the Soviet Union in the Second World War? This was a sure way to bring into play the two main ideological biases of the Wehrmacht generation, anti-Semitism and anti-Bolshevism.

In a paradoxical development in the 1960s, it was this *SN* group of journalists, and more especially Karl Heinz Ritschel, that instigated a nationwide debate on the need to reform the Austrian model of *Proporz,* to give room to more forms of participatory democracy and to reduce the influence of the political parties and of the organs of the state on decision making processes.

On the editorial team of the *Oberösterreichische Nachrichten* in Linz, Hans Behrmann, a little-known outsider with the additional handicaps of German nationality and what political observers of the time sneered at as 'Jewish looks', gained the upper hand. Behrmann, who originally hailed from Romania, had worked for the publishing house of Ullstein before the war and had survived several spells in Dachau concentration camp. In 1947 U.S. experts saw in him 'the strongest pillar of independent journalism' in Austria. At that time he was already working on a project for launching a cheap tabloid for Vienna to open up new markets for the publishing house. He was quick to organize an independent distribution system for the paper, later made use of by the *Salzburger Nachrichten* and *Tiroler Tageszeitung*. Another interesting point to note is the highly innovative model for profit sharing practised by the paper: 25 per cent of net profit was added to the operating capital, 25 per cent went to pay for social security for the staff and 50 per cent financed the publication of important books. It was Behrmann's arrest for a breach of customs regulations that was to put an end to one of the most interesting postwar media careers. Today Behrmann is one the forgotten figures of Austrian media history.

As the *Oberösterreichische Nachrichten* under Behrmann followed an independent course, with increased circulation (200,000 in 1947) and expansion to eastern Austria as its top priorities, the paper was repeatedly at loggerheads with the ÖVP owing to a clash of political and commercial interests. In the wake of the 1947 currency reform all newspapers registered a drop in circulation; printing and distribution systems alike were affected. As the de facto devaluation of the currency ate into people's disposable income, fewer newspapers were bought. In 1946 people had often bought several papers a day; now they were forced to economize and made do with one. In 1948 Behrmann's distribution organization finally filed for bankruptcy. The *Wiener Kurier* in particular threatened to start legal proceedings to recover financial losses, but Behrmann's American political network was still in place and saw off the threat.

Behrmann's role as someone who shaped media history was not yet over, even if he never managed to cease to be an outsider. When he sold his share in the *Oberösterreichische Nachrichten,* he chose not to sell to the ÖVP grandee and former concentration camp inmate Alfred Maleta, preferring Novitas Ltd., which was controlled by the head of the publishing house of *Die Presse.* It was 1954 before Maleta was finally able to purchase this share.

The crisis the *Oberösterreichische Nachrichten* was plunged into by its editor's arrest by the fraud squad in 1952 underlined how important Austria's nationalized banks were for the print media. Alfred Maleta, ÖVP general secretary since 1951, managed to obtain a bridging loan at very favourable rates from a fellow member of the ÖVP, Creditanstalt-Bankverein CEO Josef Joham. In the 'newspaper wars' that unfolded during the following years, the Creditanstalt CEO played a leading role alongside the CEOs of the Länderbank, which was traditionally close to the SPÖ, and of the trade union-controlled BAWAG. Austria's market was so undercapitalized that only the big banks and a few industrial magnates had at their disposal the capital that was needed either to keep a paper afloat or to launch a new one.

In 1955 Maleta merged the *Oberösterreichische Nachrichten* with the *Tagespost,* which had been given a new lease of life after 1953 by the publishing house of Wimmer. At the same time Behrmann was actively involved in bringing off a new project he had been mulling over since the 1940s: a tabloid for Vienna. The financiers for their part cared not only about circulation but also about political content and new, attractive packaging. Among the documents in the safe of Austria's foreign minister of the time, Leopold Figl, was a memorandum dealing with 'Projekt Bildtelegraph' that characterizes the planned paper as follows: 'A midday daily is in the planning stage that will be different from the papers already in existence – the American 'Wiener Kurier', the socialist 'Weltpresse' and the communist 'Abend' – in that it will be independent of any political party and representative in its tenor of the centre right. In addition to this it will be Austria's first illustrated paper.'

With syndicated articles from the *Salzburger* and the *Tiroler Nachrichten* and with operating capital from the same sources, half a million schillings from Behrmann and a loan of two million from the Socialist-dominated Länderbank, the paper was budgeted to become profitable once it reached a circulation of 50,000. Canaval had seconded one of his *SN* journalists to the new paper by installing Gerd Bacher as its editor in chief. The *Bild-Telegraph* was, it has to be said, Austria's first tabloid in the mould of the German *Bildzeitung,* even if Bacher today tries to pass it off in retrospect as essentially a training centre for quality journalists. Sex and sensationalism were employed to push the paper towards its break-even point.

Party politics made repeated attempts to infiltrate the media by exploiting the weak financial basis of newspapers. For instance, in 1958 Behrmann took over Canaval's share in the *Bild-Telegraph* using money supplied by the Vienna ÖVP leader Fritz Polcar. Soon afterwards Polcar had to leave the political stage because of financial irregularities. That year the paper was unable to pay the printers' bills, and Fritz Molden made use of a legal technicality to relaunch the paper, with help from Bacher, as the *Bild-Telegramm.* With the backing of the ÖVP shareholders of the *Bild-Telegraph,* Behrmann managed to persuade the owner of the *Kurier,* Ludwig Polsterer, to keep the paper afloat. A team of professional journalists from the *Kurier* – its editor in chief at the time, Hans Dichand; the assistant editor in chief, Hugo Portisch; Reinhard Hübl; and Karl Heinz Ritschel – succeeded in getting the *Bild-Telegraph* into the kiosks again two days later. Later in the same year, however, Polsterer dropped the project for good. According to Hans Dichand in his memoirs, the SPÖ had bought the newspaper licence from Polsterer. This was done to smooth the planned *Express's* path into the cramped Austrian tabloid market by removing a competitor.

When Molden appeared to be losing the first Viennese newspaper war, he switched to other financiers and tried his hand at a new venture. Working with Bacher and with capital from the Socialist branch of the trade unions, he launched the tabloid *Express*. To begin with, Bacher and Molden jointly held a majority shareholding of 51 per cent. Bacher succeeded in pushing circulation from 142,800 in 1958 to 218,700 in 1961. On the advice of Christian Broda, a lawyer and future minister of justice, the SPÖ thereupon used a clause in the original contract to buy a majority share. The paper's political function now went beyond positive reporting on the trade union movement to the downright propagation of SPÖ party politics. The SPÖ's 'T-shirt' (Bruno Kreisky's term for the *Express*, emphasizing how different it was from the party's 'tailcoat', the *Arbeiter-Zeitung*) continued to flourish and pushed its circulation through the 300,000 barrier in 1965. The *Arbeiter-Zeitung*, on the other hand, had already dropped to 123,700 in 1958 and slumped to 115,000 by 1965.

In 1968–69 the *Express* slipped down to number three on the circulation charts, having been overtaken both by the *Kronenzeitung* and the *Kurier*. Losses had been piling up since 1966 and reached 20 million schillings for the year 1969. A brief respite, largely due to the formula 'more boobs, less politics' introduced by the German tabloid expert Ewald Wilhelm Struwe (*Bild* and *Neue Illustrierte*), failed to achieve a turnaround. In December 1971 the Socialist publishing house Vorwärts sold the *Express* to the owners of the *Kronenzeitung*, Hans Dichand and Kurt Falk, who shut the paper down as a publication in its own right on 28 April 1971, merging the remnants with the *Kronenzeitung*. The *Express* shared the *Bild-Telegraph*'s fate; it was purchased and shut down by the *Kronenzeitung*, which became an ever bigger fish in a persistently small pond.

Theodor Venus[1] has produced an analysis of the 'great print solution', as it was called, which could have led to a reorganization of the still substantial Socialist press holdings under the umbrella of the Druck- und Verlagsanstalt Vorwärts AG. The BAWAG subsidiary Ingebe, which, like BAWAG itself, was controlled by the trade unions, had bought both the Elbemühl printing house and the Pressehaus in 1969. Yet neither bankers nor trade unionists were capable of coping with the grand media design that was made possible by this move or with the risks involved in such a major venture.

When Dichand and Falk were taken on board as partners on 15 July 1970, a move that was made contingent on the *Kronenzeitung*'s editors' agreement to report favourably on the SPÖ at least for a time, decay set in not only at the *Express* but also in Socialist publishing policy as a whole. The same aversion to entrepreneurial risk-taking, coupled with excessive costs and the whole system of political patronage, was ultimately also to spell the end for the *Arbeiter-Zeitung* and the publishing house of Vorwärts. If the 1969 project entertained by Kreisky and others had succeeded in transforming the *Express* into a daily free from party-political allegiances and comparable in quality to the *Süddeutsche Zeitung*, the development of Austria's press would have taken a different direction and it would arguably have been possible for a greater diversity of opinion to exist in the mass circulation market. Instead, the SPÖ indirectly and unwittingly contributed to the concentration of the tabloid market that its political strategists, notably the powerful trade union president and minister of the interior, Franz Olah, had regarded as an answer to the decline of party papers. Instead of supporting diversification the SPÖ found itself aiding and abetting the *Kronenzeitung*, which was soon to drop its favourable take on Kreisky's solo governments. Without the support it received from the Socialist Vice-Chancellor Bruno Pittermann, with whom the pro-ÖVP journalist Hans Dichand had struck up a friendship, and without the financial resources of the trade unions, which Franz Olah used for the start-up of the paper, Dichand's brainchild, the new *Kronenzeitung*, would never have seen the light of day.

At the end of the 1920s, as a child in a makeshift camp on the outskirts of Graz, Dichand had devoured the *Kronenzeitung* and had been confirmed by it in the choice of his future profession. As early as 1953 he and Fritz Molden had made an unsuccessful attempt to find financiers for a revival of the *Kronenzeitung*. The old *Kronenzeitung* had had a circulation of 100,000 in 1906, rising to 300,000 readers every Sunday in 1938, when the owner, Gustav Davis, had been forced to sell to the *Berliner Verlag* on totally ludicrous terms. After the proclamation of 'all-out war' the paper was closed down, even though it had conformed to the Nazi ideology as of 13 March 1938.

After Dichand had left the *Kurier*, Pittermann offered him the post of editor in chief of *Das Kleine Blatt*, a pioneer of the tabloid format, which had been a match for the *Kronenzeitung* prior to 1934 but had been demoted to the position of a low-circulation weekly after 1945 by Oscar Pollak, who was worried that it might encroach on the readership of the *Arbeiter-Zeitung*. Yet Dichand wanted to realize his dream of the *Kronenzeitung*. With his *Kurier* 'golden handshake' of 90,000 schillings and money from his business partner Kurt Falk, he bought the rights to the title of *Kronenzeitung* for 170,000 schillings. Even though they were then virtually broke, Dichand and Falk were granted a loan of 12 million by the *Zentralsparkasse* at the behest of the trade union president, Franz Olah. The business plan for the *Kronenzeitung* provided for an operating capital of 10 million, which in actual fact became 14, and the first net profit was expected after three to four years.

The paper in fact made a profit as early as 1962. Olah's fiat had 'solved' the issue of sureties for the required capital without the need for such traditional instruments as formal guarantees or collaterals. Olah had also found a sleeping partner for the venture in Frankfurt, who was later revealed to be an Austrian businessman, Ferdinand Karpik. Karpik played the role of financier and held a 50 per cent stake in what was to prove the last great newspaper to be founded after the war. It was also the most risk-fraught, and Karpik sold his share for 15 million in 1966 before Olah was put on trial, charged by his former employer with embezzlement of trade union funds.[2]

In retrospect it is reasonably clear that the goings-on surrounding the foundation of the *Kronenzeitung* amounted to the biggest phoney deal in the history of paper start-ups in the Second Republic. If the paper had flopped, the bank would have found it impossible to realize on the sureties. Again and again attempts were made to prove that Franz Olah in fact owned a share in the *Kronenzeitung*, for instance by a group represented by the lawyer Ewald Weninger or, as early as 1968, by Richard Drasche, whose real estate deals with the city of Vienna had made him a millionaire. Fritz Molden, too, tried his luck again, as the deal to have the *Kronenzeitung* printed at the *Pressehaus* proved none too lucrative. Yet this chapter was closed once and for all in spite of or because of, Olah's trial. Dichand cleverly reached out to Olah's successor as trade union president, Anton Benya; subsequently the ÖGB bought Fritz Molden's share in the *Pressehaus* only to resell it to Dichand and Falk via the BAWAG.

As far back as 1972 the joint proprietors of the *Kronenzeitung* tried to strengthen their hold on the tabloid and mass media market through a merger with their rival, the *Kurier*. Kurt Falk tried to pass off talks with Ludwig Polsterer, who was thinking of selling the *Kurier*, as no more than a cost-cutting exercise dealing solely with distribution. If things had gone according to plan, the ÖGB was again going to have a role, but this time its position was entirely above board as the potential financier of the merger using the BAWAG as its proxy. As the *Kronenzeitung* was still projecting a line in sympathy with the SPÖ – which did not change until the controversy surrounding the Sternwartepark in 1973 – the BAWAG-financed merger between *Kronenzeitung* and *Kurier* was considered a project of the left. In the end Falk's plan was realized with a helping hand from the German WAZ group, the Westdeutscher Allgemeiner Zeitungsverlag: in 1987, this Essen-based corporation bought 45 per cent of the *Kronenzeitung* and 49.6 per cent of the *Kurier*. The firm of Mediaprint (ownership: 70 per cent *Kronenzeitung*, 30 per cent *Kurier*) was put in charge of advertising sales, printing and distribution for both dailies.

The End of the Party Papers and the Collapse of the SPÖ Media Holdings

In the years immediately after the war the SPÖ had at its disposal Austria's largest print and publishing conglomerate, gathered under the umbrella of Konzentration, a holding company with its base in the publishing house of Vorwärts in the former Socialist Party headquarters in Rechte Wienzeile. However, in the 1980s and 1990s it was forced to shut down both its own party paper, the *Arbeiter-Zeitung*, and the Vorwärts publishers. As early as the 1970s heavy losses at the

Arbeiter-Zeitung had signalled that both the publishing house and the printing outfit were under threat. In contrast, the ÖVP was at least able to maintain a token presence in the political landscape through the medium of its ideological affiliates. One might cite in particular the Raiffeisen organization, which held the majority share of 50.4 per cent in the *Kurier*, or publishing houses with Catholic leanings such as Styria, which held the majority share of 51 per cent in the *Presse* and was sole proprietor of the *Kleine Zeitung*. While the SPÖ remained committed to its centralist ways, the ÖVP, as the opposition party, was forced to operate through a string of relatively autonomous entities, which mirrored the loosely knit structure of the party itself. From the point of view of party strategy, however, this system was becoming less reliable than it had been in the late 1950s, as was to be demonstrated by the *Kurier* campaign against the ÖVP-FPÖ coalition in 2000.

A series of newspaper wars and consolidations within the media market has resulted in Austria having a low density of nationwide dailies compared with the rest of Europe. At the same time, the *Kronenzeitung* has in the last decade gained a dominant position in the tabloid market that is without parallel. Take Norway, with its more than 100 dailies for four million inhabitants, and then consider Austria, dominated in 2006 by the *Kronenzeitung* with a reach of 43.8 per cent and sales of 1.0 million. The *Kronenzeitung* is showing a slight drop in circulation, but its closest rival in 2006, the *Kleine Zeitung*, had sales languishing at 300,000 and a reach of only 12.2 per cent.

In the weeklies market the SPÖ likewise failed to turn its considerable latent potential into tangible results. A promising project hatched by young academics and intellectuals close to the SPÖ had its operating capital withdrawn at Franz Olah's behest in a poorly attended party leadership meeting: the *Heute* had dared to publish outspoken criticism of SPÖ ministers and politicians. The *Express*, too, ultimately fell victim to Olah's heavy political hand and demand for total control over editorial policy. Molden and Bacher had been able to get the group of financiers around Christian Broda to agree to an independent, liberal line for their paper, but Olah continued to insist on his right to intervene directly in editorial matters, which in the end caused Molden and Bacher to throw in the towel at the *Express*.

By the end of the 1950s the options for the foundation of new dailies already seemed to be largely exhausted. It took until the end of the 1980s for another 'revival' to be launched. The *Standard*, founded with financial help from the German publishing house Springer and the initiative of Oscar Bronner, the founder of *Profil*, was designed to cater to a leftist, liberal readership. When *AZ*, the successor to the *Arbeiter-Zeitung*, was closed down, the list of the subscribers to the paper was handed over to the *Standard*. In 2004 the *Standard* had a circulation of 88,318 as against 97,950 for the *Presse*, which had defined a new niche for itself on the right of centre, with a reach of 5.4 per cent compared to the *Presse*'s 4.4 per cent. In 2006 the Fellner brothers launched a daily, *Österreich,* which is levelled at the target group of young readers and attempts to lure readers in this segment away from the *Kronenzeitung* and the *Kurier.*

Given the *Kronenzeitung's* market position and reach, a rightist tabloid now dominates the Austrian newspaper scene in a manner not found anywhere else. Even in absolute figures the paper is the seventh-best seller among European dailies, and when this figure is put into relation to Austria's eight million inhabitants, the *Krone's* unique market dominance becomes clear. The political consequences have been equally clear at least since the 1970s: in the long term, every political party that aspires to a mass impact has to make its peace with the idiosyncratic line of the *Krone,* which in some of its leaders is far to the right of centre. In this context it is less important for the paper to show goodwill to political top candidates – to date Viktor Klima is the last Social Democratic federal chancellor to be accorded such an honour – than to keep up a steady flow of political messages. Even the majority shareholder of the *Kronenzeitung,* Hans Dichand, got a taste of the forces of inertia at work in the paper's reporting on basic political facts and even more so in its leading articles, when he went flat out in his opposition to an ÖVP-FPÖ coalition in the weeks before that coalition became a fact – thanks in large part to the editorial line of his own paper! Both through its special 'court bulletins', featuring Jörg Haider and his indiscriminate broadsides against the Grand Coalition, and through the way it covered individual topics, the *Krone* found itself in the unlikely role of midwife to the very coalition one of its owners had sought to prevent.

Bruno Kreisky had tried to counter the development of this kind of monopoly, which began to manifest itself at the end of the 1960s and in the early 1970s. This was the reason why he did not support the plans of the ÖGB and BAWAG to finance the jumbo merger of *Krone* and *Kurier* in 1972. In retrospect his misgivings regarding market domination look like astute prognoses, yet what was foremost in people's minds in 1972 were the 1,930,000 readers of a phantom monster paper, the *Krone-Kurier* (the *Kronenzeitung* had 1,356,000 regular readers and the *Kurier* 905,000, with a further 331,000 taking both papers). State subsidies for print media were put forward as a way of saving even more papers from folding. In July 1975 a federal law was passed that provided the legal basis for daily papers and magazines to be subsidized: in 1982, for instance, the total sum earmarked for dailies was 73 million schillings, whilst magazines were to receive 7 million. This may appear a pittance at first sight, as everyone was to take a share, even if – as in the case of the mass papers – it was only a small one. Apportioning the subsidies according to actual need was obviously impossible to sell politically, but even so, the system of subsidies provided real help to small papers. Yet the underlying trend proved impossible to stem. By 1972 it was clear that print media concentration in Austria was second only to that in Ireland, where four dailies accounted for 82 per cent of total circulation: the *Kronenzeitung,*

Kurier, Kleine Zeitung and *Arbeiter-Zeitung* between them had a market share of 71 per cent.

In the same year the Catholic Church, which was economically highly successful in the publishing and printing fields, saved the *Kurier* from a dreaded takeover by the 'left', making use of the Steirische Verlagsanstalt Styria, which was owned by the Catholic Printing Association of the diocese of Graz. Joining forces with the industrialist owners of the *Wochenpresse,* the Church bought the *Kurier* for around 450 million schillings. Once again it was 'black' (ÖVP-connected) banks that were involved behind the scenes; after all, 200 million had to be raised in the form of loans. It will be found that it is always the same cast of printers and bankers that plays the decisive role in the takeovers of newspapers. This is as true today as it was in the 1970s.

Both the SPÖ and Franz Olah acting on his own tried to intervene in the struggles for the small Austrian print media market through overt, or in Olah's case covert, financial and loan arrangements. The ÖVP on the other hand promoted what was dressed up as private ownership. However, private financiers were few and far between in the undercapitalized postwar era. One way out, as happened in the case of Ludwig Polsterer, was to couple promised finance with a secret agreement to steer a course sympathetic to the ÖVP. Another option consisted in using shares in a paper to place people in strategic positions where they could channel party-political influence into the newly forming print media landscape. An example of this is the Wirtschaftsbund, which, with Julius Raab's consent and help from Fred Ungart, a highly successful public relations businessman, managed to acquire the newspaper printers Die Presse.

Media Moguls

This takeover marked the end of the first stage of Fritz P. Molden's career. He was one of the most important actors on the media stage in the 1950s and 1960s in spite of his relative youth (he was born in 1924). Molden joined the Neue Wiener Presse-, Druck- und Verlagsgesellschaft m.b.H. as head of its publishing division in 1949. His record as an active resistance fighter had given him excellent political contacts with U.S. personnel; these were further bolstered by his (brief) marriage to Joan Dulles, whose father Allen Dulles was one of the founders of the CIA and was to become its first civilian director in 1953. Molden had lobbied successfully for the licensing of the daily *Die Presse* when he was secretary to Foreign Minister Karl Gruber in 1945–46. After the death of his father, Ernst Molden, in 1953 he became the publisher of *Die Presse* and the *Wochenpresse.*

He tried his hand unsuccessfully in the political sphere by advocating the entry into government of the right-leaning VdU. More successful in the media business, Molden rented the old Steyrermühl printing shop in Vienna's Fleischmarkt and seemed to be on the way to becoming a newspaper czar. He succeeded in breaking the ÖVP and SPÖ hold on large printers. His ultimate failure, when it came, was due to party-political interventions, particularly on the part of the ÖVP and its Federal Chancellor Julius Raab. Raab had been damaged by Molden's investigative journalism – particularly in the case of Fritz Polcar and the scandal surrounding donations to the political parties made by the failed steel tycoon Haselgruber, and was determined to put an end to this kind of thing. He turned once again to Josef Joham, the CEO of Creditanstalt-Bankverein, who was asked to call Molden off. Molden's position was made clear: if he did not come to heel he would find current loans being called in with no further advances to be had from any banks close to the ÖVP.

In the *Express* Molden seemed to have a mass-circulation paper on his hands. His contacts with such SPÖ politicians as Christian Broda and Bruno Kreisky were facilitated by the record of anti-communist activity these three men had in common. In 1959, for example, with help from Broda, Kreisky and other SPÖ and conservative functionaries, Molden organized a large-scale festival to counter the communist-dominated international youth jamboree in Vienna. Julius Raab, the ÖVP chancellor, was not impressed, but the CIA obliged with substantial financial aid.

Molden, whose sympathies tended to be with the conservative half of the political spectrum, managed to acquire the financial means necessary for his projects both from the ÖVP and the SPÖ, depending on the nature of those projects. He had a way of cleverly making use of the changes in the media landscape in his search for party funds for his print media and publishing projects. Despite all this, Fritz Molden found himself increasingly confronted by both political and financial difficulties and had to sell off in steady succession the *Express, Wochenpresse, Abendzeitung* and, ultimately, *Die Presse.* In 1962 his only remaining asset was his project for Austria's only state-of-the-art large printing plant, the Pressehaus in Vienna. This, too, had to be sold to a subsidiary of the Bank für Arbeit und Wirtschaft in 1970. Soon the Pressehaus, which at that time also printed the *Express, Die Presse* and the *Wochenpresse,* was taken over by its most powerful client, the *Kronenzeitung.* There was no choice: if the *Krone,* which was threatening to build its own printing plant, had withdrawn its custom, the Pressehaus would have had to close down.

The two actors who really called the shots in the 1970s did not share Molden's Viennese upper middle-class background. They were men from the provinces: Hans Dichand hailed from Graz and Gerd Bacher from Salzburg. Both had started their careers after 1945. Molden had repeatedly risked his life as a resistance fighter during the Nazi era, while both Dichand and Bacher had conformed during the 'Third Reich' and served in the German Wehrmacht. Neither man was a stranger to conflict with the occupying authorities after the war. Dichand, starting his career in Styria under the British system, had frequently run into problems with British press officers. Bacher, operating in U.S.-controlled Salzburg as a member of Canaval's team at the *Salzburger Nachrichten,* adapted more smoothly to existing conditions, but still the U.S. press officer Abraham N. Hopman found it necessary to intervene again and again to ensure a less aggressive tone in the reporting of the Salzburg print media, sometimes even to the extent of hinting at withdrawal of the licence of the *Salzburger Nachrichten.*

Early on in their careers both Bacher and Dichand moved to Vienna. Bacher joined Canaval at the *Bild-Telegraph,* and Dichand, who was blooded at the *Murtaler Zeitung,* tried his hand at the ÖVP paper *Neue Wiener Tageszeitung* alongside Hugo Portisch in 1949–50. Dichand and Portisch both realized that little could be hoped for from the paper, whose editorial line was repeatedly thrown off course by erratic and contradictory party-political directives. For instance, 1949 had seen the ÖVP decreeing an anti-fascist election campaign following the breakdown of secret talks between the ÖVP, the VdU and ex-NSDAP functionaries: 1950 saw this edict revoked. In such conditions mass circulation was out of the question.

After four years with the *Kleine Zeitung* Dichand joined the paper that was the direct successor to the daily put out by the U.S. authorities, the *Wiener Kurier.* Once again it was Fritz Molden (this time working with Ludwig Polsterer, an industrialist with extensive holdings in mills, and a former U.S. film officer, the expatriate Ernst Haeusserman) who was pulling strings behind the scenes, persuading the State Department to allow the *Wiener Kurier* a new lease of life as the *Neuer Kurier* rather than simply closing it down. Party politics was soon to affect the new paper: the ÖVP Arbeiter- und Angestelltenbund (ÖAAB) held a 50 per cent share in the Waldheim Eberle printing plant (seized by the Nazis in 1938 but operated by its original owners between 1945 and 1948) and let it be known that the ÖVP intended to exercise concrete influence on the *Neue Kurier.* At this juncture Molden withdrew, whilst Polsterer stayed and formed a partnership with Alfred Maleta, who was already active in the media scene in Upper Austria, and with Franz Karmel, a journalist with ÖVP sympathies. In an agreement that was supposed to remain secret Polsterer promised that the paper would always support Federal Chancellor Julius Raab. Later, Polsterer was able to purchase the ÖAAB's share, and the paper's room for manoeuvre increased.

Political interventions tend to be more subtle these days, orchestrated with networking power brokers and tightly knit groups of insiders as their preferred conduit. In his memoirs Franz Vranitzky[3] has given graphic accounts of the workings of his policy of 'pragmatic discourse' with the founder and editor of the *Kronenzeitung,* Hans Dichand: in their conversations he would articulate his political positions on a number of concrete topics and was guaranteed at least a hearing and some notice of the positions the paper was planning to take. What he was unable to change was the overall editorial line of subtle rightist populism, spiralling on occasion and with some commentators into downright rightist radicalism.

Black Radio Waves, Red Screen:
How Radio and Television Evolved after 1945

In the sphere of radio broadcasting, Allied information and propaganda officers followed a course similar to the one they pursued with the print media. They took immediate control of the transmitter stations expanded and operated by the Nazi regime with such great success. The U.S. and Great Britain directly monitored the operation of the 'Rot-Weiß-Rot' group of radio stations in Salzburg and in Linz (with an additional studio in Vienna as of October 1945) and the group of stations called Alpenland Graz, whereas the Soviets contented themselves at first with inserting a 'Russian Hour' into RAVAG, which featured classical themes, and with the censorship of news programmes. RAVAG itself (Radioverkehrs-AG) was relaunched by its pre-1938 owner, Oskar Ceija, on 29 April 1945. However, the programmes needed to be submitted for approval not only to the culture department of the Red Army but also to the Amt für Kultur und Volksbildung (the Office for Culture and Popular Education) of the City of Vienna – and so faced authoritarian constraints on all levels. Ceija was quickly ousted from his position when the Communist *Volksstimme* accused him of having been close to the NSDAP. He had also filed high compensation claims against the Republic based on his ownership of RAVAG prior to 1938 and its seizure in that year. RAVAG was expropriated for a second time and, having previously been declared German property, now came under Austrian administration and Soviet control.

Until 1947 the double censorship of radio programmes according to the principle of *Proporz* as well as Soviet criteria functioned relatively smoothly. However, the Cold War saw a heightening of Soviet interference to the point of demanding (unsuccessfully) that manuscripts of speeches by Austrian politicians be subject to Soviet censorship. In the same period, the number of ideological broadcasts in the 'Russian Hour' increased, with control passing to Austrian Communists as of 1946–47. This development peaked in the controversies centring on the September and October strikes of 1950, which the KPÖ supported. However, interventions in favour of news items of predominantly Soviet interest or against specific programmes remained the exception – in general, the Soviets were content with their allotted 'Russian Hour'.

The dispensation that had been put in place in regard to Austrian radio by the Allied administration and the effects of the Cold War did not survive the year 1955. At this point the coalition government of ÖVP and SPÖ enforced a centralist model in which regional studios continued to exist but had the scope of their operations curtailed. The opportunity to create a pluralistic and regionally diversified broadcasting system comparable to the model installed in Germany was wasted. While the staff of the U.S. 'Rot-Weiß-Rot' group of stations had no problems finding employment in Austria's broadcasting corporation, the programme coordinators and artists of the 'Russian Hour' found themselves blacklisted after 1954 and thus under a virtual employment ban. To this group belonged the whole ensemble of the 'Neues Theater in der Scala'. Individuals fared differently: highly gifted and successful actors of the caliber of Karl Paryla, Otto Tausig and Hortense Raky remained stigmatized for years, whilst others, like Fritz Muliar, were soon able to shake off the stigma.

It was one of the consequences of Austria's almost total integration into the Western bloc during the Cold War that this kind of witch-hunt and employment ban went largely unnoticed by the public. Due in large part to the reporting in the *Neuer Kurier* and the *Presse,* the termination of the highly popular entertainment and literature programmes of the 'Rot-Weiß-Rot' group of radio stations that had expressed the mood of the time garnered much more attention. Under the aegis of Jörg Mauthe, writers and intellectuals such as Ingeborg Bachmann, Hans Weigel, Peter Weiser, Walter Davy, Alfred Böhm or Werner Riemerschmid made up the script department of these programmes. Highly popular cabaret programmes such as *Der Watschenmann* and *Brettl vorm Kopf,* the fruit of the collaboration of Carl Merz, Helmut Qualtinger and Gerhard Bronner, served as bulwarks against the absorption of 'Rot-Weiß-Rot' into the state-owned radio corporation. Nevertheless, lack of capital and the political tendencies of both the ÖVP and of the Socialist minister in charge of broadcasting, Karl Waldbrunner, forced the 'Rot-Weiß-Rot' group of stations to fold on 27 July 1995. Neither Ludwig Polsterer nor a group of industrialists around Manfred Mautner-Markhof, Jr., were able to raise the operating capital necessary to enable the Viennese group of stations, which had a staff of 160 and an annual budget of 20 million schillings, to remain in operation.

Back in 1951 'Rot-Weiß-Rot', with its audience of three million, was setting itself up as formidable competition for RAVAG, which had a reputation among younger listeners as a boring medium committed to the political status quo. In 1954 Vorarlberg's government petitioned the Constitutional Court, hoping for a ruling in favour of the provinces concerning the distribution of the radio licensing fees. Instead, the court found that 'the broadcasting system is in its entirety and in all its organizational, technological and cultural aspects part of the telegraph system; therefore, in accordance with Art. 10, §1, l. 9 of the Constitution, it is subject to federal authority in terms both of legislation and execution'. At the same time, the transmitter stations and studios in the Tyrol, which had been under French control until that date, were handed over to the public administration of the Austrian broadcasting system, even though this was technically still considered to be German property at the time. Vorarlberg put up only token opposition with a short-lived refusal to hand over the regional studio at Dornbirn.

After the decision in favour of a centralized monopoly, buffered to a certain extent by the regional studios, post-1955 discourse focused again and again on the issue of political control versus independence. In 1954 a social-science working group had presented three options for discussion, namely, a centralized version based in Vienna with a unified financial and technological structure, which was to include possibilities for regional productions; an extreme federalist model, with a radio station for every one of the nine provinces; and a semi-federalist compromise, with three broadcasting corporations enjoying equal status (Vienna and Lower Austria; Upper Austria, Salzburg, the Tyrol and Vorarlberg; Styria, Carinthia and Burgenland). While local radio stations are no longer an issue today, the economic problems of 1955 were such that even experts despaired of being able to finance the required technological equipment. Another obstacle that blocked a U.S.-style liberalization of radio stations was the state's monopoly on information. This held even within the U.S. zone, where U.S. information officers insisted on monopoly control and a ban on the promulgation of ideologies other than their own. There was never any attempt even within the U.S. zone to realize the U.S. model in Austria.

Both the ÖVP and SPÖ had their minds set on centralized models in the 1950s and 1960s; they differed only over what form the organizational structure should take. The SPÖ campaigned – along the lines of the first draft of the Broadcasting Law – for an institution regulated by public law comprising twenty-four representatives of the parties, two shop stewards and delegates from officially recognized religious groups and professional associations. The ÖVP, on the other hand, wanted this role to be assigned to a private not-for-profit organization. This meant in essence that the state was going to hold the majority of shares. After his success at the polls in 1956, Raab took another step backwards by demanding a legal initiative along the lines of the pre-1938 RAVAG, which was subject to state supervision in its news programmes and in the overall 'moral' orientation of programmes. Here as in other cases Raab was simply incapable of envisaging a time when the federal chancellor was not someone nominated by the ÖVP. Still less, of course, could he envisage the ÖVP being excluded even from a coalition government and thus rendered incapable of playing even the role of a junior partner in governing and controlling the country. Others in his party were less sanguine, but the vehement protests of ÖVP-dominated provinces such as Salzburg were countered by pointing to the continued existence of regional radio stations. After a protracted tug-of-war the ORF (Österreichische Rundfunk Gesellschaft m.b.H. = Austrian Broadcasting Company) finally saw the light of day on 1 January 1958.

Its complicated structure made sure that the federal authorities had the advantage over the provinces. The board was a foursome appointed by the ÖVP and SPÖ on the basis of the system of *Proporz;* unanimity was required in budget and personnel issues. When there was a hung vote, the CEO was to have a casting vote. The *Proporz* mechanism, routinely applied to personnel decisions, began to paralyse radio operations as well as the new medium of television that had started a trial operation in 1955. When the editor in chief of the *Neuer Kurier,* Hugo Portisch, together with Hermann Stöger and a number of other journalists and newspaper publishers, started to collect the signatures of protesters against a new

Proporz agreement, the *Kleine Zeitung* (Graz) and the *Wochenpresse* joined the chase. When media pressure failed to bring about any change, the group managed to organize a concerted effort in which fifty-two newspapers and magazines all demanded a referendum concerning the future of radio. A total of 832,353 Austrians were to vote in this referendum, a striking manifestation of the revulsion the system of *Proporz* had already provoked. The debate signalled clearly that the public was no longer prepared to accept the ubiquitous political influence of the two big parties in regard either to the filling of vacancies according to Austria's electoral colour scheme or the programming of radio and television. Many people were deeply impressed by this show of civil opposition against the party state; among them, incidentally, was the then seventeen-year-old Arnold Schwarzenegger, who, as has already been mentioned, sees a connection between his (unconventional) plebiscitary methods as governor of California and this experience of directly participatory democracy.

It is undoubtedly one of the merits of Josef Klaus as federal chancellor to have brought about a higher degree of professionalism in this area, particularly by installing as CEO the experienced journalist Gerd Bacher, who introduced tried and proven elements of his recipes for tabloid success into the ORF. This meant that certain topics and news items that had traditionally been suppressed were now addressed on television. It would, however, be naïve to believe that party-political considerations were therefore marginalized.

The topical news programme *Zeit im Bild* (Current Affairs on Screen) continues to be of great interest to politicians as a vehicle for off-the-cuff, ad hoc reporting. A study of its programming at the beginning of 1971 has shown that some 23 per cent of its coverage of domestic politics concerned Parliament, political controversy and elections, while 9 per cent referred to the internal mechanisms of the parties. While the 'social partners', who were important in terms of realpolitik, hardly featured at all, state institutions dominated in the 23 per cent of the information referring to domestic politics. The political parties came out on top by a wide margin with 34.5 per cent. It is interesting to note that in news items referring to the parties a balance was created by giving the ÖVP preferential treatment (14.5 per cent compared to the SPÖ's 11.5 per cent); as the ruling party the SPÖ dominated in the state-related items anyway. Another 11.5 per cent was devoted to the FPÖ, even though it was much smaller in size compared to the others. The FPÖ had a certain strategic importance because of its support for the SPÖ minority government. Extra-parliamentary initiatives were not taken note of. Today, quantitative analyses of the parties' exposure time on ORF news programmes (ZIB 1, ZIB 2, ZIB 3) show a clear preference at any given time for the party of the chancellor – the SPÖ until 2000, then the ÖVP, with the occasional glitch arising from Jörg Haider's activities. In 2006 the SPÖ moved back to centre stage with Alfred Gusenbauer as chancellor. Gusenbauer was succeeded by Werner Faymann in 2008.

Television and the Development of Democracy in Austria

Compared to the U.S., Austria is a latecomer to television. On 1 August 1955, the Österreichischer Rundfunk (ORF) started its trial television operation with four transmitter stations: Vienna-Kahlenberg, Graz-Schöckl, Linz-Freinberg and Salzburg-Gaisberg. It took until 1957 for a regular programme to be aired six days a week. In 1961 there were only 200,000 holders of viewing licences, though penetration was actually considerably greater as at least in areas of high population density programmes were routinely watched by groups of viewers in private or public settings. In 1968 a million licences were issued and the number of transmitter stations rose to 120. Finally, in the early 1980s a reasonably sized proportion of Austria was serviced with 800 transmitters in 400 locations. Today television is arguably the most important democratic political medium: 79 per cent of Austrians access television for their political information, with 52 per cent accessing print media and only 45 per cent getting such information from the radio. In 1961, before television took off, newspapers had been the more important forum for the airing of political opinions, with 61 per cent compared to radio's 59 per cent.

To begin with television had been regarded as a paragon of objective reportage: in 1976 television was held to be the most reliable source of political information by 66 per cent of Austrians, compared to a mere 14 per cent who gave their trust to the various print media. While scepticism towards television has grown in recent years, a 1999 survey showed that 54 per cent still considered television news to be objective.[4] Up until now relatively little research has been done on democracy-specific aspects of these areas, and television research in general is still in its infancy in Austria. While the legal and the political framework for the development of the television monopoly in Austria is subjected to scrutiny time and again, concrete analysis usually does not stray beyond specific events, such as the television debates between Kreisky and Klaus in 1969–70. This particular confrontation was the result of a regular 'media revolution', which at last installed television as a factor central to political opinion formation. What the Kennedy-Nixon debates had done for the U.S. in 1960 had now come to Austria: the power of these images was obvious to all who saw them.

In spite of the fact that the decision makers of the ORF, men like Bacher and Dalma, were of a different political persuasion, Kreisky managed to make excellent use of the medium of television through his highly effective self-presentation. A perfect mise en scène of his person was part of this. The chancellor at the time, Josef Klaus, was most comfortable in one-to-one talks with select journalists, whereas Kreisky delighted in supplying a whole train of journalists with information, news tidbits, sound bites and quotable interpretations. The lists of guests invited to his villa in Vienna's Armbrustergasse read like a Who's Who of Austrian journalism. The legendary 'Pressefoyer' press conference after the weekly Council of Ministers remains unsurpassed in terms of its magnetic effect on press and nation. Kreisky managed to create an atmosphere of direct, immediate involvement: his audience felt as if they were right in the thick of the action, actual witnesses to the decision making process. This was pure fiction, as decisions adopted by the Council of Ministers were a formality; the real decisions took shape elsewhere.

With the experience of totalitarian propaganda in the 1930s at the back of his mind, Kreisky worried about the power of mobilization inherent in the new medium. What finally triggered his decision to strengthen public control of radio and television was the so-called Schranz scandal. In February 1972 tempers in Austria flared following the decision of the International Olympic Committee to withdraw amateur status from the skiing ace Karl Schranz, who had connived at the commercial exploitation of his name, and to exclude him from the Olympic Games in Sapporo (Japan). Sports have played a major role in forging an identity for postwar Austria: a 1980 survey found that sport was what made 82 per cent of Austrians take pride in their country. Toni Sailer's gold medals at the 1956 Olympic Games had contributed substantially to pride in the renascent nation – particularly among young people. The postwar generation was enthralled by war heroes no longer: pride of place now went to sports heroes.

ILLUSTRATION 5.2
Bruno Kreisky, 'Chancellor of the Media' (press conference after a Council of Ministers).

In 1972 tempers ran proportionately high. Fred Sinowatz, the SPÖ minister of education who also held the sports portfolio, organized a red-carpet welcome ceremony for Schranz in Vienna. The ORF gave its unqualified support to the campaign, and its chief, Gerd Bacher, joined most of Austria's major papers in pulling out all the stops. Some 87,000 people – more than had been in the streets when the successful government delegation returned from the State Treaty negotiations in Moscow in 1955 – lined the road leading from Schwechat to Vienna on 8 February 1972, when Schranz was escorted in triumph from the airport to the Ballhausplatz, the seat of government. Kreisky did not appear with Schranz on the balcony of the Federal Chancellery until the third time of asking, and when he finally did so it was with a croaking voice, a most unusual lapse in the most media-savvy politician of the 1970s. He was acutely aware of the analogy that existed between this occasion and the night of 12 to 13 March 1938, when the National Socialist interim government of Arthur Seyß-Inquart had presented themselves on the same balcony to their bawling supporters. Kreisky realized what potential for mobilization the ORF possessed and felt a strong and emotional revulsion against it, which was only deepened by the political controversies surrounding Gerd Bacher. His decision to reform the Broadcasting Law was irrevocable.

While the ÖVP-SPÖ coalition had not dragged its feet over the broadcasting reform and had at least facilitated the creation of a second group of channels, Kreisky allowed himself all of three years' time to deal with this issue. At the Villach party congress of 1972 he declared that what was needed to neutralize the ORF's monopoly on opinion was a counterweight in the form of an additional television channel operated by newspaper publishers and of a reduction of the time allotted to commercials. Bacher in turn voiced his concern that the ORF might be harmed by the loss of revenue from advertising; in 2001, incidentally, he switched to the opposite point of view. After they learned of Bacher's cost estimate, the association of newspaper publishers dropped the idea of an independent channel. The SPÖ moved towards a reform of the broadcasting system by appointing a committee. In 1974 the new Broadcasting Law was passed, and the post of CEO was advertised. A board of trustees, on which the representatives of the SPÖ – and thus of the government – were in a majority, elected Otto Oberhammer, an undersecretary in the Ministry of Justice, as the ORF's new CEO. The body representing listeners and viewers, which had been conceived of as a democratic instrument and had been put together broadly using the criteria of the social partnership, soon saw its importance diminish.

In the secondary literature the issue of television and democracy in Austria is largely reduced to the question of how television handles politics in the narrow sense of the word, particularly with reference to party politics and electoral contests. Today the political elites are interested above all in being represented in news programmes. There is a tendency to overlook the fact that entertainment programmes, with just a scattering of covert or overt political messages, can be far more effective vehicles than classic news programmes or political documentaries. In the 1960s a cabaret sketch by Peter Wehle and Gerhard Bronner triggered a debate about Taras Borodajkewycz, a notoriously anti-Semitic economics professor at Vienna university: a televised press conference, in which Borodajkewycz drew enthusiastic reactions from frenzied supporters, turned up the heat of the debate. The programme *Wünsch dir was* (Make a Wish) with Vivi Bach and Dietmar Schönherr reflects the sociopolitical zeitgeist of the 1970s, and Franz Novotny's 1977 *Staatsoperette,* which deals with Austro-Fascism and the role the Catholic Church played in that regime, provoked battles on the letters and opinion pages of the tabloids.

The ORF has continued to be a focus of political interest for whichever party is in power. It is far beyond the scope of the present work to attempt even a summary of the numerous struggles surrounding CEOs, legislation and concrete political interventions. What is incontrovertible is the fact that the ORF will remain a bone of political contention as long as the state – in the shape of the government of the day – retains the power to exercise direct influence over it. The only alternative would be a development along the lines staked out by the BBC. While the representatives of political parties with solid majorities who decide appointments to the ORF top jobs have been replaced by people who are politically less dependent, the system remains almost as biased as ever, despite the 2002–03 ORF reform introducing a board of trustees.

Media Concentration: A Europe-wide Comparison

Supra-regional comparisons show that there is a tendency for small entities, such as Luxembourg, Austria, Ireland, the Netherlands and the Walloon and Flemish regions of Belgium, to develop a high degree of economic concentration in the media market. In Sweden, on the other hand, the market leaders' share adds up to only 36 per cent of the total market. In Europe as a whole it is common for public service radio corporations to play the most important role, and this is particularly the case in Austria. This is due no doubt partly to the belated liberalization of the granting of broadcasting licences and partly to the liberal programming practised by public-service radio stations, which has made it hard for private radio stations to make any significant inroads. In Austria, radio has successfully adapted to the interests of society.

The ORF's 54 per cent is the largest market share of all of Europe's public-service television companies, and the increasing pressure from German private companies has as yet done little to change this. As in Luxembourg and Ireland, it is only television companies from neighbouring countries sharing the same culture and language that can compete in national markets. Pressure is felt by the

ORF from satellite and cable television; there again, competition is restricted to German-language channels. In 1998 the number of households in Austria that had access to satellite television was practically the same as those with access to cable, with only one point separating them. By the fourth quarter of 1998, 39.2 per cent, or 1,188,000 of all homes with television, had opted for satellite television; 38.6 per cent or 1,171,000 homes had access to cable television. Since 1997 the operators of cable networks have been given the opportunity to create their own programmes through an amendment to the Regional Telecommunications Law. At present more than fifteen private regional stations make use of this opportunity in the networks of Austria's 275 cable network operators.

What matters most in a democratic political context is the fact that the dissemination of relevant political information is still the exclusive domain of the ORF. In spite of diminishing market shares overall, this kind of concentration has all the hallmarks of a monopoly. Austria's concentration of ownership in the print and electronic media, which is relatively high compared to other European countries, becomes a legitimate cause for concern in democratic political terms in cases of editorial intervention. Polls among representatives of the 'Fourth Estate' have shown that this kind of intervention takes place in a manner that is far subtler than old-style censorship. It works by activating journalists' internal censors where owner or advertiser interests are at stake.

Things become critical when the media monopolists, the ORF and the *Kronenzeitung,* get entangled in a web of common interests and mutual interference and grossly neglect their journalistic duty of keeping the public informed because their own interests are at play. A case in point is a documentary about Hans Dichand that was realized, in close collaboration with Dichand himself, through a generous grant from the National Film Board of Austria by the Belgian filmmaker Nathalie Borgers. Dichand saw himself unsympathetically portrayed in the finished product, which he himself had shaped all along. All that Borgers could do at the end of one year's work was to conclude: 'To begin with I thought everybody was exaggerating ... [Yet] Hans Dichand is Austria's top dog. I have never before seen the kind of power that he has.'[5] The ORF, in gross neglect of its state-regulated function, did not air the documentary about a paper that is read day by day by almost 50 per cent of Austrians above the age of fourteen. When the high-quality French-German cable station Arte aired the documentary, the *Krone* retaliated by striking Arte off the roster of television stations whose programmes the paper lists on a regular basis.

The Fourth Estate and Its Democratic Political Scope

Yet if one considers how the media have developed since 1945, it is nevertheless possible to come away with the conclusion that the scope of the 'Fourth Estate' has increased. In 1945 Allied post- and, in some cases, pre-press censorship ruled, along with party-political *Proporz;* today there is broad discretionary freedom for journalists to tackle sensitive issues, which sometimes directly concern those in power. For instance, on 3 July 1997, the editor in chief of the *Salzburger Nachrichten,* Ronald Barazon, defended one of his editors – who had reported that Wolfgang Schüssel, then Austria's foreign minister, had been bad-mouthing the president of the German Federal Bank, a representative of the Swedish government and the president of Belarus – in the face of Schüssel's denial with the words 'Schüssel is lying'. This would have been as unthinkable in 1966 as it had been in 1946. Having said this, it is important to note that political interference by all politically important groups is still the order of the day. A good example can be found in the placement of politically sensitive news items in the ORF's prime-time news programme, ZIB1, a case in point being the deletion, following interference from the Chancellery, of the name of Chancellor Viktor Klima's son from a report on a financial scandal.

Polls on the most important factors that influence journalistic work document its dependence on external forces. Primary definers (accredited sources in government and other institutions) are seen as the most important driving force behind opinion formation (84 per cent of journalists cited these, compared to the 77 per cent who cast the general public and the 72 per cent who cast their boss in that role). Roughly half the journalists experience occasional problems with their advertising department, either because of the topics they choose or the contents of their articles; 15 per cent experience such problems on a regular basis. It is equally common for PR people to provoke bouts of disinformation either by pushing alternative topics or by leaking information on other subjects, in the hope of marginalizing undesirable topics or directing the journalists' attention elsewhere. If relevant topics are nevertheless brought to the attention of the public, 61 per cent of journalists feel this is the result of indifference on the part of those concerned, whilst 84 per cent attribute it to the power of investigative journalism.[6]

The self-assessment of journalists, if realistic, is nevertheless rather sobering as far as the concrete potential of the 'Fourth Estate' is concerned in situations where there is a clash of interests between the media and the powers that be. In 1999 only 8 per cent of Austrian journalists felt that Austrian journalism had succeeded in emancipating itself from politics over the previous five years; for one in five the influence of politics had become more pronounced. The limited market and the high degree of concentration of media ownership have created a situation in Austria that makes life difficult for independent journalists, who on occasion risk their livelihood in order to fulfil their democratic political function. Only when a topic 'takes off' can it be discussed in rational terms and action and reasoned debate unfold with greater freedom.

Notes

1. Theodor Venus, 'Zerbrochene Medienträume. "Express", "Kronen-Zeitung" und "Arbeiter-Zeitung"', in *Bruno Kreisky: Seine Zeit und mehr/Era and Aftermath* (Vienna: Catalogue of the Exhibition at the Historisches Museum der Stadt Wien, 1998), 127–148.
2. Olah was sentenced only because he had not been authorized to use trade union funds worth 1,225,628 schillings and 64 groschen for his secret special project in the Cold War: establishment and armament of an anti-communist storm troop, a private army that was not controlled by state officials and institutions. The loan for Dichand and Falk already had been paid back when the trial against Olah started and was therefore excluded from the court proceedings.
3. Franz Vranitzky, *Politische Erinnerungen* (Vienna: Zsolnay Verlag, 2004), 429.
4. Fritz Plasser and Peter Ulram, *Das österreichische Politikverständnis. Von der Konsens- zur Konfliktkultur?* (Vienna: WUV-Univ.-Verlag, 2002), 33–35.
5. *Der Standard,* 24 October 2002.
6. See http://www.kfj.at/publikationen.htm (accessed 1 June 2005); Macht und Ohn- macht der Medien (Dr. Meinrad Rahofer) Key Note Lecture for the Opening of the Bischofshofener Medientage, 20 November 2002.

Neutrality and the State Treaty in a New Europe

It was not the declaration of independence that Renner's interim government issued on 27 April 1945 that was destined to become the Magna Carta of the Second Republic but the Neutrality Law passed by Parliament ten years later on 26 October 1955 and, less directly, also the State Treaty of 15 May 1955. The latter denoted the end of Allied administration and Austria's full sovereignty as a state. It is 26 October that is celebrated as Austrian National Day, acknowledging neutrality as part of the civic understanding of the Second Republic. Particularly in the 1960s and 1970s, the era of Austria's social and economic rehabilitation, that day became an important element in the self-understanding of the nation.

Until the mid 1980s, Austria's neutral status as such was never called into question by the country's experts on international law. The focus of their attention was its analysis, description (for instance, the obligations arising from neutrality in times of peace) and the interpretation of a neutrality politics that was far more active and independent than that of, say, Switzerland or Finland. It was taken for granted that joining the European Economic Community (EEC, later EC) would jeopardize Austrian neutrality and that membership was therefore incompatible with it. The catalogue of arguments (compiled by Rudolf Kirchschläger, head of the Department of International Law at the Foreign Ministry at the time, and later federal president) was valid until 1986, when Waldemar Hummer, an international law professor at Innsbruck University, produced his assessment of Austria's neutrality, commissioned by the Federation of Austrian Industry. In the years leading up to 1986 the danger of a new Anschluss with Germany had always been present, however remotely; it was also articulated repeatedly on the fringe of the debate on Austria's application for EU membership. The possibility of Anschluss had been a dominant topic in the postwar era and had caused irritation not only to the Soviet top brass but also to Austria's legal, diplomatic and political elites. (One may see a similar process in Ireland, where neutrality also contains a strong component of border demarcation vis-à-vis an overpowering neighbour – in this case, Great Britain.)

We should note in passing that other EU members, in particular France and Belgium, as well as the then EU President Jacques Delors, let it be known at the beginning of Austria's accession negotiations that they were opposed to Austria retaining its neutral status. However, as negotiations got under way, this issue did not crop up again. This was to do with the EU's Common Security Policy getting bogged down at the halfway stage. Back at home, however, it has become clear particularly over the last few years that neutral status, accepted half-heartedly in 1955 as an interim solution by a country in an exposed position, has become one of the mainstays of Austrian identity. Neutrality has become closely associated with social and economic prosperity, with internal and external security, and with peace. The success story of the Second Republic, on its way to becoming one of the richest countries in the world, is rooted, as far as public consciousness is concerned, in the small size of the country and in its neutral status.

At no stage has there been such an intense debate on Austrian neutrality as in the years before Austria joined the European Union and in the years immediately before the turn of the millennium. While the supporters of neutrality had fallen silent, its critics peremptorily demanded that Austria join NATO forthwith and overhauled their sound bites: the charge dating back to the Cold War that Austria was out for a 'free ride' was replaced by the 'neutrality lie'. Yet it is equally true that at no stage had Austria's real political situation in the first decades after the war been as consistently ignored in public debate – in spite of numerous scholarly publications. This is undoubtedly to do with radical changes on the geopolitical level, such as Austria's new position in Europe after the disintegration of the Soviet Union and its accession to the European Union.

The charge that Austria was out for a 'free ride' had long been a recurring theme in past discourses. Before assessing this charge we must return briefly to the years 1953–55 to analyse the different mindsets of the main actors and the overall geopolitical framework.

A 'Window of Opportunity': The Final Stage of the State Treaty's Genesis, 1953–55

Stalin's death in 1953 and the almost simultaneous start of the presidency of the four-star general and former NATO Commander-in-Chief Dwight D. Eisenhower created a situation that contained at least an option of détente against a backdrop of distrust and international tensions. Austria was still an occupied country, even though the remaining forces stationed on its soil were primarily Russian, with hardly any of the Western Allies still in place. The country offered itself as an ideal 'barter object' to the big players, but in the decisive negotiations it also displayed initiative and self-confidence. As early as 1953 Eisenhower signalled to his rigid foreign secretary, John Foster Dulles, that the time was ripe for détente measures (which would incidentally ease the burden on the U.S. military budget). He knew Austria's internal situation well and was aware that it served as the basis of the country's ideological, political, economic and cultural orientation towards the West. He was also well aware of three factors already in place that were congenial to the U.S. position:

i) The marginalization of the local Communist Party. In spite of, or possibly because of, the Soviet army of occupation, this was down to three MPs;

ii) A compact, extremely pro-Western and (for stringent ideological reasons) anti-Communist Social Democratic Party and trade union movement; and

iii) A stable Grand Coalition under the ÖVP Chancellor Julius Raab. Raab, to be sure, was not pro-American, yet he made up for this with his outright rejection of communism, which he was at odds with on account of his Catholic values.

It must be said that in all those years Austrian membership in NATO was not seriously considered by anyone. The economic integration into the Western bloc was as much an accomplished fact as the foreign political alliance with the U.S., so the federal government took a relatively long time, in fact until after the Communist putsch in Prague and the blockade of Berlin, to turn its thoughts to the rearmament issue. The build-up of an army had been expressly forbidden to the government of Karl Renner. However, after 1949 the U.S. considered Austria's remilitarization a core element of the conclusion of the State Treaty. The original goal, Austria's demilitarization, was given up for fear of a Communist takeover from inside the country. Towards the end of 1949 a pro-Western military force was established step by step under the guise of the B-gendarmerie, which was destined to become part of the army after the conclusion of the State Treaty and the withdrawal of the four Allies. Eisenhower was well aware of the marginal military presence of the Western Allies compared to the more than 30,000 Soviet soldiers still stationed in eastern Austria. At the end of 1953 he already saw a great advantage in a 'neutral status on the Swiss model', which would be enhanced by a small, de facto pro-American army capable of filling the vacuum of conventional armed forces in this area with up to 65,000 men. Moreover, in order to abide by the peace treaties concluded with the Eastern European countries the Soviet Union had to withdraw its units from Hungary and Romania, which had been stationed there to safeguard the supply routes for the troops in Austria; this amounted to an evacuation of Soviet troops from Central Europe.

In spite of these favourable conditions it took from the end of 1953 until May 1955 for the State Treaty to be concluded and for the preparations of the parliamentary debate on the Neutrality Law to be completed. This delay arose from a power struggle within the Soviet *nomenklatura*. While the head of the secret services, Lavrentiy Beria, was not averse in principle to a withdrawal of Soviet troops from Austria and even broached the neutralization of Germany that had also been floated by Stalin, Foreign Minister Vyacheslav Molotov was in favour of the status quo. When Nikita Krushchev emerged victorious from the power struggle consequent on Stalin's death, he realized that the 'lowest price' he would have to pay for a summit with Eisenhower was the solution of the problem of Austria. He was then clever enough to choose Molotov, an opponent of withdrawal, to start signalling Soviet readiness to agree to Austria's neutral status in a speech given on 8 February 1955. The signal was immediately picked up and interpreted correctly by Austria's ambassador in Moscow, Norbert Bischoff. Krushchev's motives were easy to understand: he needed a phase of détente in order to give the Soviet economy breathing time to develop.

In Vienna, Julius Raab, in office as federal chancellor since 1953, had made several solo attempts at bringing about a bilateral rapprochement between Austria and the Soviet Union – to the strong displeasure of U.S. observers, who were expecting unqualified loyalty to the West from Austria on the strength of its record in the past. It says a lot about Washington's assessment of the situation that when the Austrians had received an invitation to dispatch a top-level delegation to Moscow, Adolf Schärf, the Social Democratic vice-chancellor, and the SPÖ Undersecretary of State Bruno Kreisky were considered the only safeguards for U.S. and Western Allied expectations. Unlike Eisenhower, the SPÖ (whose interior minister, Oskar Helmer, had come out against the trip, saying: 'You will be stood against the wall') and U.S. Secretary of State John Foster Dulles did not see neutral status as the best possible solution. Because Communist parties in Europe, backed by the Soviet Union, had been trying since the 1950s to create a counterweight for the nuclear predominance of the West and of NATO through their demand for 'neutral zones', this term had pro-Communist ideological connotations. Schärf and Kreisky preferred to lobby for 'non-alignment' and gave in only very late – Schärf even held out until Moscow – to Raab and the Soviet Union's pressure towards accepting formal neutral status.

The upside of neutral status, as far as the Soviets were concerned, was that it effectively made Anschluss with Germany impossible and allowed the Soviet Union inherent possibilities for intervention. Soviet political experts agreed in regarding the Moscow Declaration from April 1955 in itself as already legally binding, whereas the government delegation interpreted the formal declaration of neutrality envisaged in it more as a declaration of intent (*Verwendungszusage*). Either way there was scope for the Soviet Union to argue that Austria would be in breach of contract if the declaration of intent was not honoured. A number of alternative versions of neutrality were floated in 1955: although they were ultimately to be discarded, they can at least serve as evidence for the ambiguity of this key result of the negotiations.

One example can be found in the position of Bruno Kreisky, who had come to endorse neutrality by 1955 because he was hoping to have it guaranteed by the four Allies along the lines of the Swiss model. This would have solved the security issue once and for all. However, the U.S. was not prepared to go along with this – it did not want to have its geopolitical options restricted in such a sensitive region. The U.S. Congress, which had only ever endorsed a territorial guarantee in the case of Panama, would certainly not have forfeited its say in the matter, for a territorial guarantee for Austria would have implied the necessity of a nuclear strike in the event of a Soviet or Communist intervention.

To have prevented an Anschluss with Germany, even one couched in economic terms, was of paramount importance to the Soviet leadership because any additional strengthening of Germany's economy was to be avoided at all costs. This became even more urgent against the backdrop of Western Europe's economic integration. There was nothing the Soviets could do to prevent the Federal Republic of Germany from joining NATO. Neutral status as a precondition for German reunification was no longer an option for the Soviet Union in 1955. At the same time it became obvious that the two most important U.S. conditions for the conclusion of a state treaty with Austria – the establishment of a small pro-Western army based on voluntary national service and the guarantee of internal stability held out by a grand coalition for the foreseeable future – were also acceptable to the Soviet Union.

Secret Armament Programmes and Arms Caches

The armament programme that was allegedly pursued in secret has not been secret for quite some time. As recently as 1996 this programme resurfaced when the *Boston Globe*'s CIA-prompted revelation led to the unearthing of arms caches dating back to the years before 1955. Following reports about Jörg Haider's FPÖ shifting to the right, the paper's informant was worried about the possibility of these old military depots falling into the wrong kind of hands.

Between 1950 and 1954 the CIA had installed a total of sixty-four secret arms depots in Salzburg, Upper Austria and Styria, and it had failed to remove their contents in 1955. Fearing a serious upheaval in Austro-American relations, the U.S. ambassador, Mrs Swanee Hunt, called a top-level meeting with Federal President Thomas Klestil, Federal Chancellor Franz Vranitzky, and Vice-Chancellor Wolfgang Schüssel. However, the Austrian public refused to get on board and mustered no more than mild interest in the resultant media frenzy. Neither the flagrant infringement of a neutral state's sovereignty by a superpower nor the additional fact that the Republic had in 1955 forgone all claims of damages based on the administration of the occupation attracted much attention. The relevant clause was the subject of a secret agreement that does not feature in the appropriate Austrian federal law gazettes (*Bundesgesetzblätter*); it is, however, included in the series of agreements with the UN. The fact that Austria had formed part of the Western alliance during the Cold War was taken for granted by the public, the media and the political decision makers even after forty years of neutrality and was not allowed to become a matter of debate. In 1965 Austria's Federal Army had already emptied thirty-three British-installed arms depots and taken charge of the weapons, when items from these depots appeared on the black market.

NATO's Secret Ally

From a geopolitical perspective, these 'Mickey Mouse war games' were part of a comprehensive strategy to strengthen the pro-Western alliance. In 1952–53 the U.S. military had received lists of able-bodied 'soldiers proven in World War II'; of these, 30,000 were resident in the U.S. zone of Upper Austria, 12,600 in Salzburg. The relevant plans had been hatched by Austrian military personnel close to the ÖVP Minister of Defence Ferdinand Graf. Only a few weeks after the conclusion of the State Treaty these plans entered a critical stage. Emil Liebitzky, the head of the general staff, travelled to Italy on a top-secret mission, the ultimate aim of which was to try to establish a communications headquarters involving the Italian Minister of Defence Paolo Emilio Taviani. This would have brought Austria directly into NATO planning. U.S. diplomats followed this rapprochement with great concern and ultimately put an end to the contacts, which carried with them the danger of a total erosion of Austria's neutral status. Yet until 1958 U.S. strategists were convinced that in a military conflict Austria's slowly evolving federal army would defend NATO's eastern flank and the north-south transit route connecting southern Germany and Italy against Communist Warsaw Pact troops. Eastern Austria and Vienna would have been abandoned to their fate in planning inspired by the concept of 'split neutrality'. In July 1958, a vehement controversy erupted in the ministers' council: SPÖ Vice-Chancellor Adolf Schärf and Bruno Kreisky expressed their deep concern about potentially negative consequences of this strategy both at home and abroad and demanded that planning focus on the defence of the whole territory – regardless of NATO interests. Because of the Lebanon crisis it took until July 1958 for Federal Chancellor Julius Raab's protests against unauthorized flights across Austrian airspace in the Tyrol to be heard. These were all political signals that added up to strengthen the trend towards an independent Austrian defence strategy following the Swiss model.

In this context it is important to point out that NATO's frequently mooted automatic defence of Austria during the two flash points of the Cold War in 1956 (invasion of Hungary) and in 1968 (invasion of Czechoslovakia) would have come into force only if the Warsaw Pact had attacked the north-south line of the Western alliance. Even if the Warsaw Pact troops had occupied parts of eastern Austria and Vienna and if military action had remained confined to that area,

NATO would not have reacted. Yet final certainty eludes us as long as NATO continues to hoard its superannuated deployment plans and strategy papers. It may be noted that a number of planning games of the Warsaw Pact have been made public, particularly those from archives of the former GDR. It is equally impossible to say how NATO would have reacted to a Warsaw Pact intervention in ideologically recalcitrant Romania: Viennese 'expert circles' were mooting this as an option in September 1968. According to the 'Viennese source', which is still shrouded in secrecy, the Soviets were even set to occupy parts of Austria to create bases from which their troops would be able to advance through Hungary and Bulgaria to deal with Yugoslavia as well.[1]

The invasion of Czechoslovakia by Warsaw Pact troops in 1968 took the Austrian government under Federal Chancellor Josef Klaus by surprise; at least in the short term it led to a near panic and to a number of psychological and strategic mistakes. The situation calmed down only when it became obvious that the troop advance would stop short of Austrian territory. Violations of airspace by Soviet aircraft north of the Danube (which were interpreted as reconnaissance flights) increased in number, but they stopped on September 1 following an intervention by the Austrian ambassador in Moscow. The borders with Czechoslovakia remained open in spite of the invasion, and visas continued to be granted to persons wishing to leave Czechoslovakia for Austria, provided they had a passport. A total of 93,653 Czechoslovak citizens took advantage of this and were provided with food and lodgings as they waited to see how things would turn out at home. This service ceased on 17 September 1968, and only 1,355 refugees actually sought asylum in Austria.

Time and Neutrality

It was impossible to predict the role Austria's neutrality would play in 1968, as was also the case when the Soviet Union intervened in Hungary in 1956, only a few months after the Neutrality Law had been passed. Many U.S. decision makers had initially regarded the solution of the question of Austria in 1955 as an irksome exception from the rules of the Cold War. Secretary of State John Foster Dulles was against an international upgrading of Austria, as he feared other countries in crisis regions might follow suit and suddenly decide to join the neutral or the non-aligned camps. He therefore rejected Molotov's offer in 1955 to stage the Krushchev-Eisenhower summit in Vienna. British diplomats and politicians went further still: they were convinced that Austria's geopolitical situation, coupled with its manifold contacts with its Eastern European neighbours, meant that it would inevitably become a non-aligned, pro-Communist country. Such fears were proved groundless by the unequivocal position Austria took in the Hungarian crisis of 1956.

In an unpublished manuscript Vice-Chancellor Adolf Schärf made his own criticisms of Raab's occasionally seesawing political course. He cited Raab's contradictory actions in 1959, when he gave the go-ahead to both the Congress of the Sudeten Germans and the International Youth Festival. The former was a gathering of the displaced former inhabitants of Sudetenland (Raab probably had an eye on their potential as voters) and attracted vehement Communist, Czechoslovak and Soviet protests; the latter was a Communist affair. Raab failed in his attempts to win Dulles over to his view of Austria as a mediator between West and East. Even the domiciling of the International Atomic Agency in Vienna was entirely the result of a compromise: as Dulles wanted the U.S. to be able to decide whom the key positions were going to, he had to make concessions to the Soviet Union with respect to the location. Dulles stuck to this line outside Europe, too, for instance in Latin America and in the Near East, where he refused to see a role for countries such as Costa Rica or Lebanon as mediators in armed conflicts.

This development makes it abundantly clear that neutral status for Austria was a multilayered negotiation compromise and not by any means a solution that was defined in detail by all the actors involved. The fact that no resistance stirred in the Austrian public cannot wholly be explained away, as is often done today, by a reference to the authoritarian decision mechanisms of the two big parties, ÖVP and SPÖ, in government and Parliament; it corresponded rather to a widespread desire on the part of all Europeans to be neither the object nor the subject of further military aggression. Gallup polls from the years 1952 to 1955 document this trend; Great Britain was the only country where a majority came out in favour of support of the U.S. in case of 'hot', i.e. nuclear war.[2]

Even in the Federal Republic of Germany there was powerful support for neutrality. Only the exploitation of the concept by Communist propaganda forced the Social Democrats to drop it as an option. Many observers, including U.S. experts, were concerned that the Austrian example might exercise a prejudicial influence on West Germany, yet it soon became obvious that in spite of a general longing in the populace for peace and neutrality, the West German elite remained focused on the military integration of the Federal Republic into the Western alliance. If it had been conceivable for this integration to be jeopardized by the Austrian solution, the latter would never have received the blessing of the U.S. West Germany's accession to NATO and the consolidation of the two bloc systems were required preconditions for the conclusion of the State Treaty and the end of Allied administration. Moreover, it is important to note that in the case of Austria the KPÖ had been ordered, through a directive from Moscow in 1954, to shut down its propaganda for neutrality: when neutral status did materialize in 1955, the KPÖ was no longer able to claim it as a feather in its cap enhancing its domestic political standing. The Soviet Union, too, had its own perception of neutrality in the overall context of the Cold War that was determined not by the interests of regional small states but by those of a major player on the global stage.

The 'Golden Age' of Austria's Neutrality Policy in the 1960s and 1970s

The Austrian politicians' fabled capacity for hard drinking contributed as little to the conclusion of the State Treaty as Austria's own and unaided initiative did to the international success of the policy of neutrality. In what follows we will be examining the geopolitical framework and the exploitation (or even transgression) of this international web of conditions and relations.

As has been shown above, the Eisenhower-Dulles administration played Austrian neutrality down as an isolated oddity without any genuine international significance. For the Soviet Union, on the other hand, the geographical area of Vienna became interesting after 1955 as a place where East and West mingled; its importance went beyond its role as a haunt for agents and spies. This basic positioning did not change until the Democratic administration of John F. Kennedy came into office, and it was symbolic that Vienna was chosen in 1961 as the venue for the first summit meeting between Kennedy and Krushchev. Even though the summit was a failure, Vienna and Austria continued to play a role in the détente process far transcending that of a host supplying the Hofburg setting with its imperial splendour.

Austria's Foreign Minister Bruno Kreisky was the first to realize the full scope of action now opening up for a small neutral country. In 1958 and 1959 he tried repeatedly to initiate talks between the mayor of Berlin, Willy Brandt, his close friend from the days of their Swedish exile, and the Soviet leadership, but he was held back by U.S. interventions and Brandt's personal reserve. Kreisky was more successful as a political communicator in passing on, to the U.S. and other Western countries, confidential assessments from sources in the Soviet Union and in Communist satellite states, to which he appended his own interpretations and analyses. At the end of the 1950s and in the 1960s Kreisky had good contacts to Konrad Adenauer, the Conservative German chancellor, and French President Charles de Gaulle. For Bruno Kreisky, a dyed-in-the-wool anti-Communist, the way forward lay in a peaceful erosion of the Communist bloc system. He was capable of critically interpreting relevant signals from Eastern Europe without the usual mental reservations. Only in the course of the last few years has it become clear how comprehensively the experts on Eastern Europe and the professional Kremlin watchers misjudged the social and economic developments in the Communist countries. University departments and secret services alike were so obsessed with the template of the Cold War that they fell utterly short of a realistic assessment of what was actually going on, in spite of the enormous sums of money that were sunk into this kind of 'research'.

The nature of specifically Austrian policies towards the East, which were phased in starting in 1955 under the term of *Nachbarschaftspolitik* (neighbourhood policies) and showed concrete political effects under Foreign Minister Bruno Kreisky, differed significantly from, say, the political tactics of the Adenauer government, in that they were more flexible and less ideologically determined. Raab's Grand Coalition and the later Kreisky governments not only made covert attempts at economic cooperation with Communist neighbouring countries (the Federal Republic did as much), they made such economic policies part and parcel of a much broader political approach that included clarification of unsolved border and assets disputes. This kind of *détente à l'autrichienne* was followed vis-à-vis Yugoslavia, Poland and Hungary, and included not only bilateral topics but also an intense debate on the overall geopolitical situation.

Kreisky's function as an honest broker was at no time more important than in the hot phase of the Cold War during the Cuban crisis of 1962, when he relayed a Soviet proposal aiming at de-escalation – that the Americans forgo the option of stationing Pershing missiles in Turkey in exchange for the Soviets giving up the stationing of nuclear missiles on Cuba. The proposal was accepted. In the decisive meetings of the Kennedy administration this initiative went under the name of 'the Kreisky proposal'. Even so, it might not have been possible to stave off Armageddon had it not been for the CIA's poor performance and for the failure of U.S. air reconnaissance to spot the nuclear warheads on the Soviet missiles.

Initiatives such as Kreisky's became possible on the basis of permanent and networked contacts to top-level political decision makers and an interest in international politics that was unclouded by considerations of domestic political expediency. Kreisky's attitude in that respect had been shaped by the trauma of 1938, when, as he and many other Austrians saw it, the country's integration into the Third Reich had been facilitated by the fact that no third-party country had been interested in providing help against outside aggression to a dictatorially governed country that considered itself to be within the sphere of German civilization.

UN Priority before Europe

As Austria began to develop its international contacts as a sovereign state, priority went to economic integration into the Western bloc and to membership of the UN. Whilst Austria participated intensely in the administration of the Marshall Plan within the framework of the OEEC in Paris, European policies on the whole continued to play only an insignificant role. It is therefore not surprising that the 'United States of Europe' proposed by Winston Churchill in 1946 found little resonance in Austria. Even the Joint International Committee for European Unity subsequently called into life by Churchill and others, which ultimately burgeoned into the Council of Europe, received scant attention from the Ballhausplatz. A political had-been, the 1934–38 corporatist dictatorship's press and censorship czar, Eduard Ludwig, was dispatched as an observer to the Council of Europe. The European Coal and Steel Community was likewise considered to deserve only an observer. On the other hand, Austria was immediately granted full UN membership in 1955; in Raab's eyes this was more important than membership in the Council of Europe.

In 1967, the ÖVP government of Josef Klaus decided to offer the UN a headquarters in Vienna as another essential element of Austrian security policy. At the end of the 1970s and in the 1980s, this project was realized by Bruno Kreisky, this time against massive domestic-political opposition from the ÖVP. It was only logical and by no means coincidental that Austria's foreign minister at the time, Kurt Waldheim, was elected UN secretary-general with Kreisky's active backing. Waldheim had been so active in the Austrian diplomatic service since 1946 that no one thought of checking on his own description of his role in the war years – a grave mistake in retrospect, and one that was to lead to a highly emotional debate in the 1980s.

International Détente Policies and Human Rights

Austrian politicians and political experts attributed special importance to the Organization for Security and Co-operation in Europe (OSCE), which had taken shape in the early 1970s on the basis of a perennial initiative of the Soviet Union dating back to 1953. Excluded from its agenda were nuclear disarmament issues, which were reserved to the two superpowers, but the OSCE did for the first time provide a forum for European countries to develop and shape détente matters in a coordinated manner. Neutral countries such as Austria, Switzerland, Finland and Sweden had a well-coordinated strategy and organized themselves and non-aligned countries such as Yugoslavia, Cyprus and Malta as an informal pressure group, the N + N countries. This group made significant contributions to the OSCE acts and lobbied successfully for the interests of small states to be taken into account. In addition to this the first troop reduction talks took place in Vienna in 1973.

Kreisky made his hard-line anti-Communist stance part of his party's platform through the Eisenstadt Declaration, which ruled out any kind of cooperation between SPÖ and KPÖ, but in spite of this he wholeheartedly supported the OSCE's broad initiative for détente. This intensive phase of détente, which in essence harked back to the *Nachbarschaftspolitik* of the 1960s, meant something different to Kreisky from what it did to many Western top politicians, even Social Democrats – namely, no renunciation of ideological confrontation and no soft-pedalling of the support for human rights. Kreisky advocated a continuation of the ideological confrontation 'by peaceful means', as every signatory state should be entitled freely to determine its political, social and cultural character.

In 1978 Bruno Kreisky was one of the few politicians, after the signing of the Helsinki Final Act of the Conference for Security and Co-operation in Europe, who focused on the following basic issue: '*We are therefore ready for this confronta-*

tion and one reason why we subscribe to the Conference for Security and Co-operation in Europe is because the principles that have been hammered out here have the potential to make this confrontation possible on a worldwide scale and by peaceful means. This is in any case how we interpret the passage in the declaration of principles where it is stated that every participant state is entitled freely to choose and develop its own political, social, economic and cultural system.'[3] The Soviet Union displayed all the symptoms of temporary irritation and retaliated by substantially downgrading Kreisky's imminent visit to Moscow in terms of diplomatic protocol.

This stated readiness to continue ideological confrontation was followed by practical political measures, for instance by the integration of Charter 77 members in Austria or by interventions for imprisoned human rights activists such as Václav Havel and Andrei Sakharov. Both the Czechoslovak leadership and the Soviet *nomenklatura* criticized this policy; bilateral relations with neighbouring Czechoslovakia suffered. It should however be stressed that even for small countries, the scope for foreign policy manoeuvring is by and large dependent on internal political considerations, particularly when the socioeconomic situation is taking a downward turn, as was the case in Austria in the late 1970s and early 1980s. Kreisky, for instance, warned of an escalation of the refugee influx after martial law had been imposed in Poland in 1981, as he was very much aware how negatively potential long-term immigration and integration of Polish asylum seekers was viewed by the Austrian population. On the geopolitical plane too, readiness for conflict was on the increase in the later phases of the Carter administration, a reaction to military dictatorship in Poland and the bloody Soviet invasion of Afghanistan. Austria did not support the boycott of the Olympic Games in Moscow; Kreisky's government was still trying to prevent a total breakdown of détente. Austria's political experts stressed the defensive character of the invasion of Afghanistan.

There was one more area where, at the end of the 1970s, the implications of socioeconomic crisis were plainly felt even in Austria, although its economy was affected less than those of many other industrialized nations: the ideological debate about arms exports documents the close tie between initiatives on the international stage and the economic constraints of nationalized industries. Such discussions were sparked in the 1970s by arms exports to Chile and Argentina. The international economic crisis in the wake of the second rise in oil prices in 1978 had increasingly upstaged ideological reservations against arms exports, and the vacuum thus created was exploited for lucrative arms exports despite the limitations imposed on Austria by the Neutrality Law.

From the North-South Conflict to Middle Eastern Politics

While Kreisky was able to build on ÖVP initiatives regarding détente and Cold War issues, his interest in the North-South conflict and in the Middle East was outside shared foreign political territory but germane to his basic concern with global security. In the context of development aid, Kreisky had made sure as early as the 1960s that the percentage of the budget earmarked for direct aid remained very low, as he felt that the lion's share of Austria's effort should go towards furthering intellectual and political discourse. This discourse found a base in the Vienna Institute for Development, founded in 1962, and came to fruition in the first North-South Summit in Cancún in 1981. Kreisky was involved in the preparations as co-chairman. Both the North-South conflict and the conflict involving Israel, the Palestinians and Israel's Arab neighbours had direct repercussions for Europe and Austria, as was demonstrated by the oil crises of the 1970s. In recognition of this fact Kreisky brought those two global, security-related issues within the range of Austria's concept of neutrality policies.

Once before, at the end of the 1960s, Kreisky had tried in vain to link initiatives related to the Middle East with the project of a European détente conference. He was considerably more successful in his attempt to alert Europe to the rights and problems of the Palestinians as represented by the PLO when the oil crises of 1973–74 and 1978 drew attention to Western Europe's dependency on the Arab region. Here Kreisky was able to pick up the thread of his old interests. An extended tour with opportunities for countless talks, under the patronage of the Socialist International of Israel and of all Arab countries directly involved in the conflict, finally established Kreisky as an important, if by no means universally accepted, commentator on related issues. While he succeeded in getting across his conviction that Egypt, under President Anwar el-Sadat, was ready to commit to peace negotiations, and in bringing about a rapprochement between Sadat and President Nixon, his main political message remained unheard, namely that what lay at the centre of a Middle Eastern peace solution was not Egypt, Jordan or Syria but the problem of the Palestinian refugees. This was the reason why he criticized the Camp David accord between Egypt and Israel under U.S. patronage: the Palestinian question had been left out.

In March 1980 Austria was the first Western state to grant the PLO political recognition, a daring and controversial foreign policy step at the time that was followed in quick succession by other Western European states. In this sense, Kreisky performed a pioneering role for the EEC, which was beginning to take an interest in the Middle East after the oil crises. President of the European Commission Gaston Thorn sought Kreisky's advice, as did many other leading European statesmen. Contacts to Israel, on the other hand, remained limited to the peace activists of Peace Now and to Uri Avnery. Even Shimon Peres broke off all contacts in the wake of Austria's recognition of the PLO, though by the late 1990s he was to realize that the road staked out by Kreisky was indeed the right one and received the Nobel Peace Prize for acting on that realization. Kreisky's line, which amounted to securing peace by integrating Arafat's PLO, was considered excessively utopian even by leading activists involved in the Oslo solution of the 1970s. Regarding the Middle East issue, one may safely agree with the verdict of the well-known U.S. commentator James Reston: The wise old man was far ahead of his time in 1983.

U.S. presidents from Nixon to Ford, Carter and even Reagan took note of Kreisky's assessments concerning conflict regulation in the Middle East, and although none were persuaded to abandon their pro-Israel and anti-PLO line, all of them did at least intensify their contacts with Arab states. Certainly Kreisky's political commitment was never interpreted as a breach of neutrality – on the contrary – and again and again Austria's 'good services' were either in demand or at least accepted when offered. Even Israel under the conservative Begin government asked Kreisky to mediate in successful exchanges of prisoners, and Jimmy Carter sent a special envoy to Vienna in 1979 to explore the possibility of Kreisky mediating an exchange for the U.S. hostages in the Tehran embassy. Kreisky had already obtained Arafat's consent to undertake this mission when the U.S., prodded by Israeli politicians, dropped the project on the grounds that commissioning Arafat would have amounted to a de facto recognition of the PLO by the U.S..

Kreisky maintained close contacts with other nonconformists on the question of the Middle East. One of these was the President of the World Jewish Congress Nahum Goldmann, who worked with Kreisky and Brandt to plan a by-invitation-only conference in Vienna, where Jewish and Arab intellectuals and opinion makers from the U.S., Europe and the Middle East were to have congregated. Nothing came of the project, mainly because of a lack of trust on the part of potential Arab and Palestinian partners. Goldmann had almost single-handedly negotiated the compensation settlement between the Federal Republic of Germany and Israel, and the agreement with the Jewish Claims conference in the 1950s. He was very critical of Israel's policies towards the Palestinians and its Arab neighbours. Like Kreisky, he condemned the Israeli intervention in Lebanon in 1981.

'Austria's Foreign Policy: A National Policy in the Best Sense of the Word'

For Bruno Kreisky foreign policy had been part of the process of Austria discovering its identity before the backdrop of history in a much wider context. ('Austria is the result of a more than 2,000-year-long integration process involving diverse great European populations.') In a deliberate demarcation from Germany, it was supposed to be 'the foreign policy of the Austrian people', 'a self-confident foreign policy which, while it is in keeping with the country's limited possibilities, yet ensures it a reputation which by far exceeds its economic and political potential'.[4] The policy of Austrian neutrality in this interpretation was not expected to deviate a great deal from the 'mainstream of world politics' but to develop alternative political scenarios.

Austria's refusal to join in the blockade of the Soviet Union arising from the imposition of martial law in Poland and the Reagan administration's criticism of the covert hi-tech transfer into the Communist bloc via Austria ushered in a gradual change in the external perception of Austria's neutrality. The era of détente, with its climax in the Conferences for Security and Cooperation in Europe, had come to end. Towards the end of the Carter years and especially under the Reagan administration, the NATO Double-Track Decision (as a reaction to a new type of Soviet missiles), the economic embargo after the USSR's invasion of Afghanistan and, most of all, the threat of U.S. armament spiralling into the illusory 'Star Wars' programme contributed to a build-up of pressure that increasingly reduced the freedom of movement for neutral countries like Austria and also became an important factor in a new domestic debate. It becomes evident here how the deterioration of the international climate under Reagan (aggravated in Europe by Margaret Thatcher) directly affected the manoeuvring scope of Austria's foreign and neutrality policy.

In the early 1980s all this added up to a portrait of Kreisky as an anti-American. This was heightened by Kreisky's reception of the Libyan revolutionary leader Muammar al-Gaddafi, as a guest of honour, and by his vehement criticism of the NATO Double-Track Decision. During the debate about Kurt Waldheim's war record it was argued that Kreisky's frequent criticisms of the U.S. had prepared the ground towards the end of the 1970s for America's 'east coast' (a loaded term: Austrian code for the Jewish-American intellectual and political establishment) to launch the 'Waldheim campaign'. However, a study of the evidence at the Carter and Reagan Presidential Libraries in conjunction with other documents has proved this thesis to be without substance: media confrontations of this kind had no influence whatever on the Waldheim debate as they caused controversies but no long-term image problems. It was the concept of neutrality as such that came under pressure from the West as the new confrontation between the U.S. and the USSR started to take hold in the 1980s.

In the early 1980s the ÖVP was visibly beginning to move away from the original concept of neutrality and to entertain the notion of an ideologically determined, 'hard' integration into the West without at first calling into doubt neutrality as such. In their effort to stake out for themselves positions different from the SPÖ's, the ÖVP therefore reacted positively to the Reagan administration's criticism of Austria's Eastern trade, despite its likely adverse effect on Austrian entrepreneurial interests. This divergent development became clear in the context of European integration, Austria's accession to the EU and the end of the Cold War.

Neutrality and European Integration

As has already been mentioned in passing, the European debate had initially had little or no public impact in the 1940s and 1950s compared to the soul searching connected with it in France, the Federal Republic of Germany and the Benelux states. Such issues as UN membership and the State Treaty coupled with the withdrawal of Allied troops that would follow were considered to be much more important. In 1956 it was ÖVP and SPÖ parliamentarians who pushed through the application for membership in the Council of Europe; to begin with, Chancellor Raab and other political decision makers failed to see the special significance of European developments. The Soviet Union demurred at this new round of Austria's integration into the West, but its Foreign Ministry only reacted to Austria's accession via a negative press. However, the tone and style of the confrontation changed for the worse once it became clear that the European Coal and Steel Community was going to be transformed in no time by the 1957 Treaties of Rome into a powerful, integrated European economic sphere. Leopold Figl's mere suggestion that Austria might aim at joining the European Coal and Steel Community provoked angry Soviet reactions. The protestations of the Soviet ambassador became increasingly urgent when a debate started in Austria about the need for the country to join the EEC as a consequence of Austria's growing economic dependence on Western Europe in general and on West Germany in particular; the factors that contributed most to this dependence were the Cold War and the slump in Austria's trade with the East.

The goals that had been defined for the postwar era by Stalin were still valid: he had sanctioned the separation of Austria from Germany and he had shown himself averse to Austria's integration into a conservative, Catholic bloc that was per se anti-communist. This postwar constant had also provided for a buffer zone wedged between the potential deployment areas of NATO and Warsaw Pact troops, which offered the Soviet Union the additional option of the use of a shortcut to northern Italy across Styria and Carinthia in case of an armed conflict. In addition to this, the economic and political equilibrium between France and Germany within the EEC, whose continuing existence was crucial for the Soviet Union, would be prevented from shifting towards a new 'Germanic' bloc.

In the days when Kreisky was still only an undersecretary of state, the SPÖ attempted to push the concept of an enlarged common economic area, an exercise in bridge building to bring together EEC members and non-EEC members including Great Britain; this project failed to take off. As long as Raab set the tone, the ÖVP stuck to its hard line in the matter of neutrality and did not seek a compromise. From 1960 to 1963 exploratory talks took place between the EEC and the three neutral countries Sweden, Switzerland and Austria on the subject of association, which provoked clear signals of resistance from both the U.S. and the Soviet Union.

It is remarkable how much broader Foreign Minister Kreisky's outlook was than that of his ÖVP partners in government, who saw the question of the EEC in exclusively economic terms. Some of them, like the minister of finance of the time, Reinhard Kamitz, or Minister of Trade and Commerce Fritz Bock, let it be known that in case Austria's EEC association did not materialize, there was still the last resort of economic Anschluss with Germany. Kreisky was neither prepared to accept the partitioning of Germany as irreversible (without thereby jeopardizing détente) nor to accept that Communist countries were to be permanently excluded from the process of European integration. This is why he thought aloud before the UN economic commission in Geneva about a pan-European system of inland waterways and why, in the late 1950s, he demanded the inclusion of Yugoslavia in a common European free trade zone. While the neutral countries tended in this context to be marginalized as of peripheral interest in Western European political discourse, Kreisky wanted Sweden, Switzerland and Austria to be accepted as integral parts of the 'Western cultural and social sphere'. The fact that he was opposed to communism by conviction did not prevent Kreisky from being equally opposed to the fatalistic conviction of the 1960s that the Cold War and European integration had cut Europe in two along the Iron Curtain for good. Free from ideologically motivated fear of contact, he quoted General de Gaulle's concept of Europe 'in the form of an organized association of its peoples from Iceland and Gibraltar to the Urals'.

The Kennedy administration had a clear political blueprint for Europe, which included not only an economic, but in the short term also a political and military union; neutral countries were perceived as obstacles to that project. The Soviet leadership declared itself opposed to Austria's affiliation to the EEC – which would in any case have fallen far short of conferring full membership on Austria – as they saw in it a revival of Anschluss. The Soviet postwar doctrine, which aimed at preventing a strengthening of German economic capacity, remained in force until the late 1980s. It demonstrates how deeply the thinking of Soviet decision makers had been shaped by the Second World War: from a strategic point of view, it was Austria's Anschluss that had finally primed Nazi Germany for aggression by giving Hitler access to Austria's raw materials, gold reserves, foreign currency and human resources.

As the senior partner in a coalition government, the ÖVP was ready after the departure of Julius Raab – and increasingly so under his successor's successor, Josef Klaus – to shelve neutrality and to prepare for sitting out a possible confrontation with the Soviet Union. Even when negotiations with the three neutral countries were terminated in 1963 after de Gaulle had made use of his veto in the most important part of the enlargement process, the accession of Great Britain, Klaus's government cheerfully continued to insist on negotiations – without realizing that the majority of EEC members (barring Germany) were not interested in Austria becoming even an associate member. Since then it has been obvious that Austrian decision makers are finding it impossible to accept one of the basic laws of European decision processes, namely that isolated interests of small countries are doomed if they cannot muster the support of broad coalitions. The special status that was accorded to Austria during the Cold War on account of its accidental geographic position is no longer relevant in the process of European integration. In spite of this many Austrian politicians still believe that in European politics Austria ought to be able to plead that it is a special case. This self-perception, no doubt one of the long-term legacies of the Cold War, is still active today and continues to cause serious difficulties in the decision making processes of the European Union. It is only when this self-perception has been addressed and adequately dealt with that Austria will be able to advance its agenda within the European Union more successfully.

Back in the 1960s memories of World War II were still active in shaping postwar policies. France, for instance, signalled after de Gaulle's departure in 1968 that Austria's insistence on its special role not only created problems in the country's relationship with the Soviet Union but was also having undesirable effects on the dynamics of French-German relations in that it potentially added to the strength of the 'German bloc'. True, it was Italy's veto, motivated by the terrorist attacks in South Tyrol, that put an end to the negotiations on Austria's 'going it alone', yet the Italians would not have taken that step had they not been aware of the attitude of the French. In France too, the Soviet formula 'Anschluss equals war', which dated back to 1938 and 1939, continued to play an important psychological role.

In the 1970s, after the accession of Great Britain and Ireland to the EEC, conditions for a broad solution that would include Austria appeared to have improved substantially. When the gap had been bridged between the EEC and EFTA (founded in 1960 as a pool for EEC aspirants including Austria), tariff barriers were removed in batches starting in 1972. Europe was practically non-existent as a topic in Austria; the whole issue seemed to have been resolved for the time being so that further progress could safely be put on the back burner. However, the legalistic debate as to the incompatibility of accession to the EEC with Austrian neutrality went on.

Into the EU on Stealthy Paws

Both the EC and Austria adapted to the economic pressures of globalized competition. Towards the end of 1985, the ÖVP had already given clear signals of its wish to change its position with regard to its European policy. Despite the misgivings that parts of the SPÖ harboured about too close an integration, the two parties reached agreement in 1989 on applying for membership of the EC; Austria, unlike Sweden and Finland, added – at the instigation of the SPÖ – a neutrality clause to its application. Soviet objections appeared increasingly antiquated in view of geopolitical developments, and French reservations voiced by President François Mitterrand concerning Austria's accession adding to Germany's political clout remained undiscussed, as did the question of how neutrality was supposed to coexist with the military aspects of the European Union. Since the second half of the 1980s, Austrian foreign policy has primarily taken its bearings from Brussels, and global topics and international topics that are not addressed in EU discourse (e.g. the North-South conflict, Africa, Asia) have played only the most marginalized of roles.

With the 'silk revolutions' of 1989–90 in Eastern Europe's Communist countries, the disintegration of the USSR and the manifold problems of its successor states (including Russia), the project of the EU came increasingly under the spell of factors that had not originally been taken into consideration. The Maastricht Treaty of 1992 materialized in a radically changed geopolitical environment that altered European dimensions without being properly addressed in the treaty. The goal of the European Union's foundation treaty continued to be the gradual realization of an economic and monetary union (EMU) with a common currency, a common Central Bank and common economic policies coupled with some kind of political union (institutional reforms and partial delegation of authority in such traditional nation state areas as judicial, home and police affairs). The European Economic Area (EEA) allowed EFTA countries close economic and legal participation in the European Single Market. The association agreements made with Hungary, Poland and Czechoslovakia were originally designed to facilitate trade and economic cooperation; they were not meant to be a first step towards quick full membership.

A timetable for development towards stronger internal integration of a twelve-member community with membership options for the candidates Austria, Sweden and Finland – the respective dates of whose applications were 1989, 1991 and 1992 – was already firmly in place. Further integration of the remaining EFTA states had already been conceived in the 1980s and became easier in principle when the Soviet Union gave up its traditional objections with regard to Austria and, at least in part, Sweden and above all Finland. On the other hand, the economic consequences of the reunification of Germany caused serious turbulence in the EC–EU's most powerful economy, whose repercussions are still very much with us today in the form of Germany's difficulties with the so-called Maastricht criteria. The integration blueprints of 1984–85 had not made allowances for the end of the Cold War and for the consequences that resulted from this development for Europe. Enlargement to twenty-five members has rendered this issue obsolete, even if the deepening of internal integration has ground to a halt.

The Soviet Union too was completely taken by surprise by the developments of 1989–90. As late as 1988–89 Austrian EU membership was considered by Moscow to be incompatible with the State Treaty and with neutrality. Yet in 1988 the first official relationship was established between Comecon and the EU, which was followed by direct contacts between the Soviet Union and the EU. The Soviet leadership also pinned high hopes on a conference on economic cooperation involving thirty-five OSCE countries, though at first it showed no signs of giving up its reservations concerning Austria. For the time being at least,

Moscow continued to interpret Austria's accession to the EU as a violation of its neutrality and a breach of the State Treaty.

There is no clear evidence to be gleaned from the memoirs of Austrian politicians as to who actually furnished the Russians with the arguments that enabled them at least passively to signal agreement to Austria's accession. Mikhail Gorbachev, in his memoirs, makes particular mention of Franz Vranitzky, then the federal chancellor, who had also brought his coalition colleague Vice-Chancellor and Foreign Minister Alois Mock round to seeing the merit of a demonstration of sovereignty. It was this token of an Austrian sovereign policy that served not only to convince Gorbachev, who was thoroughly aware of the objective necessity of Austria's economic integration, but also to signal to the EU members that Austria was by no means being manoeuvred into a repeat of Anschluss. It proved necessary for Vranitzky to point out repeatedly to France and especially to François Mitterrand how unfounded these misgivings were. After a state visit to Moscow on 11 October 1988, the Soviet Union's reservations remained outwardly unchanged (and were voiced repeatedly in the media), but in the realm of realpolitik the die had been cast. Alois Mock's high-profile pro-NATO line would otherwise certainly have caused much bigger problems, particularly when one bears in mind that the public positions of Paris and Moscow had changed little since the 1960s.

Austrian politicians have contributed their fair share to reviving old Anschluss anxieties in one of Europe's most recent tragic phases. By supporting Germany's lone decision to recognize the declarations of independence of Croatia and Slovenia in defiance of the EU majority, which called for certain conditions to be observed, Austria too stoked the fires in this part of the Balkans and once again provoked, quite gratuitously, criticism and historical memories in France.

The Neutrality Debate as a Domestic Political Intermezzo

Moscow's reactions to Austria's 1994 EU referendum were positive on the whole, yet divergent attitudes within the coalition that signalled contradictory positions in this respect were seen as irritating, particularly after NATO East Enlargement had added the Czech Republic, Poland and Hungary to that organization. While Vranitzky's successor Viktor Klima considered NATO membership and neutrality totally incompatible, the then Foreign Minister Wolfgang Schüssel seemed less sure, at least in the eyes of the Russian press. The FPÖ under Jörg Haider had already staked out its position in 1990 with the motto 'NATO only', and in 1997 Haider went on to announce NATO membership as imminent.

In Austria's internal debates the First Gulf War and, in 1991, the Third Balkan War led to fierce controversies, but mostly behind the closed doors of government. Neutrality no longer occupied the high ground it had held in public opinion in the 1980s, although none of the political parties – not even the FPÖ – was prepared to be seen openly advocating its abolition. A report on the options available, which was commissioned by the Grand Coalition, further cemented this stalemate. The new ÖVP-FPÖ coalition shunted the whole issue to a committee of experts, even though both parties had long been in favour of the NATO option.

In spite of the absence of a realistic foreign threat to Austria and after the evaporation of the WEU as a genuine option, many politicians, particularly in the ÖVP and FPÖ-BZÖ camps but not entirely excluding the SPÖ, consider NATO membership the move that will clinch Austria's Western integration. What shapes the issue in the eyes of some are the passionate debates on the violations of human rights and mass murders in the Balkans, as well as the necessity to demonstrate international solidarity. The SPÖ as a whole, putting the phase of a carefully devised non-position during the Klima years behind itself, has now taken a stand on neutrality and the development of a pan-European security architecture.

It is highly probable that here, too, external factors will play a decisive role in the end, as was already the case with the Neutrality Law. It becomes apparent again that Austria is either unable or unwilling to coordinate at government level its position with regard to neutrality with other EU neutrals, above all with Finland and Sweden. While the two Nordic neutrals maintain a steady flow of relevant common projects and initiatives, Austria stews in the domestic political juices of a political and legalistic debate that is not devoid of bizarre overtones. Mere participation in the NATO programme Partnership for Peace (which also includes Switzerland) is not going to solve the problem.

What has also become manifest in this context is how detached from public opinion the assessments of the political elites have become on this issue. This constitutes another difference compared with Sweden or Finland, where there is no indication of mainstream support for NATO membership, even if neutrality as such is called into question, notably in Sweden. A telling example was Thomas Klestil, who came to the presidency after many years as a diplomat in the United States, where he received the most distinctive 'Atlantic' imprint of all of Austria's politicians. Yet in spite of an ever more noticeable pro-NATO policy shift, which started out as a cautious questioning of the usefulness of the concept of neutrality in the framework of a new security system in 1992, Klestil conspicuously refrained from getting things moving in this direction.

The Austrian debate is, as one might indeed have expected, ideologically determined. In contrast to Sweden, it is not informed by the fact that the EU, under the leadership of France and the U.K., has put together a 60,000-man Rapid Reaction Force, which in effect constitutes the kernel of a European army. Andreas Khol, the parliamentary leader of the ÖVP in the coalition from 1994 to 1999, considered the lack of consensus on this issue to be the deadly virus that would finish off the coalition. (He subsequently reverted to upholding neutrality.) Yet it is a fact that the EU decision in favour of the Rapid Reaction Force, which was taken during Austria's presidency at the Pörtschach summit, has shifted the whole discourse to an entirely different level. Tensions are beginning to appear between the U.S. and the EU, as the U.S. feels excluded from this security discourse and is concerned that its dominance, which is based on superior military technology, might be endangered. Austria will put 3,500 soldiers at the disposal of this European force. The present coalition (2007), whose line can be summed up as 'NATO membership once the SPÖ says "Yes"', seems therefore to be banking on an option that is already out of date.

In the 1970s, the debate on comprehensive national defence featured as its central topics civil resistance and the anchoring of Austrian sovereignty in international politics, but all that matters for many people today is the option of NATO membership and, in a related development, access to cutting-edge military technology and the establishment of a professional army. However, this would mean an armament boost, which would not automatically be offset by NATO membership, coming at a time moreover when most other countries are disarming and reducing expenditure on armaments. It becomes more and more apparent that by contrast to the decision in favour of rearmament and the introduction of compulsory military service, the issue of NATO is not discussed in the light of foreign and security political considerations, but merely along the fault lines of domestic political ideology – which is a dangerous course for a small state to pursue.

The contradiction that has been noted by some between neutrality and European solidarity is reminiscent of the Cold War. Yet it was in the 'hottest' decades of the Cold War that Austria, without ever allowing doubts to arise as to its solidarity with the West in spite of its neutrality, played an important and constructive role. Not to replenish this position with new content but simply to pursue in ideological complacency membership in a military alliance that continues to be dominated by the U.S., which also implies the risk of military deployment outside the domain of European solidarity, appears a simplistic and by no means innovative solution.

NOTES

1. Lyndon B. Johnson Library, National Security File, Country File Austria, Vol. 1, Box 163, From U.S. Defense Attache's Office–Vienna, 19 September 1968.
2. The Declassified Documents 1992, Frame 0236, Neutralism in Europe Summary Report, drafted by the Department of State, June 1955.
3. Kreisky, *Reden,* Vol. II, (Vienna: Verlag der Österreichischen Staatsdruckerei, 1981), 756.
4. Stiftung Bruno Kreisky Archiv, Material Bundesministerium für Auswärtige Angelegenheiten, Copies of Martin Fuchs, Minutes of the Conference of Heads of Department at Schloss Wartenstein, 6 July 1961, 17.

CHAPTER 7

'Alles Walzer…'

The Politics of Art and Culture as the Early Second Republic's Elixir of Life

State Culture at Any Cost

'Austria as a cultural superpower' had already been used as a concept by the political elites of the First Republic to compensate for the country's traumatic shrinkage. Only a few days after the dissolution of the Austro-Hungarian Empire on 12 November 1918, the monarchy's executor, the state notary, announced that none of the state theatres would be closed down in the new, republican dispensation. Culture was also supposed to serve the republic, even though the state-run cultural establishment, which was concentrated in Vienna, was dimensioned so as to meet the needs of an empire of 50 million people and was, in this gargantuan form, impossible to finance through public subsidies. This political interpretation of culture was defined in exclusive terms and depended on the political and economic elites, both bourgeois and noble, for acceptance. Yet there were exceptions, such as patrons of the arts who gave moral and financial support to avant-garde artists. One might instance the Lederers, a Bohemian-Austrian-Jewish industrial family, who supported Gustav Klimt and bought his University frescoes, which had been rejected as decadent by those who had originally commissioned them for the Ceremonial Hall of Vienna University.

Austria's alleged superiority over Germany in cultural matters must be seen against the backdrop of the ideologically heterogeneous strivings for Anschluss with Germany. The claim to higher cultural refinement was supposed to ensure for Austria the role of the 'better Germany' and preferential treatment in the pan-German Reich. Ever since the middle of the nineteenth century various Austrian governments had tried to make use of Austria's cultural prowess in the country's rivalry with the militarily and economically superior Prussians. In terms of realpolitik, these strengths had enabled the German Reich to decide this rivalry in its favour long before 1914, and Germany's cultural establishment was competing on equal terms with such Habsburg cultural pillars as the Burgtheater or the Hofoper. Here too the Germans proved more than a match, at least in some aspects; moreover, they developed a multitude of cultural centres. However, the subjective feeling of superiority that distinguished Habsburg subjects, notably the bureaucratic and military elites, helped them to sublimate the political defeats that Prussia had inflicted on the Empire and to ignore its effective marginalization.

The claim to cultural superiority even managed to weather the Nazi regime, despite the Fuhrer's best efforts to the contrary. Hitler felt Austria's cultural narcissism was not conducive to the functioning of the system and set about reducing Vienna's cultural hegemony. The capital was going to be upstaged by Linz and Graz, the new centres of German cultural development. However, the advent of Baldur von Schirach changed all this, and the 'Austrian' component, notably in the culture of Vienna, was soon back in fashion: its purpose now was not to strengthen Austria's separatist tendencies but to bolster the National Socialist determination to defend the country against the Allies. In this dilemma, even some German and Viennese modern art was tolerated, including Gustav Klimt: the main proviso was that the artists passed the Nazis' racial test. Hitler and Goebbels, who were concerned about distinct separatist tendencies, criticized this cultural policy agenda, and their criticism became more urgent after the Wehrmacht's defeat at Stalingrad and the beginning of the westward push of the Red Army.

In a way, history proved Goebbels and Hitler's hunch right. In both opera and dramatic productions, as of 1941 aesthetic criteria were developed that were to be characteristic of the first postwar years in the phase of reconstruction, as will be demonstrated below for the Staatsoper (with its Mozart style) and the Burgtheater (with its cultivation of the classics). Most productions received a brittle coat of modernistic varnish, which of course fell ludicrously short of making them genuinely modern; yet it sufficed as an indication that Austria had parted ways both with her imperial tradition and with Germany. The 'Wien-Film' aesthetics of those years, with its operetta and *Wiener-Mädel* productions, left its mark on German cinema around 1941 and segued perfectly into the mainstream of the postwar film industry. For instance, Willi Forst was able to complete the film he had been forced to abandon in 1944, 'Wiener Mädeln', in 1949. It was not until the 1960s that this cloyingly sweet Viennese operetta style was finally disposed of.

It was the political officers and commissars of the Red Army – and this is no accident – who insisted immediately after the liberation of Vienna on 13 April 1945 that the institutions of high culture become operational again as soon as possible, regardless of whether or not their stars were compromised by a Nazi past. Stalin had decreed in 1941 that Austria was to revert to being a political entity independent of Germany after the defeat of the Nazi regime, and the Moscow Declaration of 1 November 1943 had informed the international community of his intention: now was the time for the Soviets to encourage Austria's cultural sovereignty with all the means at their disposal. It was therefore necessary for cultural life to boast as many prominent names as possible. People's sense of identity was thought to thrive on the manifestations of cultural life; this was, incidentally, equally true of the diverse émigré circles and associations.

It was not only the Soviets who considered the culture portfolio essential for the reestablishment of an independent small state but also the KPÖ. In the preparatory talks that preceded the formation of Social Democrat Karl Renner's interim government, the KPÖ, supported by Soviet political officers, claimed the ministry of education as their due. The portfolio was subsequently given to the literary figure and cultural politician Ernst Fischer, who had just returned from exile in Moscow. Fischer wholly embraced the Soviet line by making the earliest possible reopening of the theatres one of his top priorities and by refusing to allow any immediate addressing of the issue of artists' political past. A case in point was the Vienna Philharmonic, which had an unusually high percentage of ex-Nazis in its ranks; if it was to survive as an orchestra, it was deemed necessary to take a lenient view of this fact. (At the same time, artists who were guilty of *direct* collaboration with the Nazi regime or who had been members of the SS were suspended from their jobs.) With this climate in mind it may become easier to understand how it was possible for one of the most active NSDAP members in Berlin artistic circles in the 1930s, the actor-director and, at the climax of his career, director of the Burgtheater (1939–1945) Lothar Müthel, to continue to be active at the Burgtheater after the end of the Nazi era: of all plays, he directed Lessing's *Nathan der Weise* obviously to distract from his 1943 production of a crassly anti-Semitic *Merchant of Venice.*

As far as repertoire was concerned, it was obvious from the start that Ernst Fischer was not going to go out on a limb to promote modern, avant-garde or – least of all – anti-fascist contemporary drama; instead, he opted for the cultivation of the classics, not least by appointing as Müthel's successor Raoul Aslan, one of the legendary members of the ensemble and a dyed-in-the-wool Catholic conservative. It should be noted, however, that in the absence of suitable scripts or even acting copies in the immediate aftermath of the war, the classics were the only realistic option open. On top of this Ernst Fischer was convinced that the intensive cultivation of Franz Grillparzer and Johann Nestroy was going to do wonders for the resuscitation of the 'Austrian national character' and would finally, as a kind of cultural uber-ideology, put paid to pan-German nationalism and to 'Prussianism'. In this respect he wittingly adopted Catholic and Austro-Fascist positions.

Contemporary art and modern art of the fin de siècle and of the era after 1918 was the remit of Viktor Matejka, who was appointed to the culture portfolio in Vienna's City Council soon after he had been released from Dachau concentration camp. In Vienna too continuity was the watchword of the day, and every effort was made to give new employment to the great stars – this time even in the service of the greater glory of a new state. Nevertheless, there was a phase in

ILLUSTRATION 7.1
A curious instance of Viennese urban planning: How to revive Prater?

1945–46, which is often ignored in today's debates, in which a whole series of brave attempts were made to rehabilitate modernism and contemporary art, attempts that bore the clear hallmark of anti-Fascism. The *Neues Österreich* carried a report on 24 May 1945 about the foundation of the Internationale Gesellschaft für Neue Musik, the International Association for New Music, which was said to be planning for its first concert in June a programme consisting of Prokofiev's *Overture on Hebrew Themes,* op. 34, and works by Hindemith, de Falla, and Schönberg; further planning included Lieder by Hanns Eisler on lyrics by Brecht, Silone, etc. The programme for the first festive occasion of the Österreichische Volkspartei (ÖVP), by Kurt Maresch-Dichtl, who after much party-political extemporizing ended up, under the name of Kurt Dieman, as a political commentator in *Kronenzeitung,* was dedicated to 'Immortal masters – eternal Austria' (Beethoven, Grillparzer, Mozart, Schubert and Wildgans). The Vienna Philharmonic, on the other hand, played Gustav Mahler, who had been anathema to the Nazi regime. And the ÖVP-inspired 'Österreichische Kulturvereinigung', having outed itself as committed to Christian, occidental values, mustered the courage, at least in 1946, to swim against the current at the federal level of the party by exhibiting 'Modern Austrian Art' with Albertina prints by Klimt (who had also featured in exhibitions at the Künstlerhaus during the Nazi era), Schiele and Kokoschka; only in its next project did it revert to the traditional fare of 'Great art from Austria's monasteries'.

The ambivalence of 1945–46 was due to the loose structures of state organization of art and culture before Felix Hurdes, the ÖVP minister of education, started in 1946 to pull the reins tight again at the federal level and to steer a conservative, Catholic, rightist course. In 1945 anti-fascist manifestations were still seen using ostracized, persecuted 'modern' art; in 1946 the conservative rollback was unmistakable. The onset of the Cold War, which can be dated to February 1946 in Austria, unsurprisingly made the cultural political frontline coincide (with a few exceptions) with the ideological demarcations. The debate about the definition of 'Austrian literature', which was conducted in *Österreichisches Tagebuch* by Eva Priester, who had returned from exile in London, and Alexander Lernet-Holenia, may serve as a paradigm for the larger climate change. Priester pleaded for a new, political literature anchored in the present; Lernet-Holenia simply wanted to 'continue from where the dreams of a madman threw us off course ... There is no need for us to flirt with the future and to engage in nebulous projects, we are, in the best and most valuable sense, our past; all we need to do is to become aware that we are our past and that past will become our future'.

In 1946 Eva Priester was, as a matter of fact, already on the Cold War blacklist; as a Communist she was struck off the list of poets invited to devise the lyrics of the new anthem by Felix Hurdes; Paula Grogger was inserted in her place. Grogger felt 'akin to the whole German people' in 1946 and prognosticated a new Anschluss ('My Austrian genotype is strong enough not to be diluted by

Anschluss with our brothers'). This lack of distance from German nationalism failed to make Hurdes uncomfortable, even though he had himself experienced two spells in a concentration camp (1938–39 and 1944–45).

In late 1946 the chairman of the Association of Democratic Writers and Journalists (Verband demokratischer Schriftsteller und Journalisten), Edwin Rollett, who like Hurdes had been twice imprisoned in a concentration camp (1938–40, 1945), drew attention to the fact that Austria's postwar literary production was totally out of kilter. There was a strong preponderance of 'katholisches Schrifttum', Catholic-inspired writing of the type produced by Rudolf Henz and Paula von Preradovic, and hardly any contemporary literature. Rollett complained that this situation was made worse through diverse intrigues against individuals of 'moral integrity and with a clean record', whereas those who 'did have something to hide could count on being given a hand up in every possible way'. Another unhelpful factor was the preferential treatment given to newspapers in terms of paper rationing; only 9.8 per cent of pulp was made available for book production between April and September 1946. Diverse lists of banned books, which came into force for booksellers and lending libraries on 1 September 1946, failed to achieve their objective: in the absence of a public debate on the banned works the lists only made matters worse.

A further escalation of this development occurred in 1948 when Josef Nadler's *Literaturgeschichte Österreichs* appeared in a Linz publishing house. Nadler had been an active supporter of National Socialist ideology in his role as professor at Vienna University and had been at pains to elaborate it in the fourth volume of his *Literaturgeschichte des deutschen Volkes*. Seventy-five personalities of public life signed a memorandum that was handed by Rollett to Minister of Education Felix Hurdes, who declared himself willing to 'look into' the matter. Viktor Reimann, the star commentator of the *Salzburger Nachrichten* and later the co-founder of the VdU, a haven for ex-Nazis, and others felt it was opportune to campaign for an end to the debate on the National Socialist past. The seventy-five intellectuals, among them the playwright Fritz Hochwälder, the director G.W. Pabst and many representatives of the cultural bureaucracy, were massively attacked and pilloried in what amounted to a blacklist. The struggle for the electoral favour of the 400,000 ex-members of the NSDAP, who had been reenfranchised by the general amnesty for the '*Minderbelasteten*', the less seriously implicated, had moved into the field of culture.

'Recourse to a Reconstructed Order'

Due to extensive damage from a bombing raid on 12 April 1945, the Burgtheater was forced to relocate to the Ronacher, which had to be rented at great expense; on 30 April it reopened in its temporary new premises with Franz Grillparzer's

'Sappho'. The Staatsoper and the Theater in der Josefstadt followed on 1 May with 'Le nozze di Figaro' and Martin Costa's 'Hofrat Geiger', a film and television perennial to the present day. Because the opera building had been destroyed on 12 March 1945, the Volksoper had to stand in as a venue.

It soon became apparent that in matters of the politics of culture the decisions shaping the Second Republic's first few decades had already been preempted by both the Allies (notably the Soviets) and the Austrians: given the task of shoring up a small state in a socioeconomic crisis, conservative to postnationalistic art styles were considered to inspire more loyalty to the state than the unaccommodating 'moderns', let alone the avant-gardists. Paul Kruntorad rightly noted in 1990 that art production after 1945 was predominantly traditionalist and that reception patterns were under the spell of the 'inspired masters' concept. Even among the artists who had made it into the 'genius' category, those who had taken up ideological positions close to communism were either marginalized or cut dead. For Social Democrats it was advisable to either stay mostly in their ideological camp or to align themselves with Grand Coalition projects. The 'pillarization syndrome' of the First Republic was still very much present. 'State art' and 'state artists' had to cope with a conservative, Catholic framework until the end of the 1960s.

The most important theatrical and operatic productions of the first postwar years had already proved their power in terms of affirming the political status quo in the Nazi era, against the backdrop of the Second World War and complete with allusions to contemporary art. The famous postwar Viennese Mozart style, which was exported after 1947 when the opera toured the world to demonstrate little Austria's intrinsic loveliness and to provide a cultural safety net for its victim doctrine, had been developed since 1941 by the conductor Karl Böhm, the director Oscar Fritz Schuh and the stage designer Caspar Neher. The aesthetics of the mise en scène and of the stage design contained modern references but stopped well short of intruding on the music and the performance of the singers. It contained no potential for provocation or critique of the system, yet it was nevertheless perceived and classified as contemporary by the public.

It was in particular the reactions to the visual arts that provided seismographic signals for what was tolerable in terms of social politics. In 1943 Schirach's policy of promoting contemporary art had provoked vehement opposition from Hitler, Goebbels and numerous other Nazi potentates. Here abstract works of art by 'Aryan' painters played havoc with aesthetic demarcation lines. The exhibition 'Junge Kunst im Deutschen Reich' (Young Art in the German Reich) was shut down prematurely in 1943, and Schirach's cultural manager, the former dramaturge Walter Thomas, was replaced. After 1945, too, it was the visual arts that showed how small the space for manoeuvre was in fact for contemporary art in the young postwar democracy. Contacts to living artists were sought, but their products often proved scandalous and led to polemics, marginalization and censorship. The frescoes of the abstract painter Max Weiler in Innsbruck's St Teresa church in 1946 triggered a public debate that degenerated into personal threats against the artist. In 1947 the Innsbruck bishop, Paulus Rusch, convened a jury that forced Weiler to give God the Father more majestic features, and the three outstanding frescoes had to be presented for authorization in the form of sketches. In the same year the debate was rekindled with even greater vehemence, when Weiler's lance-wielding soldier at the crucifixion was depicted as a Tyrolean peasant. Three of his frescoes were withdrawn from public view between June 1950 and 1958, after the Vatican had intervened in 1949 and threatened the imposition of an ecclesiastical interdict. Conversely, the frescoes of Hermann Eisenmenger – who, having been sanctioned as the director of Künstlerhaus by that regime, had already been in fashion during the Nazi era – were considered to be highly acceptable. It was Eisenmenger who won the competition for the décor of Vienna's Western railway station as well as the competition for the painting on the opera's fire curtain; the wall paintings in the cinema of Wiener Künsterhaus (1949) are also his work.

Max Weiler's frescoes in the Innsbruck railway station and his abstract depiction of the Tyrol's struggle for freedom under Andreas Hofer also caused a local scandal, as did Giselbert Hoke's frescoes at the Klagenfurt railway station. These latter were at least popular with the public, but ÖVP and SPÖ politicians took umbrage and the minor storm blown up by the regional and local press took a long time to subside. When this was capped by an ink attack on the painting, the artist turned his back on Carinthia for a couple of years. The SPÖ usually cosied up to the ÖVP's aesthetic standards and remained absent from the culture political debate until 1970.

The art-political public debate was articulated extremely aggressively and without regard to manners or bourgeois etiquette in the struggle with modernism and avant-garde. The ideological mastermind behind the traditionalist, conservative drift, the art historian Hans Sedlmayr, also had his roots in the visual arts. His polemic against modernism (and against the French Revolution and its consequences), 'Der Verlust der Mitte' (The Loss of the Centre), which still resonates with some today, had originally taken shape between 1941 and 1944. As a committed NSDAP member, he was suspended from his teaching post by Vienna University and devoted himself to getting his work ready for print.[1] His editor, Taras Borodajkewycz, a Catholic pan-German and former Nazi informer, received as his share of the royalties 75,525 Austrian schillings, which would be 58,000 euros in value-adjusted terms. The political orientation becomes fully apparent from documents in the possession of the publishing house of Otto Müller, which Arno Kleibel has made available for research for this volume.

In France, 'Verlust der Mitte' was, to the annoyance of its author, ignored completely. In German-speaking countries it created a tremendous stir and sold well: 150,000 copies, including a paperback edition, by 1960. Critics paid homage to the work; even Friedrich Heer dignified it with an excursus on the significance of modern art in the Catholic weekly *Die Furche*. On the other hand, Lothar Schreyer, a Hamburg painter, writer and dramaturge, professed himself shocked that the Catholic publishing house of Otto Müller had published 'Sedlmayr's dreadful book ... which repeats all the reproaches that had been levelled at art by National Socialism (bar one, namely that it is a Jewish invention)'.

Sedlmayr's wife incidentally discovered H.C. Artmann for the publishing house of Otto Müller, which perhaps says something about the catholicity of taste in the Sedlmayr household. The publisher in his turn did a background check on the poet that classified him as 'not belonging to the left-leaning poets (an ever present danger particularly among the "moderns")'. Artmann was accepted for publication on the basis of this 'certificate' and quickly became one of the publisher's best-selling authors, particularly in the 'Alt-Reich' (original Otto Müller sound bite) from 1958. To be on the safe side, Müller gave Artmann the sobriquet 'the romantic born into another age', whose contact to the 'Art Club, where you will find the most stylish hair-dos and the tightest pants' was no more than another of many masks behind which this 'Viennese dialect poet' chose to hide.

In view of such continuities, in terms of both content and *dramatis personae,* one question becomes imperative: to what extent did the presence of the Allies, who wielded a great deal of practical political power especially during the years immediately after the war, affect the development of the arts and of culture in general in Austria? Or, to put it more radically: is it true that Austria's cultural landscape in the first post-war years was the result of the 'culture politics ... of a self-appointed bourgeois elite that prided itself on its superior education'? Was this elite 'only marginally permeable or transparent'? Did it consider its raison d'être to be the promotion of a handful of 'state artists'?[2] Finally, was it indeed obsessed with 'the struggle against "Schmutz und Schund"', filth and crap? Gerhard Rühm, speaking at a symposium in Vienna in 1996, went on to say that for the years between 1945 and 1955, with their reactionary, unreflecting tenor, the 'Four in the Jeep' had been completely irrelevant. They never amounted to much more than the possibility of borrowing a John Cage record from the Amerika-Haus, and even these hints of modernity disappeared all too quickly with the onset of McCarthyism.

France, the occupying power that has to be classified as the weakest player in Austria after 1945 in terms of both political influence and resources, compensated for its geopolitical weakness by being particularly active in matters of culture politics. After the first fact-finding missions in September 1945, direct engagement with National Socialism played a dominant role (in the sense of 'désannexion, désintoxication, démocratisation'); in 1946 a shift occurred in the ideological framework. France's cultural politics was supposed to inhabit a sort of intellectual halfway house between the new 'materialistic systems' of the mercantile 'Anglo-Saxon bloc' and the 'utilitarianism' of the Soviets. From this position France hoped both to help Austria arrive at a balanced position itself and to create a foothold for a French presence in the country. What did not escape the French experts were long-term effects of the Nazi regime. One example was found in young people in the Tyrol, among whom they found evidence of the persistence, in 1947, of 'virulent anti-Semitism and anti-Slavism'. They felt that the ideal cultural antidote to this was recourse to the baroque, Catholic values of the Habsburg Empire before 1918, even though this meant a deliberate side-lining of modern Austrian cultural developments prior to 1938 (e.g. Viennese Modernism or the achievements of Red Vienna). These retrospective, conservative efforts at stabilization partly overlapped with the cultural programme of the ÖVP and therefore reinforced, both in western Austria and in parts of Vienna (the First District was part of the French zone), trends towards the revitalization – or the creation in the first place – of a baroque, Catholic-conservative Austrian identity with a clear anti-Prussian edge.

The French cultural officers were aware – perhaps more so than their U.S. colleagues – that bureaucratic penal-law denazification measures (temporary employment bans, temporary disenfranchisement of former members of the NS-DAP and '*Sühneabgaben*', the payment of compensatory fines to the state) would not succeed in bringing about a long-term ideological reorientation. They were all the more determined to foster the 'renaissance' of a Catholic Habsburg Austrian identity as an antithesis to German-style 'pan-Germanism'.

In spite of its pragmatism and acquiescence in Austria's culture political mainstream – which was actively promoted by the ÖVP while the SPÖ and KPÖ played more of a backseat role – France contributed important long-term impulses to modernism in Austria. It is remarkable what a powerful influence French modernism exerted on Austria's artists (especially painters and sculptors) and on its elites, although public discourse (for example in Innsbruck) occasionally took a decidedly dimmer view of French contemporary art and its followers in Austria. This difference between reception by the elite and public (or rather: published) opinion accounts at least partly for cultural historiography's lack of attention to French cultural influence. It remains important not to overlook the long-term effects French models or such factors as scholarships to France had on several important key figures of the art scene in the late 1960s and 1970s.

The Allied power that appeared to be applying the most comprehensive and revolutionary concepts to Austria's cultural scene was undoubtedly the U.S.. In a way that paralleled what was happening in the British sphere of influence, the first U.S. culture-political directives, above all the 'Decree No.10', aimed at total control coupled with a temporary complete cessation of all cultural activities. Only after this were anti-Nazi 'licensees' supposed to initiate a gradual restart of cultural life. The concept behind this 'pyramid policy' was an attempt to replace the old elites with new ones by meticulously vetting and 'licensing' all individuals engaged in cultural activities, a thoroughly revolutionary idea. Yet in spite of its merits as a blueprint, the policy was undercut from the start by the Soviets and by Renner's interim government.

It turned out in practice that vetting every artist and every member of the the-atre bureaucracy along political lines was an insurmountable obstacle to a speedy resumption of cultural activities. It took several weeks for the Black, Grey and White Lists, prepared and augmented on an ongoing basis from the end of 1944 by U.S. military agencies (who relied on the cooperation of émigrés and the Se-cret Services) to become effective. The idea was that all members of the NSDAP, all active collaborators and all fellow-travellers would be banned from appear-ing in public, processed in a kind of administrative screening and, on successful completion of the procedure, declared fit to resume their professional activities.

The practical implementation of these procedures was entrusted to a section of the Information Services Branch headed by Otto de Pasetti, a singer who, as the available evidence would suggest, had emigrated to the U.S. on political grounds. Born Otto Freiherr von Pasetti-Friedenburg, he had had a modest career in Graz and Vienna, where Lotte Lenya took refuge with him after fleeing Nazi Germany in 1933. Pasetti was virtually a one-man operation for the first few weeks; nev-ertheless he tried as best he could both to carry out political background checks on the artists and to get the theatres going as quickly as possible. His outfit did not become operational until 29 May, yet on 8 July 1945, the Salzburg Landes-theater, which like all other theatres had been closed down by Goebbels in Sep-tember 1944, was already open for business. In this case the initiative proceeded from the Austrian side, with the Theatre and Music Section of the Information Services Branch supplying logistical and bureaucratic backup.

It is true for the first years that U.S., British, French and Russian authors were relatively strongly represented on Austria's theatrical stage, yet this fanning out into an international dimension was limited to the conservative range of the spectrum. The only exceptions were Vienna's Volkstheater and occasionally the Neues Theater in der Scala (from 1948); both attempted to counter this trend by putting on modern productions of plays by controversial authors that turned on contemporary issues. The Scala was promptly stigmatized as Communist-oriented and was forced to close down in 1956. Leon Epp, who took over the Volkstheater as director in 1952, realized, as Hilde Haider-Pregler has put it, 'the paradox of a vibrant theatre focused on present-day issues, yet embedded in a totally anachronistic structure'.[3]

Traces of the influence of U.S. culture at the time have survived from diverse exchange programmes, from the 'Rot-Weiss-Rot' group of German-language ra-dio stations and from the activities of Marcel Prawy, who, along with fellow émigré Ernst Haeusserman, imported the musical to Austria. All the same, the Austrians' preconceived verdict that 'Americans' were devoid of culture remained unaffected by all these activities as well as by those of the Kosmos touring theatre company. Rejection of U.S. popular culture was very much in evidence in the first years after the war. Jazz was unpopular with listeners to Rot-Weiss-Rot and was dismissed with racial stereotyping by prominent music critics until well into the 1950s.

Memory Sites of Austria's Postwar Culture

Memory sites are symbolic representations of what is stored in the collective memory of a society: events, personalities, artefacts, buildings, squares, topographical spots, etc., in the most diverse forms, contents and functions (such as memorial days, anniversaries, monuments, death rites, street names etc.). There are different methods for identifying and decoding these memory sites, whose significance is in a perpetual state of flux. In what follows, the film *Die Stimme Österreichs* (The Voice of Austria), which Ernst Haeusserman made while he was still a U.S. cultural officer, has been chosen to demonstrate what memory sites resonated most with postwar audiences. In the subject matter of its images and in its music, which accompanies Judith Holzmeister's tragically tinged commentary, it offers in an almost ideal-typical manner the entire repertoire of the core images of the postwar era.

Christian (Catholic) Popular Culture and the 'Pummerin'

As an émigré returning to his former country, Ernst Haeusserman was in a better position than many of his American colleagues to appreciate the strong dose of Catholicism in Austria's cultural life. He had been commissioned to produce a documentary on U.S. aid; in fact, Haeusserman turned *Die Stimme Österreichs* into something resembling an epic describing the cultural and political framework of the country. The opening sequences of the film are devoted to the journey on 25 April of a huge bell, the Pummerin, from a foundry in Upper Austria to its destination, the bell tower of St Stephen's Cathedral in Vienna. The original bell, which dated from 1711, had been destroyed on 12 April 1945.

The Pummerin is used in the film as a symbol of the 'good old way of life' that had fallen victim to the Second World War, which is the subject of the second sequence of the film. The devastation it caused is the second great theme, along with the symbols of the Catholic faith that crop up again and again. After a sequence that is focused on the U.S. presence, images of a Corpus Christi procession on Lake Hallstatt and of the construction of a cross on the summit of Dachstein lead up to what is the film's most substantial statement on Austrian culture. Haeusserman quite deliberately chose an approach that continued to be popular throughout the 1950s: '*Heurigen*' bliss in the Wachau, the grape harvest, dancers in traditional costumes and festival processions in Vienna's Prater. It almost looks as if the script was written by ÖVP cultural planners. Within the ruling coalition, the SPÖ, which in the years between the wars had proposed an alternative cultural programme at least for Vienna, now left the art and culture agenda – with the exception of education – completely to the ÖVP. It was up to Bruno Kreisky to bring about a change in this respect. In the meantime the typical, constantly reiterated wish, as formulated by such lights as Franz Kranebitter, an ÖVP MP, was the 'revival and appropriate make-over of our precious cultural heritage of music, folk song, folk dancing, popular drama and of the whole treasure of autochthonous customs in town and country'.[4]

Minister of Education Felix Hurdes repeatedly underscored the religious dimension in this context, for 'all creative thinking and all artistic creativity aims at proximity to God and man's embeddedness in God'.[5] The Cold War, which entailed a permanent cultural struggle against 'leftist' artists, was underpinned by a Christian humanism of the kind exemplified by Sedlmayr's *Verlust der Mitte*. This stance had been a 'decisive factor in the shaping of the Occident. Everything that we Europeans, we natives of the Occident welcome, everything that appears to be under threat from demoniac powers, is the fruit of Christian humanism and constitutes the character of Europe'.[6] These are the words of Raimund Poukar, a Catholic journalist who had survived imprisonment in a concentration camp and was the Ministry of Education press spokesman from 1945 to 1955.

In Haeusserman's documentary this retrospective position, with its heavy ideological burden, was further enhanced by emphasis on the agrarian sector. Even though this was in principle in keeping with the economic basis of a society engaged in reconstruction, it was done in a mythologizing manner that overshot the mark by far. Images such as the harvest being brought in by mountain farmers on horse-drawn carts and wood rafting on the Salzach were hardly representative of agriculture in the 1950s.

From Johann Strauss's Voices of Spring to Beethoven's Ninth Symphony: Music in the Postwar Era

In 1953, the year of Haeusserman's film, neither the Vienna Staatsoper nor the Burgtheater had yet been rebuilt; they were not yet functional as memory sites. However, this did not detract from the importance of the aesthetic role music, notably classical music, played in the postwar era. The sense of purpose felt when the old and new political and economic elites gathered for the first Philharmonic concerts on 27 and 28 April 1945 was highly significant. There was a strong admixture of the Soviet military in the audience, deliberately encouraged by the liberal dispensation of free tickets by the Philharmonic. This was followed in rapid succession by musical events staged by the Austro-French Association with works by Berlioz, Bizet, Ravel and others. The Soviet Union sent three star violinists (amongst them David Oistrakh) to claim their share in the nascent memory site of the Vienna Philharmonic. The politics of culture was, after all, not an exclusively Austrian domain.

As a collective, the Vienna Philharmonic had special meals laid on for them at the Rathauskeller, received extra rations of clothing material and fuel, and were partly exempted from denazification measures. As former NSDAP members, a quarter of the orchestra members were suspended from active service, but the purge was confined predominantly to elderly musicians. The top priority was for the orchestra not to lose too many musicians, as this would have told in its sound. The public debate concerning the orchestra's Nazi involvement got bogged down at the level of individual party memberships. A genuine debate about what had happened inside the orchestra, namely the dismissal or pensioning-off of Jewish musicians, and the artistic consequences of the banning of Jewish composers from the repertoire would arguably have resulted in deeper insight. It took a Leonard Bernstein to teach the orchestra how to perform Mahler with no holds barred. And as it was, the cachet of the orchestra's name and the political use-fulness deriving from it ultimately upstaged the government's determination to carry through its denazification programme.

The Allies also caved in from 1947 on. It was only for the orchestra's first tour abroad to France and Switzerland that ex-NSDAP members were denied visas. A 'final' line was drawn on the Nazi issue with an appearance of the orchestra at the Edinburgh Festival under the leadership of the émigré Bruno Walter, one of the most renowned conductors of the twentieth century, whose association with the orchestra dated back to the days when Gustav Mahler made him Kapellmeister at Vienna's Hofoper in 1901. The concert was cleverly used to highlight the contrast between the brilliant orchestra and its war-ravaged home. Sympathy and admiration drowned out any criticism of the behaviour of the Austrians during the Holocaust and Second World War in general. For the concert, Friedrich Buxbaum, then the cellist of the Rosé Quartet, who had been driven from Austria in 1938, even took up his former place as principal cellist.

The Edinburgh concert was managed on behalf of the Verein Wiener Philharmoniker by another Viennese émigré, Rudolf Bing, who was determined to raise the newly founded festival to a par with Salzburg and Bayreuth by involving only the very best artists. Bing, incidentally, is an example of how the exodus from Hitler's Germany brought legions of artists or people close to the arts (such as cultural managers) to the U.S. and the U.K., where they became active in making classical music a global phenomenon and in enhancing, if highly indirectly, Austria's prestige as a musical country. The fact that Austria was established, one might almost say, as a brand name for music, has to do with the acculturation abroad of thousands of its artistic elite after their expulsion, which has not received nearly the attention it would deserve. Some U.S. authors and Holocaust survivors refer to this as 'Hitler's gift to America'.

The public discourse in Austria on the 'gesture of reconciliation', which the concert in Edinburgh was supposed to constitute, remained muted, and the racist persecution that Bruno Walter had suffered was hardly ever referred to. This was business as usual: reports on Richard Tauber's reappearance on the operatic stage often contained the formula 'again … after a long interval'. The reluctance openly to address the reasons why these artists had been exiled was arguably connected to an admission of guilt that had to be suppressed in order not to jeopardize the 'victim doctrine'. When Bruno Walter signed a petition together with Alma Mahler-Werfel concerning the overdue restitution of looted Jewish property, he was attacked, under the banner headline 'Attack on Austria', as part of a 'Jewish global conspiracy' by the VdU protagonist Viktor Reimann.

The 'victim doctrine' was to be quickly and effectively installed on the international stage. The Vienna Philharmonic contributed its share during the first years. Even in the Netherlands, where Nazi and SS cliques under the leadership of the Austrian Arthur Seyß-Inquart had committed atrocities and where the Vienna Philharmonic itself had appeared in the service of the German 'Kulturmission', the 1950 tour under Wilhelm Furtwängler was highly successful. The report filed by the Austrian embassy notes with satisfaction the success of this 'goodwill tour', which was undertaken despite considerable risk – Furtwängler had been Adolf Hitler's favourite conductor and one of the figureheads of German cultural propaganda – 'in dealing with possible last repercussions caused by memories of the country's occupation under Seyß-Inquart'. As far as the internal mechanics of the orchestra were concerned, it became clear in 1953, when Helmut Wobisch, a former SS Unterscharführer (junior squad leader) and member of the Sicherheitsdienst in the Reichssicherheitshauptamt, was elected as acting head, that the policy of drawing-the-final-line had penetrated to the small world of the orchestra.

But even the Vienna Philharmonic, which, according to a self-description from 1947, was 'part of world history', was not immune to the twists and turns of Austrian history, although this did not become apparent until the 1990s. In 1992 the orchestra paid homage in a concert to the six of its members who had either been murdered or had died as a consequence of persecution after 1938, to the ten members who had been expelled – most of them had subsequently emigrated – and to the nine members who had some Jewish blood and/or were 'jüdisch Versippte' (people related to Jews by marriage) and thus had lived under the permanent threat of having their provisional exemptions withdrawn.

The psychological significance of the symbol 'Vienna Philharmonic', especially for Vienna's postwar society, has not yet been assessed, and the same applies to other postwar memory sites. In a situation marked by utter devastation, political uncertainty and social instability, in which the struggle for day-to-day survival overshadowed everything else, institutions such as the Philharmonic offered a symbolic refuge and were an indirect source of motivation for people to join in the effort of rebuilding the state. In the announcement of the first postwar Philharmonic concert on 27 April 1945, Viktor Suchy found words to describe this graphically, even if the language appears to us today to be emotionally over the top: 'This city is bleeding from a thousand wounds; from millions of eyes flow tears of suffering and bitterness about the brown plague [National Socialism] that has ravaged this city of ours until recently ... Yet they have been unable, in spite of seven years of tyranny, to rob us of the soul of Austria, which has taken shape in our beloved music.'[7] This pathos of the educated bourgeois is omnipresent in Austria's postwar discourse: a pillar of the victim doctrine, it fills the vacuum of Austrian identity with an equally vacuous construct, the notion of Austria's cultural grandeur and superiority.

In the meantime, the memory site of the Philharmonic has become part and parcel of the national culture and of the tourist industry. It is no longer the physical presence of the orchestra in the form of international tours or their recordings that matters most, but the New Year Concert. This has turned the national memory site of the Vienna Philharmonic into a global memory site and is instrumental in expanding and solidifying the myth of Austria as a musical country, even though the appreciation of classical music is on the wane here. The New Year Concert is, incidentally, another heirloom from the Nazi era: it was first broadcast as an 'extraordinary concert' on 31 December 1939; the 1941 concert, which was conducted by Clemens Krauss, was performed also on New Year's Day under the title of 'Johann Strauss Concert'. The name 'New Year Concert' first saw the light of day in 1946 and since 1959 it has been televised on a global scale.

Vienna's Staatsoper

The Soviet cultural officers were in as little doubt as the interim government of Karl Renner and the City Council of Vienna about the psychologically beneficial effects of reversing as soon as possible the 1944 ban on public operatic performances – minor events had continued to be staged at the Redoutensaal. Major Miron Lewitas used what almost amounted to coercion to enable an early restart, for which he mostly drew on wartime productions and protagonists (with the exception of the conductor Josef Krips, who, being half Jewish, had been banned from appearing in public). In a shotgun marriage the Staatsoper was administrated for a few months in tandem with the Volksoper, until this arrangement fell apart again – traditional continuities were reasserting their rights. However, Staats- and Volksoper both remained under the umbrella of the Bundestheaterverwaltung, the Administration of State Theatres, whose fold the City of Vienna–owned Volksoper joined in 1946; until 1955, the Volksoper served as an alternative venue for the Staatsoper alongside the Theater an der Wien. In the overall context of the socioeconomic crisis these developments were a clear indication that federal government (and the ÖVP decision makers) were unwilling to concede to 'Red Vienna' any substantive say in the domain of high culture. In the Nazi era, the City of Vienna had been increasingly involved in the theatre world – in 1938, the 'Neues Wiener Schauspielhaus', which had succeeded in its turn the old Volksoper after the latter's bankruptcy in 1927, was relaunched as the 'Municipal Volksoper'.

Musical culture as far as opera in Vienna was concerned was supposed to unfold under the auspices of the state, while the theatres in the provinces were allowed to go their separate ways. In Vienna this dispensation was facilitated through the ousting of the Communist acting director of the Staatsoper, Matthäus Flitsch, at the behest of the new head of the Administration of State Theatres, the ÖVP cultural functionary Egon Hilbert. Hilbert, an outspoken anti-Nazi, had been arrested in the Austrian embassy in Prague, where he held the post of press attaché, and deported to Dachau concentration camp. There he struck up a friendship with the future Chancellor Leopold Figl, which proved a stepping stone to a career within the cultural bureaucracy.

Hilbert, who was 'in thrall to opera', was also co-director of the Staatsoper with Herbert von Karajan for a spell that was to end in a fiasco. Flitsch, a former member of the Fire Brigade, had coordinated the first phase of reconstruction and followed a strict course of denazification vis-à-vis the Vienna Philharmonic, an undertaking in which he was supported by those members of the Vienna Symphony Orchestra who hoped they would be able to leapfrog over their fallen colleagues into that 'democracy of kings', the Verein Wiener Philharmoniker. Egon Hilbert, on the other hand, had already shown himself disinclined to implement a strict denazification policy when he had conducted such screenings as a U.S. official in Salzburg or, later, as the director of the Salzburg Landestheater; when he did apply the law in full force, it was usually to push through his personal preferences. His top priority was to present an ensemble of stars in Vienna as soon as possible; after all, Austria was, according to Hilbert in 1948, a 'nation of dancers and violinists'.

Two major political decisions were to affect the future of the Wiener Staatsoper, which incidentally clung to its epithet to distinguish itself from the Berliner Staatsoper, even though this was hardly necessary after the end of the Nazi era. The first decision concerned the rebuilding of the old opera house on the Ring, which gathered momentum at the beginning of the 1950s. The architect Erich Boltenstern was put in charge of the rebuilding, and administrative control lay with the ÖVP-led Ministry of Construction. Construction costs amounted to a grand total of 216 million schillings, which would be approximately 700 million dollars in today's money. The Soviet occupation force contributed 2 million Reichsmarks towards costs and supplied building materials to get reconstruction off to an early start. The first estimates of the total cost of reconstruction, by Staatsgebäudeverwaltung Wien, the Administration of Public Buildings, in September 1945, had been much too low at just below 30 million Reichsmarks.

In 1945 the fact that the use of the City of Vienna's Volksoper as a venue did not bring with it any additional costs enabled the state theatres to present a balanced budget; in 1946 the Bundestheaterverwaltung reverted to demanding the 'old' state subsidies. Until 1938, the state theatres had received an annual subsidy of between 5 and 7 million schillings. In the Nazi era this had risen to between

5 and 7 million Reichsmarks, which in 1944 dropped to 5 million as expenses were cut by the closing down of the theatres in September. The Burgtheater, the Hofoper and the Schönbrunn Schlosstheater had run at a deficit even in the days when they were still part of Hofärar, the Crown Estate Office: in the year leading up to the outbreak of the First World War, their budget required a subsidy of 7 million kronas. After 1946 budgetary requirements grew slowly but incrementally until, in 1958, they reached 128 million schillings, half the size of the budget of the entire judicial sector.

Speed was what mattered in rebuilding the opera; considerations such as faithfully re-creating the original building were downgraded. Nor was the idea of starting completely from scratch and building a modern opera house even mooted; the ostensible rebirth of the old house was supposed to signal continuity and legitimacy. However, what came into being behind the well-known façade was a house that differed from what had gone before, and not only because of Eisenmenger's fire curtain, which reminded Dmitri Shostakovich of a 'drugstore soap label'. Its seating capacity was reduced. Heinz Leinfellner's 'modern' intarsia in the interval foyer of the Marble Hall was hidden for decades behind panelling at the behest of Minister of Construction Udo Illig, whilst Rudolf Eisenmenger's tapestries managed to combine conformity with the cachet of modernity.

This reconstruction mélange with its main ingredients of semi-authentic restoration, emasculated modernism and the dominance of star artists were an excellent reflection of the state of politics of culture in the 1950s. The dominant role of Karl Böhm as both director and conductor at the inauguration of the Staatsoper on 5 November 1955 was the result of a typical cabal. Once Ernst Kolb, the minister of education, had opted for Clemens Krauss to be in charge on the occasion, a virulent campaign was launched to stigmatize Krauss as a 'traitor' for leaving Vienna for Berlin in 1935. Both Krauss and Böhm had used Nazi potentates with great skill to achieve their ends, the one in Munich and Berlin, the other in Dresden and Vienna, and both had served the regime well. The outcome of the intrigue made Böhm, the pan-German from Graz, appear more truly 'Austrian' than the 'traitor' of 1935. In this decision too, the cultural and political system of the pre-1938 authoritarian, corporatist state was still in evidence in the 1950s. 'Fidelio', the standard fare of liberation anniversaries, was performed on this occasion; it had already been abused in the old house in the context of Anschluss festivities. In 1955 matters were not helped by the fact that the director was none other than the politically compromised Heinz Tietjen, the *éminence grise* of Berlin and Bayreuth cultural life during the Nazi era. The production was considered particularly weak.

The reopening of the Staatsoper was a state occasion of the first order and symbolized the end of an era in the reconstruction of the Second Republic. From then onward the sociopolitical relevance of the Staatsoper fell into gradual decline. The running battles between Herbert von Karajan and the Staatstheaterverwaltung, coupled with the actions of the trade unions and shop stewards, pointed up the traditional weaknesses of a subsidized state operation. The hallmarks of the opera Karajan envisaged were international, preferably Italian singers, auction-style fees and no fixed schedule for rehearsals. For the staff at the Staatsoper, emphasis was squarely on the preservation of traditional work structures. Here as elsewhere, fault lines began to appear between increasingly rampant internation-alization on the one hand and Austrian traditions and idiosyncratic perceptions on the other.

The memory site of the Staatsoper continues to play an important role in a va-riety of contexts. As a general standby for official tours with an affirmative agenda, it was used in the 1970s in connection with East-West and détente politics and in 1995 in events commemorating the fiftieth anniversary of the end of the war and the establishment of Renner's interim government. In what amounted to a pre-miere, the Staatsoper did not on this occasion stage a revival of postwar emotions but a review in words and music of the Nazi bans on composers and the persecu-tion of musicians prior to 1945; the roles that Austrians played were specifically addressed. One of the consequences of this other type of commemoration of the state's foundation on 27 April 1945 was Ioan Holender's decision to have images by living artists temporarily projected onto the fire curtain, which amounted to a clear political signal without iconoclastic overtones.

The victims of the accidents that occurred during the time of the Staatsoper's rebuilding have not been properly commemorated yet. The work and time pres-sure were intense, and supervision of the works negligent: between 1950 and 1952 five workmen were killed. In 1955, no commemorative tablet was put up for them in an otherwise commemoration-happy house. High culture seems oblivious to its roots in society.

The Burgtheater

The Burgtheater, the second bastion of high culture, proved to exert a more last-ing influence on the collective memory of the Austrians. Its rebuilding consti-tuted an important agenda from the 1950s onwards. Like the Staatsoper, it had been severely damaged in a bombing raid towards the end of the war; a subse-quent fire in the costumes depot added to the damage. The plan was originally to arrive at a decision concerning the restoration of this central public symbol via a competition. It is highly unfortunate that even well-known experts on ar-chitecture have failed to provide documentation of this competition; in a wider context, too, we must note that the history of the Burgtheater is riddled with blank spaces where crucial information is nonexistent. Even the cause of the fire in the costume depot remains unclear: was it civilians who set fire to the fund of requisites off the Imperial Corridor, or was it retreating or attacking soldiers? An independent jury awarded the first prize to Otto Niedermoser, whose plan was less indebted to historical eclecticism and provided for a radical reconstruction of the auditorium, but the Ministry of Education opted for the design of Michael Engelhardt, which was 'in the historic-eclectic mould but otherwise marked by discipline and restraint'. Niedermoser's plan would have meant 500 more seats but no standing room in the parquet circle.

The low-key new architecture of the project chosen for realization was perfectly in keeping with the will to continue the theatrical tradition of the Burgtheater with its proscenium stage and the tiered boxes of the auditorium. It also accorded well with Soviet postwar politics of culture. Miron Levitas, the press secretary to Marshal Fedor Tolbukhin, outlined its principles in a speech to 'representatives of theatre, film, literature and press' in the Small Ceremonial Hall of Vienna's Town Hall: 'The cultural life of Vienna should be revived as it was in 1938. The mayor [Theodor Körner] and Councillor Matejka [Viktor Matejka, the KPÖ councillor in charge of culture in the Town Council] are prepared to do everything they can to ensure that cultural life can begin again. Let everyone do everything in their power to bring this about and to make sure that the cultural life of that bygone age is resuscitated.'[8]

Not a word was spoken about purging the elites or needing a cultural reorientation, not a hint of 'progressive culture' was evident, not a play was in sight to be the vehicle for 'contemporary, challenging ideologies', whose absence was sadly and ineffectively deplored in 1947. Even bourgeois anti-National Socialists were dismayed when, at the express wish of the Soviet cultural administration, Clemens Krauss, a conductor who had been particularly favoured by Hitler and Göring, was chosen for the first concert of the Vienna Philharmonic after the country's liberation from fascism. The audience demonstrated their displeasure before the beginning of the concert.

One of the leading NSDAP activists in Berlin's high culture sector, Lothar Müthel, who has already been mentioned in these pages as the Nazi-era director of the Burgtheater, eagerly joined in the applause during the concert whenever mention was made of the need to 'extirpate the Nazi bandits'. Cases like that of Müthel, who went on to direct Lessing's 'Nathan', where tacit 'rehabilitation' was won through ostentatious involvement in artistic production, were not uncommon: Paula Wessely took a role in the 1946 production of Bertolt Brecht's *The Good Person of Szechuan* for the same reason. Fred Hennings, another member of the Burgtheater ensemble, was the only one who publicly confronted his Nazi past, yet the example he set found few followers. He was among the first to have his name registered as a former member of the NSDAP and to report for fatigue duty. He was 'also mentally prepared to labour with the rubble clearers in St Stephen's for an indefinite period of time' and to admit to his political mistakes without ifs and buts.

It was obvious that the Soviet leadership – far from even attempting to take into consideration the repressive aspects of the Dollfuß-Schuschnigg regime's cultural politics – counted on its own retrospective policies to deliver a stabilizing effect on the situation in Austria and to enable it to gain a certain amount of indirect control. The Americans favoured a more stringently controlled model aimed at the same goals and at a democratization of society to nip authoritarian and neo-Nazi tendencies in the bud. The emphasis of the Soviets lay squarely on such institutions of high culture as the Burgtheater and the Staatsoper; they did not aspire to direct administrative control.

The Burgtheater under the auspices of its aging director Raoul Aslan was focused on the staging of German classics and on a Grillparzer renaissance. It took until the end of 1945 for two productions that had not originated during the war to be put on at the Burgtheater's alternative venue, the Ronacher. These were Franz Molnár's *Liliom* and Franz Theodor Csokor's *Kalypso*. Even these efforts to boost the production of Austrian authors of the present and the recent past were closely monitored by the political elites for correctness in terms of postwar cultural politics. An ÖVP member of Parliament noted in a speech on the budget that 'girlies, jazz music and the grotesque exaggeration' of the production of Max Christian Feiler's *Die sechste Frau* (The Sixth Wife [of Henry VIII]) were 'distinctly unwelcome' at the Burgtheater. The politician also found fault with the staging of Curt Goetz's *Der Lügner und die Nonne* (The Liar and the Nun), as it disparaged the standing of the Catholic Church.

For artists returning from exile after 1945, success hinged on becoming part of the mainstream of cultural politics, as was demonstrated by Josef Gielen, Raoul Aslan's successor as the director of the Burgtheater. He made a point of reintegrating such highly compromised stars as Werner Krauß, whose anti-Semitic interpretation of *Jud Süß* had been a high-water mark of the Nazi film industry. Authors popular in the Nazi era, such as Richard Billinger and Max Mell, were likewise revived by Gielen in 1951. There were others who made innovative contributions, such as the directors Leopold Lindtberg, Walter Felsenstein and Berthold Viertel, Gielen's brother-in-law, but these few could not prevent the perpetuation of the Burgtheater's role as a state-affirming institution. The Cold War and the Brecht boycott, which was extended in the 1960s, were important factors in this development.

The controversy surrounding the choice of play for the inauguration of the old-new Burgtheater in 1955, which pitted Grillparzer's *König Ottokars Glück und Ende* (The Happiness and Downfall of King Ottokar) against Goethe's *Egmont* – with overtones of Austrian versus German identity – was predictably lacking in any kind of style. In the end a typical compromise was adopted: the 'Austrian' option won, but *Ottokar* was censored (or worse). The last lines were deleted as politically inopportune: 'Hail to the first Habsburg in Austria! Hail! Hail! Hail to Austria! Habsburg for ever!' In keeping with the style of the time, Judith Holzmeister, whose voice featured in the above-mentioned Haeusserman film *Die Stimme Österreichs,* was cast in all three Burgtheater premieres, as Kunigunde in *Ottokar,* Princess Eboli in Schiller's *Don Carlos* and Leonore in Goethe's *Torquato Tasso.* The nation thrilled to the solemnity of her voice.

Thirty years later the memory site of the Burgtheater was at the centre of a bitter controversy caused by Elfriede Jelinek's play *Burgtheater,* in which the author focuses on the Nazi past of actor Attila Hörbiger and actress Paula Wessely, who were a couple. At least since the Bonn premiere of the play on 10 November 1985, Wessely's role in the Nazi era has been the subject of continued debate. This also has to do with the fact that, even though she passed through several denazification screenings, all the atonement that she ever made was to play a part (against Brecht's express wish) in the 1946 Josefstadt production of *The Good Person of Szechuan.* Diverse biographical accounts have done no more than gloss over the way this great actress was used (and allowed herself to be used) for Nazi propaganda purposes. Wessely's justification for her part in the anti-Polish, racist propaganda film *Heimkehr* remained a purely defensive one. She had not found the courage to decline the part, she said, 'because people knew I was not a Nazi. I was suspect owing to my Catholic faith and to my wide circle of Jewish friends'. In her confrontation with the U.S. denazification authority she claimed that had she refused to take part, she would have ended up in a concentration camp.

The way Paula Wessely dealt with National Socialism finds its equivalent in the argument of tens of thousands of Austrian men and women, who each contributed in their individual way to the legitimacy of and support for the Nazi regime. Her public standing in Germany and in Austria prior to 1938 was such that she could safely have refused to take part in a propaganda film; instead, she opted for the multiple bonus that the Nazi regime, with its expansive politics of culture, conferred on compliant artists and for the chance to strengthen her theatre and film presence. Like her husband Attila Hörbiger, she was a most welcome guest on a number of official occasions, yet by and large, and with only a few exceptions, she managed to keep her distance from the Nazi regime. Her transformation after the war is mirrored in the 1948 film *Der Engel mit der Posaune* (The Angel with the Trombone), a considerably smoothed-down version of the novel by Ernst Lothar that recounts Austria's history from the suicide of the heir-apparent, Rudolf, to the years immediately after the Second World War as seen through the eyes of a Viennese family of piano manufacturers. Wessely's performance as an actress is such that the political message of the novel is almost completely overshadowed.

The 1950s: The Peace of the Graveyard
Enveloping the Politics of Culture

According to the 1955 regional and cultural studies handbook quoted from in chapter 1 of this volume, Austria is defined as a cultural nation by the following components: 'Haydn, Mozart, Beethoven, Schubert, the Burgtheater, the Staatsoper, the Philharmonic, the Wiener Sängerknaben and the Salzburger Festspiele.' That this emphasis on tradition – all names and institutions date back to the monarchy – and the convention of the definition itself go beyond mere schoolbook rhetoric becomes apparent from a statement of Heinrich Drimmel that has also been quoted already. As minister of education between 1954 and 1964, the Catholic conservative Drimmel set the key for the official politics of culture according to his own social outlook.

The economic recovery of the 1950s was supposed to be mirrored in a traditionalist high culture, both to aid national self-confidence, as shown by the reopening of the Staatsoper and the Burgtheater, and for economic, tourist industry-related reasons. Attendance at the Staatsoper rose from 525,000 in the season of 1955–56 to 680,000 in 1957–58, but this did not signal a change in the public's understanding of high culture. The Staatsoper remained an elitist undertaking in keeping with its repertoire: in 1957–58 the traditional competition between Verdi and Mozart operas was continued (seven Verdi operas with a total of 115 performances versus five Mozart operas with 82 performances).

A similar preponderance of the classics is apparent in the 1957–58 Burgtheater season: the staging of Grillparzer, Shakespeare, Raimund and Goethe, in that order, ensured that the presentation of established culture played a dominant role. Yet not even the classics or popular plays were exempt from the exigencies of the Cold War in the 1950s: the left-leaning 'Neues Theater in der Scala' had all subsidies stopped and was forced to close down in 1956 – with a vengeance, as several of its artists and directors found themselves at loose ends for a long time. That the Scala also had artistic achievements to its credit was not conceded until the late 1970s.

The reluctance to engage openly in conflict that belonged to a different order from party-political electoral wrangling was a significant trait of postwar political apathy. The Grand Coalition filled the space of domestic politics, and the pro-U.S. orientation towards the West was practically identical with Austria's foreign relations, in spite of the permanent neutrality that the country had declared independently in 1955. In the socioeconomic area, conflict prevention was delegated to the social partners, who were assuming an increasingly important role. The late Elfriede Gerstl has described this atmosphere as 'the peace of the graveyard suffocating domestic and cultural politics alike'. Time and again the constraints imposed by reconstruction, occupation and the Cold War were invoked. Tradition ruled in an orderly manner.[9]

While the sources of working-class culture dried up completely and were being replaced by new forms of film and television consumption, government funding of the arts was confined to high culture, to the cultural establishment and to individual artists. A great deal of effort was invested in economic and social rehabilitation; official commitment to the arts stagnated or was directed at marginalizing the type of artistic potential that was unwelcome in light of the Cold War. The Brecht boycott and the branding of the Scala ensemble had sequels in the controversies surrounding Communist members of the PEN Club. In this campaign, as well as in the Brecht boycott, Hans Weigel played a leading role. In 1949 he warned in the *Arbeiterzeitung* of the 'strategy of establishing Communist bridgeheads under neutral or non-aligned camouflage'. In 1956, after the Soviet invasion of Hungary, the Communist members of PEN Austria (Ernst Fischer, Hugo Huppert and Bruno Frei) felt themselves forced to resign from the organization.

The so-called Art Club, with the artist and novelist Albert Paris Gütersloh (1887–1973) as its inspirational mentor, became a hub for all kinds of artistic experiments from 1946 onwards. Initially embracing innovative movements in the visual arts, such as expressionism, Dadaism, surrealism and constructivism, it soon widened its scope to include actionism and literary activities that criticized the restorative, conservative zeitgeist. The magazine *Neue Wege* (New Pathways) published works by emerging nonconformist talents, such as Ernst Jandl, Friederike Mayröcker, Andreas Okopenko and others. The Art Club's range included performance art and theatrical actionism; in 1959 its '2. literarisches cabaret', the 2nd Literary Cabaret, drew an audience of 700, which was sensational. The *Arbeiter-Zeitung* derided such experiments as dialect poems by Achleitner, Artmann and Rühm as 'evidence of a lack of taste'; the Graz *Kleine Zeitung,* helping itself to language from the Nazi thesaurus, spoke of 'degenerate art', of 'Unart and Unrat', perverseness and filth.

ILLUSTRATION 7.2
Protest against the 'Fab Four' from Liverpool – another facette of Austria's postwar culture.

Conclusion

Art and culture played a protective, even restorative role in the reconstruction phase of the Second Republic, which was clearly weighted in favour of Catholic conservatism. The insight into the role pre-1918 Austrian traditions were capable of playing in terms of system stabilization dated back to the Nazi era and had already been exploited by Hitler and his associates. A few attempts were made in 1945–46, mostly in urban areas, to give a new lease of life to modernism and the avant-garde of the period between the wars that had been repressed and eliminated at the time; the initiatives of the Viennese City Councillor Viktor Matejka may serve as examples. Yet very soon conservative networks took over across the board and brought artistic and cultural operations under their control. This development was exacerbated by the geopolitical climate of the Cold War and by a Social Democracy that had moved to the centre and abandoned all pretensions to a politics of art.

'Streamlined' artists, such as the painter Rudolf Eisenmenger – whose career had received a boost in the Nazi era both because of the nature of his work and for party-political reasons, and who was commissioned to beautify the fire curtain of the Staatsoper – were popular recipients of government funding. Modernity was pared back, from the point of view of the government agencies responsible for funding, to 'proven' functionality; aesthetic continuities linking the postwar years to the Nazi and the Austro-Fascist eras were hardly ever seen as a threat. The real threat was seen as coming from the 'left' and from unbridled modernism; both were marginalized, repressed and generally kept at a distance. In this respect the ideological harmony in the Grand Coalition between the dominant ÖVP and its junior partner SPÖ was easily maintained.

It took until the end of the 1950s for resistance to build up against these kinds of restrictions, intensified as they were by both published opinion in the print media and the restorative tendencies of the radio. Resistance formed not only in niches of the autonomous scene but also in the Catholic milieu and in 'hotspots' in the provinces. In the 1960s the resulting manifold forms of artistic opposition and protest were sometimes suppressed violently, occasionally with methods borrowed from the police state, which elicited applause from the media and from the public at large. However, a creeping sense of discomfort at this sort of development, part of Austria's heritage of 'pillarization' and extreme partisanship, began to assert itself across society, and in the 1970s the mould finally broke and entirely new strategies in cultural politics were formulated by the state bureaucracies and political decision makers. The conservative restorative basic mood did not, of course, disappear overnight.

Today, too, culture in all its manifestations continues to be an important factor economically, politically and in terms of identity debates. Austria also continues to present itself to the outside world as the country of music. The clash between 'modern' and 'classical' music has lost steam since the turbulence of the 1970s and 1980s. Yesterday's scandal artists, such as Hermann Nitsch, are today's model artists, courted even by conservative politicians. When one of the enemy stereotypes of the rightist populist and the conservative sector of the public, Elfriede Jelinek, was awarded the Nobel Prize for Literature, the fact was generally greeted with satisfaction, even if there were distinct differences in nuance. Productions that had been highly controversial as late as the 1970s, such as the *Staatsoperette*, which was aired by ORF in 1977, appear today to be perfectly harmless and rather lacking in fizz. At the time, the filmmaker Franz Novotny and the composer Otto M. Zykan were treated to vitriolic attacks for caricaturing Christian Social chancellors, the prelate Ignaz Seipel and Engelbert Dollfuß, in the company of bare-bosomed women. 'Pornographic distortion of Austria's past' or 'vilification of our country and of the church' was as nothing, compared to what else was said in that debate. Today this classic piece of the culture of provocation would raise no one's pulse.

Given the space, it would be interesting to discuss these developments in greater detail. What appears reasonably clear is the fact that cultural issues still command a great deal of attention in national politics, but that the urgency of the debate has evaporated and made room for market mechanisms and marketing strategies. As far as Austria's identity is concerned, music remains a constituent element – at least until further notice. Literature and the theatre still garner a great deal of interest from the German-speaking countries, but it seems that since the days of Thomas Bernhard's *Heldenplatz* and the departure of the German Burgtheater director Claus Peymann from Vienna, the controversy about who is entitled to offer politically authoritative interpretations in cultural matters has shifted to other arenas, which may well have to do with the fact that there are hardly any taboos left to lash out at in Austria's history of the recent past. Furthermore, the political elites have learned how to use artists for their own ends rather than engaging in culture political controversies, where they habitually end up cutting poor figures. Nor do the media rise to the occasion any longer, as they regularly did in the 1970s and 1980s, by lending political publicity to bar-room debates on current productions. The debates on persistent cuts in public funding for the arts and the concentration of private sponsoring on mammoth projects hardly register with the public. What does still get noticed is the wrangling between the two main cultural institutions, the Staatsoper and the Burgtheater, for the bigger slice of what subsidies are still to be had.

NOTES

1. Sedlmayr had joined the Nazi Party already before 1932, but left and then rejoined after the Anschluss of 1938. He was considered to be an 'einwandfreier' National Socialist, a Nazi beyond reproach, who commented in his lectures at the university on

day-to-day events like the failed attempt to kill Hitler and encouraged the students to report colleagues who showed anti-Nazi leanings.

2. Michael Wimmer, *Kulturpolitik in Österreich. Darstellung und Analyse 1970–1990* (Innsbruck-Vienna: Studien Verlag, 1995), 29.

3. Hilde Haider-Pregler, 'Direktion Leon Epp. Das tapferste Theater von Wien', in *100 Jahre Volkstheater. Theater – Zeit – Geschichte,* ed. Evelyn Schreiner (Vienna: Jugend & Volk, 1989), 211.

4. Cited by Ingrid Bergmann, 'Die Kulturpolitik aus der Sicht des österreichischen Nationalrates im Vergleich mit dem 3. Reich, im Umfeld des Zeitgeschehens' (Phil. diss., Vienna University, 1988), 9.

5. Felix Hurdes, 'Europa als kulturelle Einheit', *Österreichische Monatshefte* 2 (1948): 51.

6. Raimund Poukar, 'Österreichs Beitrag zur abendländischen Gemeinschaft', *Österreichische Monatshefte* 2 (1948): 2.

7. *Neues Österreich,* 27 April 1945, 4.

8. *Neues Österreich,* 24 April 1945, 2.

9. Elfriede Gerstl, 'Zwei österreichische Dichterschicksale oder wie der Kulturbetrieb seine Opfer macht und in posthumen Ehrungen sich selbst feiert', in *Literatur in Österreich von 1950 bis 1965. Walter Buchebner-Tagung 1984,* ed. Wendelin Schmidt-Dengler (Mürzzuschlag: Walter-Buchebner-Gesellschaft, 1984), 22.

CHAPTER 8

The Austrian Model of the Welfare State and Intergenerational and Intergender Contracts since 1945

In Austrian collective memory, the speedy and successful formation of a sense of identity is tied very strongly to the success of the Austrian model of the welfare state. Ultimately this model entailed a significant broadening of late nineteenth-century notions of the state as the provider of different types of benefits to combat what the liberal British social theorist William Beveridge was to call 'the five giants': illness, ignorance, disease, squalor and want. The foremost need was to alleviate the negative consequences of the industrial revolution, such as mass unemployment, homelessness, the dissolution of traditional family groups and headlong urbanization. The term 'welfare state' first appeared as a programmatic political term in a 1941 polemical pamphlet by Archbishop of Canterbury William Temple, who, in his capacity as a 'Christian citizen', demanded reforms in education and in public housing, and a participatory role in managerial decisions for blue- and white-collar workers.

In German the term '*Sozialstaat*' has negative connotations that date back to the turbulent end phase of democracy in the early 1930s. In the Weimar Republic the Brüning and von Papen governments attempted to roll back state benefits between 1930 and 1932, and corporate industry favoured their reduction to the level of poor relief: 'Social insurance is for those truly in need of help, for those who have been struck by hardship. However, great care must be taken that it is not subject to abuse, not just an evil in itself but one that has the side effect of damaging the people's morale.'[1] In Austria the Dollfuß-Schuschnigg regime likewise took steps to clear what it referred to as 'the revolutionary rubble'. Odo Neustädter-Stürmer, who provided the authoritarian constitution of 1934 with its ideological backbone, became minister of social affairs in 1934; he subsequently created the legal basis for a general reduction of state benefits whose only redeeming feature was that it removed the distinction between blue- and white-collar workers, at least with regard to social insurance. His reform entailed cuts in retirement and old age pensions and cuts in sickness benefits; it introduced three days' unpaid sick leave and cuts both in employees' annuities and in accident-related disability annuities where there was less than 50 per cent incapacity.

Dollfuß brought forward decrees aimed at controlling social insurance within a few weeks of the breach of the constitution and the suspension of Parliament in 1933. The expansion of the welfare state in Europe after 1945 was underpinned by the political agenda of keeping Communism at bay during the difficult phase of socioeconomic reconstruction; this was particularly true of Austria. Basic ideological conflicts slipped into the background as neither side was prepared to address a mutual lack of trust. To date, the Cold War has not yet received the recognition due to it as a motor both for the expansion of the welfare state and for the Marshall Plan. Before the Second World War many socialist governments and parties had regarded the welfare state as a path to a new political system; after 1945 capitalism was embraced as an integral aspect of an anti-Communist alliance. At the same time, conservative parties recognized the need for pervasive sociopolitical measures to ensure the functioning of the economy. With the exception of Friedrich von Hayek, there were hardly any well-known economists in 1945 who were pleading for the complete dismantling of the welfare state: its effects in terms of stabilizing the system were too well understood. It was generally recognized that the simple poor relief offered in the nineteenth century had not been a success.

After the break-up of the Empire in 1918 there had been intense concern about a Communist revolution in Austria. Non-communist parties, notably the Christian Socials and the Christian Democrats, cooperated to produce significant reforms. Sociopolitical regulations developed under the monarchy were improved upon and made more comprehensive (the eight-hour workday, holidays for blue-collar workers, elements of participative management, collective agreements, unemployment insurance). Setbacks, rollbacks and modifications that took place during the Dollfuß-Schuschnigg era (1933/34–38) and under National Socialism were of only marginal significance to developments after 1945. Yet the different pasts of the political parties remained subliminally stored in the collective memory. When the parties agreed in principle after 1945 to continue building on the foundations of the Austrian welfare state that had been laid under the monarchy and particularly after 1918–19, this agreement owed much to the straits the country was in at the time. The fact that the agreement did not remove the distrust between the parties meant that their historic differences simply persisted unchanged.

This becomes particularly apparent in the decision in favour of the traditional (Bismarckian) social insurance system, with its mix of public insurance governed by income brackets and private insurance for the wealthy, as opposed to the Swedish model of universal insurance. The Austrian model of the welfare state is also characterized by continuing discrimination against women in employment, professional parameters and income. This is one of the most significant differences setting Austria apart from the Scandinavian countries.

Tracing these developments from their respective sources after 1945 means reflecting on the most significant elements of what we might call the '1945 intergenerational contract' as well as the '1945 intergender contract', even if these contracts were never formally formulated.

The situation in the first months after the war was so complicated that there was no time for a thorough examination of sociopolitical structures. The two most important topics were food supply and administration. Rationing, which had been established as a wartime measure, had to be kept in place, leading to a deterioration of the food situation in 1945–46. In early May 1945, the bread ration was set at half a kilo per head per week. In Wiener Neustadt, a reporter documented the diet of an eight-year-old boy two weeks before Christmas: a cup of black coffee for breakfast, half a liter of soup from the school canteen at lunchtime, and in the evening another cup of black coffee. A girl of seven was given unsweetened tea and a slice of dry bread for breakfast, soup for lunch and three roast potatoes for supper. It took until November 1946 for the calorie level to rise to 1,500 everywhere in Austria; at the time, survival level was considered to be 1,600. By the end of 1945 the calorie level in fairly typical Wiener Neustadt had sunk to 760, which meant a weekly ration of 1,400 grams of bread, 200 grams of meat, 50 ml oil, 120 grams of coffee substitute and a handful of potatoes.

The severe winter of 1945–46 made the situation worse, particularly for people in urban centres, and in many areas survival was only possible through international aid, which came from Switzerland, Sweden, Norway, South Africa, Argentina and other countries as well as from the Allies and UNRRA. Between March 1946 and June 1947 these sources supplied food, seeds, clothing and motor vehicles worth 419 million dollars. The black market flourished and produced prices like 1,000 schillings for a kilo of lard or 600 schillings for a kilo of meat. In barter transactions a good woman's coat might have fetched a sausage and a man's suit a kilo of butter. Cigarettes were a popular alternative currency. Until the passage of the Schilling Law, the Reichsmark remained in circulation to pay for utilities, taxes and public transport; food and articles for everyday use were rationed.

Yet even the absorption of the Reichsmark and the limited issue of the new schilling currency towards the end of 1945, which also replaced the military currency of the Allies, did not change the basic dilemma: incomes lagged behind prices. The volume of money in circulation increased and so did black-market prices; the standard of living therefore remained precarious. In August 1946 the Chamber of Labour, the trade unions and industry representatives tried to buffer the food price rises, notably those of meat, by simultaneously raising wages and freezing prices; by these means they also hoped to curb inflation. The major political parties supported this kind of state interventionism without significant

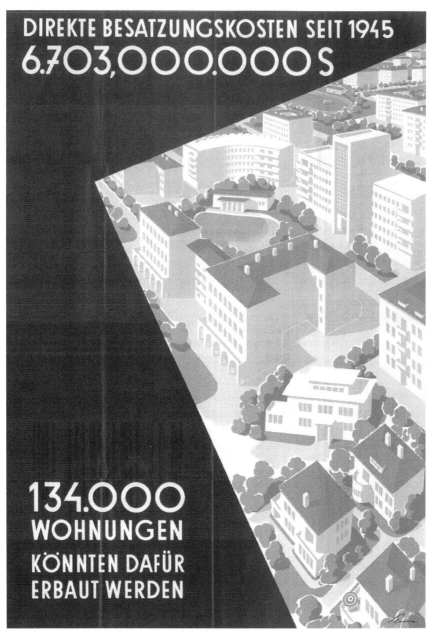

ILLUSTRATION 8.1
Occupation costs as a political argument. Poster, 1952.

ideological debates. The Allies failed to reach a unified response; in the end only the Soviets welcomed this step. Yet neither wage settlements and price caps nor the 1947 Währungsschutzgesetz (Currency Protection Law) made daily life any easier for the average Austrian. The situation eased somewhat in 1948, when black-market prices started to fall, while legitimate price indices started to rise. It took until 1954 for price developments to level off.

In this setting, state or social insurance benefits acquired a special significance. In order to produce at least a semblance of the payment of pensions and annuities, regulations dating back to the time before 1933 were revived and supplemented by German regulations where necessary. The (provisional) Administration of State Finances attempted to appeal to taxpayers' cooperation via handbills and fixed 10 May 1945 as the date on which the next payment of taxes of all kinds became due.

The patchwork character of social insurance came to an end in 1947, when the Sozialversicherungs-Überleitungsgesetz (Social Insurance Transition Law) was passed. Social insurance was cleared of the German accretions from the period of 1939–1945, and autonomy was restored to the insurance system. The autonomous tradition, which was already a feature of such sociopolitical measures of the monarchy as the first sickness insurance for workers (1888) and the first accident insurance (1898), had already been badly dented before 1938. In 1934 all Socialists were removed from the boards, and workers' representatives were nominated by the minister for social affairs on the recommendation of the streamlined trade unions. After 1938 the state was run on National Socialist leadership principles, the funds were 'depleted' and the assets transferred to Germany.

The presentation of the social insurance bill in Parliament in 1947 met with no significant hitch (one amendment sponsored by the SPÖ minority concerning an additional office in Carinthia was overruled by the ÖVP). The two parties agreed on restoration of the system's autonomy and the financial endowment of the accident and pension insurance, and on regulations concerning the transitional phase. Until 1948 a state commissar was in charge of this whole area; subsequently the social insurance institutions passed into the hands of the representatives of employees and employers. The majority of workers' representatives belonged to the Socialist lobby inside the ÖGB.

In spite of its importance for everyday life and for the future, social security played no significant role for a long time in Austria's collective memory. It was the debate on the reform of the pension and sickness insurance early in 2000 that made people aware of the extent to which they had simply taken the social security safety net for granted. An integral element of Austrian identity, it had never been subjected to close scrutiny or assessment. This may have related to the Austrian model of the welfare state simply being regarded as a byproduct of the long phase of growth between 1953–54 and 1973; maybe it was also the case that the development of a social safety net was considered the reward for the extremely heavy burden that workers had had to cope with during the first years after the war. There is no doubt that the economic success of the Second Republic rests on the exploitation factor of the postwar years, which was controlled and channeled by social partnership.

A number of other political key developments of the period 1947 to 1955 concerned the legal situation of farm labourers and home workers in respect of child and old age benefits. With regard to this agenda, the initiative within the Grand Coalition lay in the hands of the Socialist Interior Ministers Johann Böhm and Karl Maisel; both were rooted in the trade union movement, of which Böhm was also a president. His numerous bouts with representatives of employers and the ÖVP notwithstanding, Böhm was one of the pillars of the social partnership and had a great deal of pragmatic empathy for the other side, which can be seen in a speech he made to the Federation of Austrian Industry: 'No matter how many things divide the two of us, we are in the same boat, which will spill us both, if either rocks it too hard.'

The topic of pensions was very soon mined for election campaign rhetoric. In 1949 it was the housing shortage, high prices and high rents that provided the SPÖ with its main arguments against its conservative opponent, with subsidiary roles given to old age pensions for the trade sector and occasionally to comprehensive general insurance. In 1953 the emphasis was squarely on the '*Rentenklau*', the pension snatcher: 'Beware the Pension Snatcher! – Vote SPÖ!' The 'people's pension' was also discussed: jobs for the younger generations, people's pensions for the old ones. One of the great achievements of 1955 was to substitute the Allgemeines Sozialversicherungsgesetz (ASVG), the Comprehensive Social Security Law, for the sprawling jungle of more than 5,500 exceptions, exemptions and amendments that had come into being in the course of more than five decades. In the parliamentary debate this fictional intergenerational contract was described by the secretary general of the ÖAAB, Ignaz Köck, as providing an undertaking by 'the active generation to pay for the benefits for the generation of retirees, on the understanding that they in their turn will, on reaching retirement age, be treated in like manner by the generation coming after them ... All incoming payments are by and large paid out again immediately. This system, as is obvious, can only function as long as the active generation is in a position to finance the pensions of the retirees'.[2]

The problems of an aging society and the increasing burden on the gainfully employed segment of the population were already in evidence at the time. What was not yet addressed was the disadvantaged position of women with regard to both gainful employment and pensions. Pension schemes for civil servants both on federal and provincial levels were also outside the scope of the ASVG. Within the ÖVP, the Federation of Austrian Industry argued for a long time against 'excessive' pensions and social security benefits, not only because they would weigh on businesses financially but also for reasons of 'self-determination'. As late as

1956 the inclusion of the self-employed in the social security system was anathema: 'We will never give our consent to a social insurance for the self-employed, as this would be paving the way to the destruction of private entrepreneurship, to expropriation or a downward levelling.' At the same time increasing pressure was brought to bear on the ÖVP from some groups amongst its traditional constituents. For tradesmen and farmers, the demographic development of an aging society meant that handing over their business or farm was often attended by problems regarding their upkeep in old age. Because of the high incidence of pensions and annuities as one of the consequences of the Second World War, the ÖVP accepted the broadening of social security without significant ideological demur. In 1950 as much as 40 per cent of the social affairs budget was earmarked for war invalids.

In 1955 a 'comprehensive social insurance for the whole population' was promulgated and a feasibility study announced, yet the idea of the 'people's pension', which had been realized elsewhere – e.g. in Sweden or the Netherlands – as a basic pension, was not followed up. It fell victim to ideological competition. However, as the SPÖ and ÖVP learned the art of reaching compromises, the remit of social insurance was broadened step by step: in 1958 self-employed tradesmen and farmers were included (on an initially provisional basis that became definitive in 1971), and in 1979 self-employed professionals followed. In principle, however, the ÖVP continued to defend the sociopolitical position of 1955 that dates back to the fin-de-siècle days of the Christian Socials. It was then that, under the heading of '*Subsidiaritätsprinzip*' (the principle of subsidiarity), the party insisted that 'social policies should come into play only in such cases where there is an irrefutable need for the state to intervene. There are natural limits to the applicability of social policies; disregarding them would only lead to individual initiative being stamped out.'[3] Expenditure on the social affairs budget was therefore always defined as an 'obligation' and not as something demanded of the state by the people as a right.

It took tough negotiations between the social partners to ensure that the loss of the pensions' purchasing power within the framework of wage and price agreements did not become intolerable. An automatic indexing of pensions to wage rises was mooted in 1961 by the SPÖ and presented as a bill in Parliament that was to anchor this automatic indexing in accident and pension insurance. The bill did not find unanimous support until 1965, when it was passed as the Pensionsanpassungsgesetz (the Pensions Adaptation Law); in 1962 it had been rejected as 'social pie-in-the-sky'. The Bauern-Krankenversicherungsgesetz (Farmers' Sickness Insurance Law) took until 7 July 1965 to be passed, even though it affected 770,000 individuals. Here, too, an ideological controversy was fought out by proxy. Until 1966 criticism of ÖVP positions on social issues was rare. The 'social issues breathing space' and the '*Sozialstopp*', respectively ordained in 1963 by the ÖVP Finance Minister Josef Klaus and the Federal Chamber of Commerce, caused a certain amount of discussion, countered in 1968 by the SPÖ under its new leader, Bruno Kreisky. Kreisky focused on the SPÖ's differences with the ÖVP on sociopolitical topics under the catchphrase of 'dismantling the welfare state'.

In 1969 the SPÖ organized a highly successful referendum on the staggered introduction of the forty-hour work week, which found a great deal of support (889,659 signatures) and has been the fourth most popular referendum to date (2007). This achievement undoubtedly contributed to the party's electoral success in 1970. The ÖVP government of Josef Klaus (1966–70) had not called the sociopolitical consensus into question, but the SPÖ managed to project greater readiness for reform and redistribution and the will to spread the gains of the decades of growth more evenly. The 'backlog' was due not only to the ÖVP solo government but also to the 1966 agreements between the social partners that had weighted wage and price settlements to the advantage of the employers. The simplest of indicators, such as a comparison with wage settlements in Germany showing increments of 8, 10 or 12 per cent, demonstrates how restrictively wage increases were handled in Austria. Random figures from consumer statistics bear out this tendency: in 1964 one out of two households in the Federal Republic of Germany was already equipped with a television, a total of 9.4 million; in Austria the corresponding figure is half a million. By 1955 6.4 per cent of households owned a car, a figure that rose to 33 per cent by 1965; in West Germany the figure for 1955 was 1.3 million cars.

The improvement of the quality of life did not occur in all strata of society in equal measure or simultaneously. Average meat consumption did not reach its – admittedly low – prewar level until 1956–57 or, in the case of pork, 1958. At the same time people were more prepared to spend money for more expensive delicacies. The broad distribution of the profits of the growth period set in with a certain delay, for which nationalized industry was partly to blame. The state was in an entrepreneurial position and had entrepreneurial interests to tend. In Germany the SPD opposition meant that entrepreneurs were more dependent on the goodwill of the trade unions, a situation that was replicated in Austria after 1966.

In 1976 Bruno Kreisky announced in his speech to the party congress that the welfare state 'was nearing its completion'. Minister for Social Affairs Rudolf Häuser introduced a raft of reforms in labour law, social security and family politics. Labour law saw the introduction of a minimum of three weeks' holiday (1971) and the controversial 1973 Arbeitsverfassungsgesetz (Labour Constitution Law). In social security, widows' pensions were indexed in 1970, and free medical check-ups for healthy people became available in 1972, a year that also saw the introduction of optional health insurance for students. Meanwhile periods of study, illness and unemployment were allowed pensionable status. Family politics were addressed by free travel and free textbooks for schoolchildren (1972) and the indexing of family and birth benefits (1974), measures that were particularly visible and politically sensitive.

In spite of the dips in growth seen in 1974 and 1978 in the wake of the first oil crisis, the SPÖ government under Kreisky stuck to its sociopolitical guns and circumnavigated radical changes by opting for small improvements. In 1978 the first attempts were made to reduce budget contributions to social welfare in view of an improving income structure. For the SPÖ, guaranteeing old age pensions had remained a priority ever since 1949; in the general elections of 1995 this was expressed in the slogan: 'We will not be party to cuts in existing pensions.' Measures were taken to ensure full employment, which is crucial to the Austrian model. This did not take account of the so-called 'atypical' kinds of employment that are rapidly gaining in importance today, nor of women not gainfully employed, who were integrated into the model via their marital partners and subsequently via co-insurance or widows' pensions.

Detailed empirical studies show that by the end of the 1970s and in the early 1980s the expansion of the welfare state had come to an end; a phase of stabilization with minor cuts in benefits followed. This was justified with a view to consolidating the budget, for which it was necessary ultimately to cut state contributions to the social insurance budgets instead of letting them balloon any further. In spite of this the Grand Coalition under Franz Vranitzky introduced further benefits (for example the sick care benefit). As of the mid 1990s diverse austerity budgets by the same coalition reduced the adjusted social quota, and in the second year of the ÖVP-FPÖ coalition this dropped to the pre-1980 level (Figures 2 and 3).

FIGURE 2

Adjusted and non-adjusted social quota in per cent of GNP 1960–2001

Source: Martin Bolkovac, Marcel Fink: Finanzierung der Sozialdebatte.
In: http://www.voegb.at/bildungsangebote/skripten/sr/SR-13.pdf (p. 8)

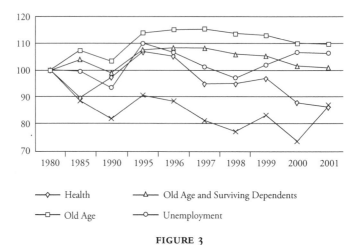

FIGURE 3

Adjusted social expenditures in per cent according to allocation in 1980–2001

Source: Martin Bolkovac, Marcel Fink: Finanzierung der Sozialdebatte.
In: http://www.voegb.at/bildungsangebote/skripten/sr/SR-13.pdf (p. 8)

In Austria the largest share of state expenditure is earmarked for pensions and annuities; health care is in second place. Expenditure on labour market policies and on unemployment benefits is marginal in practical terms but nevertheless features prominently in all debates on welfare abuse (see Figure 4). Austrian expenditure on pensions and surviving dependents, at 13.5 per cent of GNP, is well above the EU average, second only to Italy. When one takes into account its proportion of citizens aged sixty and over, Austria is in first place (see Figure 5). Expenditure on families, which has also been rising over recent years, is again among the highest in the EU.

Debates on welfare benefits are usually triggered by financial problems caused at least in part by a basic imbalance in the system that antedates the ÖVP-FPÖ governments of 2000–06: the federal contribution to the pension insurance of the self-employed and the farmers is substantially higher than the one for employees. A paltry 15 per cent of employee pensions are financed from the general tax revenue, whereas for the self-employed and farmers the figure is 60 per cent. What is apparent here is the afterlife of the power structure in the Grand Coalition after 1945, in which the SPÖ, in tandem with the trade unions, outwardly dominated social politics, whereas the ÖVP managed to insert special clauses for its traditional constituencies, which were rubberstamped by its social partners. In the days of Bruno Kreisky's solo government the SPÖ not only maintained the status quo for farmers but improved it and also transferred resources to traditionally ÖVP-dominated provinces with an eye on the general elections; the strategy

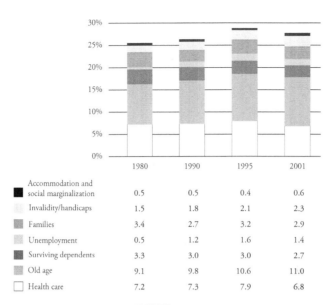

	1980	1990	1995	2001
Accommodation and social marginalization	0.5	0.5	0.4	0.6
Invalidity/handicaps	1.5	1.8	2.1	2.3
Families	3.4	2.7	3.2	2.9
Unemployment	0.5	1.2	1.6	1.4
Surviving dependents	3.3	3.0	3.0	2.7
Old age	9.1	9.8	10.6	11.0
Health care	7.2	7.3	7.9	6.8

FIGURE 4

Social expenditure by allocation in per cent of GNP in 1980–2001

Source: Martin Bolkovac, Marcel Fink: Finanzierung der Sozialdebatte.
In: http://www.voegb.at/bildungsangebote/skripten/sr/SR-13.pdf (p. 9)

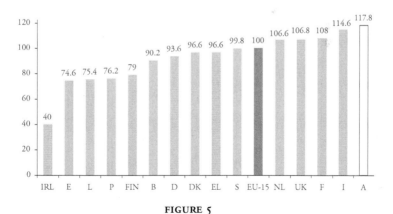

FIGURE 5

*Adjusted social expenditures earmarked for old age pensioners and surviving dependents
in per cent of GNP in 2000 (according to Eurostat); EU-15 = 100*

Source: Martin Bolkovac, Marcel Fink: Finanzierung der Sozialdebatte.
In: http://www.voegb.at/bildungsangebote/skripten/sr/SR-13.pdf (p. 13)

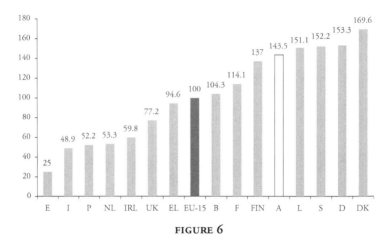

FIGURE 6

Adjusted social expenditure earmarked for families in per cent of GNP in 2000
(according to Eurostat); EU-15 = 100

Source: Martin Bolkovac, Marcel Fink: Finanzierung der Sozialdebatte.
In: http://www.voegb.at/bildungsangebote/skripten/sr/SR-13.pdf (p. 13)

worked for the party in the short term but undercut comprehensive reforms and adjustments (Table 4 and Figure 7).

The Long-term Demographic Development of the Age Structure

The pension debate in Austria is increasingly turning into a debate on the role of 'seniors' in our society. A German expert on pension issues, Bernd Rürup, estimated in 1997 that by 2030 there would be 980 old age pensioners in Austria per

TABLE 4

Federal contributions to different sectors of the obligatory pension insurance
in 1970–2002

	FEDERAL CONTRIBUTION IN RELATION TO GNP IN %	FEDERAL CONTRIBUTION TO THE PENSION VOLUME IN %	FEDERAL CONTRIBUTION TO ASVG PENSIONS IN %	FEDERAL CONTRIBUTION TO GSVG PENSIONS IN %	FEDERAL CONTRIBUTION TO BSVG PENSIONS IN %
1970	2.0	30.6	26	60	85
1985	2.6	27.8	19	72	82
2000	2.0	21.1	13	60	81
2002	2.3	23.4	16	56	88

Source: Martin Bolkovac, Marcel Fink: Finanzierung der Sozialdebatte.
In: http://www.voegb.at/bildungsangebote/skripten/sr/SR-13.pdf (S. 18)

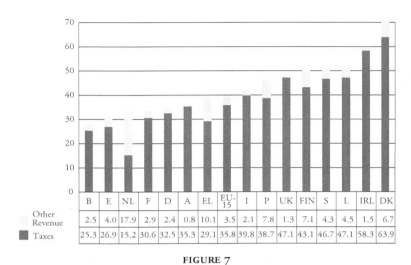

	B	E	NL	F	D	A	EL	EU-15	I	P	UK	FIN	S	L	IRL	DK
Other Revenue	2.5	4.0	17.9	2.9	2.4	0.8	10.1	3.5	2.1	7.8	1.3	7.1	4.3	4.5	1.5	6.7
Taxes	25.3	26.9	15.2	30.6	32.5	35.3	29.1	35.8	39.8	38.7	47.1	43.1	46.7	47.1	58.3	63.9

FIGURE 7

Financing social benefits through taxes and other revenue in 2000 across the EU

Source: Martin Bolkovac, Marcel Fink: Finanzierung der Sozialdebatte.
In: http://www.voegb.at/bildungsangebote/skripten/sr/SR-13.pdf (p. 20)

1,000 contributors; Österreichisches Wirtschaftsforschungsinstitut, the Austrian Economic Research Institute, later corrected that figure downward to 864 pensioners. If it proves possible to raise the quota of people in gainful employment to Northern European levels, the number of pensioners per 1,000 contributors should increase by no more than 16 per cent to 716 pensioners.

Another important factor that must not be overlooked is changes in the foundations of our society: the traditional family unit is becoming rarer or is at least undergoing a transformation. The demographer Rainer Münz points out that Austria's population growth of 13 per cent between 1961 and 2001 has been offset by a 40 per cent growth in the number of households and a 60 per cent increase in the number of flats. In other words, the rise in the number of single households is significant. In demographic terms this will mean fewer young people in the labour market, a higher average age of people in gainful employment and higher pension and sickness insurance budgets.

For politics in Austria the writing is on the wall. A radical change of trend in favour of the model noted above is needed: political momentum must be directed towards raising the employment quota; there is no room for ideological prevarication.

The debate on the changes in age structure has been overshadowed both in Germany and in Austria by fears of these societies being overtaken by old age. In 1953 Konrad Adenauer, then a youthful 77-year-old, noted an 'increasing preponderance of the older generations' at a time when those over 65 already accounted for 9 per cent of the total population. As the demographic prognoses

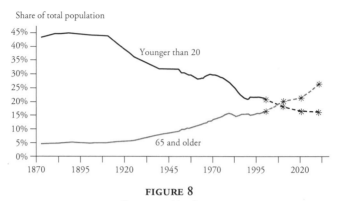

FIGURE 8
Demographic change
Source: Rainer Münz: Demographischer Wandel. In: http://www.oerok.gv.at/aktuelles/
Enquete_50_Jahre_Raumordnung/OeRok_Muenz.pdf (p. 7)

by Rainer Münz and many others indicate, the debate will have to shift towards a reassessment of old age and the roles of the older generation as regards both gainful employment and pensions. The situation that now pertains in Austria, with its low quota of people older than 55 in gainful employment, will be impossible to keep up (Figure 9).

This demographic development is of course not specific to Austria; what is specific are particularly high life expectancy prognoses. In 2007 Austrians have an

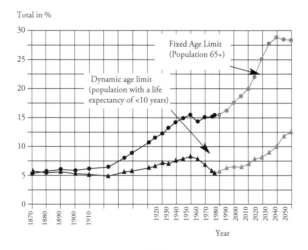

FIGURE 9
Dynamic v. statistical aging, 1870–2050
Source: Rainer Münz: Neue demographische Herausforderungen.
In http://www.wien.gv.at/who/pdf/munz.pdf (p. 27)

average life expectancy at birth of 80.7; in 2050 women can expect to live to 90, men to 86.[4] This projection shows Austrian male life expectancy bettered only in Sweden, female in France. Similar projections apply to all EU countries.

Whether the ÖVP-FPÖ government's pension reform, which became effective in 2005, will really be the end of the debate remains to be seen. It seems unlikely. The homogenization of the different pension systems – ASVG, self-employed, farmers, civil servants – will not be in place before 2050; until then the different groups remain. In the third attempt at a reform of the pension system there are basically three groups who do not have to regard themselves as losers: those who have already retired, people over 50, who with a few exceptions need not be concerned about a deterioration in their situation and those who did not start on their working lives until 2005; this group will have a manageable pension law to rely on, which will be – more or less – the same for everyone in the form of a pension account. For everyone else, i.e. for people not belonging to one of these three groups, the reform entails a complicated transitional system with quite a few 'bumps' and iniquities. The fact that average pensions vary a good deal has only been brought home to many people by this debate and will no doubt remain on the political agenda for the foreseeable future.

By and large one cannot help agreeing with Emmerich Tálos's thesis that the welfare state is on the retreat; there have been both shifts in the ideological paradigm and international/European developments since the 1980s that account for this state of affairs.[5] The postwar decades were characterized by the establishment of the welfare state and by the permanent expansion and refinement of eligibility criteria for benefits, whereas since the mid 1980s social transfer has been put into reverse and since 2000 the ÖVP, first in an FPÖ, then in a BZÖ coalition, has used this instrument to implement major structural changes. In Sweden it was possible to introduce a comprehensive pension reform without any damage to the social structure as a whole, but in Austria this appears impossible. The international debate – above all the one in Germany's Red-Green coalition – on the difficulties of financing the high costs of old age pensions has triggered neoliberal cuts in Austria. In a remarkable act of political brinkmanship, the government of the time used the German coalition's policies as a model while concurrently painting the coalition itself as a bogeyman. It was the trade unions' and the social partners' continual erosion, a process that started in the late 1980s, and the SPÖ's exclusion from government that made a change of paradigms possible. It should not be forgotten in this context that up to 1999 the SPÖ had been in charge of social affairs for fifty-four years (bar only the four years of the Klaus government from 1966 to 1970). It is up to the political powers to decide whether the reduction of the system of welfare benefits will continue, in which case the reduction would have to be offset by a broadening of private and individualized insurance tied to gainful employment. The latter option takes into account the current changes in the global economy, in the labour market and the age structure by providing a wider financial basis. The decision as to what direction to take will no doubt be influenced by what happens in Europe at large; the European context was after all what was decisive in the unhampered development of the welfare state. That the welfare state was deemed ideologically acceptable was ultimately one of the consequences of the Cold War and of the necessity to stabilize the Western European nations (France, Italy) as quickly and comprehensively as possible in order to forestall an internal Communist takeover. When this pressure fell away after 1990, the retreat of the welfare state gained momentum.

The Intergender Contract

In 1945 two thirds of those eligible to vote were women, who, by taking upon themselves an excessive workload both in household and workplace, were the agents of survival. Yet the structures of a classic patriarchal society remained completely untouched by these facts. With only a hint of the provocative, one might say that the so-called intergender contract was a unilateral one, with a great number of obligations for women and few formal rights, which were moreover almost impossible to realize in practice. Even as far as equality before the law was concerned it took until 1975 – fifty years after the Social Democratic MPs Adelheid Popp and Gabriele Proft had presented the first draft of the relevant bill in Parliament – before the principle of partnership and the self-determination of women were anchored in new family law formulations.

The 'reconstruction role' delegated to women was clearly shaped by traditional gender relations: women were primarily responsible for the family and the household without thereby acquiring any independent income or pension. Where this was feasible, they were expected to help their husbands in their businesses, again for free. If they chose careers independent of their male consorts, let them make sure it was done in a manner that was compatible with the primacy of family and household. Employers in their turn set wage and income levels for women that were substantially below those of comparable male employees. In 1953, female employees earned slightly above 73 per cent of male incomes, and by 1963 this had dropped to 60 per cent.

The same discrimination against women is to be found in the field of education. Until the late 1960s the female quota of GCE holders and university graduates remained low.

Male dominance in the Second Republic's political elites is evident. Only one woman was included in Karl Renner's provisional government: Hella Postranecky, KPÖ. The statistic in Table 5 shows that women were not represented in government until 1966. In the Kreisky years the situation improved to a certain extent, yet female representation remained extremely low compared to Northern European countries. In Parliament female representation was initially even lower

ILLUSTRATION 8.2
*The first mayoress in Austria: Zenzi Hölzl, SPÖ, in Gloggnitz, Lower Austria
(1948–1958).*

than in the first stages of the First Republic (5.5 per cent compared to 5.8 per cent). Between 1945 and 2000 it rose by 21.3 per cent, with 49 female MPs out of a total of 183 in 2000. An international comparison shows it is the Northern Europeans' different concept of the welfare state that has resulted in a different gender distribution. Yet Austria has caught up somewhat in recent years, as becomes apparent from a comparison of 1999 data with those of 2004 (Table 6).

The difference in the two big parties' positioning of themselves vis-à-vis this obvious gender gap was, as far as realpolitik was concerned, merely rhetorical, at least to begin with. After 1945 the SPÖ attempted once more to project an image of itself as the party with the reform of women's position at heart. However, when the key issue of food rationing came up, housewives and domestic help were classified as normal consumers along with the unemployed and pensioners – in spite of their multiple workload in an economy dominated by scarcity.

If it had not been for women's survival strategies of juggling the black market, bartering and improvisation, there would have been no such thing as reconstruction. This did not deter decision makers on the political and administrative levels from banking on male stereotypes, an undertaking that was abetted by the senes-

TABLE 5

Women in the Austrian government 1945–2000 (in absolute numbers)

GOVERNMENT (NAME OF FEDERAL CHANCELLOR)	IN OFFICE AS OF	TOTAL NUMBER OF MEMBERS OF GOVERNMENT	FEMALE MINISTERS	FEMALE UNDER-SECRETARIES OF STATE	TOTAL NUMBER OF WOMEN IN GOVERNMENT
RENNER	1945	39	0	1	1
KLAUS	1966	20	1	0	1
KREISKY I	1970	15	1	1	2
KREISKY II	1971	18	2	1	3
KREISKY III	1975	18	2	1	3
KREISKY IV	1979	23	2	5	7
SINOWATZ	1983	24	2	2	4
VRANITZKY I	1986	22	1	2	3
VRANITZKY II	1987	17	2	1	3
VRANITZKY III	1990	20	2	1	3
VRANITZKY IV	1994	22	4	1	5
VRANITZKY V	1996	16	3	1	4
KLIMA	1997	16	3	1	4
SCHÜSSEL	2000	16	4	1	5

Source: Barbara Steininger: Feminisierung der Politik?
In: www.salzburg.gv.at/pdf-steininger.pdf (S. 9)

TABLE 6

Women in National Parliaments (1999 and 2004)

RANK		FEMALE SHARE IN PERCENTAGE POINTS	
		1999	2004
1	SWEDEN	42.7	45
2	DENMARK	37.4	38
3	FINLAND	37.0	38
4	NORWAY	36.4	36
5	NETHERLANDS	36.0	37
6	ICELAND	34.9	30
7	GERMANY	30.9	32
8	SOUTH AFRICA	30.0	33
9	NEW ZEALAND	29.2	28
10	ARGENTINA	27.6	34
11	CUBA	27.6	36
12	AUSTRIA	26.8	34
13	VIETNAM	26.0	27

Source: Barbara Steininger: Femininisierung der Politik?
www.salzburg.gv.at/pdf-steininger.pdf (accessed 1 June 2005)
http:www.globalpolicy.org/socecon/inequal/gender/tables/womeninparliament.htm (accessed 1 June 2005)

cence of these same decision makers. It took until 24 May 1948 for a housewife, provided she 'had at least two children, no domestic help and did additional temporary work of at least 2 hours a week', to be allotted the same food coupons as a female employee.

This obvious discrimination was not only the result of traditional political structures but also of male dominance being even more rampant inside the hierarchies of the social partners. None of them, neither the Federal Economic Chamber nor the Chamber of Trade and Commerce nor the trade unions nor the Chamber of Labour, had women in leading positions. This was compounded by a key problem that has beset trade unions to this day: they consider themselves as exclusively representing wage earners and take classic gainful employment for granted. Unpaid housework falls outside their scope.

Continuities within society, the comeback of religion after the war and the 'male-dominated' political climate ensured that individual attempts at emancipation did not add up to sociopolitical reform movements. The fact that many war veterans returning from captivity found themselves unable to communicate with their empowered wives led to a sharp rise in the divorce rate, a sociopolitical crisis that politics did its best to camouflage. The former POWs were much sought after as potential voters. They were integrated into society as quickly as possible, and welfare benefits were used for this purpose to the extent they were available. Reconstruction was given a male face again in terms of public relations, even though the female contribution was worth at least as much. In the political interpretation of the past and the present, it was only the men that counted. In Germany, the 'Trümmerfrauen', the women clearing debris, were at least etched into the collective memory; in Austria this role was taken by homecoming POWs and 'the men of Kaprun', and these images were repeated and reinforced again and again. The true heroines of the period of reconstruction have remained unsung to this day. In popular perception they have instead been reduced to the well-known graphic artist Theodor Slama's 'Kübelweiber' (bucket women), who were cast in a role subservient to the 'Mauerhelden' (brick-laying heroes).[6]

It did not take long for a counterstrategy to emerge among men dealing with the postwar image of 'empowered woman': young women who consorted with American or other Allied soldiers were branded as representatives of female moral decadence. Apart from the fact that only a small number of women were in that position in any case, the arguments cited in that context appear completely out of place, even if the superior material status of Allied soldiers played an undeniable role. The criticism that was brought to bear on these women draws heavily on National Socialist stereotypes, which had earlier been used against millions of foreign male labourers.

Diverse reforms in the 1970s have made discrimination against women less glaringly obvious. Yet even in Bruno Kreisky's SPÖ solo government, women's issues came up short against an inert, powerful male lobby. Kreisky wanted to emulate the Swedish model in this respect; on finding that his own party refused to follow suit, he diagnosed a 'conservative strand' in the SPÖ as far as women's issues were concerned. By way of therapy he created four female undersecretaries of state. One of them, Johanna Dohnal, who was put in charge of women's issues, caused a great deal of commotion in politics, in the bureaucracy and in public. She proved one of the mainstays of Austria's autonomous women's movement, and between 1990 and 1995 she was the country's first minister for women's affairs.

In 2005 discrimination issues were still a source of justified criticism in respect of both the pension system and the labour market. The EU commission in its report on employment noted that the distribution of income along gender lines is still unjust.[7] As regards the difference in wages, Austria is in third place after Great Britain and Ireland. According to the commission there has only been 'limited progress' in this area. Neither the government nor the social partners (employers, trade unions) seem willing to tackle a comprehensive reform.

NOTES

1. Präsidium des Reichsverbandes der Deutschen Industrie (ed.). 'Denkschrift "Aufstieg und Niedergang"', (Berlin: Selbstverlag, 1929).
2. Emmerich Tálos, *Staatliche Sozialpolitik in Österreich. Rekonstruktion und Analyse,* 2nd ed. (Vienna: Verlag für Gesellschaftskritik, 1981), 309.
3. Alfred Klose, 'Neue Dimensionen der Sozialpolitik', in *Zwanzig Jahre Zweite Republik. Österreich findet zu sich selbst,* ed. Ludwig Reichhold (Vienna: Herder Verlag, 1965), 263.
4. *Die Presse,* 30 October 2007, 1.
5. Emmerich Tálos, *Vom Siegeszug zum Rückzug. Sozialstaat Österreich 1945–2005* (Innsbruck-Vienna-Bozen: Studien Verlag, 2005), 38–82.
6. Wolfgang Kos, *Eigenheim Österreich. Zu Politik, Kultur und Alltag nach 1945* (Vienna: Sonderzahl, 1994), 123.
7. See http://www.orf.at/050129-83242/index.html (accessed 1 June 2005).

CHAPTER 9

The Shadow of the Past

At first sight it might appear that the current debate on National Socialism and the degree to which Austrian men and women were complicit in its horrific and genocidal regime points towards an enhanced role for the past in topical political discussion. However, the fact is that such debates have been repeated in a cyclical fashion ever since the denazification debates of the years immediately after the war, the amnesties of the 1950s, the acquittals of the 1960s, the Wiesenthal-Kreisky-Peter affair of 1975 and the Waldheim affair of 1986. In 1995 this development seemed to acquire an altogether new quality through Franz Vranitzky's deliberate, critical statement. Only three years later the debate was restarted, this time as fall-out from the global debate on the so-called ownerless bank accounts in Switzerland and the indemnification scheme for forced labourers in Germany. The Nazi past is not over yet for Austria: the jury is still out, and the discourse is ongoing.

The collective memory of the Austrians, which originally claimed victim status for the country (to which parts of the political elites were in fact entitled on the basis of their persecution and incarceration by the Nazi regime), has begun since the 1980s to disintegrate into several distinct strands, which may be virulently at odds with each other. It is remarkable that the erosion of national mainstream self-perception – Austria as a collective victim of Germany and its handful of Austrian accomplices – has as its by-product a most extraordinary fixation on an Austrian small-state identity. The more this sense of Austrian identity is in evidence, the less need there is to cling to that postwar doctrine. Since the 1950s bursts of critical reflection have occurred roughly in ten-year cycles, which began to register in sociopolitical terms in about the mid 1980s. All opinion polls since 1946–47 have demonstrated quite clearly how an Austrian sense of identity has gradually evolved and how this identity is particularly independent of Germany in the field of culture. Today Austria belongs to those countries in the world that take the most pride in their nationhood, which has the downside, in Austria's case, of a powerful latent chauvinism. In the meantime even formerly professing pan-Germans who saw themselves as belonging to a unified German civilization have mutated, at least in public discourse, into radical small-state Austrians.

This means on the other hand that the 'victim only' theory is no longer the linchpin of Austrian identity, as the latter is no longer defined negatively as the antithesis of German identity. In addition to this factor, which is integral to the current reassessment of the history of the Austrian contribution to National Socialism and the Holocaust, it is important not to overlook the role external factors played in shaping historical memory after 1945. In 1945 it was by no means obvious which of the two clauses in the 1943 Moscow Declaration, the victim or the co-defendant clause, the Allies were going to opt for when it came to reconstructing the country. Yet it was already obvious from the declaration of Karl Renner's provisional government that the SPÖ, ÖVP and KPÖ were all banking on the victim doctrine. The Cold War and Austria's devastated economy contributed their share so that a differentiated perpetrator-victim doctrine, which was articulated in the first years after the war by the media, the judiciary and the political elites, was not adopted by society as the mainstream interpretation.

Austria is of course no exception. If one looks at France's struggle with the echoes of Vichy and the role of French men and women in stripping French Jews of their possessions and in their deportation, one realizes that the Résistance was the dominant political force only for the first few months after liberation and that it was very soon shouldered aside amid calls for an end to soul searching and to further debates. The French war crimes trials of the 1950s are comparable with those in Austria in that there appeared to be a consensus that proper processing of the collaborators was against the public interest. The role that was played in Austria by the victim myth fell in France to the myth of the Résistance, which has only been subjected to closer inspection within the last few years. The French archives of the Vichy period remained classified until fairly recently, which is in keeping with the overall development. The same applies to Switzerland's extremely restrictive asylum and refugee policies. This was moved centre stage only towards the end of the 1980s to be scrutinized in a critical public debate that moved beyond the narrow confines of intra-academic discourse.

As in other European countries, public memory was shaped by those who had stayed put and by the soldiers. Emigrés and victims (Jews, Roma and Sinti, physically and mentally handicapped victims of euthanasia programmes, deserters, homosexuals, Jehovah's Witnesses etc.) remained marginalized. The memory of the Wehrmacht generation came more and more to be the dominant force and was kept alive through the politics of history as orchestrated by associations of veterans from the 1950s onwards. It formed a layer of remembrance that all but stifled the memory of the victims and the survivors of the Holocaust. Commemoration of both the fate of the Jewish victims in the Nazi extermination camps and that of the surviving émigrés was outsourced to 'memory happenings' linked to particular sites or to anniversaries. Nevertheless – and this is of great significance – these memories remained unconsciously and indirectly ever present.

Every generation confronts those chapters of the past that are constitutive for the rebirth of its society, and it does so in different ways. This is apparent in today's post-transformation regimes. South Africa has sought through its Truth and Reconciliation Commission to implement an open and public confrontation between perpetrators and victims in order to turn 'truth' into a political tool with which to build bridges between the races. In practice this means that all those perpetrators who own up publicly to their wrongdoings and admit their guilt thereby escape punishment; this applies of course also to criminals from the group that has suffered discrimination. The crucial difference in the case of Austria is that after 1945 it was not the confrontation with National Socialism as part of the Austria's national memory that was declared all-important but the reconciliation between the two political camps, which had fought each other since the 1920s not only politically, but physically, with paramilitary units and in a bloody civil war. The truce between 'Red' and 'Black', enforced by the constraints of Allied occupation and administration and of social and economic reconstruction, developed into the basis of a stable society. The postwar project of establishing democratic structures has been successful, even though there is still much to do in the field of political culture.

The year 1984, one of the anniversaries mentioned above, saw an exhibition on the Civil War of February 1934. This exhibition signaled on a symbolic level the end of the interwar years as the most pressing historical issue of the time. In the same year came the first signals that Austrians had become aware of their need to reexamine another part of their history: their share in National Socialism and the way they had dealt with it since 1945. It was time to confront the many blank patches that continue to feature in individual memories and remembrance to this day. This shift in the interpretation of history in Austrian public discourse also has to do with changes in the international perception of the Holocaust: until the end of the 1970s, U.S. society did not fully appreciate the dimensions of the Holocaust, of the extermination or expulsion of European Jewry by the Nazi extirpation industry. This intra-American shift, which found its outward expression in the Holocaust Memorial Museum, was influential for the European and Austrian discourse. Whereas after 1945 Austria was seen in the U.S. as a victim of Nazi aggression – an astonishing 19 per cent of citizens polled were able to locate Austria geographically – the 1980s saw the beginning of critical questions about the actual political contribution of Austrian men and women. A remarkable fact that has not yet received the attention it deserves in academic discourse is that the question of Austria's co-responsibility for the First World War has not been raised in the U.S. in the same way it has been raised with reference to the German Reich. Be that as it may, it is certainly true that the U.S. sees a common thread in Austria's foreign policy dating back at least to 1918. This continuity of perception in the U.S. also accounts for the quick change in U.S. policies regarding political reeducation in Austria. Owing to the smallness of the country and to its difficult socioeconomic situation, the stringent denazification and reeducation policy had already been replaced before the Cold War by a policy of political reorientation, which aimed primarily at ensuring that Austria would side firmly with the Western alliance both ideologically and politically. By as early as 1949, even former NSDAP members were welcomed into positions of power.

What was of concern to U.S. diplomats were the scandalous acquittals of Austrian war criminals by Austrian juries in the 1960s, as well the latent anti-Semitism that, in the Borodajkewycz affair, led to the first casualty of Nazi revisionism. However, this did not at the time produce repercussions in the U.S.: National Socialism and the Holocaust were not yet socially relevant topics.

As is evidenced by the reactions to an article in *Art News* about 'Jewish assets without traceable inheritors' (primarily paintings and other art objects) stored in the Carthusian monastery of Mauerbach, public opinion in the U.S. was beginning to change by 1984. The current debates on looted art and its restitution, the agreements on reparation payments to surviving former forced labourers and decisions in favour of the victims of Nazi Aryanization policies have been shaped by the globalization of the remembrance of recent history. Austria has only become active of its own accord in the case of artworks that were looted or that were sold by their rightful owners under duress. A law has been passed that facilitates restitution to survivors of the Nazi regime or their heirs. In all other respects, as in the creation of a committee of historians to analyse the Nazi forced labour regime, Aryanization and restitution, the Republic has been following examples set by other countries. In the case of the 'Reconciliation Fund' Austria has followed the German model but has been considerably more comprehensive as regards forced labour in agriculture, notably by women (especially mothers).

What has been lost sight of in the current debate is the fact that the FPÖ again exacted a political price: indemnification was to be extended to former Austrian POWs, even though there had been no mention of them when the Reconciliation Fund was conceived. In keeping with the old rules of *Proporz,* the FPÖ tied its consent to this concession. Like the former VdU and the FPÖ of the 1950s, it wished to assume the mantle of protector of the Wehrmacht generation.

It is a fact that Austria has begun to react to changes in the global reception of memory. Yet this does not mean that this accommodation to global political correctness automatically translates into a modification of national historical memory. As always it is primarily the political elites who are concerned with averting economic or political setbacks and sometimes act out of open political opportunism. Yet in the last resort collective memory is neither determined by politics nor mediated by school education. It is shaped by what happens in the family and in the personal sphere of each individual. For a critical analysis of the recent past to remain active, enlightened politics must gain a foothold in these areas. Then we will perhaps be spared the spectacle of national debates being galvanized into life by outside interference, only to peter out again in amnesia or the formation of prejudice. Historiography in its turn has focused increasingly on studying social historical memory over the last few years; it proved especially helpful in many areas in the 1970s and 1980s with its study of anti-Semitism and National Socialism. The postmodern breathing space in many historical disciplines is drawing to an end.

At the same time we must be clear about the fact that National Socialism and the Holocaust are by no means the only chapters of the past that are relevant to our present. One might consider how powerful attitudes and assessments based on the past are for our Eastern European neighbors. This is documented among other things by the debate on the Benes Decrees and the ethnic cleansing of the Sudeten Germans, a topic deliberately ignored by the postwar elites in 1945. This historical topic was instrumentalized as part of the debate on EU enlargement.

It would of course be utterly naïve to believe that collective myths and stereotypes can be made to vanish overnight. Yet it is precisely the context of EU enlargement that makes it imperative to counter the national compulsions of historical memory and to strive for a broad, critical reassessment of the twentieth century's manifold facets in the interest of a shared European past. Raul Hilberg, arguably the most knowledgeable expert on the Shoah, who was forced to leave Austria in 1938, has coined the phrase 'the destruction of the European Jews', the title of his standard work on the subject. It is this European dimension that Austrians must not lose sight of in reflecting on their own past. An isolated memory that remains constricted by national boundaries is worthless for the future; this is as evident as the fact that there can no longer be such as thing as a monolithic historical memory. Austrians will have to accept this challenge, even if this is the last thing they want to hear at a time of rampant Austro-centrism.

The Victim Doctrine of 1945 Revamped

In 1988, the fiftieth anniversary of Austria's Anschluss, Alois Mock, then minister of foreign affairs, signalled his displeasure at the impending publication of a research report on the reconstitution of Austria's foreign service in 1945. By means of sources that had then become newly available, the author of this book was able to demonstrate how the victim doctrine was construed in 1945, how unstable it was, how it was only one option among several others and how uncertain a reception it was likely to meet with in international circles. The author was also able to show that it was by no means the case that Austria's diplomatic service and its leading representatives were recruited at that juncture exclusively from among diplomats who had been persecuted by the Nazis. The original (1988) plan had been for a plaque to be unveiled at the entrance to the Foreign Office at the Ballhausplatz with a text saying that all the ministry's general secretaries had either been persecuted by or opposed to the Nazi regime. However, research had revealed that in some cases the opposite was true and that some of the ministry's employees had actually been members of NSDAP. The wording of the plaque was altered accordingly.

The Foreign Office, which was predominantly staffed with Conservatives at the time (with the exception of its political director, Norbert Bischoff, who referred to himself as an 'unaffiliated leftist', occasionally also as a '*salon* bolshevist'), clung to the victim doctrine in its most comprehensive form. This form was to remain valid until the 1980s, and it is only in recent years that it has been subjected to reassessment. In June 1945 Bischoff asked the international law expert Alfred Verdross, who had shown Catholic-nationalist leanings prior to 1945 and had been cleared by the Nazi regime, to opt for the victim doctrine on the basis of the Moscow Declaration of 1 November 1943 and for what had become known as the occupation theory. Verdross's own inclination had been to postulate Austria's co-responsibility, following the annexation variant. This move on Bischoff's part may appear subjectively justifiable if one bears his own past in mind: a committed anti-Nazi, he was immediately removed from the Foreign Service in 1938. Yet it goes without saying that his biography differs in that vital respect from those of the vast majority of Austrians. In the case of Renner, for instance, who had not only publicly voted for the Anschluss in 1938 but had argued in radically nationalist diction for the Anschluss of Sudetenland in a propaganda pamphlet (which has only survived in the form of a galley proof), the subjective status of a victim was simply nonexistent; yet many civil servants and a number of politicians in 1945 were unquestionably in the same position. Some of them, for instance the young Christian Social diplomat Josef Schöner, a staunch opponent of the Nazi regime, were horrified when Stalin accepted Renner as chancellor. At the same time it was committed opponents of the Nazis such as Schöner who prevented an open discussion of the implication of Austrians in war crimes. In the western half of Austria it was the resistance movement of Karl Gruber that was averse to addressing the political past of some of their comrades of the previous few years. That quite a few Resistance fighters who joined up after 1944–45 were reformed Nazi criminals remained unnoticed. Joining a resistance group, an act that entailed a high degree of risk, was apparently considered to be the equivalent of confession and to confer absolution for all previous crimes.

The declaration of 27 April 1945 made by Renner's provisional government, whose tone is clearly the chancellor's, meticulously avoids naming any victims, even the Jews, and camouflages the depth of Austrian implication with references to the sole responsibility of the Germans and of Austrian Nazis acting outside the law. The key issue in it is the question of reparations. This question jogged Renner's historical memory: he wanted to prevent at all costs a replay of 1918, when the devastated economy was burdened with reparation payments that only served to make the crisis permanent. Renner was unaware at the time that the Allies had agreed long beforehand to reestablish the rump state within the boundaries of 1918; a clear economic agenda had as yet been missing. This was a point emphasized by the legal experts of the Amt für die Auswärtigen Angelegenheiten der Staatskanzlei, Renner's provisional Foreign Ministry, in a directive dated June 1945. On the one hand the demand was voiced that Jewish and Christian victims should be entitled to the same treatment, which was misleading in that the Nazi regime proceeded along racist and not religious categories; on the other it was clear that international pressure could not but result in indemnification acts in the long term. The advice was therefore – contrary to Renner's plans – for a restitution of the looted assets.

Nor was the Soviet Union interested in 1945 in either a comprehensive denazification programme or an indemnification programme with reference to Nazi crimes. Until the elections in November 1945 it was individual war criminals that had an exclusive claim on Soviet interest, and it took until 1946 for wider issues to be considered. For the time being these were left to the three political parties.

The victims too, notably the politically active émigrés, emphasized Austria's victim status through their activities and publications. This approach, although a reflection of actual fact as far as the responsibility of the structures of the state is concerned, still manages completely to ignore the involvement of countless former Austrian citizens in the Nazi regime and the broad acceptance of its systemic injustice. The Social Democrat Friedrich Adler did not abjure his German nationalism even after 1945 and called the viability of an independent small Austria into question; he even went so far as to reduce the political responsibility of the Germans to that of a criminal core group centring on Adolf Hitler. His flag-waving publication *Gerechtigkeit für Österreich* (Justice for Austria) was based on material that, had it been presented in full, would have led to an identification of Austrian culprits. As published, it limited itself largely to the cataloguing of German involvement, and a planned second volume never appeared.

During the state treaty negotiations Yugoslavia demanded that parts of Carinthia's territory be ceded to it and published lists of Austrians charged with having committed war crimes in Yugoslavia; most of these charges were never investigated. In the Cold War they were indiscriminately classified as Communist propaganda, only to resurface in a spectacular manner during the Waldheim affair. A number of Austrians were tried as members of the Wehrmacht in Yugoslavia and found guilty; many were executed or imprisoned. Their cases were never politically evaluated in Austria.

One case among many was that of the CEO of Creditanstalt Bankverein Josef Joham, one of the most important, if today nearly forgotten, economic decision makers of the Second Republic, who was considered a convicted war criminal well into the 1950s because of his bank's involvement in Yugoslavia. The charges were never investigated.[1]

All such charges were rebutted summarily as Communist propaganda. It is in such summary treatment that the problem of the victim doctrine resides. When

Joham was arrested in his native Carinthia by the British authorities, he was immediately released again following a U.S. intervention; the reason that was given was that Joham had identified strategic bombing targets for the Allies. Even prior to the Moscow Declaration of 1 November 1943, Joham had in fact begun to relay information on strategic bombing targets and on the effect of bombing raids on armament-related industrial sites to Allen Dulles's CIA through an intermediary in Switzerland, Kurt Grimm. In effect, he laid the foundation for his postwar career by putting his life on the line. If the National Socialists had sprung his cover, he would have been executed – as was the CEO of the Semperit AG, Franz Josef Messner. Joham could not be sure whether his past might not be exposed to public scrutiny, and he therefore successfully blocked his mooted appointment as finance minister. He did not want to be dragged into the limelight immediately under the eyes of the Allies.

In literature too the summary excuse soon raised its head. In the words of the writer Rudolf Brunngraber, this reads as follows (in a pamphlet published by the three-party publishing house Neues Österreich): 'That an Austrian Fifth Column and Austrian fellow-travellers contributed to this misery pales into insignificance in view of the magnitude of the tragedy.' He goes on to further obfuscate the issue of political responsibility by alleging that there had been 350,000 Belgian collaborators and 77,000 SS volunteers in the Netherlands.

It was no coincidence that Brunngraber, who had a knack of delving into the history of Austria's empire as far back as the Babenbergs and the *Nibelungenlied,* was one of the two script authors for a film that was symptomatic of Austrian self-perception at the time, *1. April 2000,* commissioned by Bundespressedienst, the Federal Media Service, in 1948 and presented in 1952. Brunngraber, nominally a Social Democrat, formed a grand-coalition duo with Ernst Marboe, an ÖVP civil servant; their script was then handed to one of the most important directors of Nazi propaganda films, Wolfgang Liebeneiner. The fact that Liebeneiner was a native of Germany was obviously no longer considered relevant, and his marriage to the Austrian star actress Hilde Krahl helped. This trio, a symbol of what could be achieved through 'integration', represents a snapshot of the social mainstream towards the end of the 1940s. In the film, merry Austria, still under Allied occupation in 2000, dances rings around the occupation forces; among other things, it has managed unilaterally to cancel the Allied Control Agreement. The reasons why it should have been necessary for the 'others', i.e. the Allies, to remain in Austria so long remain in the dark; it was not causes that counted but effects.

In 1945 the government elites displayed at least a fitful interest in reacting to the consequences of the Nazi regime with educational and judiciary measures and by means of the denazification legislation, but from 1946–47 onwards a great deal of Allied pressure was required to keep them on track. Whoever sided with the 'others' was taught a lesson by the voters. In 1945 it was above all the turn of the KPÖ, which had failed to distance itself from the lootings and massive gang rapes carried out by soldiers of the Red Army. The ÖVP, the party that signalled the most understanding – often couched in the Catholic code of absolution – for ex-members of the NSDAP (at this time not yet eligible to vote), was the most successful. The SPÖ, overruling the opposition of Renner and Schärf, adopted a tough stance vis-à-vis this group, which arguably cost it votes in the 1945 elections, where women were by far the most important constituency. This signal given by women voters clearly pointed towards a speedy integration of the former Nazis without further ado.

As the State Treaty negotiations were drawing to an end, Leopold Figl, Austria's foreign minister, managed with U.S. help to persuade the Soviets to allow the co-responsibility clause to be deleted from the preamble of the treaty. This was presented as an expedient to forestall potential Soviet interventions, for the Soviet Union had, in an unexpected about-turn, suddenly discovered anti-fascism as a political topic. At the same time it was of course the internationally sanctioned ringing down of the curtain (at least for the time being) on Austria's debate concerning its concrete co-responsibility for the Second World War and the Holocaust. It is noteworthy that the Foreign Ministry repeatedly fielded the argument that the deletion of that clause was going to erect a wall between the Federal Republic of Germany and Austria, which would finally dispose of all kinds of Anschluss pipedreams on the one hand and on the other open up the way to a non-German armed forces tradition. Molotov may indeed have found the definitive separation of Austria from Germany, which had been the key objective of Soviet policies towards Austria since 1943, the clinching argument. The metaphorical wall very quickly lost its importance in terms of both domestic and foreign policy after 1955, and the development of a strong Austrian identity in the 1970s made it completely obsolete. By the 1980s the very ink on the original document was beginning to fade. The agreement of 23 January 2001 between the U.S. government, victim organizations, lawyers and the Israelitische Kultusgemeinde in Vienna contained a new declaration, following the statements made in the 1990s by Franz Vranitzky and Thomas Klestil.

Notes on the Perpetrator Myth

Both in the debates conducted in the media and in historical research focusing on Austria's Nazi past, a position diametrically opposed to the victim doctrine has been gaining prominence since the 1980s. Again, as was the case with the victim doctrine, case histories of individuals or of groups are given preference over a comprehensive study of the total picture. In the political debate of 1999–2000 on retrospective restitution, Aryanization and forced labour it was repeatedly put forward that a disproportionately high percentage of Austrians had been involved in the expropriation and destruction of European Jewry: it was claimed that one in five concentration camp guards had been Austrians.

This claim is not new. It first became politically relevant in 1952, when German politicians tried to exclude the claims of Austrian Jews from the restitution negotiations between the Jewish Claims Conference and the Federal Republic of Germany. The German position prevailed, even though the Jewish Claims Conference had included the claims of Austrian Jews in its figures. On 12 October 1966, Simon Wiesenthal, the director of the Documentation Center of the Association of Jewish Victims of the Nazi Regime, repeated this claim in his memorandum 'Crime and Punishment of Nazi Perpetrators from Austria' and used a number of isolated case histories as his primary corroboration. Wiesenthal did this in order to motivate the ÖVP solo government of the day to take a critical look at the pending lawsuits against Nazi war criminals and at the scandalous acquittals of Austrian Nazi criminals. U.S. publications have often quoted from what are alleged to be Wiesenthal's findings; the latest person to do so was the then U.S. Undersecretary of State Stuart Eizenstat, supporting his own claim that Austrians had held a disproportionate number of key positions in the extermination machinery of the Nazi regime.

It is remarkable that nobody seems to have bothered to read Wiesenthal's original documentation. In it Wiesenthal wanted to draw attention to the high percentage of Austrian culprits who had not been subjected to judiciary proceedings. He himself questions the arithmetical correctness of the disproportionate percentage of Austrians involved. Wiesenthal wanted to draw attention to the former National Socialist *Gauleiter* of Vienna, Odilo Globocnik, who had played a leading role in Lublin's 'Aktion Reinhardt', in whose course between 1.8 and 2.2 million Jews were murdered. The head of the staff responsible, which included at least another twenty-five Austrians, was Heinrich Höfle, who committed suicide in prison.

The first empirical studies were limited to a small group of around fifteen men from the entourage of Adolf Eichmann, who were charged with helping organize the persecution of Jews in Vienna, Prague, Thessalonika, Paris, Bratislava and Budapest. (Eichmann, a salesman from Linz, considered himself a German and spoke with a North-German accent.[2]) Without underestimating the importance of this Austrian clique, it would appear that studies focusing on nationalities will have to be integrated into the overall context of the Nazi extermination machinery if they are to be fruitful in terms of Holocaust research.

The crucial shortcoming of the Austrian judiciary and Austria as a whole is this: only a fraction of the individuals who are suspected of having been implicated during the Second World War in capital crimes committed outside the country's current boundaries have been indicted. This is a chapter of legal history that as yet remains to be written. By the mid 1960s only forty people had been identified as having been concentration camp guards: no one was ever brought to justice. Accurate group analyses of the people involved in crimes are a prerequisite to any determination of the actual proportion of Austrians involved.

Initial empirical research was too inaccurate for the thesis of a disproportionate recruitment of Austrians to SS guard units to hold. In his study *The Camp Men*, made on the basis of 61,000 microfiched SS leader profiles, the U.S. troop inspector for Europe, French L. MacLean, identified 967 officers (from the rank of SS-Untersturmführer or junior storm leader upwards) serving in SS concentration camp guard units. Of these, according to MacLean's analysis, 4.65 per cent were of Austrian extraction. In a recent analysis Stefan Kupska[3] has revised this figure upwards to at least 7.41 per cent, this against an Austrian population that comprised 8.81 per cent of the population of the Reich. What additionally hampers more accurate analysis is the fact that a number of birthplaces have not yet been identified with any certainty. A reasonable correspondence can also be found amongst those officers who were actually in charge of concentration camps, 6 per cent of whom were Austrian. Christopher Browning and Daniel Goldhagen have drawn attention to police battalions that were involved in brutal annihilation campaigns against civilians in Eastern Europe and in Russia. Three of them were recruited in Vienna; in at least one of them, Police Batallion 311 (Vienna-Kagran), there were only two reserve officers from Austria and only a third of the enlisted men were natives of what is today Austria. Wiesenthal does not mention this example in his memorandum, but he does mention another one and five other police and gendarmerie units with Austrian recruits in them – without, however, quantifying their relative group sizes. Among the officers of the special units, who were active with devastating consequences in the Soviet Union and the Balkans, 3.9 per cent were Austrian; further research is needed before any figures concerning enlisted men can be given.

However, even if it is at present impossible to prove with empirical methods that Austrians played a disproportionately large role in mass exterminations, and despite the questionable nature of much of the analysis done so far, the collaboration of Austrians with the Nazi regime during the Second World War and in the Holocaust remains all too manifest. Equally clear is the inefficiency of the judiciary, which did not follow up the information gathered by the police both in Austria and in Germany. Immediately after 1945 the difference from both the Federal Republic and the GDR lay in the extent to which the Austrian judiciary (in the context of war crimes trials and people's courts trials) was prepared not only to indict Austrian citizens for crimes committed within the boundaries of today's Austria but also to follow up crimes committed by Austrians in the East.

It is true that the stringent first phase of judicial processing, particularly in the people's courts, means that the Austrian judiciary takes precedence even over

Germany when one considers the average of guilty verdicts. Out of a total number of 134,567 suspects, a guilty verdict was handed down in 13,852 or 10.2 per cent of cases; for Germany the figures are a total of 89,789 suspects and 6,469 or 7.7 per cent found guilty. However, closer inspection of individual cases reveals that in many cases the Austrian trials concerned illegal status, i.e. political NSDAP activities in the era before 1938, when the party was banned; they did not concern involvement in atrocities outside Austria. Furthermore, the 1960s in Germany saw the Auschwitz trials, whereas in Austria mass murderers such as Franz Murer, the slaughterer of Vilna, or Franz Novak, who played a leading role in the deportation of Hungarian Jews, were tried by juries in 1963 and 1964 and acquitted. Erich Rajakowitsch, who was involved as a 'lawyer' in robbing Jews of their property and helping to organize their deportation in the Netherlands, was sentenced to a mere two and a half years.

Out of sixteen lawsuits, eleven ended in acquittals. A leading member of the Flemish SS, Robert Jan Verbelen, who had worked both for the Austrian state police and, after 1945, for the U.S. Military Secret Service, CIC, was not extradited to Belgium, where he had been sentenced to death. Instead, he was tried by jury in Austria and acquitted on the grounds that he had acted under duress. His lawyer, Erich Führer, had defended one of the Dollfuß assassins after 1934 and had taken an active and substantial part in the spoliation of Jews. The SS-Oberführer Gustav Franz Wagner was tried for his part in the murder of 150,000 Jews in the Lublin district; proceedings against his superior, the SS senior storm unit leader, Ernst Lerch, a Klagenfurt coffeehouse operator, were dropped. While it is true that the Federal Republic of Germany was late in initiating proceedings for crimes committed outside its boundaries and that the business was left unfinished, at least an effort was made.

The miscarriages of justice in Austria were registered with disgust outside the country, but even in the U.S. no attempt was made to address the issue at a government level. The indignation of Jewish organizations was voiced only in their own internal media and pamphlets.

Generation Wehrmacht

In political discussions about the Nazi era there was a strong tendency for summary judgments to be passed on the Wehrmacht generation. Here too, the Cold War posed a problem. After an initial phase in 1945–46, in which they had shown little interest in the issue, the Soviets began at the Nuremberg war crimes trials to underscore the role Austrians had played within the Wehrmacht in the devastation of large parts of the Soviet Union. This summary verdict ruined all chances of a differentiated debate. The blurring of differences resulted also in such shameful cases as that of Heinrich Gross, a medical doctor involved in the Nazi euthanasia programme, who escaped the first round of strict indictments for Nazi crimes because he was still a Russian prisoner of war at the time. After his return he had hopes – justified at the outset – of finding the courts much more lenient.

Around 17 million men had been drafted into the Wehrmacht, almost 1.3 million from Austrian territory and from annexed territories in the north and south. In the casualty rate there was a difference: whereas 29 per cent of Germans died in action, the figure for Austrians is lower by 10 per cent, which may very well indicate a certain distancing from 'pan-German' aggression – although such statistics must be used with caution. It remains a fact that at least 8 per cent of the Wehrmacht came from Austria; at leadership level, 207 generals were Austrians, as were 326 holders of the iron cross. That units of the Wehrmacht were involved in war crimes is also a fact that every knowledgeable military historian and expert on military law can document on the basis of overwhelming evidence. In the Waffen-SS Austrians may well have been represented to an extent that is significantly higher than the Austrian population share in the Reich of 8.81 per cent: 60,000 Austrians belonged to the Waffen-SS.

The prisoner of war issue was one of the most important of the postwar era, particularly with respect to the Soviet Union. All parties established sub-organizations for the integration and political education of war veterans. In the 1940s and early 1950s the Second World War had not yet been romanticized, but in 1953, when rearmament was a foreseeable fact, a number of associations for the cultivation of war memory set up shop, amongst them the Kameradschaftsbund (Association of War Veterans). Today the Kameradschaftsbund has 250,000 members, of whom only a fraction, as is documented at various jamborees, are actively involved; only 30 per cent belong to the actual war generation. After 1945, more than 400,000 Austrians were the recipients of war, invalid, widow or orphan annuities (figure given as in 1948); many of these annuities dated back to the time of the First World War.

From the end of the 1950s onwards, public remembrance again took the form of the traditional 'veterans' commemorations' with the attendant marginalization of those who had engaged in resistance against the Nazi regime or had been persecuted by it. A majority of veterans dominated the discourse, and deserters from the Wehrmacht were still regarded as traitors. The Cold War and the splits in diverse special interest groups contributed to the marginalization of the Resistance. It took until the late 1980s and the 1990s for these memory patterns to disintegrate, usually under the impact of public debates, such as the one on the Hrdlicka memorial in Albertina Square or Rachel Whiteread's Holocaust memorial in the Judenplatz. Currently initiatives are under way to create some kind of visual memory of victims in a public space.

The Aftermath of the Victim Doctrine:
The Wiesenthal-Kreisky-Peter Debate

Simon Wiesenthal, an ÖVP sympathizer, had hoped that the Klaus government was going to make sure in 1966 that proceedings pending against Nazi war criminals were speeded up; in this, he was disappointed. His memorandum, which has already been quoted here, produced no effect in spite of repeated interventions. After 1970, the social and political framework that had been created by the grand coalition's amnesty and its abolition of the people's courts no longer allowed for a confrontation of the Holocaust with any semblance of justice. However, this was not what Wiesenthal criticized; his criticism was directed against the SPÖ. It was true that between November 1945 and 1966 the SPÖ had held tenure at the Ministry of the Interior; Oskar Helmer, a conservative Social Democrat who was not averse to the occasional anti-Semitic joke, was at the helm until 1957. Yet when it was the turn of the ÖVP to provide ministers of the interior between 1966 and 1970, they showed no more interest in following up Nazi crimes. The ministers of justice, such as Josef Gerö and Hans Kapfer, were independents and themselves victims of the Nazi regime (Gerö had been held at Dachau, Kapfer in Theresienstadt). It was precisely their status as victims that made them only too willing to implement amnesty legislation; in practice, of course, drawing a line between fellow-travellers, who were eligible for amnesty, and perpetrators, who were not, proved tricky. Worried about losing votes, politicians failed to provide for adequate legal tools, even though it was evident to everyone that juries would not act objectively and correctly in the upcoming trials.

Against this background Simon Wiesenthal shifted the whole burden of postwar responsibility to Bruno Kreisky's 1970 minority government. Bruno Kreisky, a man with Jewish roots, had been incarcerated both in the days of Austro-Fascism and in the Nazi era before exiling himself to Sweden until 1951, and yet, as was immediately reported in *Der Spiegel*, he had co-opted four former NSDAP members into his cabinet. Kreisky had to cope with anti-Semitism in Austria all his life and had been attacked as late as 1965 at an electoral convention by a senior functionary of the Lower Austrian Farmers' Association as a 'Saujude' (Jewish pig). Kreisky was afraid that Wiesenthal was trying to turn his Jewishness into a political issue; after all, in 1970 the ÖVP had fielded the slogan 'Ein echter Österreicher' (A genuine Austrian) for Josef Klaus, which was designed to mobilize subliminal prejudice against Kreisky, the Jewish émigré. Kreisky defended the incriminated ministers with more vigour than would presumably have been forthcoming from someone with a different history, but at the same time he saw to it that one of them, Johann Öllinger, who was new to him and turned out to have been a member of the SS, was dismissed forthwith from his post as minister for agriculture. There is no indication that Kreisky had co-opted these 'formers' into his government as a calculated signal to former National Socialists.

The short-lived Öllinger had been made minister more or less by chance: in an intraparty balancing act the trade union organization had rejected the agriculture portfolio offered to its own Josef Staribacher as insufficiently prestigious. There had then been a frantic last-minute search culminating in the discovery in Carinthia of one of the few SPÖ experts on agriculture – agriculture being traditionally an ÖVP domain. Minister of the Interior Otto Rösch had belonged to several governments prior to 1966. His NSDAP membership was well known, as was his implication and acquittal in a 1947 neo-Nazi trial; neither had elicited any reaction from Wiesenthal or from anyone else before 1970.

The whole topic of NSDAP membership was taboo for Kreisky. On his return to Austria in the 1950s he was given to understand that the reintegration of the 'formers' was a fait accompli. He had had to accept this in order to continue to be politically active. He was determined to avoid at all cost any semblance of partisanship due to his Jewish origins; for this reason he left the so-called restitution negotiations to others for a long time. His emotional reaction in 1970 no doubt had much to do with Wiesenthal's breaking this taboo, but it is clear that he also suspected Wiesenthal of having a hidden party political agenda. This was a reasonable assumption: at the time of the ÖVP-led grand coalition Wiesenthal had abstained from criticizing members of the government for their former NSDAP membership, as is evidenced by the case of Reinhard Kamitz, an important ÖVP finance minister, whose Nazi past was an open secret.

However, in 1975 Wiesenthal wanted to forestall any attempt by the SPÖ to rely once more on the support of the FPÖ under the leadership of Friedrich Peter. He therefore informed Federal President Rudolf Kirchschläger of the fact that Peter (as was apparent from then newly discovered evidence) had belonged to an SS unit that had been involved in liquidations. Wiesenthal had already been in possession of this information at the time of the election campaign but had chosen not to pass it on. Had he wanted to prevent a pro-Peter debate, whose acrimony he could foresee? Or had his primary motive always been to prevent a second edition of Kreisky's minority government? If he had remained consistent with himself, he would have published the information without delay as soon as he had obtained it.

Kreisky's reaction was extreme and disproportionate, particularly when he indirectly accused Wiesenthal of collaboration with the Nazi regime. Kreisky's overreaction is often linked to his presumed intention to use the incident in order to win over the 'formers' as voters. In this case, however, it was a personal taboo that Wiesenthal had hit upon – knowingly or unknowingly. Bruno Kreisky did not want to be played off as a Jew against that stable bloc in society that advocated the reintegration of ex-members of the NSDAP and of former soldiers of the Wehrmacht in the 1970s. It was quite simply a gut reaction.

In the meantime Kreisky had received allegations about Wiesenthal's activities as a Nazi collaborator; traces of this are now beginning to emerge in secret service

archives in Warsaw and Prague. The allegations had to do with Wiesenthal's precarious status as an anti-communist. In 1960 he had published a documentation
Judenhetze in Polen (Anti-Jewish Hate Campaign in Poland), in which he attacked the Communist regime; at a press conference in 1968 he had presented a
study focusing on totalitarian continuities linking the Nazi era to the GDR, 'Die
gleiche Sprache: Erst für Hitler – jetzt für Ulbricht' (The Same Language: First
for Hitler, Now for Ulbricht).

Kreisky too was in the sights of the Communist secret services, since Social
Democrats per se were classified as dangerous to communism. Willy Brandt was
also notoriously targeted in a secret service operation that eventually led to his
resignation as federal chancellor: in late 1972 East Berlin State Security had managed to place Günter Guillaume in Brandt's immediate vicinity as his personal assistant in the Federal Chancellery; Guillaume reported intimate details of Brandt's
private life. On 6 May 1974, Brandt resigned. The Czechoslovak secret service
had compromised Austria with great efficiency, infiltrating the top echelons of
the bureaucracy and the media: witness the reaction to allegations that Helmut
Zilk, a journalist and television personality who was later to become mayor of
Vienna, had engaged in espionage. It is certain that a spy ring was cracked in
1968 but equally clear that this did not spell the end for this particular network.
The case of Wiesenthal v. Kreisky meant a loss of status for both men.

Rumour had it, according to diverse pieces of information that reached
Kreisky, that there was an informant who was prepared to appear as chief witness
against Wiesenthal: Theodor Oberländer, the highly controversial and quarrel-
some German CDU minister for displaced persons. Kreisky remained convinced
to the end (there was a second lawsuit in the 1980s on the grounds of reiteration
of a false accusation) that his testimony was truthful. It was highly unusual, to say
the least, that Wiesenthal had defended Kreisky's chief witness, whose name was
not made public until decades later, against charges of war crimes in Poland and
entered into a correspondence with him. In other words, the Polish secret service
exploited Kreisky's overreaction in order to discredit Wiesenthal. Wiesenthal's
anti-socialist leanings prevented him from establishing with Kreisky the kind of
contact he had forged with the ÖVP in 1966. Maybe he also felt that this particular avenue was now closed to him. To make matters worse, both men hailed,
in Wiesenthal's phrase, 'from the same tree'. Yet Kreisky defended his personal interpretation of Jewishness, which largely corresponded to that of an assimilated,
non-religious Jew in Vienna around 1900, both fiercely and passionately. Wiesenthal lived another form of Jewishness, which put the Holocaust at the centre
of everything. At the same time he was unable to overcome his Bolshevist trauma,
which led him to attribute the legislative and political shortcomings of Austria's
confrontation with the Holocaust and National Socialism primarily to the SPÖ.

The conflict between Kreisky and Wiesenthal was defused – by Karl Kahane,
one of Austria's foremost industrialists and a close personal friend of the chan-

cellor, and by Iwan Hacker, the president of the Kultusgemeinde – but a reconciliation worth the name never took place.[4] Intellectual reflection on the uproar
that followed the Wiesenthal controversy usually stigmatizes Kreisky as its prime
cause. However, such judgments tend to overlook the personal and political background to his overreaction, which is itself a snapshot of the social mainstream of
the 1970s. They also miss the fact that it was the Cold War that had provided the
fuse. What Kreisky did was to fall into a trap set by an agent provocateur.

The Wiesenthal controversy attracted a certain amount of attention, particularly in the U.S. and U.K., but was quick to disappear from the media agenda.
Austria's image was not tarnished by it, and Kreisky continued to be accepted as a
dialogue partner until he crossed the line for the majority of Israelis by recognizing the PLO in 1979–80. It remained unsaid that the onus of a critical confrontation with National Socialism continued to lie with Austria. The international
public was not yet really interested in a debate focused on the Holocaust and
National Socialism.

The Waldheim Debate

If Kurt Waldheim, a meticulous career strategist second to none in Austria, had
had an inkling of the rancorous debate that would be triggered by his prettified
biography – let alone by his declaration that all he had done as a soldier 'was his
duty', he would probably have thought twice about his candidacy. He had always
been in the right place at the right time, but it was this very capacity that led to
his brief term during the war as defence officer in the vicinity of General Alexander Löhr of Army Group E. The atrocities of the brutal Balkan warfare were
referred to in the reports that crossed Waldheim's desk, and he dutifully marked
them with his abbreviated signature. After 1945 he very quickly found himself
a new job as 'secretary' in a group that happened to consist of former Resistance
fighters such as Fritz Molden, gathered around the Minister for Foreign Affairs
Karl Gruber. His first curriculum vitae – which was simply copied subsequently
– mentioned only his Wehrmacht service on the 'Eastern front', a war injury and
his studies in Vienna; the Balkan War chapter had been inked over by the internal censor. Yugoslavia did not drop its territorial claims with regard to Austria
until 1948, by which time Löhr had been executed as a war criminal. Still, there
always remained the distinct possibility that Waldheim's early history would be
used against him should the need arise. The 'smoking gun' was planted, as was
discovered in the 1980s, in the shape of a file of the War Criminals Commission.
That this file shared the same New York address with UN Secretary-General Kurt
Waldheim for decades is one of the quirkier aspects of the whole affair.

Immediately after the war Waldheim was as yet too insignificant, and the Cold
War too omnipresent, for anyone to take an interest in war crimes in Yugoslavia

and Greece. When Tito set out on his non-aligned course in opposition to the Soviet Union as of 1948, the issue looked dead and buried. Until recently the historian Robert Hertzstein was convinced that the CIA had used the information to get a handle on Waldheim or that it had in fact even used him as a spy. Newly declassified CIA files disprove this theory: Waldheim himself was too much obsessed with his career to take any risk. In retrospect, the career that Waldheim subsequently made displays evidence of almost strategic planning. He quickly rose to the rank of head of personnel in the Federal Chancellery and the Foreign Ministry and began setting his sights on a UN position. His closeness to the ÖVP did not prevent him from seeking – and finding – close personal contact with Bruno Kreisky, then minister for foreign affairs.

During his spell as ÖVP foreign minister (1968–70) Waldheim proved embarrassingly deficient in his response to the Czechoslovak crisis. He did notch up several successes in the South Tyrol question, but in 1970 his career seemed to be on its last legs, at least as far as traditional party political nepotism was concerned. In the end Kreisky came down fully in favour of Waldheim's candidacy for the post of UN secretary-general because he wanted to add another component to Austria's international prestige.

It is still a moot point who was actually the first person to draw attention to the inked passage in Waldheim's curriculum vitae. Usually it is the SPÖ that is mentioned as the 'culprit', in particular the head of Chancellor Fred Sinowatz's cabinet, Hans Pusch, with the motive of influencing the upcoming presidential elections. What is not usually taken into account is the fact that the welcome-home reception given to the war criminal Walter Reder by FPÖ Defence Minister Friedhelm Frischenschlager had already set alarm bells ringing in the media outside Austria. A similar incident was the plaque planned by air force romanticists for the war criminal Alexander Löhr, who was to be remembered for his role as head of the completely inferior Austrian Air Force until 1938. This climate of complete insensitivity to issues of guilt and responsibility set not only journalists in the U.S. and in Austria but also people in the U.S. judiciary on Waldheim's track; via Löhr they caught up with him.

This successful playing of the Nazi card against a federal president – a move until then unheard of in the history of the Second Republic – made it clear that the taboo of addressing NSDAP membership in a political context was broken. The whole business was analogous to Wiesenthal's incriminations in the 1970s, but this time things had moved on to the big stage. The choreography unfolded as planned: particularly after the intervention of the World Jewish Congress (for whom the Waldheim case meant an opportunity to garner publicity for the Holocaust debate in the U.S.), postwar reflexes set in yet again. The 1986 election saw the ÖVP playing the 'So what?' card adroitly, without worrying whose bed it was therefore sharing. What really mattered to the electorate was that the SPÖ had a severe credibility problem with its newly rediscovered anti-fascist stance –

having fostered the NSDAP taboo from 1945 onwards in tandem with the ÖVP, the VdU and the FPÖ. Waldheim was reelected with a clear majority.

In 1986 Austria woke up to a completely changed situation. Its postwar role as the darling of the Cold War had come to an end. There was no longer any geopolitical necessity to bypass the political confrontation on the extent of implication in the Holocaust and the Second World War in order not to hurt the feelings of an ally. The differences between Austria and the new political debate in the U.S. were thrown into sharp relief. The whole development peaked when Kurt Waldheim's name was put on a watch list of people who were to be refused entry into the United States. This was done on the basis of a dossier that appears rather incomplete when examined today. Moreover, it connected Waldheim directly with war crimes. In the light of what we know today, this had not been the case. This state of affairs proved impossible to change – despite cost-intensive efforts made by Foreign Minister Alois Mock to have Waldheim removed from this list.

The reason for this obduracy on the part of the U.S. is clear: the original listing was politically motivated, arising under a new U.S. code that subsequently manifested itself in the 1990s in vehement debates concerning Swiss banks, Nazi forced labour and the practice of 'Aryanization'. Waldheim fell foul of this code by claiming to have had no knowledge of either the deportation of Jews from Thessalonika or any other wartime atrocities perpetrated in the Balkans. Conflict

ILLUSTRATION 9.1
Many protest rallies took place after the presidential election of Kurt Waldheim.

with this new code for both himself and his supporters was, in the end, down to his personal version of the victim doctrine (subsequently reinforced by several special envoys) and to his own assertion that he had been 'in duty bound' to carry out all his wartime activities.

That it was an ÖVP-FPÖ coalition that continued the erosion of the victim doctrine demonstrates quite clearly the potency of the external forces at work here. It remains to be seen whether this externally motivated revision of history will really be accepted by society.

Denazification or Continuity of the Elites

It is noteworthy that the Waldheim debate did not lead to a full-scale confrontation on the nature of Austria's postwar elites and their pasts. What followed were analyses in general terms, while the debates on National Socialism and anti-Semitism were overly concerned with Waldheim as a person. It was the trial in 2000 of the former euthanasia doctor Heinrich Gross that caused a political earthquake. It was as though the fifty-five-year development of denazification in the Second Republic flashed across the mind of the Austrian public in a single instant.

After Viktor Klima's resignation, Alfred Gusenbauer – the predecessor of Austria's current chancellor, Werner Faymann – was elected leader of the SPÖ. Among the items on his initial agenda were an apology to the surviving victims and the families of the children murdered at the Klinik Spiegelgrund and a self-critical examination of the 'brown stains in the SPÖ'. In 2005 two publications presented the results of historical research projects headed by Wolfgang Neugebauer for the Bund Sozialistischer Akademiker (BSA, Association of Socialist University Graduates), and by Maria Mesner for the SPÖ. This triggered a debate about former NSDAP members in the SPÖ and a bout of Nazi-bashing within the party. This last was also remarkable for its context: the ÖVP was mentioned only in passing in media reports on the issue in deference to the power structure of the ÖVP-led coalition, while the VdU, the ancestor party of the FPÖ, was left out completely, even though it was this party that had sought the bulk of its support and recruits among former NSDAP members. Particularly in the 1950s both the VdU and its successor party, the FPÖ, had agitated for an amnesty of NSDAP members in their election platforms and in their propaganda. They had also been radically opposed to restitution and indemnification legislation and had been a constant thorn in the flesh of the two major parties on these issues. This situation also accounts for the general amnesty of 1957, which made legal proceedings against Nazi war criminals virtually impossible.

But the whole issue was not primarily about such things as party membership. Of greater concern was that the prejudices and kindred attitudes that had come blatantly to the fore under National Socialism – racism, anti-Semitism and xenophobia – had been a problem in Austria before National Socialism and have continued to be one since. This state of affairs was not addressed as part of the SPÖ's 'brown stains' debate. To persist in laying the blame for it on one or two political parties would be not only politically unwise but also historically incorrect. What we should be concerning ourselves with is the analysis and assessment of both the transformation of these prejudices and the resistance to them seen in the generations that have come to maturity since 1945.

The idea of a kind of 'retribution law' was first mooted in the 'Proklamation der Vorstände der antifaschistischen Parteien Österreichs', a statement issued as early as 27 April 1945 by the leaders of Austria's anti-fascist parties that was in fact the first programmatic declaration of the provisional government. It was to have been applied as a kind of emergency law to those former members of the NSDAP, 'who, out of contempt for democracy and democratic rights, established and upheld a regime in Austria based on violence, denunciation, persecution and repression and who had recklessly plunged the country into a disastrous war and laid it open to devastation'.[5] The plan provided for 'fellow-travellers' to be reintegrated into society as quickly as possible. A similar message can be found in Order No 1, issued by the representatives of the Red Army's High Command, with its dictate that ordinary NSDAP members were not to be incriminated by the Red Army simply on the basis of their 'party membership ... provided they show themselves to be loyal to the Red Army'. Karl Renner, chancellor of the provisional government, floated the idea of 'barring all fascists (members of the *Heimwehren* and clerical and nationalistic fascists) who were not simply taking orders from their superiors ... from exercising their democratic rights for a ten-year probation period'. Although this idea coincided with recommendations advanced by U.S. experts, it was dropped after being aired in political discussions. Renner's proposal of getting *Zensurkommissionen* (review committees) to draw up complete lists of former NSDAP members was taken up and put into action.

The *Verbotsgesetz*, a constitutional law dated 8 May 1945 concerning the banning of the NSDAP, and the War Criminals Act, dated 26 June 1945, created the basis for the legal processing of ordinary ex-members and of ex-functionaries of the Nationalsozialistische Deutsche Arbeiterpartei in legal and administrative terms instead of in political and revolutionary ones. All persons who had been formally in contact with the NSDAP (as members, candidates for membership, members of paramilitary formations, members of the SS or candidates for SS membership) between 19 June 1933 (when the NSDAP was banned as a party in Austria) and 27 April 1945 (Austria's declaration of independence) were put under an obligation to register with the authorities. Registration was followed in a number of cases by *Sühnefolgen* (retribution measures) aimed above all against former illegal Nazis – those who had belonged to the NSDAP between the banning of the party in 1933 and 13 March 1938 – and against party functionaries and members of the SS. The *Sühnefolgen* could take the form of a temporary loss of civic rights, a temporary employment ban, confiscation of property or the imposition of a fine. A further sanction was for the offender to be interned in an *Anhaltelager*. These camps were located in Glasenbach, Wolfsberg, Tulln and Korneuburg; by 15 September 1946 a mere 258 individuals were interned in the Soviet zone, compared to 11,234 in the U.S. zone, 7,186 in the British and 1,871 in the French zone. Registered individuals were banned from voting in the general elections in November 1945.

Until the beginning of 1946 both the Austrian authorities and the Allies actively pursued an agenda of getting heavily incriminated people discharged from their jobs, making arrests and organizing trials of war criminals; initially the Americans and the British were particularly active in their pursuit of employment bans and discharges. With the onset of the Cold War the Western allies started toning down their denazification efforts in favour of an inclusive anti-communist movement and left the whole business of denazification to the Austrian authorities and parties. The Soviet Union in its turn seized on denazification to argue the need for the continued administration of Austria by the Allies. The total number of Austrians to be registered in this way in 1946 was 536,660. After a legislative change in the form of the Nazi Act of 1947 this figure was reduced; this also entailed a reduction of the *Sühnefolgen,* as it was now no longer the 'illegal' Nazis who appeared primarily culpable but rather those who had held real functions within the NSDAP.

Once the first administrative obstacles had been cleared and the implementation instructions for the *Verbots- und Kriegsverbrechergesetz,* the Prohibition and War Criminals Act, had been issued, it was observed that bureaucratic implementation itself met with great obstacles. The main reasons for this were that no comprehensive debate was encouraged, that no reeducation campaign on fascism and National Socialism had taken place and that the crimes the Nazis had committed against the Jewish part of the population were perceived as the exclusive responsibility not of Austrian society as a whole but rather of the 'Reichsdeutsche' (German Nazis), who had been aided and abetted in their crimes by Austrian accomplices acting outside the law. Karl Renner left no doubt about this interpretation in his postwar agenda: 'For the damage done to the Jews the people as a whole shall not to be made liable.' Nonetheless provisions were made for the restitution of some assets.

By 1946 it was clear that a relatively small number of former Nazis was going to be indicted, but that there would be no ideological confrontation with the phenomenon of National Socialism as such, on the grounds that this would have interfered with a controlled economic and social reconstruction programme. As an inevitable side effect of this, many people who were temporarily suspended from their jobs or had been handed down other *Sühnefolgen* began to see themselves as the real victims, since the basic culpability of the Nazi regime, with its endless ramifications in everyday life, had not been spelled out for them. A process of discussion and reeducation involving the whole of society would have been required for such categories as individual responsibility to become a living reality. Such a discussion would have had to include everyone, even non-NSDAP anti-Semites and racists, in order for the whole of society to be evaluated.

The tendency to want to 'draw a line under the past' was increasingly in evidence from 1947–48 onwards. Even in the field of penal justice the people's courts stepped up the number of acquittals to 52 per cent (compared with 26 per cent in the period from 1945 to 1947). At the same time the two big parties, the ÖVP and the SPÖ, openly discussed an issue that had a direct bearing on their election strategy: a large number of former NSDAP members were going to be reenfranchised for the 1949 general elections. As a result of the amnesty for less incriminated former NSDAP members, there was to be an influx of 500,000 new voters, which was bound to have a significant impact on the political landscape. In Lower Austria alone this meant 74,000 additional votes. The two major parties tried in different ways to secure the votes of the 'formers' for themselves – even where this involved giving up on denazification altogether. The grand coalition had originally intended to phase out denazification by 1947 but had been compelled by Allied pressure to persist. Even the KPÖ made secret contributions to the campaign budget of the VdU in Upper Austria in order to prolong the duration of Soviet occupation: the more prominent the role aspired to by neo–National Socialists, the more imperative it became for Soviet troops to remain stationed in the country. The fourth political party was in fact nothing but a lobby group for that part of the population who were targeted by denazification legislation. It had treated itself to a pseudo-liberal leadership in the persons of Viktor Reimann and Herbert Kraus, whose popularity as journalists was almost entirely due to their incessant criticism of the denazification measures of the Austrians and the Allies.

In 1945 the U.S. administration had drawn up the blueprint of a strict denazification programme that specified reeducation goals aimed at the establishment of a democratic elite. The idea was to replace not only former members of the NSDAP, SS and SA, but all other functionaries of the Nazi regimes as well, at least temporarily. These plans were frustrated at the very outset, when, on 27 April 1945, the Soviet Union presented Karl Renner's provisional government with all the powers it needed to become fully functional within the Soviet zone. This was done without prior consultation with the other Allies. The U.S. continued to maintain a strict military regime in its zone until August, but in that month the High Commissioner Mark W. Clark signalled acceptance of the newly established parties in his opening speech at the Salzburg Festival. That fall he also recognized the Austrian government, already augmented by members from western Austria. Compared with the Federal Republic of Germany, Austria in 1945–46 was already capable of exercising a certain amount of influence on Allied decision making by means of its own deliberations.

In 1946–47 the Cold War caused Austrian interests to stabilize to such a degree that the U.S. withdrew completely from the denazification discourse, insisting only on monitoring the application of more stringent criteria than those proposed by Austria. The sudden anti-Nazism of the Soviets was quickly 'turned round' by the Americans to serve as an additional argument in the Cold War: it was widely felt that the 'formers' must be integrated in order to strengthen the anti-communist bloc. The few U.S. reeducation initiatives in the western Austrian media evolved along unforeseen paths to give comfort to the 'formers': Herbert Kraus, who has already been mentioned, used open programmes of the U.S. radio station 'Rot-Weiß-Rot' to become a well-known radio personality by criticizing denazification policies and demanding an end to measures against former members of the NSDAP. He continued to pursue this line in a monthly paper licensed by the U.S. Viktor Reimann was equally active in the *Salzburger Nachrichten,* which had been licensed by the U.S. as an independent paper. Kraus and Reimann, as has been noted above, were soon to become the figureheads of the political ragbag of the 'formers'. The licensing of a 'lobby' for former NSDAP members, though based on the approval of the U.S. State Department, was done against the advice of the U.S. high commissioner. It ensured the persistence of ideologically warped structures. The first postwar anti-Semitic incidents had occurred by 1946. Even one of the highest-ranking ÖVP politicians from Christian Social times, Leopold Kunschak, was not above making anti-Semitic allegations on public occasions.

The amnesty of 1948 and the election campaign of 1949 put an end to denazification in all its forms, even though the people's courts remained in session until 1955 and a number of government agencies continued to make use of the *Sühnefolgen.* The *Verbotsgesetz* in its 1947 version was repealed almost completely by the Nazi amnesty of 1957, as was the entire War Criminals Act, so that as of that year Nazi crimes were dealt with under Austrian penal law and the Austrian code of criminal procedure.

The Continuity of Prejudice in the Second Generation

The continuity of racial prejudice up to the present day is part of Austria's history. It is no coincidence that someone whose father was involved in a Nazi putsch in 1934 should feel that he has been socialized in a democracy that was forced upon him; it is no coincidence that this person's mother should refer to the Allied detention camp where her father was held for two years without being charged as a 'concentration camp', thereby playing down the horrors of National Socialist concentration camps; nor is it coincidental that her son referred to the Nazi extermination camps as 'prison camps'. Tens of thousands of NSDAP and

SS members who were held prisoners for a time but never charged frequently felt themselves to be 'victims of liberation'. This warped perception of history has been passed on to their children and has, particularly since the Waldheim debate, generated an unending series of readjustments. Too many children have had to listen to this kind of *Geschichtsbewältigung* (coping with the past) from their stigmatized fathers or mothers. The son described above, one among many who listened quietly and receptively, was Jörg Haider.

Yet Jörg Haider was no isolated case. More than 500,000 party members were caught up in the works of denazification after the war; roughly a fourth of Austria's postwar society had to undergo a direct and close confrontation with that issue. This still does not take into account the hundreds of thousands who were not accepted into the NSDAP because of a temporary stop on membership but whose membership applications are stored in the U.S. National Archives in College Park, Maryland. The reactions of the sons and daughters, or of the grandchildren, are by no means all the same, even if the Waldheim affair opened up fault lines indicating that there was a pro-Waldheim majority. Franz Vranitzky, whose roots were in an anti-fascist environment, had a different take on the Nazi topic altogether.

More questions need to be asked about Wolfgang Schüssel, chancellor between 2000 and 2006. How was it possible for a politician who had never given any indication of Jörg Haider's kind of historical revisionism to demonstrate such a blatant lack of historical awareness as to toy again with the idea of Austria's victimization in 1938? The journalist Joachim Riedl was the first to point out that Schüssel's father had vacillated between the Christian Socials and the NSDAP; his son, who grew up apart from his father, nevertheless felt emotionally close to him. Riedl lacked the documentation to interpret Ludwig Schüssel's complex socialization. It appears likely that it was the father's ambivalence that made Schüssel junior, in the teeth of better knowledge, so tolerant of Jörg Haider's historical perceptions.

Ludwig Schüssel could just as well have been a Social Democrat or a pan-German: the biographies of such people are often interchangeable. It was not NSDAP membership that was a problem for many Austrians but the vacillation between political extremes, which also entails – as was obvious after 1945 – a readiness to pardon the political hardliners, of whom Haider's father was one. Ludwig Schüssel, editor and civil servant, joined the NSDAP in 1932; the party did not honour his membership in 1941 as he was considered to have renounced it through his involvement with the Vaterländische Front. In 1938 he tried to paint himself into the role of an 'illegal' fighter, which earned him an employment ban after 1945.

Haider and Schüssel had fathers with the same problems, even though the two received politically diverse socializations. Once again sons look only ahead and not back – a dilemma that has contributed to Austria's postwar history.

ILLUSTRATION 9.2

The report of the 'three wise men' was an important precondition for the annulment of the 'sanctions' against Austria imposed in February 2000 by the EU-14. From left to right: FPÖ Defense Minister Herbert Scheibner, Jochen Frowein, Martii Ahtisaari, ÖVP Chancellor Wolfgang Schüssel and Marcelino Oreja.

Forgotten Fascism

U.S. planning experts believed that establishing democracy – once the war and National Socialism were finished – was going to be more difficult in Austria than in Germany, since the Christian Social and the Social Democratic camps had fought each other in the era between the wars; the Dollfuß dictatorship and the Civil War of February 1934 were still well within living memory. By contrast with Germany, Austria had gone through two different dictatorships, even if the Dollfuß-Schuschnigg regime was for a number of reasons not in the same league as the Nazi terror regime. It had nevertheless instilled fear in tens of thousands of people and had left a record of killings, politically motivated executions and thousands of people driven into exile.

The former Christian Socials made an adroit move by founding a new party, the Österreichische Volkspartei, which refrained from declaring itself a successor to such pre-1938 organizations as the Vaterländische Front, etc. There was continuity of leadership to an extent, but it was rather marginal on the whole and in some cases, as with Leopold Figl, who had belonged to the Ostmärkische Sturmscharen, concentration camp imprisonment was considered to have been sufficient atonement. Emphasis on the 'Geist der Lagerstraße', a certain esprit de corps among former internees from different parties,[6] was a bargaining counter particularly for the ÖVP to avoid having to confront questions on the *Ständestaat,* the corporatist regime of 1934–38.

Another argument used for strategic purposes was the highlighting of Social Democratic pan-German leanings prior to 1933 or Karl Renner's attitude in 1938, when he had made a public show of voting for the Anschluss. This was brought home to him in the first round table in the presence of Soviet officers. Renner kept on addressing the issue of 'clerical fascism' in the first months after the war, but every time he did so he was rebuffed by Soviet political officers, who were not interested in the issue.

The U.S. very quickly reshuffled its plans and adapted them to this tacit postwar pact, for which Ernst Fischer found a memorable, ultra-terse formula: 'The one side were no democrats, the others no patriots.' A last vehement row was sparked in 1947 by the trial of former Foreign Minister Guido Schmidt. Schmidt had been the mastermind behind the July Agreement of 1936 and the appeasement policy towards Hitler's Germany, which put an end to Schuschnigg's shortlived radical anti-Nazism and paved the way to Anschluss. A close personal friend of Göring's, Schmidt was later put in charge of high positions in the Hermann Göring Werke and also played a role as the administrator of 'enemy assets' in the occupied protectorates of Bohemia and Moravia. The postwar elite of the ÖVP was called to the witness stand, and their testimony reflected their own close involvement with the pre-1938 *Ständestaat* as well as their belated efforts to bridge the gap that divided them from the Social Democrats at the end of 1937.

Schmidt was represented by a leading ÖVP counsel and was acquitted – with political caveats – for lack of evidence.

After 1947 the issue of Austro-Fascism was reduced by and large to occasional appearances on anniversaries and at the inauguration festivities of monuments; it was hardly ever addressed directly. Negotiations within the grand coalition about the restitution of Social Democratic assets confiscated in 1934 and indemnification for wartime losses incurred dragged on into the 1950s, when they were ultimately settled. With reference to this issue, the *Burgfrieden,* a code word for mutual tolerance, was observed as the unwritten basis of the coalition. When Chancellor Alfons Gorbach and SPÖ Vice-Chancellor Bruno Pittermann shook hands at a memorial festivity for the victims of the Civil War on the thirtieth anniversary of 12 February 1934, the symbolic gesture had more to do with the crisis sparked by the Habsburg question and the parlous state of the grand coalition. It failed to achieve its aim: eleven days later Gorbach resigned.

The debate on Austro-Fascism reignited briefly after the ÖVP's electoral victory in 1966, when the possibility of a continued coalition was discussed by the SPÖ leadership; a group round Bruno Kreisky was in favour as there were fears that an ÖVP solo government might entail authoritarian developments. Subsequent developments showed that these fears were unfounded.

In the 1970s Kreisky realized a long-cherished research project of his concerning Austro-Fascism or, more broadly speaking, the time between the two wars and the First Austrian Republic's political structures up to 1938. The means for this project came from the Leopold Kunschak and Theodor Körner foundations. In a first phase the focus was on 1927, a year whose political turmoil had culminated in the fire that was laid at the Justizpalast (the Palace of Justice) after a trial by jury had ended in a politically motivated miscarriage of justice. Subsequently the time limit was extended to 1938. The result is a useful collection of material and interpretative studies. The conferences that involved historians and contemporary witnesses yielded clear findings without the blinkers of *Proporz* historiography. Kreisky's interests subsequently moved on to other institutions, and in 1982 he founded the Gesellschaft für politische Aufklärung (Society for Political Education), which was to devote itself to the study of phenomena that continue to be latent in Austria, such as right-wing radicalism and anti-Semitism, and to assume the function of a scientific seismograph for the Second Republic's political culture. Nowadays, the era from 1918 to 1938 has dwindled into a chapter in history textbooks. Its relevance, so palpable in the years after 1945, is hardly discernible anymore.

The Habsburg Question: A Non-starter

In 1945 political observers both in Austria and abroad had their eyes fixed on members of the house of Habsburg, whose every move was noted. The U.S.

Secret Service filed reports on alleged or actual visits of Felix Habsburg to the Tyrol, which was particularly annoying for the Social Democrats. After all, Otto, the pretender to the throne, had gained access to President Franklin D. Roosevelt by cleverly exploiting private contacts and his post-imperial aura, and Austrian legitimists and supporters of the monarchy had been active in various émigré movements.

In 1935 the Schuschnigg regime developed close contacts with the Habsburg family to provide an additional option against Nazi pressure from inside and outside. A small part of the family assets that had been confiscated in 1919, the so-called 'family fund', was restored, and hundreds of small townships conferred honorary citizenship on diverse archdukes and archduchesses. Schuschnigg did not in the end take up Otto's offer to serve as a sort of state notary with special powers. The Nazi regime mercilessly persecuted all supporters of the monarchy and confiscated the family fund anew. After 1945 the Republican axis was too powerful for a restoration to stand any real chance. Otto's denunciatory letter to Roosevelt, in which he called Renner a crypto-Communist, made no difference. In the debate on the national anthem the ÖVP would have loved to reintroduce the Kaiserhymne, the imperial anthem, but the SPÖ was categorically opposed to any such move.

When the crisis of the grand coalition was at its worst in the early 1960s, the SPÖ withheld its consent to Chancellor Alfons Gorbach's motion that the government accept a declaration from Otto von Habsburg renouncing all claim to a (hypothetical) throne but upholding his right to become politically active. In 1963 this escalated further when the Administrative Court overruled a decree of the SPÖ minister of the interior banning Otto from entering Austria. In Parliament, keeping Otto von Habsburg out of Austria was the first key issue to unite the SPÖ and FPÖ in a vote against the ÖVP. The 'Pretender' was thereby compelled to delay his homecoming until another legislative period in 1964.

In the 1970s Bruno Kreisky made gestures of reconciliation towards Otto von Habsburg; this had to do with the fact that the chancellor thought highly of the Austro-Hungarian monarchy as a cultural and economic entity. The move was arguably also designed to compensate for the pan-German predilections of many other Social Democrats. However, neither the return of Kaiser Karl's wife, Zita, nor her funeral, which was staged as a major media event, enabled the monarchist movement to gain any momentum; moreover, the movement thought it expedient to don an alias, calling itself the Paneuropa Movement. The Austrians had in the meantime fully accepted their republican status. Neither the television appearances of Otto's son, Karl, nor ÖVP patronage for him have been able to make the least difference in that respect. Many different incidents have played their part in putting an end to this one-man show.

The monarchist tradition has come to fruition in the tourist industry, and also in Austrians' understanding of their culture, without there being the slightest indication of an inclination towards restoration. One could say, however, that there are few democracies in Europe that are as reliant on monarchic foundations as Austria.

Another of Austria's legacies from its tradition is its entanglement in a conflict of nationalities of another kind that still hails from the days of the monarchy. The vehement reactions against the nuclear power station of Temelín going into operation can only be understood against the backdrop of Austria's inability to empathize with any Czech position. Prejudices against the 'perfidious Czechs' that were preserved in the ice of the Cold War have come to light again. As far as eastward enlargement of the EU was concerned, strategies of demarcation and procrastination determined the discussion, which in the asylum and migration debate of 1989 had already robbed Austria of all credibility as an honest broker in favour of Eastern European accession application. It would appear that the Austrians have – with obvious exceptions, of course – learned little beyond the pronouncements made in Sunday speeches from the history of the Austro-Hungarian monarchy, an economic area that had, after all, the potential to become Europe's first integrated market. The monarchy failed because it failed to unravel the knotty nationality issue, which lit the fuse for the First World War. This fact is not generally acknowledged today. Awareness of this historic culpability exists only in the muted discourse of historical research.

NOTES

1. Gerald D. Feldman, Oliver Rathkolb, Thedor Venus and Ulrike Zimmerl, *Österreichische Banken und Sparkassen im Nationalsozialismus und in der Nachkriegszeit* (Munich: Beck Verlag, 2006), 680–684.
2. Hans Safrian, *Eichmann und seine Gehilfen* (Frankfurt/Main: Fischer-Taschenbuch-Verlag, 1997).
3. See www.doew.at (accessed 1 June 2005).
4. Evelyn Adunka, *Die vierte Gemeinde. Die Wiener Juden in der Zeit von 1945 bis heute* (Berlin-Vienna: Philo, 2000), 431.
5. Csáky, *Der Weg zu Freiheit*, 36.
6. Lagerstraße or Camp Street was the name given to the main thoroughfare in various prison camps, notably the concentration camps at Dachau and Auschwitz.

CHAPTER *10*

Austria's Political Future: Some Trends

Prognosis, we keep on being told, is tricky, 'particularly about the future'. A case in point for us is the end of the Cold War and the reunification of Germany. Very few people had the perceptiveness of Paul Kennedy, a British historian teaching at Yale who foresaw the disintegration of the Soviet Union and the Communist bloc, although even he saw the process as taking rather longer than it did. The problems accompanying (German) reunification certainly owe much to the fact that no advance planning of any kind was made for this development. It might nevertheless be interesting to add a postscript that looks at a prognosis of where Austria's political structures are heading.

More Equality of Opportunity – and More Political Ennui

In 2004 a study by the Metis Institute made an attempt to gauge the basic mood of Austria's 15- to 35-year olds from a sample of 2,500 individual interviews and group associations.[1] The results reinforce impressions that have been gaining ground since polls in the 1980s: not only the tax system but politicians themselves are perceived to be faults in the system (64.3 per cent). Only 12.9 per cent expect that by 2050 'visionary and idealistic politicians' would be at work.

These attitudes are mirrored by an increasing disinclination towards political engagement (echoed in many other countries besides Austria). Readiness to become politically engaged ranks below such goals as power and influence (33 per cent) or tradition (31 per cent), scoring only 22 per cent on personal life-planning agendas. Health (98 per cent) and the protection of the environment and the countryside (40.3 per cent) are considered particularly important, with 31 per cent believing that saving the environment is a realistic proposition. These youngsters of today, who will be between fifty and seventy years old in 2050, are by no means short of political ideas. They feel strongly about openness to the world, equality of opportunity, access to education and the fair distribution between the sexes of housework, bringing up children and the process of earning a living.

A look at the 2002 distribution of wealth in Austria underscores how justified the younger generations are in pressing issues of equality of opportunity and of distribution: the richest 10 per cent of the population held 69 per cent of private assets; the other 90 per cent therefore had to make do with 31 per cent. Furthermore, those same 90 per cent have an average per head income running at a mere hundredth of that of the top-earning 1 per cent. Capital gains and income from real estate had risen twice as fast as the total sum of salaries and wages (29 per cent), and the purchasing power of employees had fallen by 7 per cent since 1992. In 2000 taxes on profits accounted for 9.2 per cent of all taxes and revenues in the average of the EU Fifteen; for Austria that figure was 4.7 per cent, which left it at the bottom of the list in an OECD study. The share of property tax puts Austria at the bottom of that table as well; at 1.3 per cent it trails Hungary's 1.7 per cent; EU average is 5 per cent. In 2005 the corporation tax rate was lowered from 34 per cent to 25 per cent; Switzerland has 24.1 per cent, Germany 39.58 per cent and Italy 38.25 per cent; this, incidentally, is one of the reasons why Bank Austria-Creditanstalt's new parent, UniCredit, moved the seat of its Eastern European Holding from Milan to Vienna. Whether Austria can benefit in terms of jobs and general economic development from the low corporation tax – Hungary (16 per cent), Slovakia (19 per cent) and Slovenia (20 per cent) are all lower – remains to be seen.

Less Authoritarianism, More Individualism

A poll commissioned by the author at the end of 2004, repeating a 1978 questionnaire on authoritarian attitudes, provided clear evidence of Austria's continued evolution in democratic political terms, coupled with an increasing general disenchantment with politics or politicians. Perhaps, though, such opinions are simply a reflection of a general increase in critical competence among Austrians.

In August and September 2004 1,420 persons above fifteen years of age, selected on the basis of Stratified Multistage Clustered Random Sampling, were interviewed face to face (no telephone interviews) by IFES, which had been entrusted with the project by its initiator. The introductory statement, 'Obedience and respect for those in authority are important virtues that children should acquire', met with 68 per cent approval in 2004, falling only slightly from the 74 per cent seen in 1978. However, this was offset by a pronounced decline in the acceptability of such authoritarian codes as the reintroduction of the death penalty, the unwillingness to take responsibility or an emphasis on society being split into strong and weak individuals.

Among statements concerning the Nazi past, the claim 'There are worse things than the emergence of another Hitler' met with significantly reduced approval (84 per cent disagree as against 62 per cent in 1978; in 1978, 19 per cent signalled agreement, which had shrunk to 4 per cent in 2004). The same applies to the 'glorification of the Nazi past': the statement 'Obviously there were aberrations in the Third Reich but it is certainly not true that six million Jews were killed' was rejected by 61 per cent and accepted by only 5 per cent. In 1978 the equivalent figures were 35 per cent and 21 per cent. That there is still a certain amount of leeway for revisionism in this area is shown by the response to the statement 'In view of the way they behaved, Jews are not entirely without blame for their persecution'. In 2004, 52 per cent signalled total disagreement and 12 per cent total agreement, compared to 29 per cent total disagreement and 25 per cent total agreement in 1978.

The idea that the death penalty should be reintroduced 'to put an end to terrorism' was welcomed unconditionally by 60 per cent in 1978. It should be remembered that the reform of the judicial system was in full swing at this time. In 2004, despite the impact of the events of 11 September 2001, the approval rate had shrunk to a mere 12 per cent; 66 per cent disapproved completely, compared to a meager 19 per cent in 1978. That the context of migration continues to be beset by prejudices is borne out by the fact that approval rates remained roughly the same on the question of whether 'vagabond foreign youths' should be barred from entering the country: in 2004, 45 per cent were unequivocally in favour and only 21 per cent totally opposed. In 1978 the corresponding ratio was 68 per cent versus 16 per cent. Sex with juveniles below the age of consent was still felt to warrant severe punishment: in 2004, 42 per cent agreed, in 1978, 67 per cent; the figure of those totally opposed remained almost the same: 13 per cent in 2004 as against 12 per cent in 1978. The topics addressed in the poll – migration, crime rate and sex with underage juveniles – had been at the focus of media and political attention in the period between the two polls.

A clear breakthrough was achieved regarding the status of women: in 1978, 51 per cent came out in favour of the 'nature given role of housewife and mother' as holding out the only hope of 'real fulfilment' for women; in 2004 this had shrunk to 13 per cent; disagreement rose from 16 per cent to 65 per cent.

In view of these and comparable data I for one would not be inclined to interpret the sociopolitical sea changes in the mid 1960s and mid 1980s as an integral concomitant of the significant improvement in democratic attitudes. The authoritarian potential was still extremely high in 1978, a year that marks the climax of the Kreisky era with his dictum of 'drenching all areas of life with democracy'; the only reason why this potential would have been impossible to radicalize was the containment of discontent through welfare measures. Democratic maturity and socioeconomic development do not go hand in hand by any means. Democratic maturity takes time to evolve.

A further indicator of this time delay in the area of political participation is the readiness of collective historical memory to tackle taboo topics. In light of this I would suggest the mid 1980s as a possible terminus *post quem* for the shrinking of the authoritarian shadow that blocked the evolution of Austria's democracy. This was brought about not by the 1964 *Rundfunkvolksbegehren,* the radio referendum, as this was primarily an initiative by which the print media elites targeted the Grand Coalition and the state radio, but by the broad movement against the Hainburg power station and the establishment of the Greens as a political party. The defeat of the SPÖ and Bruno Kreisky in the referendum on the Zwentendorf nuclear power station (5 November 1978) was a by-product of that process, but more significantly it was the result of ÖVP tactical manoeuvring and of the intransigence of Kreisky, the SPÖ, the trade unions and the social partners. How else does one account for Kreisky's 1979 electoral victory?

While the putsch-like establishment of the youthful Jörg Haider as the leader of the FPÖ is in a league of its own, the successful strategies with which he attacked the social partnership and the Grand Coalition are a further indication of voters' readiness to switch camps. Other authoritarian codes in the same league as the Haider coup were welcome in this transformation phase, provided they combined rightist populism, up-to-date trappings and cool, young leaders. This Janus-faced development – the gradual disappearance on the one hand of the authoritarian undercurrent in society, on the other a rising tide of new authoritarian codes directed against aliens, migrants, criminals etc. – was a characteristic of the late 1980s and of the 1990s.

What Is Paradoxical about the Second Republic? A Summary

The contradictions that have been shown to characterize central aspects of Austria's political culture, and of its democratic development since 1945, change at different speeds; at the same time new contradictory patterns emerge. Let us briefly summarize the most significant paradoxes of Austria's postwar history.

There are few examples in history of a small-state society forming an identity as quickly as did Austria, which had to cope in addition with the traumata of two world wars and the loss of its status as a major power. National pride in Austria, highly developed even by international standards, has never been more powerful than it is today – at a time moreover when Austrian identity has not yet found its place in the European debate. Austrian businesses display flexibility and great skill in exploiting shared cultural codes in Southern, Central and Eastern Europe; history seems almost to stage a replay of the time when 'the Balkans began at the Rennweg in Vienna', a leitmotif in great vogue with marketing managers. Meanwhile the Austrian ego keeps up a lacklustre grating against the European Union.

The reason for this development lies on one hand in a sense of belonging to one's birthplace that is again gaining in importance. It has served as the basis of the Second Republic's sense of identity and as a kind of shield against the negative side effects of integration and globalization. On the other hand, the identity kit hardly contains any components apart from ones in the national colours. Even in primary school kids are treated to large helpings of the scenic beauty and the cleanliness of island Austria, where life is good and tourists turn up by the millions. In this basic grounding in national identity no reference is made to the hosts of migrants with other cultural backgrounds and national traditions, nor to the facts of Austria's international networking and European integration. Only those who are fortunate enough to get the chance to live and study abroad for a length of time will have the chance to develop more complex identities. Change will presumably be some time coming in this area and will perhaps be brought about by stronger emotional ties to European institutions and by an end to arm-chair criticism of the European Union.

The second area, another postwar paradox, concerns the intensity of democratic culture and the readiness to muster civic courage in resistance to non-legitimate demands and coercion. Prone to obedience and to extremely authoritarian attitudes in important social questions and averse to conflict throughout the first postwar decades, Austrian society has undergone a gradual transformation in those respects since the 1970s. This is not to say that opposition to the authoritarian societal mainstream was not present as early as 1945, or that there were no 'islets of innovation' from the very beginning of the new republic. These took a little time developing before manifesting themselves in the 1960s in the spheres of art, 'actionism' and youth protest movements. The driving forces in society have tended to arise from the young (also as first-time voters) and from women, as these groups were the most exposed to the constraints imposed by the hierarchical system and also by the dominance of the two main political parties.

As far as welfare and education were concerned, the Kreisky era staked out a course without any immediate effect on the basic structures. For instance, it proved impossible to introduce sexual education in the schools of western Austria; teachers who went out on a limb lost their jobs. Even in the SPÖ there were very few women to be found as party officials or decision makers. Only towards the end of 'state reformism'[2] did the dominance of the Catholic-conservative and Socialist-authoritarian paradigms begin to crumble, and as has so often been the case, there was a clear East-to-West progression. By 1980, the old political camps started being eroded by both a strong environmental movement, which was to spawn a political party, and the successful rightist populism centring on Jörg Haider and the FPÖ.

The real extent of the postwar thaw is demonstrated by the debate on the Austrian National Socialist past that has been going on since 1984–85. It was against this background that the post-1986 Grand Coalition launched Austria's most important postwar reforms and turned accession to the EU into the greatest success of the social partnership – without, however, being able to stop the rise of Europe's most successful right-wing populist party, Jörg Haider's FPÖ. It was only when the FPÖ joined the government that it too was subjected to the general process of political erosion, which took place in this case to a background music of vehement internal conflicts and revelations both ideological and structural in nature. Side by side with these developments there arose an alternative public sphere independent not only of the government but in many cases also of the opposition, which indicated increasingly potent trends towards a civil society and a further erosion of the authoritarian position. Particularly notable in this context was the opposition to the nuclear power plant at Zwentendorf and the Hainburg Au power station, both serious stand-offs ending in the first significant defeats for the social partnership.

The Economic Miracle

Arguably the greatest success story since 1945 is the development of the Austrian economy. The economist Hans Seidel has estimated that the total liquidity of private households amounted to 5 per cent of GNP after the stabilization of the schilling in 1952; the same figure for 2004 is 130 per cent.[3] In the collective consciousness this development has been stylized as an exclusively homegrown achievement, but it is in fact the result of a number of positive supranational factors related to Austria's integration into the economy of the West, which sheltered it from competition for a long time. These factors included tightly knit corporatist structures, global growth, Marshall Plan aid during the Cold War, the transformation for civilian purposes of the infrastructure and trained workforce created by the Nazi armament industry, nationalization along lines controlled by social partnership, and political organization of the economic framework and individual labour input. Until the early 1950s regular incomes trailed prices, and the gap had to be bridged by people taking on additional jobs in reconstruction.

Supranational factors were again to the fore in the slump of the 1980s that affected not only the nationalized industries but also the economy in general, hampered as it was by cartels, monopolies and overregulation. These included integration effects prior to Austria's EU accession and the onset of globalization, heightened by a changing international climate. It was possible to contain unemployment through substantial public expenditure, but the ideological controversy between supporters of undiluted market forces and active state interference is an ongoing one. The easing of tensions caused by the Cold War has only exacerbated this controversy. In contrast to Sweden, Austria has opted since 2000 for a savings and redistribution policy instead of a growth-oriented, offensive economic strategy with appropriate investment in research, education and infrastructure.

Putting it in a simple formula, one might say that if some budget deficits in the 1980s were too high, they have been too low since 2000, which hampers progress through innovation. While in the highly market-oriented U.S., conservative administrations (Ronald Reagan, George Bush and George W. Bush) have had no problem deliberately running up deficits, Austria has applied the maxim of the lowest possible budget expenditure since 2000. What is often ignored is the fact that this often motivates consumers to reduce spending, which slows down the market even further. Rates of growth have been correspondingly low, while the rise in unemployment, particularly among the young, is correspondingly high. Hannes Androsch, minister of finance between 1970 and 1981 and today one of Austria's leading industrialists, has formulated the following recipe for Europe's future economic growth: 'subsidies for initiatives, coupled with investment both in human capital and in infrastructure' combined with 'European engagement' and the fostering of a 'purpose-oriented immigration policy instead of xenophobic resistance to migration'.[4]

One fundamental change from the time immediately after 1945 is the fact that in economic and financial matters the really important decisions are made today on European and global levels. While this reduces manoeuvring space for a small country like Austria in many respects, appropriate initiatives and networking open up entirely new horizons. Prim and proper budgets may not be appropriate in this situation, if Austria is to overcome its economic solipsism and its navel-gazing and adapt to reality.

The Fourth Estate and Its Woes

No modern democracy can function without an independent, professionally organized media sector, the so-called Fourth Estate. Investigative journalism and its untrammeled access to publication are at the centre of the demand for unrestricted freedom of speech and of the press. This demand has remained a theatre of conflict in Austria's democratic development ever since it was first articulated in the upheaval of 1848; steady progress has been punctuated by many backslidings. Both the Dollfuß-Schuschnigg and the Nazi regimes so drastically curtailed the freedom of the press that in 1945 the demand for independent media was central. Nevertheless it was only partly fulfilled. There was Allied interference both in newspapers and in radio. Party ownership of newspapers was another obstacle, as was the new Austrian state's controlling policy towards radio. New possibilities opened up with the advent of the tabloids and the decline of the party newspapers at the end of the 1950s; regional papers had also struggled for – and achieved – greater independence. Quality journalism improved in the course of time. The struggle for the independence of a centralist radio and television corporation went to a referendum, whose success was limited in the end to independent monitoring of government influence. One of the more blatant instances of that influence can be seen in the ORF's decision to reschedule a programme featuring Jörg Haider's speech to a gathering of SS veterans in Carinthia's Krumpendorf from immediately before the 1995 general elections to the Tuesday following the polling day. That the programme was in fact aired before the polling day by the German ARD highlighted the new opportunities to bypass the ORF monopoly offered by cable and satellite television. Public opinion and the print media continue to nudge ORF towards independence but with little result.

It is a fact that Austria belongs among the European nations with the highest concentration of media ownership, along with Bulgaria, Estonia, Hungary, Ireland, Luxembourg and Belgium.[5] Data from 2003 and the first half of 2004 document that the *Kronenzeitung* has a reach of 43.8 per cent, reaching the whole country and rising to 50.6 per cent when one adds in the *Kurier*. These two papers, which share the same distribution organization, Mediaprint, also control 41.1 per cent of the advertising market. The second-largest print conglomerate, Styria Medien AG, has a reach of 17.5 per cent, with a 20 per cent share of the circulation market and 25 per cent of advertising. The viewer quota of ORF 1 and 2 in the age group twelve and above was 42.5 per cent; the advertising market share, 76 per cent. ORF radio accounts for 81 per cent of listeners, with 69.6 per cent of advertising. The question is whether it would not make sense in the medium term to create a level playing field for competition by means of appropriate European anti-cartel legislation.

At the same time eastward expansion of Western European print conglomerates such as *Westdeutsche Allgemeine Zeitung* (*WAZ*), which is also a shareholder of Mediaprint and *Kronenzeitung,* strengthens the tendency towards concentration of media ownership in the new EU member states and in the neighbouring countries in Eastern and Southern Europe. This is one of the reasons why Austria is only fourteenth in the 'World Democracy Audit' of OECD countries, a long way behind Finland, Denmark, New Zealand, Sweden and Norway; for freedom of the press, its ranking, at nineteenth, is even worse.[6] However, concentration of media ownership is not necessarily an indicator of a lack of freedom of the press – witness Belgium, which comes in third for press freedom despite media ownership every bit as concentrated as in Austria.

The democratic reform backlog in the areas of print media and television is acknowledged even by some of the people who benefit from it. Witness the assertion of Horst Pirker, the CEO of Styria Medien AG, that there were two great topics that needed to be tackled, one being ORF – 'there is no question that it needs to be pruned back' – and the other the media concentration, 'in particular the Mediaprint, the Styria and the News Groups. These three conglomerates are each too big for this country'.[7]

Criticism of the public broadcasting system led to the 1998 'Initiative Öffentlicher Rundfunk', which demanded more democracy along the lines of the BBC. Its stated aims include 'sustaining citizenship and civil society' and a reduction of ORF's focus on generating revenue. Old hands like Teddy Podgorsky, himself a one-time ORF CEO, remain sceptical.

The Chancellors of the Second Republic

The chancellors of the Second Republic are perceived as figures embodying their respective eras. Karl Renner stands for the switchback to the beginnings of the

First Republic and to the monarchic past of the country. Leopold Figl has been everyone's darling in the Second Republic right up to the present day: a concentration camp inmate in the Nazi era, he proved a resourceful player in the match with the Allies while retaining the bonhomie and down-to-earth qualities so attractive to Austrians. Julius Raab, who can be credited with greater merit in terms of realpolitik than Figl, lacked his predecessor's emotional appeal. Raab was respected but lost to Adolf Schärf in his bid for the presidency when he refused to be deterred from running by the onset of a serious illness. Alfons Gorbach was a mere transitional figure. Josef Klaus held out the first hope for many that it would be possible to push through a radical reform of social and political structures, though these hopes did not come to fruition until the 1970s.

The Jewish émigré Bruno Kreisky, an intellectual with a man-of-the world bourgeois appearance, had to struggle hard to win the hearts of the Austrians. Even after he had won, not all the prejudices against his person disappeared. On the international stage he remains the most widely recognized Austrian politician of the Second Republic. After another – underrated – transitional figure, Fred Sinowatz, Franz Vranitzky, who kept his distance both from his party and from the voters, implemented a host of reforms and presided over EU accession. He also acknowledged Austria's co-responsibility for the crimes of the Nazi era; his international reputation is comparable to that of Kreisky. Viktor Klima, the first spin-doctor chancellor, remains no more than an interlude. His successor, Wolfgang Schüssel, broke a European taboo by entering into a coalition with the right-wing FPÖ. This coalition was arguably instrumental in bringing down the FPÖ, though whether this had been part of Schüssel's strategy is difficult to tell at this stage. It also remains to be seen what consequences his neoliberal policies and his partnership with a rightist, populist and rather chaotic party will have with regard to society and economy.

In general it must be said that there is a clear trend among Austrian voters to reward leadership qualities and the will to lead, rather than likeability. Sympathy alone does not decide voter behaviour, as was last demonstrated in the case of Viktor Klima. Wolfgang Schüssel, on the other hand, was not much loved as a chancellor but was trusted by many people for his leadership qualities. The way he is perceived on the big stage is different because echoes still linger of the breaking of the coalition taboo in 2000, even among some of his EU Christian Conservative party colleagues. Apart from Kreisky, Vranitzky, Schüssel and perhaps – in the odd flashback – Renner, none of the chancellors of the Second Republic feature in international debate.

Neutrality and Identity

Austria's international position is still a determining factor in identity formation. The country was forced to travel along the international highway by Allied liberation and administration; then the option for neutral status in 1955 prolonged the need to remain engaged in the international context. The political decision makers were only too aware that in the worst-case scenario of a 'hot' war between the two blocs, the military aspect of neutrality was going to count for nothing. It was therefore all the more important that Austria became a member of the UN, that international organizations established their headquarters in Vienna and that it remained a player in the context of détente policies. The more people endorsed these activities, the more neutrality became a catalyst for the development of a positive and active small-state sense of identity, which started in the mid 1960s and reached its climax in the 1970s and early 1980s. Austria reaped the full benefit of its geo-strategic position between the blocs, soon latched on to integration into the Western economy and played a largely autonomous role in terms of its social and economic politics. An exception that immediately comes to mind is of course the schilling's being pegged to the deutschmark.

It was the problems posed by the reforms of the 1980s that made a reorientation towards the EU imperative, and the end of the Cold War only served to speed up Austria's total integration. Collective consciousness – which applies even to some decision makers – has not yet caught up with the incisive changes in the country's manoeuvrability in international waters. The special role Austria played in the Cold War still lingers in people's minds, as does the belief that it is possible for the country to determine the course of events in an international context either unilaterally or with a handful of allies. It is only within the last few years, most notably since the diplomatic sanctions against Austria by the then EU Fourteen, that a reassessment has set in, and that people have begun to be aware that European politics should no longer be considered foreign, but rather domestic politics. Austria is of course not the only country that has had to come to terms with such a development.

In the last few years the assessment of Austria's influence on European policies has oscillated between a sense of inferiority and utter powerlessness and unbounded euphoria. The bits and pieces of neutrality that have survived the EU accession of 1995 have had a certain stabilizing function, and the loud calls for NATO membership have subsided. Neutrality, which was defined in 1965 as part of the Magna Carta of Austrian identity by being given its own memorial day, 26 October, has left its marks in the fabric of society as a symbol of economic progress safeguarded by the welfare state and, above all, of military non-intervention. A mere 15 per cent were in favour in 2004 of giving military support to another EU member state. In the same poll 82 per cent of Austrians said they harboured positive feelings towards neutrality.[8] It is clear that even though neutrality was not declared until 26 October 1955, ten years after the foundation of the Second Republic on 27 April 1945, it has nevertheless become an integral part of Austria's foundation legend. To an extent it serves to offset the close association of the founding day with the complex involvement of the Austrians in the Second

World War and the Holocaust, which makes it almost something of a national *dies nefastus*.

'Heimat'

An important factor on the road to truly autonomous nationhood, as well as a significant economic motor for the Second Republic, was the whole area of culture. In the first decades culture was, as far as the remit of the state carries, under the control of the ÖVP, which had already laid down the law in its party platform of 1945: 'Purpose-oriented cultivation of the spirit of Austria and a sharp emphasis on autonomous Austrian cultural heritage, which has its roots in the occidental Christian wealth of ideas that has come to us as our patrimony. Unlimited scope of development for the Church and the religious communities as the most important agents of culture'. This meant not only a switchback to the time before 1938 but also a continuation of the repression of modernism and the avant-garde and a licence for the Catholic Church to intervene in aesthetic matters.

The SPÖ was wary of getting involved in a debate on the subject, which could well have entailed having to confront its own traditional pan-German nationalism dating back all the way to the Revolution of 1848. *Heimat* as a discourse topic was therefore left to the exclusive use of the ÖVP for several decades. The experiments of 'Rotes Wien' in the areas of the arts and culture were all but discontinued. Politically stigmatized initiatives such as the communist-led 'Neues Theater in der Scala' were closed down after 1955. It took until 1958 for the SPÖ to take note of cultural matters in a principled way as part of its party programme, and it was again Bruno Kreisky who discovered the importance of this topic for political discussion. He sought alliances with artists, supported initiatives that took up the thread of modernism and the avant-garde from before 1938 and ensured that a clause stipulating the freedom of the arts was included in the country's constitution. In this way he ended the ÖVP hegemony in cultural matters.

What was not called into question was the ÖVP monopoly of high culture represented by those erratic blocks from the days of the monarchy, the Staatsoper, the Vienna Philharmonic and the Burgtheater. Giving the 'old order' a new lease of life was supposed to guarantee stability and bolster the dominant position of the ÖVP within society. In structural terms these decisions of principle have remained effective to this day: in spite of an above average overall share allotted to the arts and culture sector in the budget, there is little leeway for subsidizing independent small initiatives and activities. Nevertheless, small refractory creative nuclei have formed to foster innovative impulses or to counteract in an 'actionist' manner the state culture prescribed from above. Even though they differ in intensity and outward effect, such alternative worlds or countercultures are to be found in all areas of art, from the visual arts to film and literature, and in many guises other than those supplied by the 'Wiener Gruppe', which has recently achieved almost mythical status. The Austrian *Heimatfilm,* a type of sentimental film in idealized regional settings, was by far the most popular cinematic fare in the '50s and '60s, yet there were exceptions. *Flucht ins Schilf* (1952–54), in which a pair of unmarried lovers are allowed the ultimate treat of a night together, called the Church's traditional moral teaching into question. This was in marked contrast to sex education films of the type of *Vom Mädchen zur Frau* (From Girlhood to Womanhood), where the slightest deviation from the straight and narrow path calls down vengeance in the form of venereal diseases and unwanted pregnancy.[9] Helmut Käutner's 1954 take on partisan warfare, *Die letzte Brücke/Poslednji Most* (The Last Bridge), was another controversial film; it was the first attempt to do justice to both sides and had a Yugoslav co-producer.

The more a conservative or even restorative climate came to overwhelm literature, the more aggressive the countermovement became in the 1960s, 1970s and 1980s. The *Heimatroman,* which painted simplistic bittersweet idylls, found more than its match in the savage realism of such novels as Hans Lebert's 1960 *Wolfshaut* (Wolfskin) or Gerhard Fritsch's 1967 *Fasching* (Carnival).[10] Towards the end of the 1970s and in the 1980s, at a time when Austria's presumed total innocence with regard to the war was first called in doubt, writers such as Thomas Bernhard, Peter Turrini and the Nobel Prize-winning Elfriede Jelinek, who were to become extremely successful outside Austria, were beginning to find their voice. The pioneering cabaret of such highly gifted comedians as Helmut Qualtinger, Carl Merz and Gerhard Bronner had blazed its own trail in the 1960s. *Herr Karl,* the chilling portrait of a '*gemütlich*' (good-natured and complacent) opportunist, is a classic of retrospective analysis ranging over the monarchy, the Dollfuß-Schuschnigg regime, National Socialism and the postwar era.

The resilience of published opinion and increasingly also of politics is such that over the last years, cultural provocation has been countered with appropriation. Plays such as *Heldenplatz* (Bernhard) or *Burgtheater* (Jelinek) sparked vehement discussions and political reactions in the 1980s; since then they have become de rigueur as showpieces of national exhibitionism. In the last resort Austrian solipsism is hooked on success and international applause, even if their basis is a critique of the country. In addition to this, the fact that social taboos are played down in public lessens their effectiveness as literary dynamite. While the arts and literature have lost a great deal of their sociopolitical clout, artists and literary figures remain important participants in the debates of society. In 2004, 57 per cent of the Austrian population, predominantly women slightly older than the population average and domiciled in eastern Austria, classified themselves as interested in culture.[11] The central memory sites are the same as in 1945 and 1955: the Salzburg Festival, the Staatsoper and the concerts of the Vienna Philharmonic. Needless to say, only a fraction of the population ever attends an actual performance.

Culture in the broadest sense is extremely important for the way Austria presents itself to the world, particularly in the tourist industry. In addition, if one includes entertainment and sports, culture makes a substantial contribution in terms of the labour market, even though some other European countries do even better in this respect. All this might tempt one to overlook the fact that, as far as actual consumption of culture is concerned, Austrians depend largely on imports. It is enough to look at music by living composers, i.e. music that still generates royalties: in the pop music sector Austrian productions have a market share of a meagre 13.7 per cent; among European countries, only Belgium and Switzerland fare worse.[12] As regards the import of recent releases, Austria is up in third place behind Ireland and Switzerland; 90 per cent of all royalty payments go to the EU or the U.S. Composers such as Mozart or Johann Strauss and musical institutions like the Vienna Philharmonic and the Staatsoper continue to be important codes for Austria's perception of itself as a cultural nation, yet they are codes that reach back to the nineteenth century and beyond.[13] The numbers of those learning to play a musical instrument or joining a choir have been steadily declining, and the 'greatness' of Austria as a musical country has largely been reduced to passive consumption.

Sport is an integral part of culture. In the collective consciousness the Austrian obsession with alpine skiing easily bests interest in musical institutions. Like music, sport has – belatedly – become important economically. Music as a business proposition dates back to the monarchy, and volumes increased steadily throughout the interwar years and the Nazi era. Sport, however, in spite of the first signs of professionalization in the interwar years and the nationalistic hype surrounding it in the Nazi era, spent the early postwar years in the role of a useful political tool with a largely amateur identity. The exploitation of sporting successes in the media was already in evidence at the alpine world championships in Innsbruck in 1933; by 1948 and the Olympic winter games in St Moritz, medals were headline stuff. Climaxes and anticlimaxes, such as Toni Sailer's triple gold medal in Cortina d'Ampezzo in 1956 or Karl Schranz's disqualification from the games in Sapporo (which united the whole nation behind its suffering hero) are as much part of the history of sport as of the media in Austria.

The 1990s saw commercialization of skiing as a sport, initiated in the 1970s by equipment suppliers, spiralling ever higher. The business profile of Peter Schröcksnadel, president of Österreichischer Skiverband (ÖSV) since 1990, may serve to illustrate the fusion of Skiverband (Austria's skiing association), media and public funds at the communal, regional and federal levels. Schröcksnadel is the majority shareholder of Feratel Media Technologies Inc. (which operates more than 200 summit and panorama cameras), founder and owner of Sitour Management PLC (market leader in piste demarcation signposts), owner of Hinterstoder-Wurzeralm Funicular Inc and Vereinigte Bergbahnen Inc., and president of the ÖSV. Though he holds this last post in an honorary capacity, he has nevertheless succeeded in raising a racing budget of 10 million euros.[14]

The downside of this development is that identity clusters in the sectors of sport and culture both tend to get coddled by the media, business interests and politics. This promotes a narrow nation-state identity. Hyphenated identity with regard to Europe is nowhere visible yet in these sectors.

Values

Among the values that polls have consistently shown to be considered essential for a functioning society, pride of place goes to basic social needs (accommodation, health care): in December 2004, 91 per cent of women and 77 per cent of men put this at the top of what they considered the most important glue holding Austria together.[15] Religious values such as belief in god are important only for a predominantly female minority (37 per cent). Fairness, equality of opportunity and intact family life continue to have high priority. As far as domestic politics is concerned, worries about job security are uppermost in people's minds (36 per cent), followed by pensions (28 per cent), national security (23 per cent), the neutrality issue (9 per cent) and immigration (4 per cent) in that order.[16] This survey, which accords with earlier polls, shows that though neutrality has ceased to matter as an issue of international law it continues to have some importance as a symbol of a functional welfare state. For this reason no party in Austria is likely to risk significant structural changes either to the welfare state or to the country's symbolically highly charged neutrality, however much of a dead letter it may have become internationally.

To some extent Austria's surprising post-1945 socioeconomic success was based on hope: the system of the welfare state was continuously being expanded, which helped people put up with lower wages and occasional unemployment. In the 1950s the social quota was a mere 5 to 7 per cent of GNP; by 2001 that figure had risen to 27.5 per cent. The EU average was then 27.5 per cent, which meant that Austria was in fifth place behind Sweden (31.3 per cent), France (30 per cent), Germany (29.8 per cent) and Denmark (29.5 per cent). In spite of an extremely unpromising start after 1945, it was no coincidence that 1955, the year of the State Treaty, also saw the creation of the legal framework for social transfer in the form of the Allgemeine Sozialversicherungsgesetz (ASVG), the Comprehensive Social Security Law .

Even though background conditions have improved beyond recognition today compared with the 1950s, when people often did not live to reach pension age, the mood is now one marked by great pessimism. Limited reforms in the 1980s were quite obviously insufficient to make the welfare system immune to criticism, either in the area of state and employment-related insurance, which is to be supplemented through private insurance, or in reductions in health and unemployment insurance. It is obvious that this constitutes a break with postwar developments, but it is as yet less obvious which way the road ahead will ultimately twist. One of the possibilities, as summarized by Emmerich Tálos, one of the country's leading politologists, is for the direction 'to be determined by today's internationally dominant neoliberal options with their preference for market-mediated, private and individualized insurance'; another would be 'for the dominance of gainful employment to be offset by increasing *Grundsicherung* (people's pension) and a change in the financial structure by broadening the financial basis beyond the wage bill'.[17] Several important clauses of the *Wiederaufbauvertrag* (Reconstruction Contract) of 1945 have undoubtedly been cancelled and are being renegotiated; in the course of these negotiations the traditional ideological differences about just distribution and the role of the state will become much clearer than they were in the compromise of 1945.

The Politics of History

One last question needs to be asked. In view of the fact that an IMAS poll of February 2005 found only 8 per cent who had frequent conversations about the recent past and the Second World War, why should discussions of that past be so important in Austria? Forty per cent occasionally talk about this subject, whereas for 52 per cent it is 'practically non-existent'.[18] There are several reasons for this paradox. One is the after-effect of the excessive role retrospection played in the reconstruction after 1945; this slide-back is still manifest. A second factor is that the confrontation with the Nazi past and the Holocaust, after an intense postwar discussion, was delegated to a kind of private do-it-yourself history workshop, where the administration of liberal doses of self-justification was the rule. These 'dead letterboxes' were rediscovered by a new generation and in a new setting determined by international attention. Moreover, the more individualized society has become, the more human rights issues have gained in importance, including violations of human rights in the past and the projection of human rights violations of the present (as in the civil war in the former Yugoslavia) onto the past.

The past has increasingly been accorded a place in the media, and politics involving the past has enabled the breaking of political taboos both in the context of reinterpretations of historical perceptions (as in the case of the Greens) or of revisionist attempts (as in the case of the FPÖ). The Second World War and the Holocaust are invariably at the centre of direct debates, while the civil war of February 1934 and the Dollfuß-Schuschnigg regime have been consigned to 'cold' history along with the Habsburg monarchy. There is a growing East-West divide regarding these topics, as many historical debates are considered irrelevant in western Austria. Another factor that is steadily gaining in importance is migration, which, again particularly in eastern Austria, notably in Vienna, ensures that the most diverse historical perceptions and experiences mix in school. For many pupils, the Holocaust and the Second World War belong to 'other people's' history; there is little in the past of their own families that would enable them to empathize. If a politics that takes its bearing from the past should attempt to install a national reconstruction of history in the school curriculum without taking into account the diversity of pupils' cultural backgrounds, national history and the sense of identity will be eroded even further in the pupils' minds.

But if it is possible to pay more attention to European and international contexts, there is hope for ideas about history to become more differentiated and to reflect what actually happened in Austria. This would enhance the development of hyphenated identities, which have existed on a local and regional level for a long time, and of cultural competence. Success in a globalized and integrated world will ultimately come more easily to those whose understanding of their traditional nation-state past is augmented by the acceptance and creative interpretation of their European and global environment.

NOTES

1. Barbara Tóth, *Der Standard,* 24 December 2004, and Harald Mahrer, ed., *Österreich 2050* (Vienna: Czernin Verlag, 2000).
2. Ernst Hanisch, *Der lange Schatten des Staates. Österreichische Gesellschaftsgeschichte im 20. Jahrhundert* (Vienna: Ueberreuter, 1994), 469–470.
3. See wko.at/wp/extra/wipolb/2005/t_2005_I_Kronberger-schediwy.pdf (accessed 1 June 2005).
4. Hannes Androsch, *Wirtschaft und Gesellschaft. Österreich 1945–2005* (Innsbruck-Vienna-Bozen: Studien Verlag, 2005), 77.
5. Data from Harald Fidler, *Im Vorhof der Schlacht. Österreichs alte Medienmonopole und neue Zeitungskriege* (Vienna: Falter-Verlag, 2004), 322–333.
6. http://www.worldaudit.org/democracy.htm (accessed 1 June 2005).
7. Clemens Hüffel and Anton Reiter, eds., *Medienpioniere erzählen ... 50 Jahre österreichische Mediengeschichte – von den alten zu den neuen Medien* (Horn: Braumüller, 2004), 170.
8. Otmar Lahodynsky, 'Patriotismus. Vernetzter Nationalstolz', *profil* 21, 23 May 2005, 22–24.
9. Nina Schedlmayer, 'Ausnahmefälle. Gegenentwürfe zur österreichischen Mainstream-Produktion zwischen 1945 und 1955', in *Besetzte Bilder. Film, Kultur und Propaganda in Österreich 1945–1955,* ed. Karin Moser (Vienna: Verlag Filmarchiv Austria, 2005), 258–259.
10. Robert Menasse, *Das Land ohne Eigenschaften* (Berlin: Sonderzahl, 1992), 114.
11. See www.uniqagroup.com/uniqagroup/cms/de/press/pressrelease/archive/pa_salzburger_festspiele_2004.jsp (accessed 1 June 2005).
12. Reinhold Wagnleitner, 'Von der Coca-Colonisation zur Sili-Colonisation', http://www.uni-koeln.de/phil-fak/histsem/anglo/kbaag/wagnleitner.pdf (accessed 1 June 2005).
13. Cornelia Szabo-Knotik, 'Mythos Musik in Österreich. Die zweite Republik', in *Memoriae Austriae I. Menschen, Mythen, Zeiten,* ed. Emil Brix, Ernst Bruckmüller and Hannes Stekl (Vienna: Verlag für Geschichte und Politik, 2004), 265.
14. See http://www.wirtschaftsblatt.at/cgi-bin/page.pl?id=200805 (accessed 1 June 2005).
15. *Der Standard,* 8 January 2005.
16. *profil* 12, 21 March 2005.
17. Tálos, *Vom Siegeszug zum Rückzug,* 81.
18. IMAS International Report No. 10, June 2005, 3a.

Bibliography

Adunka, Evelyn. *Die vierte Gemeinde. Die Wiener Juden in der Zeit von 1945 bis heute,* Berlin-Vienna: Philo, 2000.

Aichinger, Wilfried. *Sowjetische Österreichpolitik 1943–1945,* Vienna: Österreichische Gesellschaft für Zeitgeschichte, 1977.

Androsch, Hannes. *Wirtschaft und Gesellschaft. Österreich 1945–2005,* Innsbruck-Vienna-Bozen: Studien Verlag, 2005.

Arnold, Sabine R., Christian Fuhrmeister and Dietmar Schiller (eds). *Politische Inszenierung im 20. Jahrhundert. Zur Sinnlichkeit der Macht,* Vienna-Cologne-Weimar: Böhlau, 1998.

Ausch, Karl. *Erlebte Wirtschaftsgeschichte. Österreichs Wirtschaft seit 1945,* Vienna: Europa-Verlag, 1963.

———. *Licht und Irrlicht des österreichischen Wirtschaftswunders,* Vienna: Verlag der Wiener Volksbuchhandlung, 1965.

Bader, William B. *Austria between East and West,* Stanford, CA: Stanford Univ. Press, 1966.

Bergmann, Ingrid. 'Die Kulturpolitik aus der Sicht des österreichischen Nationalrates im Vergleich mit dem 3. Reich, im Umfeld des Zeitgeschehens', Phil. diss., Vienna University, 1988.

Bischof, Günter. *Austria in the First Cold War 1945–55: The Leverage of the Weak,* Basingstoke: Macmillan, 1999.

Bischof, Günter, Anton Pelinka and Ruth Wodak (eds). *Neutrality in Austria,* New Brunswick-London: Transaction Publishers, 2001.

Bischof, Günter and Dieter Stiefel (eds). *80 Dollar. 50 Jahre ERP-Fonds und Marshall-Plan in Österreich 1948–1998,* Vienna: Ueberreuter, 1999.

Blasi, Walter, Erwin A. Schmidl and Felix Schneider (eds). *B-Gendarmerie, Waffenlager und Nachrichtendienste. Der militärische Weg zum Staatsvertrag,* Vienna-Cologne-Weimar: Böhlau, 2000.

Brandstaller, Trautl, ed. *Österreich 2 ½. Anstöße zur Strukturreform,* Vienna: Deuticke, 1996.

Brix, Emil, Ernst Bruckmüller and Hannes Stekl (eds). *Memoriae Austriae I. Menschen, Mythen, Zeiten,* Vienna: Verlag für Geschichte und Politik, 2004.

Brix, Emil, Thomas Fröschl and Josef Leidenfrost (eds). *Geschichte zwischen Freiheit und Ordnung. Gerald Stourzh zum 60. Geburtstag,* Graz-Vienna-Cologne: Styria, 1991.

Bruck, Peter A. *Die Mozart-Krone,* Vienna-St. Johann im Pongau: Österreichischer Kunst- und Kulturverlag, 1991.

Bruckmüller, Ernst. 'Die ständische Tradition – ÖVP und Neokorporatismus', in *Volkspartei – Anspruch und Realität. Zur Geschichte der ÖVP seit 1945,* ed. Robert Kriechbaumer and Franz Schausberger, Vienna-Cologne-Weimar: Böhlau, 1995.

———. *Nation Österreich. Kulturelles Bewußtsein und gesellschaftlich-politische Prozesse,* Vienna-Cologne-Weimar: Böhlau, 1996.

Bubenik, Peter. '1938 – Gefahr und Lehre', in *Julius Raab, Aussaat und Ernte,* Catalogue of the exhibition at the Benedictine monastery of Seitenstetten May 15 – October 26, 1992.

Buchegger, F. and W. Stamminger, 'Anspruch und Wirklichkeit: Marginalien zur Geschichte der SPÖ', in Gerlich, Peter and Müller, W. C. (eds). *Österreichs Parteien seit 1945: Zwischen Koalition und Konkurrenz,* Vienna: Braumüller, 1983, 17-51.

Bundeskanzleramt (ed.). *Kulturpolitik. Kulturverwaltung in Österreich,* Vienna: Österreichische Kulturdokumentation, Internationales Archiv für Kulturanalysen, 1998.

Bundesministerium für soziale Verwaltung (ed.). *Soziale Struktur Österreichs. Soziale Schichten – Arbeitswelt – Soziale Sicherung,* Vienna: Verlag für Gesellschaftskritik, 1982.

Bundesministerium für Wissenschaft und Verkehr (ed.). *Dokumentation 5: Ästhetik und Ideologie. Aneignung und Sinngebung, Abgrenzung und Ausblick,* Vienna: Selbstverlag, 1996.

Busek, Erhard and Thomas A. Bauer (eds). *Politik am Gängelband der Medien,* Vienna: Jugend & Volk, 1998.

Butschek, Felix. *Die österreichische Wirtschaft im 20. Jahrhundert,* Vienna: Österreichisches Institut für Wirtschaftsforschung, 1985.

———. *Vom Staatsvertrag zur EU. Österreichische Wirtschaftsgeschichte von 1955 bis zur Gegenwart,* Vienna-Cologne-Weimar: Böhlau, 2004.

Butterweck, Hellmut. *Verurteilt und begnadigt. Österreich und seine NS-Straftäter,* Vienna: Czernin Verlag, 2003.

Büttner, Elisabeth and Christian Dewald. *Anschluß an Morgen. Eine Geschichte des österreichischen Films von 1945 bis zur Gegenwart,* Salzburg: Residenz-Verlag, 1997.

Chorherr, Thomas. *Wir Täterkinder. Junges Leben zwischen Hakenkreuz, Bomben und Freiheit,* Vienna: Molden Verlag, 2001.

Claus, Thomas, Ferdinand Karlhofer, Gilg Seeber and Cocky Booy, 'Jugendliche im Spannungsfeld von Demokratie und Extremismus. Tirol, Sachsen-Anhalt und Holland im Vergleich', in *Demokratie, Modus und Telos. Festschrift für Anton Pelinka,* ed. Andrei S. Markovits and Sieglinde Rosenberger (Vienna-Cologne-Weimar: Böhlau, 2001); http://homepage.uibk.ac.at/homepage/c402/c40205/JuP.pdf. (accessed 1 June 2005).

Csáky, Eva-Marie (ed.). *Der Weg zu Freiheit und Neutralität. Dokumentation zur österreichischen Außenpolitik 1945–1955,* Vienna: Österreichische Gesellschaft für Außenpolitik und Internationale Beziehungen, 1980.

Dachs, Herbert, Peter Gerlich and Herbert Gottweis (eds). *Handbuch des politischen Systems Österreichs,* Vienna: Manz Verlag, 1991.

Dachs, Herbert, Peter Gerlich and Wolfgang C. Müller (eds). *Die Politiker. Karrieren und Wirken bedeutender Repräsentanten der Zweiten Republik,* Vienna: Manz Verlag, 1995.

Denscher, Barbara and Carl Aigner (eds). *Kunst und Kultur in Österreich. Das 20. Jahrhundert*, Vienna-Munich: Brandstätter, 1999.

Deutsch-Schreiner, Evelyn. *Theater im Wiederaufbau. Zur Kulturpolitik im österreichischen Parteien- und Verbändestaat*, Vienna: Sonderzahl, 2001.

Dichand, Hans. *Im Vorhof der Macht. Erinnerungen eines Journalisten*, Vienna: Ibera & Molden, 1996.

———. *Kronenzeitung. Die Geschichte eines Erfolgs*, Vienna: Orac Verlag, 1977.

Dinklage, Karl and Ernst Peyker. *Des Österreichers wirtschaftlicher Aufstieg*, Klagenfurt: Sozialgeschichtliches Archiv, 1979.

Dörfler, Edith and Wolfgang Pensold. *Die Macht der Nachricht. Die Geschichte der Nachrichtenagenturen in Österreich*, ed. Wolfgang Vyslozil, Vienna: Molden Verlag, 2001.

Ederer, Brigitte, Wilhelmine Goldmann, Elisabeth Beer and C. Reiterlechner. *Eigentumsverhältnisse in der österreichischen Wirtschaft. Wem gehört Österreichs Wirtschaft wirklich?* Vienna: Wirtschaftsverlag Orac, 1991.

Eigner, Peter and Andrea Helige. *175 Jahre Wiener Städtische Allgemeine Versicherung Aktiengesellschaft. Österreichische Wirtschafts- und Sozialgeschichte im 19. und 20. Jahrhundert*, Vienna: Brandstätter, 1999.

Enderle-Burcel, Gertrude, Rudolf Jerábek and Leopold Kammerhofer (eds.). *Protokolle des Kabinettsrates der Provisorischen Regierung Karl Renner. Vol. I*, Horn-Vienna: Verlag Österreich, 1995 ff.

Enderle-Burcel, Gertrude and Rudolf Jerábek (eds.). *Protokolle des Ministerrates der Zweiten Republik. Kabinett Leopold Figl I, Vol. I*, Vienna: Verlag Österreich, 2004.

Etzersdorfer, Irene. 'Persönlichkeit und Politik. Zur Interaktion politischer und seelischer Faktoren in der interdisziplinären "Political-Leadership"-Forschung', *Österreichische Zeitschrift für Politikwissenschaft* 4 (1997): 377–392.

Fabris, Hans Heinz and Fritz Hausjell (eds). *Die vierte Macht. Zur Geschichte und Kultur des Journalismus in Österreich seit 1945*, Vienna: Verlag für Gesellschaftskritik, 1991.

Feldinger, Norbert Peter. 'Das Prinzip "Regional" im Österreichischen Rundfunk. Ein Beitrag zur Geschichte eines Mediums von 1945 bis 1957', PhD diss., Salzburg University, 1987.

Feldman, Gerald D., Oliver Rathkolb, Thedor Venus and Ulrike Zimmerl, *Österreichische Banken und Sparkassen im Nationalsozialismus und in der Nachkriegszeit*, Munich: Beck Verlag, 2006.

Dr. Fessel & Co. Institut für Meinungsforschung, *Österreichbewußtsein 1987*, Vienna: Dr. Fessel & Co, 1987.

Fessel GfK Institut für Marktforschung, *ORF Qualitätsmonitoring 1999. Das Kunst- und Kulturverständnis der Österreicher*, Vienna: GfK, 1999.

Fidler, Harald. *Im Vorhof der Schlacht. Österreichs alte Medienmonopole und neue Zeitungskriege*, Vienna: Falter-Verlag, 2004.

Fidler, Harald and Andreas Merkle. *Sendepause. Medien und Medienpolitik in Österreich*, Oberwart: Ed. Lex Liszt 12, 1999.

Fischer, Ernst. *Das Ende einer Illusion. Erinnerungen 1945–1955*, Vienna: Molden, 1973.

Fischer, Heinz. *Die Kreisky-Jahre 1967–1983*, Vienna: Löcker Verlag, 1994.

Fleming, Donald and Bernard Bailyn (eds). *The Intellectual Migration: Europe and America, 1930–1960*, Cambridge, MA: Harvard University Press, 1969.

Fritz, Wolfgang. *Der Kopf des Asiaten Breitner. Politik und Ökonomie im Roten Wien. Hugo Breitner – Leben und Werk,* Vienna: Löcker Verlag, 2000.

Gehler, Michael. *Der lange Weg nach Europa,* vols. 1 and 2, Innsbruck-Vienna-Munich-Bozen: Studien Verlag, 2002.

———. *Europa. Ideen, Institutionen, Vereinigung,* Munich: Olzog Verlag, 2005.

Gehler, Michael and Hubert Sickinger (eds). *Politische Affären und Skandale in Österreich. Von Mayerling bis Waldheim,* Thaur-Vienna-Munich: Kulturverlag, 1995.

Gehler, Michael and Rolf Steininger. *Die Neutralen und die europäische Integration 1945–1995 – The Neutrals and the European Integration 1945–1955,* Vienna-Cologne-Weimar: Böhlau, 2000.

Gehrlich, Peter and Wolfgang Müller (eds). *Zwischen Koalition und Konkurrenz. Österreichs Partreien seit 1945,* Vienna: Braumüller, 1983.

Gerstl, Elfriede. 'Zwei österreichische Dichterschicksale oder wie der Kulturbetrieb seine Opfer macht und in posthumen Ehrungen sich selbst feiert', in *Literatur in Österreich von 1950 bis 1965. Walter Buchebner-Tagung 1984,* ed. Wendelin Schmidt-Dengler, Mürzzuschlag: Walter-Buchebner-Gesellschaft, 1984, 189–194.

Goschler, Constantin. *Wiedergutmachung. Westdeutschland und die Verfolgten des Nationalsozialismus (1945–1954),* Munich: Oldenbourg, 1992.

Grünwald, Oskar. 'Austrian Industrial Structure and Industrial Policy', in *The Political Economy of Austria: A Conference Held at the American Enterprise Institute in Washington, DC, on October 1–2, 1981,* ed. Sven W. Arndt, Washington, D.C.: American Enterprise Institute, 1982.

Guger, Alois. *Umverteilung durch öffentliche Haushalte in Österreich,* Vienna: Österreichisches Institut für Wirtschaftsforschung, 1987.

Hachmeister, Lutz and Günter Rager. *Wer beherrscht die Medien? Die 50 größten Medienkonzerne der Welt,* Munich: Beck, 1997.

Haerpfner, Christian. 'Die Sozialstruktur der SPÖ. Gesellschaftliche Einflußfaktoren der sozialdemokratischen Parteibindung in Österreich 1969–1988', *Österreichische Zeitschrift für Politikwissenschaft* 4 (1989): 373–394.

Haider-Pregler, Hilde and Peter Roessler (eds). *Zeit der Befreiung. Wiener Theater nach 1945,* Vienna: Picus-Verlag, 1998.

Haller, Max (ed.). *Identität und Nationalstolz der Österreicher. Gesellschaftliche Ursachen und Funktionen. Herausbildung und Transformation seit 1945. Internationaler Vergleich,* Vienna-Cologne-Weimar: Böhlau, 1996.

Hanisch, Ernst. *Der lange Schatten des Staates. Österreichische Gesellschaftsgeschichte im 20. Jahrhundert,* Vienna: Ueberreuter, 1994.

———. 'Überlegungen zum Funktionswandel des Antikommunismus. Eine österreichische Perspektive', in *Zeitgeschichte im Wandel. 3. Österreichischer Zeitgeschichtetag 1997,* ed. Gertraud Diendorfer, Gerhard Jagschitz and Oliver Rathkolb, Innsbruck-Vienna: Studien Verlag, 1998.

Hannak, Jacques (ed.). *Bestandsaufnahme Österreich 1945–1963,* Vienna-Hanover-Bern: Forum-Verlag, 1963.

Heer, Friedrich. *Der Kampf um die österreichische Identität,* Vienna-Cologne-Weimar: Böhlau, 1981.

Heiss, Gernot and Oliver Rathkolb (ed.). *Asylland wider Willen. Flüchtlinge in Österreich im europäischen Kontext seit 1914,* Vienna: Jugend & Volk, 1995.

Herz, Martin F. 'The View from Vienna', in *Witnesses to the Origins of the Cold War,* ed. Thomas Taylor Hammond, Seattle: Univ. of Washington Press, 1982.

Herz, Martin F. and Reinhold Wagnleitner (eds.). *Understanding Austria. The Political Reports and Analyses of Martin F. Herz,* Salzburg: Neugebauer, 1984.

Honner, Franz. *Probleme der österreichischen Währungspolitik,* Freiburg/Schweiz-Zell am See, unpublished dissertation, University of Fribourg, 1965.

Horak, Kurt (ed.). *… glaubt an dieses Österreich! 50 Jahre ÖGB,* Vienna: Verlag des Österreichischen Gewerkschaftsbundes, 1995.

Horvath, Elisabeth. *Die Seilschaften. Das Spiel der Mächtigen in Österreich,* Vienna: Kremayr & Scheriau, 1999.

Hüffel, Clemens and Anton Reiter (eds). *Medienpioniere erzählen … 50 Jahre österreichische Mediengeschichte – von den alten zu den neuen Medien,* Horn: Braumüller, 2004.

Hurdes, Felix. 'Europa als kulturelle Einheit', *Österreichische Monatshefte* 2 (1948): 49–54.

Institut für die Wissenschaften vom Menschen (ed.). 'Die Zukunft des Wohlfahrtsstaates', *Transit* 12 (1996).

Institut für Publizistik- und Kommunikationswissenschaft der Universität Wien, Cornelia Brantner and Wolfgang R. Langenbucher (eds). *Medienkonzentration – Kontrollmechanismen innerhalb der EU. Vergleichendes Forschungsvorhaben,* Commissioned by Bundesministerium für Justiz/Präsidialsektion, Vienna: 2003.

Ivan, Franz (ed.). *200 Jahre Tageszeitung in Österreich 1783–1983. Festschrift und Ausstellungskatalog,* Graz: Österreichische Nationalbibliothek, 1983.

Janitschek, Hans. *Nur ein Journalist. Hans Dichand – Ein Mann und drei Zeitungen,* Vienna-Munich-Zürich: Orac Verlag, 1992.

Jetschgo, Johannes, Ferdinand Lacina, Michael Pammer and Roman Sandgruber. *Österreichische Industriegeschichte 1948–1955. Die verpaßte Chance,* vol. 2, Vienna: Ueberreuter, 2004.

Jochum, Manfred (ed.). *Reden über Österreich,* Salzburg-Vienna, Residenz-Verlag, 1995.

John, Michael and Roman Sandgruber. *Tradition – Innovation. Ausstellungskatalog im Rahmen der Oberösterreichischen Landesausstellung 1998,* Steyr: 1998.

Karner, Stefan, Barbara Stelzl-Marx and Alexander Tschubarjan (eds.) *Die Rote Armee in Österreich. Sowjetische Besatzung 1945–1955. Dokumente,* Graz-Vienna-Munich: Verein zur Förderung von Forschung von Folgen nach Konflikten und Kriegen, 2005.

Keck, Edi, Karl Krammer, Heinz Lederer, Andreas Mailath-Pokorny and Oliver Rathkolb (eds). *Die ersten zehn Jahre Franz Vranitzky,* Vienna: D + R Verl.-Ges., 1996.

Kerschbaumer, Gert and Karl Müller (eds). *Begnadet für das Schöne. Der rot-weiß-rote Kulturkampf gegen die Moderne,* Vienna: Verlag für Gesellschaftskritik, 1992.

Kienzl, Heinz and Susanne Kirchner (ed.). *Ein neuer Frühling wird blühen. Erinnerungen und Spurensuche,* Vienna: Deuticke, 2002.

Klambauer, Otto and Ernst Bezemek. *Die USIA-Betriebe in Niederösterreich. Geschichte, Organisation, Dokumentation,* Vienna: Selbstverl. d. NÖ Inst. für Landeskunde, 1983.

Klaus, Josef. *Macht und Ohnmacht in Österreich. Konfrontationen und Versuche,* Vienna-Munich-Zürich: Molden Verlag, 1971.

Kos, Wolfgang. *Eigenheim Österreich. Zu Politik, Kultur und Alltag nach 1945,* Vienna: Sonderzahl, 1994.

Kramer, Helmut (ed.). *Perspektiven der österreichischen Industrie*, Vienna: Österreichischer Wirtschaftsverlag, 1982.

Kreisky, Bruno, *Zwischen den Zeiten. Erinnerungen aus fünf Jahrzehnten*, Berlin: Siedler, 1986.

Kreisky, Bruno. *Reden*, Vol. II. Vienna: Verlag der Österreichischen Staatsdruckerei, 1981.

Kreissler, Felix. *Der Österreicher und seine Nation*, Vienna-Cologne-Weimar: Böhlau, 1984.

Krejci, Herbert, Erich Reiter and Heinrich Schneider (eds). *Neutralität. Mythos und Wirklichkeit*, Vienna: Signum-Verlag, 1992.

Kriechbaumer, Robert. *Von der Illegalität zur Legalität. Die ÖVP im Jahr 1945. Politische und geistesgeschichtliche Aspekte des Entstehens der Zweiten Republik*, Vienna: Multiplex Media Verlag,1985.

———. *Parteiprogramme im Widerstreit der Interessen. Die Programmdiskussionen und die Programme von ÖVP und SPÖ 1945–1986, Österreichisches Jahrbuch für Politik* spezial edition 3 (1990).

———. *Die Ära Kreisky. Österreich 1970–1983 in der historischen Analyse*, Vienna-Cologne-Weimar: Böhlau, 2004.

Kriechbaumer, Robert and Franz Schausberger (eds). *Volkspartei – Anspruch und Realität. Zur Geschichte der ÖVP seit 1945*, Vienna-Cologne-Weimar: Böhlau, 1995.

Kunz, Johannes and Gerhard Friedrich (eds). *Bevor die Zukunft vorbei ist. Österreich 2000*, Vienna: Kremayr & Scheriau, 1998.

Kuretsidis-Haider, Claudia and Winfried R. Garscha (eds). *Keine Abrechnung. NS-Verbrechen, Justiz und Gesellschaft in Europa nach 1945*, Leipzig-Vienna: Akad. Verl.-Anst., 1998.

Lahodynsky, Otmar. 'Patriotismus. Vernetzter Nationalstolz', *profil* 21, 23 May 2005, 22–24.

Langer, Edmond. *Die Verstaatlichung in Österreich*, Vienna: Verlag der Wiener Volksbuchhandlung, 1966.

Liegl, Barbara and Anton Pelinka, *Chronos und Ödipus. Der Kreisky-Androsch Konflikt*, Vienna: Braumüller, 2004.

Luif, Paul. *On the Road to Brussels: The Political Dimension of Austria's, Finland's and Sweden's Accession to the European Union*, Vienna: Braumüller, 1995.

Lyon, Dirk, Joseph Marko, Eduard Staudinger and Franz Christian Weber (eds). *Österreich'bewußt'sein – bewußt Österreicher sein? Materialien zur Entwicklung des Österreichbewußtsein seit 1945*, Vienna: Österreichischer Bundesverlag, 1985.

Mahrer, Harald (ed.). *Österreich 2050*, Vienna: Czernin Verlag, 2000.

Maimann, Helene. *Politik im Wartesaal. Österreichische Exilpolitik in Großbritannien 1938–1945*, Vienna-Cologne-Weimar: Böhlau, 1975.

Maimann, Helene (ed.). 'Die Rückkehr beschäftigt uns ständig. Vom Flüchten und vom Wiederkommen', in *Die ersten 100 Jahre. Österreichische Sozialdemokratie 1888–1988*, Vienna: Brandstätter, 1988.

Massiczek, Albert and Wilfried Daim (eds). *Die österreichische Nation*, Vienna: Europa-Verlag, 1967.

Matis, Herbert. 'Handel, Gewerbefleiß und Industrie', in *Die wirtschaftliche Entwicklung Österreichs*, ed. Hannes Androsch and Helmut H. Haschek, Vienna: Brandstätter, 1987, 136–158.

Matis, Herbert and Dieter Stiefel (eds). *Österreich 2010. Die wirtschaftliche und soziale Zukunft unseres Landes*, Vienna: Linde Verlag, 2004.

Mayer, Klaus M. *Die Sozialstruktur Österreichs*, Vienna: Österreichischer Bundesverlag für Unterricht, Wissenschaft und Kunst, 1979.

März, Eduard and Maria Szecsi. 'Stagnation und Expansion. Eine vergleichende Analyse der wirtschaftlichen Entwicklung in der Ersten und Zweiten Republik', *Wirtschaft und Gesellschaft* 2 (1982): 321–344.

Meissl, Sebastian, Klaus-Dieter Mulley and Oliver Rathkolb (eds). *Verdrängte Schuld, verfehlte Sühne. Entnazifizierung in Österreich 1945–1955*, Vienna: Verlag für Geschichte und Politik, 1986.

Menasse, Robert. *Das Land ohne Eigenschaften*, Berlin: Sonderzahl, 1992.

Mesner, Maria. *Frauensache? Die Auseinandersetzung um den Schwangerschaftsabbruch in Österreich*, Vienna: Jugend & Volk, 1994.

Mesner, Maria and Matthew P. Berg (eds). *Entnazifizierung zwischen politischem Anspruch, Parteienkonkurrenz und Kaltem Krieg. Das Beispiel der SPÖ*, Vienna: Oldenbourg, 2005.

Mesner, Maria, Margit Niederhuber, Heidi Niederkofler and Gudrun Wolfgruber. *Das Geschlecht der Politik*, Vienna: Bundesministerium für Bildung, Wissenschaft und Kultur, 2004.

Meyer, Thomas and Martina Kampmann. *Politik als Theater. Die neue Macht der Darstellungskunst*, Berlin: Aufbau-Verlag, 1998.

Molden, Fritz. *Besetzer, Toren, Biedermänner. Ein Bericht aus Österreich 1945–1962*, Vienna-Munich-Zürich-New York: Molden Verlag, 1980.

Moser, Karin (ed.). *Besetzte Bilder. Film, Kultur und Propaganda in Österreich 1945–1955*, Vienna: Verlag Filmarchiv Austria, 2005.

Müller, Wolfgang. '"Genosse Filipov" und seine österreichischen "Freunde". Kommunikationslinien, Strategiedebatten und Entscheidungsmechanismen im Verhältnis zwischen KPÖ, Sowjetbesatzung und UdSSR 1946–1951', in *Osteuropa vom Weltkrieg zur Wende*, ed. Wolfgang Müller and Michael Portmann, Vienna: Verlag der Österreichischen Akademie der Wissenschaften, 2007, 133–161.

Müller, Wolfgang C. and Kaare Strom (eds). *Koalitionsregierungen in Westeuropa. Bildung, Arbeitsweise und Beendigung*, Vienna: Signum-Verlag, 1997.

Neidhart, Peter. 'Historische Analyse ausgewählter österreichischer Interessensvertretungen anhand der Erklärungsansätze von Douglass North und Mancur Olson', Phil. diss., Vienna University of Economics and Business, 2003.

Neugebauer, Wolfgang and Peter Schwarz. *Der Wille zum aufrechten Gang. Offenlegung der Rolle des BSA bei der gesellschaftlichen Reintegration ehemaliger Nationalsozialisten*, ed. Bund Sozialdemokratischer AkademikerInnen, Intellektueller und KünstlerInnen, BSA, Vienna: Czernin Verlag, 2005.

Nowotny, Ewald (ed.). *Sozialdemokratische Wirtschaftspolitik. Die solidarische Leistungsgesellschaft*, Vienna: Löcker Verlag, 1992.

Nowotny, Thomas. 'Aber was macht der Dumme schon mit dem Glück? Politische Leadership durch Bruno Kreisky', *Österreichische Zeitschrift für Politikwissenschaft* 4 (1997): 393–406.

Ogris, Günther. 'Einstellungen der österreichischen Bevölkerung zur Demokratie. Demokratietheorie und Demokratieverständnis in Österreich', in *Demokratietheorie und Demokratieverständnis in Österreich,* ed. Manuela Delpos, Vienna: Passagen-Verlag, 2001, 57–102.

Österreichische Akademie der Wissenschaft/Kommission für historische Pressedokumente (ed.). 'Relation. Medien – Gesellschaft', *Geschichte* 2 (1996): 25–56.

Österreichische Gesellschaft für Europapolitik. *Die EU-Erweiterung aus der Sicht der Österreicher und unserer Nachbarn,* Vienna: Selbstverlag, 1999.

———. *Osterweiterung am Prüfstand,* Vienna: Selbstverlag, 2001.

Österreichische Gesellschaft für Kommunikationsfragen (ed.). 'Medienkultur nach 1945', *Medienjournal* 1–2 (1986).

Palme, Lieselotte. *Androsch. Ein Leben zwischen Geld und Macht,* Vienna: Molden 1999.

Pelinka, Anton. *Zur österreichischen Identität. Zwischen deutscher Vereinigung und Mitteleuropa,* Vienna: Ueberreuter, 1990.

———. 'Leadership. Zur Funktionalität eines Konzepts', *Österreichische Zeitschrift für Politikwissenschaft* 4 (1997): 369–376.

Pelinka, Anton, Fritz Plasser and Wolfgang Meixner. *Die Zukunft der österreichischen Demokratie. Trends, Prognosen und Szenarien,* Vienna: Signum-Verlag, 2000.

Pelinka, Anton and Sieglinde Rosenberger. *Österreichische Politik. Grundlagen – Strukturen – Trends,* Vienna: WUV-Univ.-Verlag, 2000.

Pelinka, Peter. *Österreichs Kanzler. Von Leopold Figl bis Wolfgang Schüssel,* Vienna: Ueberreuter, 2000.

———. *Wolfgang Schüssel. Eine politische Biografie,* Vienna: Ueberreuter, 2003.

Pelinka, Peter, Wolfgang Duchkowitsch and Fritz Hausjell (eds). *Zeitungs-Los. Essays zu Pressepolitik und Pressekonzentration in Österreich,* Salzburg: Müller Verlag, 1992.

Petritsch, Wolfgang. *Bruno Kreisky. Ein biographischer Essay,* Vienna: Kremayr & Scheriau, 2000.

Pichler, Rupert (ed.). *Innovationsmuster der österreichischen Wirtschaftsgeschichte. Wirtschaftliche Entwicklung, Unternehmen, Polititik und Innovationsverhalten im 19. und 20. Jahrhundert,* Innsbruck: Studienverlag, 2003.

Plasser, Fritz (ed.). *Politische Kommunikation in Österreich. Ein praxisnahes Handbuch,* Vienna: WUV-Universitätsverlag, 2004.

Plasser, Fritz and Peter Ulram. *Das österreichische Politikverständnis. Von der Konsens- zur Konfliktkultur?* Vienna: WUV-Universitätsverlag, 2002.

Plasser, Fritz, Peter Ulram and Franz Sommer (eds). Das österreichische Wahlverhalten, Vienna: Signum-Verlag, 2000.

Poukar, Raimund. 'Österreichs Beitrag zur abendländischen Gemeinschaft', *Österreichische Monatshefte* 2 (1948): 2–9.

Prader, Hans. 'Die Angst der Gewerkschaft vorm Klassenkampf. Der ÖGB und die Weichenstellung 1945–1950', *In Sachen* 1, Vienna: Arbeitsgemeinschaft für Sozialwissenschaftliche Publizistik, 1975.

Präsidium des Reichsverbandes der Deutschen Industrie (ed.). 'Denkschrift "Aufstieg und Niedergang"', 2 December 1929, Berlin: Selbstverlag, 1929.

Rathkolb, Oliver (ed.). *Gesellschaft und Politik am Beginn der Zweiten Republik. Vertrauliche Berichte der U.S.-Militäradministration aus Österreich 1945 in englischer Originalfassung,* Vienna-Cologne-Weimar: Böhlau, 1985.

———. *Führertreu und gottbegnadet. Künstlereliten im Dritten Reich,* Vienna: Österreichischer Bundesverlag, 1991.

———. *Washington ruft Wien. US-Großmachtpolitik und Österreich 1953–1963. Mit Exkursen zu CIA-Waffenlagern, NATO-Connection und Neutralitätsdebatte,* Vienna-Cologne-Weimar: Böhlau, 1997.

Rathkolb, Oliver, Johannes Kunz and Margit Schmidt (eds). *Bruno Kreisky. Zwischen den Zeiten. Der Memoiren erster Teil,* Vienna: Kremayr & Scheriau, 2000.

——— (eds). *Bruno Kreisky. Im Strom der Politik. Der Memoiren zweiter Teil,* Vienna: Kremayr & Scheriau, 2000.

——— (eds). *Bruno Kreisky. Der Mensch im Mittelpunkt. Der Memoiren dritter Teil,* Vienna: Kremayr & Scheriau, 2000.

Rathkolb, Oliver, Theodor Venus and Ulrike Zimmerl (eds). *Bank Austria Creditanstalt. 150 Jahre österreichische Bankengeschichte im Zentrum Europas,* Vienna: Zsolnay Verlag, 2005.

Rauscher, Hans. *Vranitzky. Eine Chance,* Vienna: Ueberreuter, 1987.

Reich, Simon. *The Fruits of Fascism: Postwar Prosperity in Historical Perspective,* Ithaca, NY: Cornell Univ. Press, 1990.

Reichhold, Ludwig (ed.). *Zwanzig Jahre Zweite Republik. Österreich findet zu sich selbst,* Vienna: Herder Verlag, 1965.

Reiterer, Albert (ed.). *Nation und Nationalbewußtsein in Österreich,* Vienna: Verband d. Wiss. Ges. Österreichs, 1988.

Riedl, Joachim. *Der Wende-Kanzler. Die unerschütterliche Beharrlichkeit des Wolfgang Schüssel. Ein biographischer Essay,* Vienna: Czernin Verlag, 2001.

Ritschel, Karl Heinz (ed.). *Demokratiereform. Die Existenzfrage Österreichs,* Vienna: Zsolnay Verlag, 1969.

Roussel, Danièle. *Der Wiener Aktionismus und die Österreicher. Gespräche,* Klagenfurt: Ritter Verlag, 1995.

Rudas, Stephan. *Österreich auf der Couch. Zur Befindlichkeit eines Landes,* Vienna: Ueberreuter, 2001.

Safrian, Hans. *Eichmann und seine Gehilfen,* Frankfurt/Main: Fischer-Taschenbuch-Verlag, 1997.

Sandgruber, Roman. *Österreichische Geschichte. Ökonomie und Politik. Österreichische Wirtschaftsgeschichte vom Mittelalter bis zur Gegenwart,* Vienna: Ueberreuter, 1995.

Scharpf, Fritz W and Vivien A. Schmidt (eds.). *Welfare and Work in the Open Economy,* vol. 1, Oxford: Oxford University Press, 2000.

Schärf, Adolf. *Österreichs Erneuerung 1945–1955. Das erste Jahrzehnt der Zweiten Republik,* Vienna: Verlag der Wiener Volksbuchhandlung, 1955.

Schmidlechner, Karin M. *Frauenleben in Männerwelten. Kriegsende und Nachkriegszeit in der Steiermark,* Vienna: Döcker Verlag, 1997.

Schmidt-Dengler, Wendelin (ed.). *Literatur in Österreich von 1950 bis 1965. Walter Buchebner-Tagung 1984,* Mürzzuschlag: Walter-Buchebner-Gesellschaft, 1984.

Schnitzler, Arthur. *Tagebuch 1917–1919,* Vienna: Verlag der Österreichischen Akademie der Wissenschaften, 1985.

Schreiner, Evelyn (ed.). *100 Jahre Volkstheater. Theater – Zeit – Geschichte,* Vienna: Jugend & Volk, 1989.

Schuster, Walter and Wolfgang Weber (eds). *Entnazifizierung im regionalen Vergleich,* Linz: Archiv der Stadt Linz, 2004.

Seidel, Hans. 'The Challenge of Small Size. Austria's Economy – Today and Tomorrow', in *Austria. Past and Present,* Hannes Androsch and Helmut H. Haschek (eds.), Vienna: Brandstätter, 1986, 158–186.

———. *Österreichs Wirtschaft und Wirtschaftspolitik nach dem Zweiten Weltkrieg,* Vienna: Manz Verlag, 2005.

Sieder, Reinhard, Hans Steinert and Emmerich Tálos (eds). *Österreich 1945–1955. Gesellschaft, Politik, Kultur,* Vienna: Verlag für Gesellschaftskritik, 1995.

Solsten, Eric and David E. McClave (eds.). *Austria: A Country Study,* 2ⁿᵈ ed., Washington, D.C.: Headquarters, Department of the Army, 1994.

Sozialistische Partei Österreichs (ed.). *Dr. Bruno Kreisky – Vom Heute ins Morgen. Rede vor dem Villacher Parteitag 1972,* Vienna: Sozialistische Partei Österreichs, Zentralsekretariat, 1972.

Spevak, Stefan. *Das Jubiläum '950 Jahre Österreich',* Vienna: Oldenbourg, 2003.

Stadler, Karl R. *Adolf Schärf. Mensch, Politiker, Staatsmann,* Vienna: Europa Verlag, 1982.

Stadler, Friedrich and Peter Weibel. *Vertreibung der Vernunft – The Cultural Exodus from Austria,* Vienna-New York: Springer Verlag, 1995.

Stearman, William Lloyd. *The Soviet Union and the Occupation of Austria: An Analysis of Soviet Policy in Austria, 1945–1955* (Bonn-Vienna: Siegler, 1962.

Steiner, Gertraud. *Die Heimat-Macher. Kino in Österreich 1946–1966,* Vienna: Verlag für Gesellschaftskritik, 1987.

Stiefel, Dieter. *Entnazifizierung in Österreich,* Vienna-Munich-Zürich: Europaverlag, 1981.

Stiftung Bruno Kreisky Archiv, Material Bundesministerium für Auswärtige Angelegenheiten, Copies of Martin Fuchs, Minutes of the Conference of Heads of Department at Schloss Wartenstein, 6 July 1961.

Stourzh, Gerald. *Um Einheit und Freiheit. Staatsvertrag, Neutralität und das Ende der Ost-West-Besetzung Österreichs 1945–1955,* Vienna-Cologne-Weimar: Böhlau, 1998.

Stourzh, Gerald. *Vom Reich zur Republik: Studien zum Österreichbewußtsein im 20. Jahrhundert,* Vienna: Wiener Journal Zeitschriftenverlag, 1990.

Stourzh, Gerald and Peter A. Ulram. *Österreichbewußtsein 1987,* Vienna: Dr. Fessel & Co, Institut für Meinungsforschung, 1987.

Sturmthal, Adolf. *Zwei Leben. Erinnerungen eines sozialistischen Internationalisten zwischen Österreich und den USA,* ed. Georg Hauptfeld and Oliver Rathkolb in cooperation with Christina Wesemann, Vienna-Cologne-Weimar: Böhlau, 1989.

Szuszkiewicz, Hans. *Reporter war … 10 Jahre Österreichischer Rundfunk 1945–1955,* Vienna: Kaltschmid, 1963.

Tálos, Emmerich. *Staatliche Sozialpolitik in Österreich. Rekonstruktion und Analyse,* 2nd ed., Vienna: Verlag für Gesellschaftskritik, 1981.

———. *Vom Siegeszug zum Rückzug. Sozialstaat Österreich 1945–2005,* Innsbruck-Vienna-Bozen: Studien Verlag, 2005.

——— (ed.). *Der geforderte Wohlfahrtsstaat. Traditionen – Herausforderungen – Perspektiven,* Vienna: Löcker Verlag, 1992.

Thaler, Peter. *The Ambivalence of Identity: The Austrian Experience of Nation-Building in a Modern Society. Central European Studies,* West Lafayette, IN: Purdue Univ. Press, 2001.

Thurner, Erika. *Nationale Identität und Geschlecht in Österreich nach 1945,* Innsbruck-Vienna-Munich: Studien Verlag, 2000.

Thurnher, Armin. *Franz Vranitzky im Gespräch mit Armin Thurnher,* Frankfurt/Main: Eichborn, 1992.

Tichy, Frank. *Friedrich Torberg: Ein Leben in Widersprüchen,* Salzburg: Otto Müller Verlag, 1995.

Ulram, Peter A. *Hegemonie und Erosion. Politische Kultur und politischer Wandel in Österreich,* Vienna-Cologne-Weimar: Böhlau, 1990.

Utgaard, Peter. *Remembering and Forgetting Nazism: Education, National Identity, and the Victim Myth in Postwar Austria,* New York-Oxford: Berghahn Books, 2003.

Venus, Theodor. 'Zerbrochene Medienträume. "Express", "Kronen-Zeitung" und "Arbeiter-Zeitung"', in *Bruno Kreisky: Seine Zeit und mehr/Era and Aftermath,* Vienna: Catalogue of the Exhibition at the Historisches Museum der Stadt Wien, 1998, 127–148.

Veselsky, Ernst Eugen (ed.). *So leben wir morgen. Österreich 1985. 110 Fachleute analysieren unsere Zukunft,* Vienna: Orac Verlag, 1976.

Vidal, Jean-François. 'Internationalisierung, Regulation und politische Ökonomie. Ein Vergleich der Perioden 1880–1913 und 1970–1995', *Kurswechsel* 1 (1998): 23–33.

Vollnhals, Clemens (ed.). *Entnazifizierung. Politische Säuberung und Rehabilitierung in den vier Besatzungszonen 1945–1949,* Munich: Dt. Taschenbuch-Verlag, 1991.

Vranitzky, Franz. *Politische Erinnerungen,* Vienna: Zsolnay Verlag, 2004.

Wassermann, Heinz P. *Naziland Österreich!?: Studien zu Antisemitismus, Nation und Nationalsozialismus im öffentlichen Meinungsbild,* Innsbruck-Vienna: Studien Verlag, 2002.

Wasmair, Martin. *Österreich, schau auf deinen Schilling und behüte den lieben Gott! Kulturpolitische Rückschau auf ein Erfolgsrezept der ÖVP,* see http://www.igkultur/kulturrisse/1046078977/1046162765 (accessed 1 June 2005).

Weber, Andreas (ed.). *Streitfall Neutralität. Geschichten – Legenden – Fakten,* Vienna: Czernin Verlag, 1999.

Weber, Fritz and Theodor Venus (eds). *Austro-Keynesianismus in Theorie und Praxis,* Vienna: Jugend & Volk, 1993.

Weber, Stefan. *Nachrichtenkonstruktion im Boulevardmedium. Die Wirklichkeit der 'Kronen-Zeitung',* Vienna: Passagen-Verlag, 1995.

Weber, Wilhelm. *Wirtschaft in Politik und Recht am österreichischen Beispiel 1945–1970,* Vienna: Europa-Verlag, 1972.

Weibel, Peter and Christa Steinle (eds). *Identität: Differenz. Tribüne Trigon 1940–1990. Eine Topographie der Moderne,* Vienna-Cologne-Weimar: Böhlau, 1992.

Weinzierl, Erika and Kurt Skalnik. *Österreich. Die Zweite Republik,* vols. 1 and 2, Graz-Vienna-Cologne: Styria, 1972.

Weiss, Hilde. *'Alte und neue Minderheiten. Zum Einstellungswandel in Österreich (1984–1998)',* *SWS Rundschau* 40 (2000): 25–42.

Werkner, Patrick (ed.). *Kunst in Österreich 1945–1955,* Vienna: WUV Universitätsverlag, 1996.

Wimmer, Michael. *Kulturpolitik in Österreich. Darstellung und Analyse 1970–1990,* Innsbruck-Vienna: Studien Verlag, 1995.

Wodak, Ruth. *Zur diskursiven Konstruktion nationaler Identität,* Frankfurt/Main: Suhrkamp, 1998.

Name Index

Pusch, Hans 121, 254

Qualtinger, Helmut 158, 278

Raab, Julius 44, 50, 58, 69, 74ff., 98ff.,
  101ff., 104ff., *106,* 107ff., 110f., 114,
  120, 132ff., 135f., 142, 144f., 154ff.,
  159, 170f., 173, 175, 177f., 183f.
Raimund, Ferdinand 212
Rajakowitsch, Erich 248
Raky, Hortense 158
Ravel, Maurice 202
Reagan, Ronald 181f., 272
Reder, Walter 20, 121f., 125, 254
Reimann, Viktor 144f., 195, 204, 259f.
Renner, Karl 2, 13, 22, 38f., 44f., 47f.,
  50, 54ff., 57, 61, 68f., 71, 93f., *95,*
  96, 98f., 104, 132ff., 141, 168, 170,
  192, 200, 205, 208, 232, 238, 242f.,
  245, 257ff., 263, 265, 274f.
Reston, James 181
Richter, Horst Eberhard 13
Riedl, Joachim 261
Riemerschmid, Werner 158
Ritschel, Karl Heinz 146, 148
Rohracher, Andreas 111, 144
Rollett, Edwin 195
Roosevelt, Franklin D. 265
Rösch, Otto 251
Rosenzweig, Wilhelm 97
Roszenich, Norbert 116
Rothschild, Alfons 63
Rothschild, Louis 63
Rudas, Andreas 127
Rudolf, Crown Prince 211
Rühm, Gerhard 198, 213
Rürup, Bernd 228
Rusch, Paulus 197

Sadat, Anwar el *119,* 180
Sailer, Toni 162, 279
Sakharov, Andrei 179
Salcher, Herbert 80, 122
Sallinger, Rudolf 50
Sanford, Nevitt 31

Saragat, Giuseppe 113
Schachter, Herbert 85
Schärf, Adolf 23, 44, 48ff., 64, 69, 76,
  96ff., 105, 107f., 113, 115, 120, 171,
  173, 175, 245, 275
Scharf, Erwin 98
Schaumayer, Maria 131
Scheibner, Herbert *262*
Schieder, Peter 122
Schiele, Egon 62, 194
Schirach, Baldur von 191, 196
Schleinzer, Karl 46, 110
Schmidt, Guido 102, 263
Schmidt, Heide 134
Schmidt-Chiari, Guido 84
Schmitz, Bruno 39
Schnitzler, Arthur 23
Schönberg, Arnold 194
Schöner, Josef 242
Schönherr, Dietmar 164
Schorsch, Friedl 97
Schorske, Carl E. 26
Schranz, Karl 162f., 279
Schreyer, Lothar 198
Schröcksnadel, Peter 279
Schröder, Gerhard 83, 128f.
Schubert, Franz 19, 194, 212
Schuh, Oscar Fritz 196
Schumpeter, Joseph A. 61
Schuschnigg, Kurt von xiv, 1, 32f., 49,
  102, 113, 144f., 209, 217f., 263, 265,
  273, 278, 281
Schüssel, Ludwig 261
Schüssel, Wolfgang 46, 126ff., *129,*
  130ff., 133ff., 136, 166, 172, 187,
  261, *262,* 275
Schwarzenegger, Arnold 110f., 160
Sedlmayr, Hans 197f., 202
Seeber, Gilg 34
Seidel, Hans 78, 272
Seipel, Ignaz 103, 215
Seitz, Karl 47
Seyß-Inquart, Arthur 102, 163, 204
Shakespeare, William 212
Shevardnadze, Eduard 77